The
SOCIAL
HISTORY
of
ANCIENT
ISRAEL

The
SOCIAL HISTORY
of
ANCIENT ISRAEL

An Introduction

RAINER KESSLER

Translated by Linda M. Maloney

Fortress Press
Minneapolis

THE SOCIAL HISTORY OF ANCIENT ISRAEL
An Introduction

Translated from Rainer Kessler, *Sozialgeschichte des alten Israel: Eine Einführung*
(© 2006 by Wissenschaftliche Buchgesellschaft, Darmstadt).

Line drawings on pp. 43, 47, 115, and 116 taken from Othmar Keel / Christoph Uelinger, *Göttinnen, Götter und Gottessymbole* © 1992, Verlag Herder Freiburg im Breisgau, Germany. Used by permission.

Line drawings on pp. 52, 80, 107 by Christa Rubsam, © Augsburg Fortress.

Maps © 2008 Lucidity Information Design, LLC. Used by permission.

Cover image: *Milk Vessel,* © Carolyn Brunelle. Used by permission.
Cover design: Diana Running
Book design: The HK Scriptorium, Inc.

Library of Congress Cataloging-in-Publication Data

Kessler, Rainer.
[Sozialgeschichte des alten Israel. English]
The social history of ancient Israel : an introduction / Rainer Kessler ; translated by Linda M. Maloney.
p. cm.
Includes bibliographical references and index.
ISBN 978-0-8006-6282-0 (alk. paper)
1. Sociology, Biblical. 2. Jews—Civilization—To 70 A.D. 3. Palestine—Social life and customs—To 70 A.D. I. Title.
DS112.K45513 2008
933—dc22   2007044771

Manufactured in the U.S.A.

12 11 10 09 08 1 2 3 4 5 6 7 8 9 10

Contents

Publisher's Foreword

WE CAN ASK MANY QUESTIONS OF THE TEXT we call the Old Testament. Among them are: How did ancient Israel organize its society? Who were its leaders? How were families structured? How were gender relations constructed? Did the nature of Israelite society evolve over time? And how does the structure of that society relate to its theology and its relationship to God?

Rainer Kessler uses the discipline of social history to describe ancient Israel by answering these and other related questions. The currency and sophistication of his argument makes this book a valuable resource for scholars and students of the Hebrew Bible and ancient Israel. But as Kessler points out in chapter 1, he is also keenly aware that the last question asked above is an important reason why many readers will be drawn to this book. Because of the claims made in Judaism and Christianity about the biblical God's involvement in human history, questions of social history are for many people of tremendous theological importance as well.

The Social History of Ancient Israel falls into three parts. First, in chapter 1, the author discusses the social history method itself by describing it as a historical discipline and method of biblical exegesis, reviewing the different rhythms of history, describing the two ways of doing social history, and reviewing the

history of scholarship on the analysis of biblical social history.

In part 1, chapters 2–5 review the available methods for studying Israelite social history: the geographical and historical environments of ancient Israel, the material remains we have from archaeology and epigraphy, the nature of the Hebrew Bible texts, and useful analogies for studying ancient Israel derived from its cultural environment and the work of modern ethnology and sociology.

In part 2, chapters 6–11 use social history methodology to review Israelite history, from its earliest origins as a kinship-based society in the Levant through the beginning and full development of the monarchy and a class-based society in both the south and the north, the exilic and post-exilic periods and their social consequences, and finishing with Israel under Alexander the Great and his successors and the development of the independent Jewish Hasmonean state.

The book concludes, in chapter 12, by describing the features of Israel's society that persisted throughout history, discussing the identity of the entity Israel, and examining the theological relevance of social history.

This fine translation by Linda M. Maloney is supplemented by maps and illustrations throughout, and a glossary of terms. Special thanks go to Andrew De Young, Lynn Kauppi, Joshua Messner, Bob Cronan, Christa Rubsam, and the HK Scriptorium for their careful, conscientious, and creative work bringing the book to print.

In the text, asterisked passages are those that the author considers later, secondary additions to the original text: for example, "Micah 1—3*" indicates that the author understands these chapters to be a later addition to the book of Micah that do not go back to the prophet Micah himself.

Additional resources for professors and students using this book are available on the Web at www.fortresspress.com/kessler.

Neil Elliott
Fortress Press

Preface

MY INTEREST IN THE SOCIAL HISTORY OF ancient Israel began in the early 1970s, when I was doing my doctoral work. At that time, Frank Crüsemann, Christof Hardmeier, and I met regularly in Heidelberg to discuss new methodological approaches to the Old Testament. After some major interruptions in my life, my interest in social history received a new impetus through Willy Schottroff's invitation to me, in 1985, to undertake some regular teaching in Frankfurt am Main. After that, my position as assistant to Frank Crüsemann at the Kirchliche Hochschule in Bielefeld, from 1987 to 1991, made it possible for me to devote myself entirely to this topic in writing my Habilitationsschrift. Since being appointed to Marburg in 1993, I have had repeated opportunities to discuss social-historical themes in my lectures and seminars. The open atmosphere that characterizes the faculty at Marburg, and good interdisciplinary work, especially with colleagues from social ethics, ancient Near Eastern studies, Semitics, and archaeology have given me a multitude of ideas that have issued in the present work.

Since 1985 I have also participated in a pleasant little circle that has called itself, from the outset, the "Heidelberg Working Group." Once a year, exegetes of both Testaments meet together with colleagues from the field of social ethics and people doing practical church work to discuss questions of social-historical interpretation of the Bible and their significance for theology and the churches. Innumerable ideas emerge from these meetings, and I, also, come away with many new thoughts.

However, it was only when Eckart Otto invited me to describe Israel's social history in ninety lines for the article "Israel II.4" in the fourth edition of *Religion in Geschichte und Gegenwart* that I finally decided to write a separate volume entitled *Social History of Ancient Israel*. It was an easy decision: if over a thousand years of social history can be compressed into ninety lines, they can certainly be described in two hundred pages. I am grateful to the Wissenschaftliche Buchgesellschaft in Darmstadt for accepting the idea immediately and for successfully bringing the work to completion.

Besides what has already been said, special thanks are due to my previous graduate assistant, Dr. Uta Schmidt of Giessen. She read the whole manuscript and made many valuable suggestions that sometimes led to substantial changes and revisions. I also thank my undergraduate assistants Silke Arendsen and Christian Vosloh, who assisted in preparing the manuscript.

It is my hope that students of theology, pastors, teachers, and colleagues in the field of Old Testament may be able to derive something useful from this book to assist them in their work with the Hebrew Bible.

1

The Social History Method

KEY POINTS

- Social history is the history of a society's organizational development.
- Social history investigates the social conditions that created the contradictions in biblical texts.
- Different "speeds" of history (Fernand Braudel):
  - natural phenomena (ice ages, climactic change)
  - (individual) events
  - social history (the development of a society over time)
- Types of social history:
  - the history of social institutions
  - the history of eras or time periods
- The history of biblical social-history scholarship:
  - "Biblical antiquities" approach—Roland de Vaux's *Ancient Israel: Its Life and Institutions*
  - Sociology of ancient Judaism—Max Weber; influenced Albrecht Alt and Martin Noth
  - Post-1968—liberation theology; use of sociological and anthropological theory; Marxism

Social History as Discipline and as Method

Social History as a Subdiscipline of Historical Studies

THE SOCIAL HISTORY OF ANCIENT ISRAEL IS treated in these pages as a discipline of historical study. At the same time, it is an essentially theological discipline, because the Hebrew Bible, as the fundamental theological document of Judaism and Christianity, tells the story of God—but not "mythically," as is the case with the legends of the gods. Rather, the Bible tells the story of God as the history of God's interaction with human beings, focused on the history of God's interaction with God's people, Israel.

Without understanding the history of this people, it is impossible to understand the history of God's interaction with them. Israel's social history is therefore necessary for an understanding both of ancient Israel as a historical entity and of the theological reality that is the Hebrew Bible, a document of that ancient Israel.

The history of a people in a particular era, here the history of Israel in the time to which the writings of the Hebrew Bible refer and the period in which they were composed, is always social history to the extent that a people is a social entity. Nevertheless, social history as a discipline within historical studies has an object of its own. It stands alongside other special historical fields such as history of religions, literary history, or art history.

1

However, in this case the particular object is less evident than in other specialized fields of historical study. We cannot speak about the social structures of a society without taking into account its economic system, which is the subject of economic history. Nor can we leave out of view the system of laws, the object of legal history. The same is true of political structures and institutions, the description of which falls within the field of political science.

Despite a certain blurriness, which we concede, the subject of social history can, nevertheless, be limited in the sense that it does *not* have to do with any particular *statements* of a society or primarily with particular *events*. The subject of social history is, rather, the *form* of a society itself. Of course, the word "form" suggests something static, which is not at all the case. A society's form is subject to constant change, often proceeding nearly unnoticed, but sometimes dynamic and intensely rapid. That is why social history, as its name implies, is always concerned with the form of a society as it evolves throughout history.

Social History as an Exegetical Method

In discussions of Israel's social history over the last thirty-five years, of course, scholars have not been content to regard social history as a subdiscipline of historical studies whose purpose was to describe the shape of society in ancient Israel. For as a theological discipline, a subdiscipline of Old Testament exegesis, it was also always concerned with biblical texts. And here the newer, social-historical oriented exegesis inquired not only about the setting in life of a particular genre (its *Sitz im Leben*), as earlier form criticism had done, but about the *interests* traceable in the texts. This question was associated with the reverse inquiry: how

did the religious views we can discern in the texts in turn affect the social developments of the period?[1]

Since social interests are traceable in the biblical texts, this type of exegesis, working with social-historical methods, proposes that a society contains a variety of partly overlapping, partly coexisting interests, which are capable of diverging or sharply conflicting. And it presupposes that texts also participate in this interweaving of interests, though as a rule not in the sense of simply reflecting a particular interest in a particular text. "Contradictions between different statements in the Bible prove . . . as a rule to be occasioned by the different social origins of the texts in question."[2] If the questions are posed in this way, this interweaving of interests has to be described, the social and historical circumstances of the different interests have to be investigated, and the interaction of these interests and the dynamics of their changes must be understood.

We have to be content here simply to indicate the consequences of such a conception of social-historical interpretation. They affect our relationship with the biblical texts, so that social-historical biblical exegesis "in contrast to all the ideological tendencies to cover up, excuse, and harmonize that are to be found at all times in the history of human societies . . . names the real social conflicts of the past and present and so acts as a critique of ideology."[3] The consequences of a social-historical biblical exegesis thus conceived extend even to social-ethical and practical theological questions so that, not to put too fine a point on it, one may say that "social-historical biblical exegesis" reveals "itself to be an aspect of liberation theology."[4]

We cannot draw out this line of thought here,[5] nor is it necessary to share all the implications and consequences of this understanding of social-historical biblical exegesis in order to enunciate what follows. I will, however, mark what I myself am interested in knowing by stating that in my own conception, the "social history of Israel" encompasses more than what I am about to attempt in these pages, which is to reconstruct the social history of Israel as a subdiscipline of the history of ancient Israel.

The History of Events and "the Long Term"

Defining social history as an investigation of a society's social structure within history is an attempt to join a static and a dynamic element. In the real world of living organisms, the dynamic element of time does not proceed as a steady continuum, but moves with different intensities. Periods of accelerating change alternate with long phases of relative stability in which, at least on the visible surface, almost nothing changes.

Every type of historical study must take account of these differing dynamics in or

speeds of history. Since the foundational 1946 work of the French historian Fernand Braudel on the Mediterranean, it has been customary to distinguish three differently paced rhythms in history: "history over the long term" describes people's relationship to their natural environment; since the latter is a given, this kind of history moves "at an unaltered and even pace" (at least that was true, to a degree, when Braudel wrote his book). The "history of events," the object of traditional historical writing, by contrast, concerns itself with individual events, rapidly shifting surface movements. Social history, which Braudel called "that of groups and groupings," lies between the two. It must take into account the natural conditions that are not perceptible in themselves. But it must also have an eye to "events" (in our case, for example, the successive conquests by the Assyrians, Babylonians, Persians, and Greeks) and investigate their effects on the community's social organization.[6]

Every form of historical writing must take these different rhythms into account, but each has a different focus. In the sphere of history of events,[†] for example, there is a contentious

The Rhythms of History		
Type of History	Historical events covered	Examples
History over the long term	Natural events	Ice ages, climatic changes, ecosystem changes, changes in Palestinian ecology over time
Social history	Social changes, major historical eras	The history of the family, the history of a government, the history of the twentieth century, the history of the evolution of Israel's monarchy
History of events	Specific historical events	Wars, assassinations, elections, new discoveries, the fall of Jerusalem in 587/6.

[†] Translator's note: The author speaks of "history of events" (*Ereignisgeschichte*) to refer to what is commonly called in English "political history" or more often, and inaccurately, simply "history."

discussion about whether the conquest of Jerusalem took place in 587 or 586. For social history this one-year difference is inconsequential. For literary history it is interesting to consider whether prophets like Amos or Micah wrote down their oral statements themselves or whether that was the work of their disciples and adherents after the death of the individual prophet. But for social history, which uses these texts as its sources, the question is incidental.

Examples could be multiplied but should not create the impression that questions of political or literary history are inconsequential, since whether a prophetic text is preexilic or represents a projection backward from a postexilic time is, of course, relevant for social history as well.[7] And whether the military, diplomatic, or commercial-political incidents reported of David or Solomon rest on historical facts or represent literary fictions is interesting for social history, too.

Nevertheless, it must be said that social history is "a history of slow rhythms."[8] Certainly, insofar as it is a form of historical writing it is concerned with changes. But in the first instance it intends to apprehend the form, or better, the different forms, assumed by the society being studied, and that have remained stable over certain longer periods of time. Therefore it need not concern itself with every event and does not require a precise dating in terms of the decade for its sources. Social history can permit itself a certain controlled vagueness for the dating of events and sources.

A Description of Social History

Since it is the task of social-historical writing to link the static moment in which a society's form is described with the dynamic description of its historical development, two approaches to that description are, in principle, possible. Social historical description can begin with the form of society and explicate this amorphous phenomenon, "form of society," or it can begin with historical development and offer a division by epochs "with a slow rhythm."

Social History as the History of Institutions

Society is a very broad and abstract concept. If we try to characterize a particular society using a single concept (for early periods we may think of concepts like "agrarian society" or "feudal society," and for the present expressions such as "consumer society" or "experiential society")—as a rule we only succeed in capturing one particular feature of the society, even though our intention is to typify it. But this method does not bring the whole fabric of social relationships into view by ignoring gender, family structure, military organization, and similar such factors.

Hence we are invited to differentiate this abstract and amorphous phenomenon called "society" into constituent parts. If we consider the whole society as a grand system, we could speak of subsystems. Following the tradition of French sociology, I will employ the concept of *institution*, which is broader in scope than the corresponding popular expression in German.[9]

If we begin our social-historical description with institutions, the static element necessarily dominates. However, the dynamic element is not absent since, first of all, every institution has, in turn, its own history, and second, particular institutions, such as kingship in Israel and Judah, are limited to particular historical locations. These two circumstances constitute the strength of a social-historical account based on institutions. It can take into account that various institutions develop according to a variety of rhythms. Thus, for example, familial structures are stable over extended periods of time, while military institutions were subjected to numerous changes during the relatively short period of the monarchy. A further and closely allied advantage is that we can establish a certain hierarchy of institutions. So, for example, Erhard Gerstenberger precedes his "theologies in the Old Testament" with a "summary of the social history of Israel" and divides it as follows: family and clan; village and town; tribes; the monarchical state; confessional and parochial communities.[10] The first three represent basic institutions that, although they change, are relevant for the whole era covered by the Old Testament, while the monarchical state or the confessional and parochial communities are obviously secondary to the former and only exist at one time or another during limited periods.

This last example shows that even a depiction of social history oriented to institutions must have a general notion of the periods into which it will divide the era in question. This suggests the possibility of making the period division itself the starting point for the description.

Social History as the History of Time Periods (Epochs)

If the depiction of social history always begins with one period's institutions, that represents an alternative form of presentation, but by no means the *right* in contrast to the *wrong* method. Both belong together; it is only that the accents are differently placed. As the description of institutions must always have a concept of time periods, so a description that follows time periods must always have a concept of the institutions it intends to depict.

The method of presentation we have chosen here, following time periods, emphasizes historical development; the description of social structures is subordinated to the division of time periods. Otherwise one would have to speak of a sociology of Israel rather than a social history. The weight of this presentation thus lies more on the radical shifts within society and what is characteristic of a particular period than on the continuing features such as family structures. This is intended to sharpen awareness that even a premodern society underwent altogether dramatic developments in the thousand years or so to be described here.

The choice to pursue a description following time periods in no way way devalues a presentation according to institutions; rather, it remains in many ways and at multiple points related to and dependent on it. But it does represent a choice that implies a certain position as regards the history of scholarship. I will explain this more fully in the next section.

History of Scholarship

The history of Israel in biblical times as well as the so-called *realia*—the material objects, places, and social institutions mentioned in the Bible—have been of interest ever since there was a canon of the biblical writings that required interpretation. For, despite teachings about multiple meanings of Scripture, the *sensus literalis* has always played a deciding role, and no such sense can be derived from the text without knowledge of history and material remains. In his own description of "Hebrew Archaeology," Immanuel Benzinger gives a short summary of the history of this discipline from ancient times onward.[11]

Chronology

The historical value of the stories of the patriarchs is uncertain.
Modern scholars have often proposed a date of 1800 BCE for Abraham.

1250 BCE (approx.)	Exodus from Egypt (disputed)
1250–1000	Emergence of Israel in the highlands of Canaan
1000–960 (approx.)	King David; beginning of monarchy in Jerusalem (disputed)
960–922 (approx.)	King Solomon; building of the Jerusalem temple (disputed)
922	Division of kingdom: Israel in the north, Judah in the south
722/721	Destruction of Samaria, capital of Israel, by the Assyrians
	End of kingdom of Israel
621	Reform of Jerusalem cult by King Josiah
	Promulgation of "the book of the law" (some form of Deuteronomy)
597	Capture of Jerusalem by Babylonians
	Deportation of king and nobles to Babylon
586	Destruction of Jerusalem by Babylonians
	More extensive deportations; beginning of Babylonian exile
539	Conquest of Babylon by Cyrus of Persia; Jewish exiles allowed to return to Jerusalem; end of exile; Judah becomes a province of Persia
520–515	Rebuilding of Jerusalem Temple
458	Ezra sent from Babylon to Jerusalem with a copy of the Law
336–323	Alexander the Great conquers the Persian Empire
312–198	Judea controlled by the Ptolemies of Egypt (also a Greek dynasty, founded by one of Alexander's generals)
168/167	Persecution of Jews in Jerusalem by Antiochus IV Epiphanes, king of Syria; Maccabean revolt
63	Conquest of Jerusalem by Roman general Pompey
66–70 CE	First Jewish revolt against Rome
	Destruction of Jerusalem Temple
132–135 CE	Second Jewish revolt under Bar Kochba; Jerusalem rebuilt as Aelia Capitolina, with a temple to Jupiter Capitolinus

However, since the nineteenth century this discipline has enjoyed an unexampled upswing. The deciphering of hieroglyphics and cuneiform writing, excavations in the Near East, the increased travels of European scholars and new forms of documentation (for example, photography) augmented knowledge in such quantity that a new quality arose as well. For whereas previously the Bible itself was almost the only source for the history and material lore of ancient Israel, it now became one source among many others whose value had first to be determined.

This new situation led to the appearance, beginning at the end of the nineteenth century, of a flood of summarizing works that, however, stood entirely within the tradition of older investigations of biblical antiquities.

The Tradition of Biblical Antiquities

Immanuel Benzinger, already mentioned, begins his *Biblische Archäologie* (its first edition appeared in 1893) with a definition. Biblical archaeology, he says, is the name "of a special historical discipline whose task is the scientific depiction of all the living conditions, customs and usages, civil and religious institutions of the Hebrews."[12] On the one hand, this is a much broader notion of archaeology than had been used heretofore, as it had previously been limited to excavations and their results. On the other hand, however, it was still only a subdiscipline "of the whole, still to be sought, of a cultural history" from which, in such a concept of biblical archaeology, "political history, literary history, and religious history" can be derived.[13] The structure of Benzinger's work can serve as an example of such presentations. It contains four parts: land and people, private antiquities, public antiquities, and sacred antiquities.

Benzinger's demand that a comprehensive presentation should also consider "political history, literary history, and religious history," was fulfilled in a sense by Rudolf Kittel. In his *Geschichte der Hebräer* ["History of the Hebrews"], the first edition of which appeared in 1888–92, he undertook to integrate elements of a history of culture and religion, in that each section of the work, which divided chronologically according to political history, was supplied with a description of the culture and religion of the period.[14]

What for Kittel is part of the overall history of Israel becomes the title of the work of Alfred Bertholet. He called his 1919 book *Kulturgeschichte Israels* [*Cultural History of Israel*].[15] But the major impetus to a cultural history of Israel was developed in the work of the Dane, Johannes Pedersen—whose first volumes appeared in Danish as early as 1920—in its English translation, *Israel: Its Life and Culture*, published in four volumes 1926–40.[16] Here, for example in the 160-page section dealing with the Hebrew idea of the soul,[17] we find integrated into social history what French historiography has called the history of mentality. Sal Wittmayer Baron undertook something similar in his monumental *Sozial- und Religionsgeschichte der Juden* [*Social and Religious History of the Jews*] in 1937, which, however, remained almost without influence in Europe.[18]

The writing of social history in the tradition of biblical antiquities reached a certain climax with Roland de Vaux's *Institutions*. If we consider the subtitle of the two volumes, we find once again the same structure as in Benzinger's *Biblische Archäologie*: volume 1 treats "Nomadism and Its Survival; Family Institutions; Civil Institutions," while volume 2 deals with "Military Institutions" and "Religious Institutions."[19]

The works described here have two consistent similarities. They are, first of all, descriptive in their form and avoid any attempt to construct theories about the form of ancient Israelite society they describe. Frants Buhl, who presented an analysis of "Israelite social conditions" in 1899, expresses it this way: his intention was to give "a simple and clear presentation of the material in the Old Testament, devoid of any theories and constructs."[20] Second, the presentations, with the exception of Kittel's *Geschichte Israels*, are kept historically flat. In his *Die biblischen Altertümer* (1914),

Paul Volz asserted: "Within the individual sections, material from very different periods has often been brought together without hesitation."[21] There were two reasons for this: namely, that diachronic development (development through history) within social institutions is often hard to follow, and that ways of life have in any case changed very little in the course of time. A third, and probably unconscious, reason may be added: the historical picture in these presentations is exceedingly biblical to the extent that the early period, which is equated with what is depicted in the Pentateuch, plays the decisive role. As a rule there are only two eras, namely before the occupation of the Land and after. As a late phenomenon of the Romantic longing for origins, there is genuine interest only in the early period up to the monarchy. So Kittel ends his history of Israel with the destruction of Jerusalem in 587.

In contrast to the authors to be treated next, the works in the tradition of biblical antiquities can thus be summarized as "descriptive works with a general abstinence from theoretical construction."[22] Works of this type should rather be categorized with presentations of social history as history of institutions than with its depiction in terms of time periods. But just as an orientation to periods does not devalue an orientation to institutions, so also the descriptive portrayals of conditions in ancient Israel are not outdated, which is why, in the most recent state of research, such depictions are still again and again necessary.[23]

The Religious Sociology of Ancient Judaism

Biblical archaeology, as characterized above, has always regarded the investigation of material facts and social relationships as merely an auxiliary science, subordinate to the purpose of understanding the biblical writings.[24] Religious sociology's view of ancient Israel is quite different: its purpose is to understand the religion itself and the society that produced it. For this field of scholarship the biblical writings are not the real aim of the work, but the source and at most a part of the religion and society being studied. This is exemplified by Max Weber's posthumous (1921) study, *Ancient Judaism*.[25] The very fact that it appeared as the third volume of his collected essays on religious sociology shows that its systematic location is not within biblical scholarship, but rather in the sociology of religion.

Of course, Weber relies on the works of biblical scholars, as he acknowledges in a six-page note on the title "ancient Judaism."[26] But Weber is posing a different set of questions, which arise from the observation that, "from a sociological point of view," the Jews were a "pariah people,"[27] something that, according to Weber, has been true of Judaism from the Babylonian exile to the present. "Thus the problem is: how did the Jews become a pariah people with this highly specific and unique character?"[28]

In attempting to answer this question, Weber begins with the upper classes of the pre-national society, the Bedouins, the city dwellers, the farmers, and the semi-nomads. But he is not content with a superficial description of the various groups; he posits a constellation of interests: "However, over against the city patricians and the Bedouins stood two groups: farmers and herders in equal opposition, and in this opposition to the first two groups, the latter two developed a community of interests."[29] Weber then, beginning with the concept of "covenant," calls the social form within which this constellation of interests reached a relatively stable balance a "confederation."[30] This confederation is "a military covenant under and with YHWH as the war god of the covenant."[31] "This fragile Israelite community had, until the royal period, as far as we can see, no enduring political organs at all."[32]

This characterization already implies that the rise of the monarchy brought with it a new epoch in the social history of ancient Israel. That was not yet true of Saul's kingdom or David's early years, but was so in the "altogether different structure of the kingdom that began when David took up residence in the city, and became definitive from the time of Solomon."[33] What was decisive about this new structure was the city location, as well as the "resulting change in the organization of the army."[34] "Out of the loose confederation of farmers, herder tribes, and small hill towns, Solomon . . . sought to create a tightly organized political structure."[35]

Naturally the end of the kingdom constituted the transition to the third epoch, that of what Weber called the "pariah people," even though the roots of that existence were to be found earlier, especially in the preexilic prophets. "Pariah people" was to be understood as "a nation of resident aliens, separated ritually, formally or actually, from its social environment," from which could be derived "all the essential characteristics of its relationship to its environment, especially its . . . self-chosen ghetto existence and the nature of the dualism between its internal and external morality."[36]

Weber's thesis about a pariah people cannot be discussed here; as a matter of fact, it found no followers.[37] What is important for us is the overall evaluation of Weber's initiative that arises from it. Unlike the descriptive presentations of biblical antiquities, Weber's work focused on a theoretical conception of the society under study; he calls it a confed-

eration, a monarchy, and a pariah people. And unlike the ahistorical depictions, or those that distinguished only a period before entrance into the Land and the time of existence in the Land, Weber was interested in the characteristics of the epochs as such and in the transitions, and he did not (in contrast to Kittel's *Geschichte des Volkes Israel* ["History of the People of Israel"]) stop with the end of the monarchy, but devoted the second of two parts of his study entirely to the topic of "The Establishment of the Jewish Pariah People."

Weber's work had a profound influence on German Old Testament scholarship, even though the authors affected by it seldom acknowledge this explicitly. Above all, Albrecht Alt and Martin Noth took up Weber's theoretical interest in social formations and their developments and transitions. Likewise, individual theories such as the transhumance of nomadic herders, the tribal military confederation of the pre-national period, the importance of the contrast between city and country in the royal period, or the description of postexilic Israel as a cultic community can be traced without difficulty to Weber. Add to these some new theories such as the thesis of an amphictyony in pre-national Israel or the categories drawn from the Middle Ages and applied to Israel's royal period (vassal status, fiefdoms, royal estates, and similar medieval categories.).[38] These theories and categories are not found in Weber's work, it is true, but they are certainly "influences . . . derived from Weber's thesis."[39] As with Weber, they aid the attempt to understand the social and religious reality of ancient Israel with the assistance of sociology, especially the sociology of religion.

Although no notice was taken of it in Germany for a long time, there developed in France, from the end of the nineteenth to the middle of the twentieth century, an altogether independent image of ancient Israel that, nonetheless, can be compared in its basic intent and structures to that proposed by Max Weber. Its most important results were found in the work of the Strasbourg Protestant Old Testament scholar Antonin Causse, *Du groupe éthnique à la communauté religieuse. Le problème sociologique de la religion d'Israël.* The book's dedication page shows the tradition within which Causse stood and how it differed from the German scholarly trend represented by Weber. That is, the book is dedicated to Professor Lévy-Bruhl, the "master of studies of the primitive mind."[40] And Causse also sees in the deficient "attention to the primitive structure of the mentality, of the social order in Israel" the weakness of Weber's study, even though he shows a great deal of admiration for his "intuitive" grasp.[41]

In spite of this weight given to the history of ways of thinking, which characterizes French historiography to the present time, Causse continually pursues a goal comparable to Weber's: "The principal problem is in recognizing how the transition from this primitive, pre-logical, and group mentality to more developed ethical, rational, and individualistic ideas took place. In studying, in the following pages, the crisis of social groupings in ancient Israel and the origins of the Jewish community, I have attempted to point out some aspects of that transition."[42] As with Weber, there are two points to this agenda. On the one hand the social structures and the mentalities associated with them in the several epochs are to be described in sociological terms ("ethnic group," "religious community," "nation,"[43] "sect"[44]). On the other hand, there is a fundamental interest in the transitions. This is clear from the occurrence already in the title of the formula (which then recurs so frequently) of "from . . . till." Again and again he speaks of

"passage," that is, transition, as in the sentence quoted above, and the title of two out of four major sections contains the phrase "the crisis of social groups."[45]

Thus it is entirely appropriate that Peter Welten, after "descriptive works that as a general rule fashion no theories," links the works of Weber and Causse as a second "related group" of predecessors of the newer social history under the rubric of "works presenting a non-Marxist theoretical construction."[46]

Since 1968

It was characteristic of the period after World War II that the images of ancient Israel that had been developed in the inter-war period were at first unquestioningly regarded as valid. References to Alt and Noth in German-language scholarship, to Pedersen among Scandinavian, English-speaking, and Dutch scholars, and to Causse and related authors in the French-dominated Romance-language realm[47] indicate a broad consensus. Certainly there were always critical voices, but they remained in the minority, and on the whole interest in social history was minor—so minor that after the emergence of the "new social history" the dominant impression was often that this was something entirely new and without precedent.[48]

This movement to a new social history was related in a twofold way to the—real and symbolic—year 1968. In the first place, 1968 was the year in which a nonelectoral political, social, and cultural movement took the field in most of the Western nations. Part, though certainly not an especially large part, of that movement in Germany was made up of students of theology, members of student groups who were also active in church organizations, especially the synods (church districts). In critiquing the political and social situation and striving for changes in society and church, they rediscovered with special enthusiasm, among other biblical traditions, the prophets' social critique. The "Critical Papers" that appeared that year in Westphalia adopted the programmatic name "AMOS."

Likewise, in an intensification of symbolism, 1968 was the year that Latin American liberation theology was born.[49] In that year the second conference of the Catholic bishops of Latin America, at Medellín in Colombia, following Vatican Council II, officially sanctioned the new position of the Bible and the preferential option for the poor. In 1970, then, the programmatic *Teología de la liberación* by Gustavo Gutiérrez was published in Spanish in Lima, Peru; by 1973 it had been translated into English, and also into German.[50]

The larger part of the extra-parliamentary movement's publications in Germany (and other Western countries), as well as an important segment of what took place in the base communities in Latin America under the name of *lectura popular,* belongs to the realm of "gray literature."[51] As far as the history of scholarly research is concerned, such pamphlet literature[52] had at first only an indirect influence, but its impact was all the broader for that. It found expression in a multitude of articles on the subject of prophetic social criticism.[53] To a lesser extent they employed this newly awakened interest in a positive sense, but the majority rejected the implied or expressed claims that the Old Testament prophets were something like social revolutionaries or liberation fighters.[54] The flood of literature shows what a stimulating effect this external impulse had, in spite of the fact that it was not even aimed at scholars. At the same time this should not be overemphasized, since the studies of the late

1960s and early 1970s dialogued with their scholarly predecessors.[55]

After the initial reaction to the new social developments, first recorded in some fairly short articles, there began to appear from the mid-1970s onward some works that renewed engagement with questions that had been proposed since the 1920s. The older theories were tested, and dismantled, for example, Noth's "amphictyony" by C. H. J. de Geus (1976) and Weber's "confederation" by Christa Schäfer-Lichtenberger (1983).[56] But in spite of the critique of the specifics of the older proposals, their interest in a theoretical understanding of social structures was seen in a positive light. In particular, Max Weber's sociologically oriented initiative was retained, as evidenced especially by the cooperation of many biblical scholars in the two volumes on Weber's studies of ancient Judaism and on his view of ancient Christianity, edited by Wolfgang Schluchter in 1981 and 1985 respectively.[57]

Of course, dismantling the old theories was not the end of research; new proposals took their place. On the basis of the works of the sociologist and anthropologist Christian Sigrist, Frank Crüsemann and Rainer Neu described pre-state Israel as a segmentary lineage-society and a regulated anarchy.[58] Oswald Loretz introduced the concept of sharecropping, borrowed from Hans Bobek, to describe the social relationships in the background of the prophets' social critique, while Hans G. Kippenberg preferred, following Karl Marx, to speak of an ancient class society.[59] Again, postexilic Israel was described by Joel Weinberg as a citizen-temple community.[60]

The influence of Marxism on the new theoretical constructions was relatively small.[61] It is true that many authors use the concept of social classes and attempt to understand social developments in terms of the dynamics of class conflict; likewise, great weight is given to economic and social conditions, with special attention paid to property relationships. But all that is found in Max Weber as well. Thus the decidedly Marxist sixty-four page study by Moscow professor M. Lurje on the "economic and social conditions in the Israelite-Jewish kingdom" remains an exception (published in 1927 in the series Beihefte zur Zeitschrift für die alttestamentliche Wissenschaft[62]). Instead, we should reckon rather with a vague influence of Marxism mediated by works that were written in conversation with Marxism.

Naturally, the newly awakened interest in social history was not restricted to theoretical proposals. Most of the work is found in a multitude of individual studies. These concentrate on particular epochs, such as "The Formation of the State in Ancient Israel," or "State and Society in Pre-exilic Judah";[63] they investigate particular institutions: for example, "Officialdom in the Israelite Royal Period," or the "concept of the social type" of the "foreigner" (ger);[64] or they study particular biblical texts with a special social-historical interest such as "The Social Criticism of the Book of Amos in Historical-Critical, Social-Historical, and

Archaeological Perspective" or "Social Justice in Israel's Prophets."[65] These are some examples of monographs among a great many, to say nothing of the multitude of essays and dictionary articles.

However, there has been some hesitance to attempt an overview of Israelite social history. A first, important impulse came in 1988 from Niels Peter Lemche, who subtitled his *Ancient Israel* "A New History of Israelite Society."[66] In German, we may mention Rainer Albertz's 1992 *Religionsgeschichte Israels* and Erhard Gerstenberger's 2001 *Theologien im Alten Testament.*[67] It is true that these belong to a different field, but they describe their respective subjects against the background of social-historical developments in the several epochs of Israel's history. In English-language literature, two books in the American series Library of Ancient Israel, *Reconstructing the Society of Ancient Israel* by Paula McNutt (1999) and *The Politics of Ancient Israel* by Norman K. Gottwald (2001) deserve mention.[68] And much as in the case of Albertz and Gerstenberger, J. David Pleins' study of *The Social Visions of the Hebrew Bible* (2001), although devoted to ethical concepts, may be seen as social history.[69]

PART ONE

Methods for Studying the Social History of Israel

NOW THAT WE HAVE INTRODUCED THE question of *what* a social history of Israel will deal with, we must consider *how* to achieve a social history of Israel. We must take into account three multiple overlapping fields. First, there is the framework within which the social history of a community develops, its geographical and historical environments. Then we must have proper methods for dealing with the archaeological, epigraphic, and literary sources on which the description must draw. Finally, and intimately related to the question of sources, issues of theory and especially the search for analogies and the appropriateness of categories that may be used in the social history also play a role.

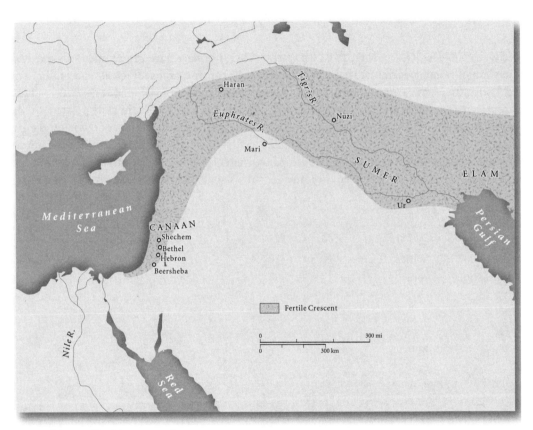

Map of the world of the patriarchs

2

Environment as Living Space

┌───┐
KEY POINTS

- Geography of ancient Palestine
  - Broken terrain, hills and valleys, coastal plain
  - Population living in small isolated units
  - Resulting commercial exchange
  - Unequal development with settlement and organized states first appearing in the flatlands
  - Highly diverse population

- External cultural influences
  - Early period: Egypt
  - Around the turn of the first millennium—regional power vacuum; Israel and Judah developed
  - After the eighth century: Assyrians and Egyptians, Babylonians and Persians, Greeks and Romans
└───┘

LET US RECALL THE DISTINCTION BETWEEN differing "rhythms of history," discussed in the Introduction, which according to Fernand Braudel must be considered by every descriptive history. First, he says, is "history over the long term."[1] Here geography forms part of the historical account. Every society exists under particular geographic conditions. But every society also exists under particular historical conditions and, as with geography, in a state of reciprocal influence with those conditions. I will summarize both under the concept of the environment as living space.

The Geographical Environment

Ancient Israel was already aware that the geographical and environmental conditions in which a people lives are not a negligible factor, as is clear from the lovely contrast between the irrigation culture in the Egyptian riverine landscape and the rain-dependent agriculture of Canaan's hills in Deut 11:10-11:

> For the land that you are about to enter to occupy is not like the land of Egypt, from which you have come, where you sow your seed and irrigate by foot like a vegetable garden. But the land that you are crossing over to occupy is a land of hills and valleys, watered by rain from the sky.

This contrast permits certain conclusions about social history to be drawn from the different geographical conditions. It is no accident that the world's great river valleys contained the places in which the earliest high cultures flourished. Irrigation systems had to be provided there. Since the water of the rivers was used more efficiently to the extent there was better social organization, it was in these valleys that the first states were created.

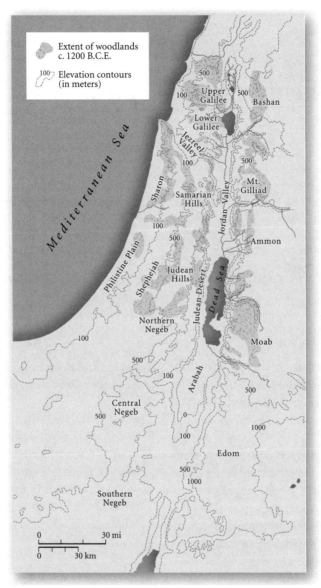

2.1 Topographic map of Palestine

It is true that even in a land "watered by rain from the sky" people have to remake nature to improve their conditions of life, for example by constructing cisterns and terraced fields. But in this rugged and broken country, this "land of hills and valleys," the inhabitants could easily exist in small groups, isolated from one another, and, at least for a time, they were not compelled to construct larger societies. The southern Levant, the land of Canaan,[2] is marked by its variety of landscapes. Beginning from the hill country of Ephraim and Judah and the uplands of Shephelah, a fertile, level corridor follows the coast; there are also level places in the hill country, of which the most impressive is the Jezreel plain in the north.

This geography of small, isolated social units with very different environmental and agricultural conditions, in close proximity to one another, had consequences for social development as well. For one thing, it calls for commercial exchange, something that played an important part in every epoch of Israel's history, from the time when the hill country was settled at the beginning of the Iron Age[3] to the regulation of commerce in Nehemiah's time (Neh 13:15-22). It also promoted unequal development. Settlement began earlier in the flat country than in the hills, and cultures organized as states also developed earlier there. The consequence was that the rise of states in Israel and Judah took place only as a "secondary creation of states," ones that presupposed the prior existence of other states.[4] Finally, the geography of the small social units caused the political units of the region also to remain, for the most part, fairly small, from the Canaanite city-states of the late Bronze Age and the Philistine cities to the provinces of the Persian period—and very often there were different structures existing in close proximity—to the settlement areas of the various peoples and the Greek πόλεις (city-states) of the Hellenistic epoch.

The fact that Israel and Judah achieved only a secondary or later state-creation was not only an indirect consequence of the region's internal geographical structure, but at the same time a consequence of the larger geographical situation. Syro-Palestine is a broad open space, a transit corridor on the road from Mesopotamia to Egypt. The states that rose at an early period in those river valleys regarded the region as within their sphere of influence and used it as a corridor for invasion and a buffer zone. These uses of the land took different forms and were more or less intensified at different periods throughout history, with different forms and intensities through the rhythms of history.

At the same time, the land's borders lay open. In the second and first millennia BCE, there were movements of peoples across the Mediterranean, just as there were from the eastern steppes. The population of the land was mixed. Not without reason did the late biblical texts describe the previous inhabitants of Canaan in terms of long lists of peoples (Gen 15:18b-21; Exod 3:8, 17; and frequently elsewhere). Historicity played no part in the situations presumed by these lists. What was important was the awareness that this was a mixed population.

With this last observation we have already broached a sphere that is not part of the geographical conditions in the narrow sense, but rather belongs to Israel's historical-environmental circumstances.

The Historical Environment

Israel itself had always preserved an awareness that when it appeared on the stage of history in the land of Canaan it did not encounter there a *tabula rasa*, a land totally devoid of people. The narratives of the origins of the people who were led out of Egypt and took a land for themselves, a land whose previous inhabitants were exterminated, expelled, or subjected, attest to this. Even if, contrary to this historical construction in the biblical text, current knowledge asserts that Israel arose more or less autochthonously in the Land itself, and that the population elements coming from outside are estimated in relatively small numbers, the narrative retains the memory that this Israel was not always present. Among the most important historical-environmental conditions for Israel was that, long before its existence in Canaan, there was already present there a colorful world of states with developed cultures. And that Mesopotamia and Egypt possessed high cultures with varied state structures, with systems of laws and administration, elaborate literatures, and well-developed high forms of religion, to which were later added the Hittite culture of Asia Minor. All these cultures left traces in the Syro-Palestinian land of passage, a corridor that has been well-traveled by armies, migrants, and traders.

For Israel's early period, the influence of Egypt was of special importance, for from the time that the Asiatic Hyksos dynasty was driven from Egypt, the realm of the pharaohs dominated the Canaanite states of the southern Levant. The collapse of those states and, connected with it, the direct influence of Egypt, was one of the conditions that made it possible for independent states to arise in the region, in Israel and Judah, around the turn to the first millennium BCE In fact, their rise was only possible because there was a temporary power vacuum in the great powers of the ancient Near East. But that vacuum was only momentary. From the eighth century onward, without interruption, the region was in the thrall of the ambitions of major external powers to seize dominance, and most of the time it was directly subject to them.[5] From that point on, no history of Israel can be written without reference to Assyrians and Egyptians, Babylonians and Persians, Greeks and Romans. And of course the social history of Israel did not remain untouched by the course of this larger history.

3

Material Remains

KEY POINTS

- Three sources for a social history of Israel:
  - Primary: artifacts from archaeological excavations
  - Secondary: the biblical texts
  - Tertiary: ethnological analogies
- Criteria for primary sources:
  - Datability: dated with relative precision
  - Temporal proximity: "originated during or shortly after reported event."
- Three levels of interpretation:
  - Reconstruction
  - Dating
  - Theoretical interpretation
- Palestinian epigraphy:
  - Vast sources of information from Egypt and Mesopotamia: hieroglyphics and cuneiform writings
  - Much smaller amount of material from ancient Israel: mostly ostraca, papyrus, and bullae
  - Coins from the Persian and Hellenistic eras useful for social history

GEOGRAPHY AND THE HISTORICAL environment constitute the frame, the living space, within which Israel found and developed its social structure. But how can we grasp that structure itself? We are faced with the question of the *sources* for a social history of Israel. They are very varied, and that variety requires careful weighing of the relative value of each source. Essentially, the sources divide into three types: material remains discovered by archaeology, biblical texts, and the conclusions we can draw by analogy from other societies regarding conditions in Israel.

The sequence of this list is not arbitrary; it is conceived in terms of primary, secondary, and tertiary sources. In recent historiographical discussions the awareness that we must distinguish between primary and secondary sources, and that the biblical texts are secondary sources, has prevailed.[1] In this understanding,

primary sources are those whose origins can be "dated with relative precision . . . on the basis of archaeological criteria" ("criterion of datability") and that "originated during or only shortly after the reported events" ("criterion of temporal proximity").[2] Neither of these applies to the biblical texts. They were, as a rule, composed a long time after the events recounted, the time of their composition can be reconstructed only hypothetically, and even when authentic documents have been retained in biblical texts we have only "copies of copies" of the texts themselves.[3]

Nevertheless, the distinction between primary and secondary sources is only a formal one; it says nothing about the historical reliability of the sources.[4] Bismarck's *Gedanken und Erinnerungen* (Thoughts and Reflections, Otto von Bismarck's memoirs), undoubtedly a primary source for the second half of the nineteenth century, certainly offers, from one point of view, less reliable information than a historical study of the same period written a hundred years later. The decision about reliability demands a critical evaluation of each individual source, whether primary or secondary.[5][†]

Archaeology: Artifacts and Interpretation

If primary sources are distinguished, according to the above definition, by the criteria of datability and temporal proximity, we are in the realm of archaeology, which excavates the remains of the older societies that produced those sources, thus opening for us a window into the past.

Of course, not all the results of archaeological work are equally significant for the special interest of social history. Certainly, monumental edifices such as temples and palaces are important for their very existence in that they presuppose a certain level of social organization. In social-historical terms one must ask who built them, under what circumstances, and for whom, and yet these are questions that archaeology itself is in no position to answer. On the other hand, it is a matter of indifference for social history whether the temple is of the long-body or broad-body type or whether the

palace had an upper story or not. Entire city layouts that permit conclusions to be drawn about social structure are much more interesting for social history than monumental structures.[6] Likewise, highly relevant for social history are the surveys of whole regions that give us information about the distribution of settlements, agricultural production, and changes to these over the course of centuries.[7] Here archaeology and the geography of settlement come very close in their interests and studies. And other remains besides architecture have varying degrees of value for social history. Thus the presence of signet seals permits conclusions about writing culture. The wealth of pictorial material on these seals also opens up a new and highly fruitful access to the history of religion. But nothing that bears directly on social relationships can be gleaned from the images. The same is true for practically all important iconographic remains.

If the remnants of ancient Israel uncovered by archaeology are of different value than the special interests of social history, their use as primary sources is likewise subject, methodologically, to the objection that material remains as such are dumb and *only interpretation* can make them speak.[8]

Since it is only in the rarest cases that archaeology discovers intact remains, the first act of

Definitions of Criteria for Primary Source	
Criterion of datability	Identifies a source that is "dated with relative precision" by archaeological methods
Criterion of temporal proximity	Identifies a source that "originated during or only shortly after the reported events"

Adapted from Christoph Uehlinger, "Gab es eine joschianische Kultreform? Plädoyer für ein begründetes Minimum," in *Jeremia und die "deuteronomistische Bewegung"* (ed. Walter Groß; BBB 98; Weinheim: Beltz Athenaeum, 1995), 59–60.

[†] Editor's note: In the American context, we may make similar comments about the memoirs of the Civil War general, Ulysses S. Grant, *Personal Memoirs of U. S. Grant*, published 1885–1886.

Writing a Social History of Ancient Israel: Types of Sources		
Source	**Type of Source**	**Examples**
Archaeological and epigraphic remains	Primary	Excavated houses, temples, ancient coins, pottery, ancient tools, ancient graffiti, ancient inscriptions
Texts	Secondary	The canonical "Old Testament" or Hebrew Bible, the Apocrypha, the pseudepigrapha
Socio-ethnological analogies	Tertiary	Theories derived from modern sociological/anthropological research, for example, segmentary lineage society, acephalic rule, regulated anarchy, tribal class society

interpretation is *reconstruction*. The degree to which such reconstructions of the same material may differ is illustrated by the discoveries on Mount Ebal dated to ca. 1200 BCE. Those on the dig interpreted the structure as a sanctuary with side rooms and a wall surrounding the sacred space.[9] Others read them as a farmstead with work buildings and an enclosing fence to hold the animals within.[10] It is obvious that the value of the excavated primary sources will be judged quite differently, depending on the reconstruction.

A second act of interpretation requires *dating* the reconstructed remains. In this regard, there has been a heated argument within the archaeological guild in recent years over *high* or *low chronology* in dating monumental structures, especially in the north of Israel. The question is whether these buildings should be dated to the tenth century or no earlier than the eighth. In the former case they would be evidence of the building activity of Solomon, as depicted in the Bible; otherwise the biblical accounts would be shown to be backward projections of building work that in reality was carried out by the rulers of the Northern Kingdom.[11] This shows how inseparable archaeology is from the interpretation of the biblical texts, for whether I regard the latter

as historically reliable or as later projections into the past, I must attempt to make my case plausible on the basis of the texts themselves. Simply refusing to take the texts into account, sometimes suggested as a way of escaping the circle of archaeological interpretation and textual interpretation, is no solution.

Finally, in a last act the archaeological findings form the basis for a theoretical interpretation. The excavation of the city of Tell el-Farʿah (north), from the eighth century, revealed sectors with two different kinds of houses, the larger with foundations measuring 100 to 110 square meters and the smaller only 65 to 80 meters square. For the archaeologist Roland de Vaux this was evidence for "a radical social change," to which references are also found in the eighth-century prophets.[12] But that proposal does not result from the archaeological findings themselves, which can certainly be interpreted differently. Thus Abraham Faust suggests that those who lived in the larger houses still retained the social form of the extended family, while small or nuclear families dwelt in the smaller houses.[13]

What is true of archaeological discoveries in general applies likewise, with appropriate caution, to a special group of findings, namely those that preserve written texts.

Epigraphic Material from Israel and Its Environment

There is an abundance of written records from Israel's environment, primarily from Egypt and Mesopotamia.[14] Although we have here a rich mine of sources, they are only indirectly useful for reconstructing the social history of Israel, for whatever we can draw from these texts about social, economic, and legal conditions can only be used directly to reconstruct the social organization of the society that produced the documents. Only at a second stage can we attempt, by analogy, to transfer what we have learned to Israel. We will address this question below.[15]

In contrast, the quantity of inscriptional material in Israel itself is much thinner.[16] This paucity of remains results not only from the fact that these societies had much less developed governmental structures in comparison to Egypt and Mesopotamia and therefore produced fewer writings. But also the dearth of findings was caused primarily by the writing materials used. For ordinary texts (letters and official documents) these were mainly ostraca, shards written on with ink. We have a vast number of these, especially ostraca from Samaria,

Arad, and Lachish that are likewise of interest to social history.[17] But we must suppose that in previous excavations many inscribed ostraca whose ink had faded or been obscured by dirt were unwittingly erased by washing. The other important writing material, especially for documents, was papyrus (see Jer 32:11-14, 44). An archive destroyed during the conquest of Jerusalem in 587–586 yielded a large number of *bullae* (seal impressions in clay), and still visible on the verso are the threads that once held the sealed rolls together, as well as the crossed-fiber pattern of the papyrus that made up the rolls.[18] But all the papyrus rolls were burned, and in general papyrus did not survive well in the climate of Syro-Palestine.

However, inscribed seals play an important part in the study of Israel's social history. The major corpus of West Semitic seals lists 1217, including 711 described as Hebraic.[19] The collection in the *Handbuch der Althebräischen Epigraphik* (2003) speaks of a "corpus of about 945 seals, *bullae,* and jar seals."[20] Especially important for social-historical reconstruction are the seals that contain not only the name of the owner, but also a title.

As with the non-written remains, the mere presence of inscribed monuments is significant,

Types of Archaeological and Epigraphic Data	
Type of data	**Examples**
Material remains	Houses, temples, vases, kitchen utensils, altars, oil lamps, human and animal remains (mummies, skeletons)
Epigraphic (inscribed or written) material, that is, written material on pottery, stone, or objects, but not preserved on papyri, scrolls, or in books.	Inscriptions: the Rosetta Stone, Merneptah stele, Moabite stone Graffiti Ostraca (pieces of pottery used as a surface for writing letters, contracts, and so forth) Inscriptions on Signet Rings Inscriptions on coins

Interpretation of Archaeological Remains
Discovery → reconstruction of remains → dating → theoretical interpretation of remains

because whether much or little is written, whether many people or only a few had seals, or whether private individuals as well as civil officials had them, whether those who owned seals included women—all this is material for evaluating the form of a society.

As we have said above, both written and non-written evidence constitutes primary source material. Occasionally it has been asked whether it should not be possible to write a history of Israel from primary sources alone.[21] As a thought experiment, it is certainly tempting. But I would not consider it an advance if we were to rely solely on the accident of archaeological findings and the restricted realm of social reality that reveals itself only in material remains to the exclusion of the theologically colored biblical tradition.

For example, the existence of slavery in Israel is attested epigraphically only by the documents from Elephantine and the Samaritan papyri from the fifth and fourth centuries. But if we assume that there was also slavery in the land of Israel itself, we do so because we rely on other sources, namely on the one hand the analogy to comparable ancient societies on the one hand, and on the other hand biblical texts that speak of slaves.

Finally, let me refer, for the Persian and Hellenistic era, to a special kind of "written" remains, namely coins. In this case also, their mere existence is significant.[22] Coins were first introduced in Asia Minor in the sixth century by the Lydian king Croesus, and their use was adopted by the Persians. The advantage of coins over the unmarked silver that was in use beforehand was that the tedious process of weighing was eliminated and the monetary value of the silver was indicated and guaranteed by the stamp. Of course, that does not mean that coins were immediately introduced in great numbers. The Persian imperial coins existing since 521 BCE, the gold *daric* and the silver *siglos,* were much too valuable to be in everyday use. Only from the mid-fifth century onward were smaller coins minted, a variety of local money, satrapy coins, and provincial coinage. Obviously this had consequences for commerce, and thus for social relationships.

4

The Texts of the Hebrew Bible

KEY POINTS

- Aspects of the Hebrew Bible relevant to social history:
  - A theological book
  - Largely fictional: contains its own narrative world
- Historical minimalism:
  - Relies solely on extra-biblical evidence
  - Is represented by Philip Davies, Niels Peter Lemche, Thomas Thompson, Keith Whitelam
  - Rejects the historicity of biblical narrative texts
  - Must speculate about the origin of such texts
- Social-historical data in biblical narratives:
  - Concerning the time of narrating
  - Concerning the narrated time
  - Unintentional tradition of more value than intentional
- Legal texts:
  - contain information about social institutions and processes more than most other texts
  - provide an idealized portrait of reality
- Dating biblical texts:
  - Distinguish narrated time from time of the narrative
  - Distinguish original prophetic texts from their later edited versions
  - Test legal texts
  - Use poetic and wisdom texts for entire historical periods

HAVING FIRST EXAMINED MATERIAL remains, we now turn to the biblical texts—in that order because of the formal distinction according to the criteria of datability and temporal proximity.[1] But that is not the only reason. "The Old Testament is a theological book."[2] It is true that, to a greater degree than almost any other work in the literature of the world religions, it engages with history, but it is a history that is interpreted theologically. It is precisely when one takes seriously this deeply theological character of the Hebrew Bible that one recognizes that its texts are historical sources only in a secondary or indirect sense.

Moreover, the biblical texts are in large part fiction.[3] That is a statement about the genre of the texts. The truth of the fictional accounts does not lie in their agreement with a reality external to the narrative. That would the truth of a report, for example a police report or the minutes of a meeting. A fictional narrative, by contrast, describes its own world, and its relationship to the world outside the text is quite flexible and in any case cannot be captured by the categories of "true" and "false."[4] In truth, there are only a very few biblical texts that could be called reports (some annals that can be extracted from 1 and 2 Kings), and even those are embedded in the larger fictional contexts of the theologically interpreted histories of Israel and Judah in the books of Kings.

Other biblical texts are neither reports nor narratives. We can think, for example, of legal texts, wisdom sayings or great wisdom poems like the book of Job, psalms, or sayings of the prophets. In the case of these texts it is quite obvious that they were not written to convey reliable historical information. Nevertheless, they, too, are highly valuable for attempts at social-historical reconstruction.

But what is the value of biblical texts for the reconstruction of ancient Israel's social history? What has already been said makes it clear that this is to be judged differently according to the kind of text in question.

The Historical Reliability of the Biblical Accounts

In spite of their theologically motivated and fictional character, the biblical texts do contain reliable information. A whole series of events from the royal period onward is attested by extra-biblical sources. There is agreement not only in the framework of the dates, but also in a surprising number of details, if one is able to read both the biblical and extra-biblical texts critically.[5]

Since all historical researchers have access to the same source material, differences in evaluation of those sources must be methodologically grounded. This can be illustrated by the example of so-called historical minimalism.

It is to the credit of the painstaking deconstruction of the "history of Israel" in the works of Philip Davies, Niels Peter Lemche, Thomas Thompson, or Keith Whitelam, to mention only the most prominent names, that they leave nothing unquestioned. That is the duty of critical scholarship. However,

their treatment of the sources is not entirely unproblematic. What is "accepted" is only what is attested by "external evidence." For Lemche that means the Merneptah stele, the Mesha stele, the reference to Ahab in Assyrian sources, Sennacherib's siege of Jerusalem, and Nebuchadnezzar's conquest of the city.[6] The possible methodological conclusion would be that if the biblical texts that speak of events confirmed by "external evidence" contain a historical kernel, this may be asserted of other narratives by analogy—though not without critical examination in each individual case. But Lemche seems to draw the opposite conclusion: Everything that is not obviously incontestable is suspect of being unhistorical. Such a methodology is also defensible—if one is in a position to explain how such narratives came to be. And at that point, unfortunately, Lemche abandons the ground of scholarly argumentation and enters the field of speculation. According to him, the mention of building works in Egypt in Exod 1:11 is a backward projection from such works "that may have happened in the days of Pharaoh Necho" (at the end of the seventh century). But we know absolutely nothing about any such building. As to the traditions about David and Saul, he speculates: " . . . it is possible that traditions which had originally nothing to do with Judah or conditions in Jerusalem in the 10th century BCE were simply transformed into Judean traditions."[7] Of course, with "may have happened" and "it is possible" one can posit pretty much anything.[8]

There are also other reasons to believe that biblical texts contain reliable information about historical events. The Jewish monarchy in Jerusalem was part of an ancient cultural tradition that maintained a written correspondence with the Pharaoh as early as the late Bronze Era.[9] We may scarcely suppose

Types of Social Historical Sources in the Hebrew Bible		
Genre	**Social Historical Information Contained**	**Examples**
Reports/annals	Accurate information about historical events and social institutions external to the text: the exile of Israel and Judah, the siege of Jerusalem, assassinations, lists of reigning kings, trade relations	1 Kgs 14:25–26
Fictional narratives	A self-contained narrative world whose connection to the external history of Israel/Judah is flexible; but may contain data about family structures, gender roles, travel, the economy, and so forth	The stories of Saul, David, and Solomon (1 Sam 10–1 Kgs 11)
Legal texts	Prescriptions and proscriptions for forming an ideal Israelite society; real issues facing society at the time of writing	Leviticus
Poetry	Information about the nature of Israelite worship and conceptions of the deity, thoughts about sex in ancient Israel, concerns about society and government and the nation's future	Psalms, Song of Songs, prophetic oracles
Wisdom	The nature of daily life: what do husbands/wives/children do? What are their responsibilities? How do social superiors/inferiors relate to one another? What are the signs of social success?	Ecclesiastes, Proverbs, Job

that that tradition broke off when new elements entered the culture, especially since, demonstrably, a great many Jerusalem traditions were adapted for use within the cultural sphere. The note in 1 Kgs 14:25-26 may serve as evidence for written annals, and from this we learn that Pharaoh Shishak received a massive tribute from Jerusalem during his historically attested campaign at the beginning of the last third of the tenth century, but did not take the city. Form and tradition criticism as well as the general rules of cultural memory dictate that such a notice, not narratively developed, can only have been handed down in written form.[10]

If we may accept that there is a body of reliable information (to be critically evaluated) about historical events, this is all the more true of social history, which inquires about social structures that are not dependent on individual events.

Fiction and Milieu

We begin with the abundance of material that can be called historical in the broadest sense. These books (Genesis–2 Kings; Ezra; Nehemiah; Chronicles; Ruth; Esther; Maccabees; Judith; Tobit) are, as we have seen, not reports, but narratives, and to that extent they are fictional. But as a rule they are not fictional in the sense of the modern genres of fantasy or science fiction, which invent the world in which they locate their stories. The biblical narratives, instead—and increasingly from the point at which Israel was living in the Land, the time with which we must also associate the authors—are located in a very real world. They are more like a novel by Dostoevsky: all the characters may be invented, but we learn a great deal about social conditions in nineteenth-century Russia. In this case we are not interested in the historicity of the actors, but in the milieu within which the authors place them.[11]

Of course, as regards biblical narratives we cannot assume, without further examination, that the milieu presumed by the narrative is that of the time period described; it may also be the time of the person or persons writing. It is not like Dostoevsky's situation: he places his characters in their own contemporary milieu. Instead, this is historical narrative, in which we must make a stringent distinction between the time of narrating and the narrated time.

We are thus confronted with the problem of anachronistic backward projection, so that every single case must be tested. For example, when the author of Genesis 24 depicts Abraham as the wealthy owner of many camels, our knowledge of the history of the domestication of these animals, which did not take place until the first millennium, leads us to suspect an anachronism here. It is a different matter when the author of Jeremiah 32 describes how, in a business transaction, the agreed-upon selling price is weighed on a scale, a bill of sale is prepared with two copies, one open and one sealed, and it is signed by a group of witnesses (vv. 9-12). We know that at the beginning of the sixth century (that is, at the time of the narrative) there were no coins, so that uncoined metal was weighed, and on the basis of the discovery of a great many *bullae* with traces of papyrus and threads on the verso, as well as by somewhat later analogous procedures in neighboring cultures we may assume that in fact bills of sale were prepared in just

this way. Whenever an author tells a story, he or she describes a milieu as it existed in narrated time, the time of the narrator.

The Problem of Narrative Anachronism

| | are projected back | |
| Events in the narrator's time | | to the narrative's time |

The narrator projects social conditions at his time of writing into a narrative about past events. In Genesis 24, for example, Abraham is the wealthy owner of many camels. Yet, the camel was not domesticated until the first millennium BCE, and Abraham is described as living before that time.

So a testing of whether an anachronistic backward projection is present must be conducted in every individual case. And yet there is no reason for a generalized suspicion that all descriptions of milieu are unreliable. This is connected to the following point.

Intentional and Unintentional Tradition

Almost everything that interests us in our attempt at social-historical reconstruction appears only incidentally in the texts we use as our sources. The just-mentioned narrative in Jeremiah 32 is not meant to inform us about mercantile activity in the early sixth century; its purpose is to attest that the prophet Jeremiah, even during the siege of Jerusalem by the Babylonians, expressed the hope that at a later time normal business dealings would be possible once again. The material side of the action, that is, especially the question that is so interesting for social and economic history— whether silver was weighed or paid in coin—is not of the slightest interest to the narrator.

In general, we can say that the narrative texts of the Old Testament are interested in events, and simply assume the circumstances within which the events occur as background.[12] Something similar is true for other groups of texts. Prophetic sayings are handed on for the sake of the divine message the prophet transmits. That the message was spoken in a concrete, historical world is also evident from the texts, but telling about that is not the point of the text. The same holds for wisdom sayings: the worldly knowledge they wish to convey presumes the world in which it is to be applied, but that world itself is only unintentionally—on the side—the subject of the tradition. Helmut Seiffert expresses this in theoretical terms as a distinction between intentional and unintentional tradition.[13]

Social history is interested precisely in what is handed on unintentionally, the background situation. This has two consequences. In the first place, it means that the knowledge we can derive from the texts is only spotty. On the other hand, however, we must assume that while texts intend the things they mean to convey to appear in a certain light, we should not presume that they have an equal interest in the implied circumstances. Thus the direct intention of Jeremiah 32 is that Jeremiah's message be shown to be reliable, but the circumstances in which that takes place are unimportant.

Like the distinction between fiction and milieu, the differentiation between intentional and unintentional tradition is suggestive, but it is not an absolutely secure indicator of historical reliability. We can never avoid the task of comparing the evidence of biblical texts

with other evidence. At the same time, we are again faced with the question of dating. Before we turn to that, however, we need to give some attention to a group of texts that, as with narratives, prophetic sayings, and wisdom texts, poses the question of the relationship between text and reality, but in a different way. I am referring to legal texts.

Norm and Reality

Legal texts are not narratives that may or may not take place in a milieu that is interesting for social history. Nor do they offer information, unintentionally and incidentally, that can be used for social-historical reconstruction. Rather, they are meant to influence the social world of the people for whom they are written. Therefore they contain information about social institutions and processes to a greater extent than almost any other group of texts.

The information in these texts is extremely useful for social-historical reconstruction. While I could say above that we would know nothing about slaves in ancient Israel if we had only archaeological or epigraphical sources,[14] that false conclusion is excluded by the biblical laws concerning slavery in Exodus 21, Deuteronomy 15, and Leviticus 25, as well as other regulations concerning slaves.

But let us be clear that legal texts do not simply reflect reality. Anyone who tried to reconstruct the social reality of the German republic from its constitution and the individual laws in accord with it would get a distorted picture. The same is true for biblical laws. They all contain an ideal picture, a program for what Israel's social and religious form ought to be, and so do not permit a direct conclusion about the real situation. The extent to which that program was enacted must be determined by

4.1. Scene on a *pithos* from Kuntillet ʿAjrud. A portion of the inscription reads "For Yʜwʜ and his Asherah." The meaning of the inscription is not clear, but many scholars conclude that Yʜwʜ is represented with a consort—an idea completely at odds with the writings in the Hebrew Bible.

comparison with sources other than the law texts themselves.

But if the biblical collections of laws must be read primarily as programmatic, and not as a reflection of reality, they are by no means a utopian program in the strict sense; their intention is to shape the world as they find it. They must therefore both take account of its institutions and address its problems. The question of norm and reality in legal texts can be illustrated by a law that concretely refers to slavery. Deuteronomy 23:16 requires that the Israelite it addresses should not hand over a slave who has escaped from his or her master, but permit the slave to dwell in a place of his or her choosing. We may conclude from this that at the time this rule was made that institutionalized slavery existed and

the problem was that slaves ran away from their masters; since laws only regulate things that are socially relevant, we may assume that this happened often. But we cannot learn from the text whether its prescription, which is unique in antiquity and in fact would result in the abolition of slavery, was put into effect. We would need other sources to demonstrate that.

While the relationship among institution, problem, and prescription can be quite accurately determined, for an interpretation of legal texts that addresses not only institutions but their history we would also need to know the dates of the texts. That, of course, is an issue that legal texts share with all other kinds of texts, even though the question is differently posed with regard to different kinds of texts.

4.2 Ink pot found in the excavations at Qumran, Israel, 3rd cent. BCE–1st cent. CE. Shrine of the Book, Jerusalem. Photo © Erich Lessing / Art Resource, N.Y.

Dating Biblical Texts

All questions of fiction and milieu, intentional and unintentional tradition, and the relationship between norm and reality come together in the issue of the dating of texts. We should first repeat what we said above under the rubric of history of events and "the long term": for the questions of social history it is not a matter of fixing a year and a month, and the question of the identity of an author (for example, a prophet), so interesting for literary criticism, is altogether unimportant. And yet the issue of dating is not merely incidental.

The question is posed differently depending on the kind of text at issue. For *historical-narrative texts*, the distinction between narrated time and the time of the narrative is fundamental. It is true of every narrative that these two are not identical, but it is interesting to know how far apart they are and what degree of reliability should be attributed to the narrative as we have it. We need to determine whether the

narrative, for example, in the books of Kings, uses older sources, and perhaps even has access to official documents. The possibility of reliable oral tradition cannot be excluded, either. And finally, we may attribute to the authors something like an awareness of historical distance: when they speak of what they call the "time of the judges" they know that they cannot place a king of Israel in that time period. Ultimately, every individual case needs to be tested. But one thing is sure: the narrated time cannot be more recent than the time of narration.

This fixing of a starting point behind which we cannot go is especially important for the *prophetic texts,* each of which is presented under the name of a prophetic author. The collected texts can hardly be older than that author. But they can, of course, be more recent, since in most of the prophetic writings we must reckon with a process of handing on and augmentation that extends in some cases over centuries. Here, too, the question of dating requires testing in individual cases.

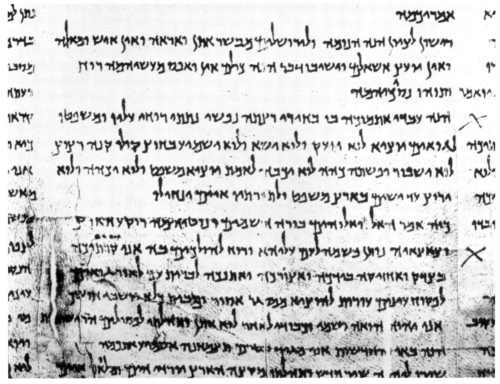

4.3 Lines (in Hebrew writing) from one of the two scrolls of Isaiah found at Qumran, Israel. Herodian period. Israel Museum (IDAM), Jerusalem. Photo © Erich Lessing / Art Resource, N.Y.

The biblical law texts, unlike the Mesopotamian *corpora,* are not attributed to kings whose dates we know; according to the Pentateuch's narrative of origins they all stem from the period between the exodus from Egypt and the entry into the Land. That this is a fiction—a highly important theological fiction—has long been recognized. But how are we to date the texts, then? Here a certain consensus has emerged as regards the relative sequence of the texts. As a rule it is assumed that the Book of the Covenant in Exodus 20–23 is older than Deuteronomy, and Deuteronomy in turn is older than the priestly laws. But a relative chronology still does not tell us anything about absolute dates; can we use the Book of the Covenant to reconstruct the conditions pre-state ancient Israel, or

does it reflect the society of the eighth century? It is not surprising that considering the legal texts yields the conclusion that a testing of individual cases is indispensable.

From their very genre, the poetic and wisdom texts are most resistant to dating. These texts engage fundamental aspects of faith, life, and relationship to the world, not datable events. In contrast to the prophetic sayings, which address a historical situation, these lay claim to a certain timelessness. Nevertheless, they are not without value for social-historical reconstruction because in any case they reflect certain fundamental realities that we may presume are valid for whole epochs (for example, sayings about the poor and the rich) or for a certain sector (for example, the royal proverbs).

Although the question of dating leads to a checking of individual cases there is still, in my opinion, no reason to trace almost all the texts to the post-exilic period (as one faction of Old Testament scholarship does) and to treat the pre-exilic epoch as a dark period and sweepingly exclude it from all attempts at reconstruction. Certainly, most of the Old Testament writings achieved their final form only in the post-exilic period. But that does not mean that they are entirely backward projections from that period. Against such an opinion are, first of all, the observation that most of the texts are not from the same mold but reveal clear signs of development; where there is recent addition there must be older portions as well. Second, against a general thesis of backward projection stands the variety of the material; the fact that the writings attributed to Amos and Hosea, Isaiah and Micah, Jeremiah and Ezekiel have such a fundamentally different character scarcely can be explained otherwise than by supposing that they are traceable to different prophetic figures. Third, a closer look at the word choices is required in order to make it possible to distinguish continuous basic vocabulary combinations, which by their very quality are hard to date, from elements shaped by a particular time.

So, on the basis of the combination of rich landlords and debt-laden peasant farmers, which predominates throughout antiquity and is reflected in Nehemiah 5, the latter text has been used as a key for dating prophetic texts that contain the same combination to the Persian period.[15] But this overlooks the fact that in Neh 5:7 the members of the upper classes are called *khorim* and *seganim,* an expression that never appears in texts that are traced to the pre-exilic prophets. Contrariwise, Isa 3:14, for example, speaks of "elders and princes," who do not appear in Nehemiah 5. Just such details speak against deriving all texts from one and the same epoch.

J. Maxwell Miller's question quoted above, "Is it possible to write a history of Israel without relying on the Hebrew Bible?"[16] may be addressed again here. I have already said that, because of the accidental nature of the findings and the restricted range of real objects available from archaeological remains, it would not necessarily represent progress to do without the biblical texts. But more needs to be said. Even if it were *possible* to write a (social) history of Israel without reference to the Hebrew Bible, from the point of view of historical methodology it would be *impermissible.* For no historical work may deliberately deprive itself altogether of part of its sources. It must regard them critically, and in individual cases there may be disputes about the results of the critical testing. But if we take careful note of their fundamentally theological character, the different forms of the texts, and their historical origins, there is no reason to exclude the texts of the Old Testament in general from the reconstruction of the social history of Israel.[17]

5

In Search of Analogies

KEY POINTS

- Data derived from archaeology and the biblical texts requires interpretation
- This interpretation must rely on structural analogies from ancient Israel's neighboring societies and the results of ethnological study
- Because of the geography of Syria-Palestine, Israel was influenced by other cultures
- Israel and Judah were always the weaker

cultures, incorporating or resisting to the dominant culture's power
- Ethnologic comparisons require theory construction
- Social history requires generalizations that are often anachronistic
- Using such theories in historical reconstruction must guard against projecting our concerns onto the past

IN TREATING MATERIAL REMAINS AS THE sole primary source for Israel's social history we repeatedly come back to the issue that these remains require both interpretation and augmentation from other sources. When we have recourse to the biblical text to augment our resources, the question of interpretation of the archaeological findings—and, incidentally, the biblical ones as well—lies methodologically on a different plane. We could say that archaeology and biblical texts present data, but the issue now is what interpretative framework do we organize the date within?

Such a framework cannot be derived solely from observing the society under investigation, for every term I use presumes the comparison that, at the outset, permits us to construct concepts by means of generalization and delimitation. If, for example, I refer to a "state," I am generalizing from a variety of concrete political forms and at the same time I am eliminating nonpolitical social entities

(such as the family) and non-state forms of society (such as a tribal community). I will say more on this below.[1]

On the general level of conceptual construction, for example, in the case of the concept of "state", one must in principle include all societies past and present. But if we want to describe the particular social organization of ancient Israelite society we will have to concentrate on societies that, because of temporal or material similarity, allow us to justly suspect that there may be structural analogies. For ancient Israel that means that we must consider, on the one hand, the societies in Israel's own environment, and, on the other hand, historical and recent societies studied by ethnology.

In both cases, certainly, we must note that even when structural analogies can be demonstrated, comparisons always have only a heuristic function. For example, the significance of genealogies for the organization of segmentary societies in modern Africa may raise the question whether there was something comparable in ancient Israel, but it cannot prove that such was really the case. The same is true of ancient Near Eastern law codes and legal institutions.

Societies in Israel's Environment

What was just said about the heuristic value of analogies must now be expanded and made more precise. The societies surrounding Israel were close to it in time and space, which is why we pay attention to them. But the extent to which they are close to Israel in their social structures must be examined separately in each case. We already pointed out above the reasons why, for geographical reasons alone, we must presume different social developments in the river valleys of Egypt and Mesopotamia and in the hill country of the southern Levant.[2] This circumstance suggests that we should, when possible, compare not only the smallest, isolated segments, but more complex systems also.

At the same time, a look at the geographical-environmental conditions showed that the region of Syria-Palestine is a broad, open space[3] in which influences from all the surrounding cultures mingled. Added to that, for Israel and Judah, is the fact that, historically speaking, they arose relatively late.[4] We must therefore calculate that from the beginning they were marked by elements of other cultures. In the early period, that would have taken place primarily through the influence of other Canaanite societies, but very soon, quite obviously from the eighth century onward, Israel, and then Judah, lay under the direct influence of Assyria and Babylon, Persia and Greece, and finally Rome. This forbids any attempt to try to understand the development of Israelite and Judahite society in isolation, simply on the basis of internal laws.

And yet, even when the dominant powers are shifting, the overall structure must always be taken into account. Israel and Judah were always the weaker, dominated cultures. Whatever influence the dominant culture exercised, it did not make Israel itself culturally dominant. Therefore at every individual point of comparison, this deep structural inequality must be taken into account, and we must reckon with the fact that Israel developed not only by incorporating, but also by resisting, the culture of the dominant power.

Ethnology: From Empirical Studies to Theory

What is true of a comparison with the societies surrounding Israel is still more valid for the comparisons to be made with societies studied by ethnologists. Here, too, comparisons have at most a heuristic value and are not probative. And here, to a still greater degree, there can be no comparison between isolated phenomena without regard for the overall social context.

This is especially true when ethnology—as is its primary task—studies recent societies (that is, those that still exist at the time they are studied). Here one can certainly find a great many analogies, in family systems and genealogies, in the forms in which authority is exercised and in the functions of gifts and exchanges, in legal systems and the organization of production.[5] And yet in every individual instance the whole society must be kept in view, and its interaction with other societies must also be considered. Family systems may be comparable in details, and yet it is not irrelevant that in a society without a central government the family is the only organizing principle of the society. This is true whether it is the form of organization of a people in an early form of the state, standing over against the political authority, or if, under imperial rule, a subject people maintains its identity by means of its familial relationships. Likewise it makes a fundamental difference whether societies develop in isolation (as was sometimes the case in Oceania) or other societies in different stages of development are in close contact with one another, and are also confronted by European colonial power (as in Africa beginning in the nineteenth century).

For ethnology, even more than in the historical examination of roughly contemporary ancient societies, comparisons require the construction of theories. Thus we cannot directly compare African peoples such as the Nuer, Tiv, or Dinka, studied by twentieth-century anthropologists, with the ancient Israelites and Judahites of the first millennium BCE. But on the basis of studies of recent African peoples, one can construct a theory about segmentary lineage societies and acephalic rule that makes it possible to gain a better understanding of certain phenomena from the period of Israel's development into a political state.[6] It is not so much the empirically observable phenomena that are placed in relationship to one another as it is the theories derived from them that are used as a framework for understanding and interpretation of both the recent and the ancient societies. Methodologically, one must make a firm distinction between the empirical findings derived from study of archaeological primary sources, analysis of secondary sources, and ethnological comparisons, and the theories by means of which these findings are interpreted. It is true that individual theories are ultimately derived from comparison of empirically observable phenomena, but they are not the phenomena themselves.

This brings us to a point that takes us beyond ethnology as a science of the study of peoples in the recent past.

Sociological Categories

Social history as the study of a society's form through its history cannot be accomplished without generalizing categories. This is true even of the empirical description of particular phenomena. For example, the descriptions in the "biblical antiquities" tradition, described above in our retrospective on the history of research, all had chapters on "marriage" and "family."[7] Hebrew has no equivalent word for "marriage." In the case of "family" one ordinarily thinks first of the "father's house" (*bet ʾav*), but here again the terms are not simply equivalent. When the descriptions in question then have subsections on "polygamy and monogamy" or "Levirate" marriage,[8] it is completely obvious that these categories have not been derived from the texts, but imposed on them.

The farther we move from the description of individual phenomena and the more we try to understand the form of a society as a whole, the more are we forced to use such categories not derived from the texts. The very word "society" does not exist in Hebrew. Sometimes it coincides with the Hebrew word for "people," but "people" is also an ethnic category—which society is not—and as a sociological category it can refer only to that part of the society that is "people" in contrast to the ruling house. Whether we describe Israel at the end of the second millennium BCE as a segmentary lineage society, a regulated anarchy, or a tribal class society, whether we call Judah and Israel at the beginning of the first millennium an empire or a chiefdom or an early state, whether we speak of post-exilic Judah as a the-ocracy or a pariah people or a citizen-temple community, we are using categories derived from sociology's theoretical constructions.

We certainly could not succeed, then, in describing Israel's social history without using categories borrowed from sociology.[9] But that should not be misunderstood as a license to project the business of making history relevant to our current situation—which has its place in preaching and teaching—back into histori-cal reconstruction. Although we cannot work without modern categories, our description must attempt to discover and depict what is different and strange in the society of ancient Israel. We could certainly translate Hebrew *sar* as "official."[10] But at the same time we must explain that the function of an official in a soci-ety that is less thoroughly regulated by laws and is constructed in a fundamental sense on honor, prestige, and personal relationships is something different from a modern, bureau-cratic political office.

PART TWO

The Epochs of Israel's Social History

WHAT HAS BEEN SAID THUS FAR ABOUT the object and methods of social-historical work is true as a whole for social-historical study of every (ancient) society, even though the examples have been drawn from Israel's social history. As we now turn to a material description of Israel's social history in particular, we must at the outset clarify what we understand by "Israel."

In biblical literature, the name *Israel* is used for the whole people from the time of their sojourn in Egypt. It marks the transition from the book of Genesis to that of Exodus. While this portrayal applies the name *Israel* from the beginning to all the tribes, including Judah, the usage becomes more differentiated as the royal period begins. Now, when the text speaks of political entities, it distinguishes between Judah and Israel. Judah is the southern kingdom, Israel the northern kingdom.[1] This begins even with David: according to 2 Sam 2:4 he is anointed first by "the men of Judah" to be "king over the house of Judah," and later he is anointed by "all the elders of Israel" to be "king over Israel" (2 Sam 5:3). At the same time and in the same textual context, however, "Israel" can also mean the whole people, including Judah, when the elders of the northern tribes remind David of God's promise that he will shepherd "my people Israel" (2 Sam 5:2). This double meaning then continues through the whole deuteronomistic depiction of the history of the royal period.

The usage shifts and becomes still more complex from the end of the eighth century as a consequence of the exile. Does the population in the former northern kingdom, where the Assyrians settled other peoples alongside those who did not pass into exile, belong to Israel? Do those who remained in the territory of the former southern kingdom belong to Israel? Or is the concept to be restricted to the members of the Babylonian diaspora? Does it become detached from the Land if those who remained in Babylon, but not all those who live in the territory of the earlier kingdoms, are "Israel"? These are questions that will need to be addressed again when we come to describe the Persian period. But the fact that it has been asked here already is meant to show how vague the concept "Israel" is in any description of the social history of "Israel."[2] In what follows it will be used in such a way as to keep in view three components that are, as a rule, essential when one speaks of "Israel." These are, first, the consciousness of an ethnic solidarity expressed primarily in the construction of a common genealogy. Second is the relationship to the Land, which was basically retained even by those in the diaspora. Finally, we cannot speak of Israel apart from its relationship to its God, YHWH, quite apart from the question whether, alongside and with him, there may legitimately have been other divinities before and even during the royal period.

In addition to these three internal aspects, this presentation is limited to the period covered by the Old Testament writings. This sets an end-point for the account drawn not from social history itself, but from the development and canonization of the texts of the Hebrew Bible.

But when can a description of the (social) history of Israel begin? According to the biblical picture, the history of Israel begins with the prehistory of the ancestral families, and that picture has been adopted in many scholarly depictions of Israel's history.[3] The *Biblische Enzyklopädie,* appearing since 1996, also treats "Israel's Prehistory" in its first volume,[4] but it has nothing to do with the biblical historical picture, but is "an account of the history of the Near East from ca. 2300 to ca. 1200 BCE, at which point we are at the beginning of the history of Israel proper."[5] We are still farther along if we take "the Davidic-Solomonic kingdom"[6] or even the middle of the royal period ("toward the end of the 9th century and in the 8th century")[7] as a starting-point.

The distinction between Israel's "prehistory" and "history" underlies this discussion.[8] It is not very helpful because, as the preceding remarks show, it is not fully clear in any epoch what is "really" Israel. History is a continual process of change, and to that extent every epoch is the prehistory of future developments. If we abandon this distinction, there remains the empirical fact that the name *Israel*—whatever social entity that may refer to—appears for the first time at the end of the

thirteenth century BCE on a Pharaoh's stele.[9] That, then, is the period in which the description of Israel's social history must begin.

More problematic still, methodologically, is the initiative of some recent historians who consider Israel's history before the Persian period to be altogether a Persian-era construct, its historical value approximately the same as that of Vergil's *Aeneid* for the history of Rome.[10] Certainly the history of Israel is part of the history of the ancient Near East and has no greater dignity than that of the other peoples of the region. And certainly the picture of Israel's history, like every historical account, is constructed by the historian. But these two insights have been positivistically reversed: because Israel's history is embedded in that of the Near East, and because every historical account is constructed, suddenly we have a difference between a "history of Israel," which is an "invention," an "imagined past," while the "history of Palestine" is a matter of "realities."[11] The fact that this positivism is used to legitimate current Palestinian claims challenging the state of Israel does not increase its plausibility.[12]

With the mention of the name *Israel* at the end of the thirteenth century, we arrive in the epoch that archaeologists regard as the transition from the Late Bronze Age (1550–1200) to Iron Age I (1200–1000). Here we must seek Israel's beginnings.

Meaning of "Israel" in the Hebrew Bible			
The whole people (as sharing a common genealogy), from the sojourn in Egypt on	The people as they relate to the Land (which is also called "Israel")	The northern kingdom as opposed to the southern kingdom, Judah, in the time of the divided kingdom	The people in relationship to YHWH

Chronological Table for Palestinian/Israelite Archaeology in the Second and First Millennia				
Periodization Employed in the *Encyclopedia of Archaeological Excavations in the Holy Land*		Periodization Employed Here	Dominant Factors, Characteristics	
Middle Bronze IIA	2000–1750	2000–1750	Egyptian Middle Kingdom, 12th Dynasty	
Middle Bronze IIB	1750–1550	1750–1550	Canaanite city-states; 13–15th Dynasties	
Late Bronze I	1550–1400	1550–1400	[Egyptian]	Earlier 18th Dyn. (to Amenophis II)
Late Bronze IIA	1400–1300	1400–1300	[New]	Later 18th Dyn. (from Thutmose IV)
Late Bronze IIB	1300–1200	1300–1150	[Kingdom]	19th–20th Dynasties— Ramessides
Iron IA	1200–1100	1250–1100	Deurbanization phase; "settlement"	
Iron IB	1100–1000	1100–1000	Growth of settlements, regional centers	
Iron IIA	1000–900	1000–900	"United Monarchy" (David, Solomon)	
Iron IIB	900–800	925–720/700	Nation-states (Israel, Judah, Ammon ...)	
Iron IIC	800–586	720/700–600	Assyria, provinces, vassal states ...	
Babylonian-Early Persian	586–333	600/587–450 (Iron III)	Babylonian, early Achaemenid Periods	
		450–333 (Persian Period)	Persian Province of Yehud, from Artaxerxes I	

6

Israel's Origins as a Kinship-Based Society

KEY POINTS

At the start of the second millennium BCE:
- Egypt dominated the small city-states of the Levant politically
- Two other major social groups in ancient Palestine:
  - Shasu nomads
  - The 'Apiru—a marginalized social, not ethnic, group
- During the Late Bronze Age, the Merneptah stele records the presence of a group called "Israel"

Around 1200 BCE:
- Egypt's influence in the Levant waned; many Canaanite city-states collapsed and the influence of the remaining ones decline; the Sea Peoples, the Philistines, settled in the coastal areas
- During the early Iron Age, new settlements appeared in Palestine's hill country
  - Their economies were based upon vineyards, fruit orchards, and olive tree cultivation
  - These settlements developed commercial contacts with the remaining Canaanite cities
  - It is unclear who developed these settlements—possibly the Shasu nomads, survivors of the abandoned Canaanite cities, and the 'Apiru
  - The "Israel" on the Merneptah stele was part of these newly emerging small hill-country cities
- The evidence of the biblical text:
  - Ethnically diverse population in Palestine

- A group of nomadic herders who entered Palestine from the east
- A group of escapees from Egyptian slavery, the "Hebrews," who conquered Canaan for themselves
- Scholarly models of early Israel:
  - Most twentieth century scholarly models are monocausal
  - The best models for Israel's earliest development envision multiple causal factors
- "Pre-state" Israel (the period of the judges):
  - Best described using archaeological data interpreted through social history and ethnographic models
- Results:
  - Israel's small hill settlements were more or less egalitarian, and were probably related
  - larger settlements contained people from different clans
  - the family was defined by its male head
  - gender relationships were relatively egalitarian
  - A clan shared a common ancestor
  - The tribe's role is unclear but tribes formed ad hoc coalitions during times of crisis
- Israel's unity was probably genealogical
  - "Israel" regarded as the common ancestor of all the tribes
- Pre-state Israel was still part of Canaan, though independent and recognizable
- Pre-state Israel seems to have been a segmented lineage society

---

- Pre-state Israel's economy:
  - Mostly agricultural—farming and animal husbandry
  - Some work on Phoenician ships
  - Some were Canaanite slaves.
- Leadership structures:
  - A lack of organized leadership structures
  - "The men of the city" and the "elders" as decision-makers in cities
  - No evidence for an authoritative tribal leader
  - "Judges" military leaders for the duration of a military crisis
- Social stratification:
  - Large farmsteads owned by the "big men," that is, the wealthy
  - Individuals on the economic margins fleeing family conflicts, in economic distress, or involved in crimes

"Israel" does not appear on history's stage as a finished entity. Rather, it was built up out of a variety of elements in a process lasting about two hundred years (which is not to say that after that time the entity "Israel" was defined for all time). If it is the task of social history to describe the social form or organization of a society in its historical development, there is no epoch in which the dynamic moment of social change and the static form of social stability are more difficult to distinguish than that in which Israel came to be. If in what follows we nedvertheless treat the beginnings of Israel and the structures of the kinship-based society sequentially, we do so only for reasons of clarity. If anyone were to get the impression that first there was a dynamic epoch of origins that was then replaced by a static phase with stable structures, that impression would be false. Israel's existence throughout the epoch was an existence in the process of constant development.

The Beginnings of Something Called Israel

What is the political, social, and cultural milieu in which we find ourselves at the time when the first contours of emerging Israel are visible?

Canaanite Society in the Late Bronze Age (1550–1200)

We can clearly discern, from the beginning of the second millennium BCE onward, that in the Bronze Age the Levantine region was characterized by numerous city-states, each of them independent, living alongside each other in a tense relationship of cooperation and competition. This is signaled by the imprecatory texts from the Middle Kingdom in Egypt. These incantations indicate Egyptian interest in the region, and in fact the Pharaohs of the Middle Kingdom proceeded to extend their hegemony over the Levant. Pharaoh Thutmose III (1479–1425), in his first campaign, finally secured the New Kingdom's rule over Palestine. The Egyptians were content to establish outposts in some cities and to use the rivalry among the individual rulers to cement their own dominance over the region. The Amarna correspondence from the palace of Pharaoh Amenhotep IV Akhenaten (1351–1334), named for the place where it was found, confirms the picture of fragmentary city-states. This correspondence also enhances this picture by showing that at that time, especially in the hill country, there are discernible larger spheres of political dominance that already have the character of territorial states. We will have to return to this picture when we speak of how Israel and Judah became states.[1]

For reconstructing the internal social conditions in Canaan at that period, the lists of prisoners in the reports of the campaigns of Thutmose's son Amenhotep II (1428–1397) are very revealing.[2] These—augmented by other reports and archaeological findings—reveal a complex society. Numerous ruling houses in the individual tiny states relied militarily on professional charioteers and were surrounded by specialists in cultic affairs and general administration. They were associated with people who are called Canaanites in the prisoner lists and who, since they are few in number, must have been wealthy merchants and traders. The mass of the population, the farmers, formed the economic basis for the city-states.

Besides the city-states, with their monarchical and centralized organization, probably similar from one to the other, there are two groups in the lists that are not identical with this resident population and are distinct from each other: the ʿApiru, and the Shasu nomads. The Amarma letters also mention the ʿApiru as an independent social group. Who are the people concealed behind this significant (so the sources lead us to believe) social group?

The Shasu mentioned in the Egyptian sources were nomads,[3] more properly sheep- and goatherders (camel herders, comparable to modern Bedouins, appear only later).[4] Such nomadic herders are already attested in the Near East in the second millennium, as is evident especially from the Mari texts.[5] On the spectrum of lifestyles from settled residence to pure homelessness, there was a broad range of possible nomadic types: movement with the herds between residences, a shift from settlement to nomadism in accordance with the seasons, irregular nomadism, and other forms of nomadic life.[6] Nor should the difference between nomads and settled people be seen as fundamentally and inimically opposed to one another; it was, rather, a symbiotic relationship.

Michael B. Rowton has described in a series of articles[7] the intertwining of urban settlement and nomadism between and among the urban areas as a "dimorphic social and political structure," or more briefly as a "dimorphic structure."[8] Since nomadism is related to the cities, Rowton calls it "enclosed nomadism," in contrast to the nomadic systems in the steppes of Central Asia and Arabia.[9] In speaking of a "dimorphic society," Rowton is seeking a concept that can apply, at a high level of abstraction, to all the societies of western Asia over a long period. Since the city and the (nomadic) tribe furnish the basic structure of the societies, but the grid is very loose because of the desired high degree of abstraction, it is possible to speak not of a "dimorphic" but of a "polymorphic" society.[10]

It is known that the nomads in the region where Israel was later established, the place that interests us most, sometimes moved from southern Palestine to the Nile Delta in search of food. This is attested for the whole of the second millennium. The nomads are painted in color in Khnumhotep of Beni Hassan's tomb in the nineteenth century BCE, being brought by Egyptian officials to their district commander, with women and children, herds and gifts.[11] Later, in the twelfth century, a border official writes to his superior that he has registered Shasu tribes from Edom and directed them to public lands assigned to them.[12] As Amenhotep II's prisoner lists show, such Shasu also entered the land of the Nile as prisoners of war.

6.1. An ivory from Megiddo shows a prince in a victory procession with Shasu captives going before him (above); (below) left side of the ivory, showing a victory celebration.

Besides the Shasu, the prisoner lists also mention the ʿApiru. What social entity lies behind this group?[13]

The first thing we know about the ʿApiru is that the sources always distinguish them clearly from the Shasu. These two social groups are not only nonidentical; they do not even overlap. Alongside the settled peoples and the nomads, the basic groups of Canaanite society in the Late Bronze Age, the ʿApiru constitute a kind of "third power" that is clearly distinct from both.[14] In the Amarna correspondence the ʿApiru are described as an unruly element and as enemies of Egypt who sometimes ally themselves with rebellious kings. They are mentioned very frequently as hill-dwellers. Since such ʿApiru appear in the sources of

any number of Near Eastern cultures in the second millennium (besides Egypt we may mention Nuzi and Mari, Ugarit and Alalach, as well as Hittite texts and Hebrew Bible texts that look backward to the second millennium[15]) this picture is easily enhanced. The ʿApiru are evidently not an ethnic, but a social category standing for migrants, people who have unstable living conditions either for economic or political reasons. They lead their lives as thieves on the margins of society or, when more deeply integrated, either as mercenaries in the service of individual city rulers or as resident aliens with minimal rights.

As Amenhotep II's prisoner lists show, such ʿApiru sometimes entered Egypt as prisoners of war.[16] Two model letters from the time

6.2. "Israel stela" of Pharaoh Merneptah, on which he claims to have defeated Israel in the fifth year of his reign (1207 BCE). This is the earliest recorded mention of "Israel" on a monument.

of Ramses II (1279–1213) show the fate that awaited them there: ". . . give provisions of grain to the people of the army and to the ꜤApiru who are drawing stones . . . for the great pylon of 'Ramses Miamun.'"[17] Thus the ꜤApiru are different from the Shasu in this respect as well. The latter seem to have received only a right of residence that was regarded as temporary. When the cause of their migration to Egypt has ceased to exist they can evidently return to their home region. But for the ꜤApiru, who were being used as forced labor, that was scarcely a possibility.

Somewhere around 1200 BCE, fundamental changes began in the society of Canaan we have just described. But before that, at the end of the epoch called the Late Bronze Era, the name "Israel" appears on a stele of Pharaoh Merneptah. What can we learn from this?

"Israel" on a Stele of Pharaoh Merneptah

The victory stele of Pharaoh Merneptah (1213–1203) bears a long account of the Pharaoh's Libyan campaign in the fifth year of his reign. Added at the end is a short hymn summarizing the ruler's victories in the Levant,[18] which is described in general terms as "Canaan." Then follows a list of three cities: Ashkelon, Gezer, and Yanoam, followed by the statement about Israel: "Israel is laid waste, his seed is not." At the end, Khor stands for "Khurri-land," the land of the Hurrians.

Of prime importance for the interpretation is that each of the three cities has the hieroglyphic determinative for a foreign land next to its name, while "Israel" is accompanied by the sign that indicates persons, and thus is thought of as a group of people. Hence the three cities, on the one hand, represent the traditional Canaanite city-states, while "Israel," on the other hand, designates a population group that is not restricted to a particular, geographically definable region within Canaan and is clearly distinct from the populations of the city-states.[19]

The statement that "Israel is laid waste, his seed is not" contains very strong phraseology; "seed" is probably understood to mean "progeny."[20] Therefore, we can by no means conclude that the stele refers to a purely agricultural people; nomadic or semi-nomadic lifestyles would not be excluded.[21] Noteworthy in any case, however, is "the deviation from the previous usage for describing elements of the population outside the Canaanite city-states."[22] Whoever carved the stele evidently did not consider the expressions ʿApiru or Shasu appropriate to describe the population group he was referring to. And he names "Israel" as a single entity alongside the three city-states.[23]

There are a number of possible answers to the question of what "Israel" on Merneptah's stele has to do with the later Israel. The stele itself can offer no solution. It is interesting that "Israel" contains the theophoric name element "El," while in later documents "Israel" is always closely associated with the God YHWH. This is true not only in the Bible, but also especially in the chronologically closest inscriptional evidence, the Mesha stele from the ninth century. This favors, on the one hand, the idea that worshipers of YHWH in the ninth century bore a name handed down in tradition, but on the other hand indicates less an unbroken ethic

identity and speaks more for the proposition that the "Israel" on Merneptah's stele later joined or was dissolved into a group for which the God YHWH was constitutive, and gave its name to that group.

The fact that between the end of the thirteenth century and the next inscriptional mention of Israel in the middle of the ninth century there stretches a gap of nearly four hundred years cannot be interpreted to mean that the Israel of the Merneptah stele had nothing to do with the Israel of the Mesha stele. Rather, it indicates that the Israel we find widely attested in extra-biblical sources from the ninth century onward already had a four-hundred-year history behind it. In reconstructing it, of course, we are dependent on archaeological material and the biblical texts. The reason for the great gap in inscriptional evidence is not that in the mean time the Israel of the Merneptah stele had disappeared or sunk into complete insignificance.[24] It is due, rather, to the fact that in the transition from the Late Bronze Era to the First Iron Age, around 1200, Near Eastern society underwent profound changes; a (secondary) result was that there are almost no monumental inscriptions from the early Iron Age. We will now take a look at these changes.

Transformations of Canaanite Society in the Transition to the Iron Age

What happened around 1200 BCE in the southern Levant can rightly be described in such words as "collapse,"[25] "dissolution,"[26] "ruin,"[27] or "radical change."[28] There were many aspects to the process that mutually affected and intensified each other.

Until the end of the thirteenth century, Egypt and the Hittites divided control of the southern and northern Levant. But then the internal ability of these empires to maintain their imperial interests outside their own borders rapidly collapsed. After the death of Ramses II in 1213, Egypt had increasing difficulty in holding its empire together. Merneptah was able to intervene in the southern Levant once more with success, but his victory stele attests above all that he had to expend great effort to beat back the Libyans who were attacking Egypt from the west. Merneptah's successors still undertook advances into southern Canaan; documents showing Egyptian presence are attested here and there throughout the twelfth century.[29] But Egyptian influence in the region was steadily declining, and we can no longer speak of Egyptian rule there.

The internal developments in Egypt were not caused by, but were certainly intensified by the advance of the so-called "Sea Peoples." These were groups from the Aegean region, traveling by sea to seek new places to settle. After Ramses III (1183/82–1152/51) succeeded in keeping them out of Egypt a group of them, the Philistines, settled in the southern coastal plain of the land later named for them (Palestine) and erected city-states on the Canaanite pattern. We would certainly not be wrong to assume that Egypt approved of these settlements, and that the Philistine states are to be seen more as substitutes representing Egyptian interests than as Egypt's competitors. Nevertheless, these events also testify to the decline in direct Egyptian influence in Canaanite territory.[30]

Profound revolutions in the internal conditions in Canaan accompanied these changes in the Levantine-political situation. It is, of course, an exaggeration to speak of the "ruin of the Canaanite city-states" at this point,[31] since by no means did all the cities collapse. But the dense network of city-states, the system as such, did enter a profound crisis, at the end of which—in the first millennium—the dominance of the city-states had given way

to territorial states. The development was different from place to place. Important cities like Hazor, Sichem, and Aphek were already destroyed by about 1200, and afterward were vacant or thinly occupied. Other centers like Beth-Shean and Lachish, Megiddo, and Gezer retained their inhabitants through the twelfth century. In the cases of Megiddo and Beth-Shean, we can even deduce from the material culture that the occupants were still Canaanites, even after the collapse of the Bronze Era settlement. Other cities, in contrast, remained entirely unoccupied as late as the tenth century.[32]

Parallel to the collapse of the Bronze Era cities of Canaan, and certainly connected to causes for the collapse, was the land's resettlement during the early Iron Age. New settlements arose throughout the hill country that were significantly different from the old cities. They were smaller, and they lacked city walls and towers as well as monumental buildings. In general, we can discern no deliberate planning, something that would be shown by street layouts or the arrangement of open squares. The types of houses that dominated in these new settlements were also different from those predominant in the old cities. To the extent that the region's surface has been explored, we find an evenly spaced pattern of settlement—except for the coastal plain and the Plain of Jezreel. Even the Negeb, where there were no old cities, was included in this settlement.[33]

The newly settled regions were clearly different in their economic geography from the lands surrounding the old city-states. In the plains, the most important agricultural activity was planting and harvesting grain. There was relatively little land in the hill country suitable for such planting. But the high plains and especially the slopes were well suited to cultivating olive trees as well as fruit trees and vines. In particular, the building of terraces in

6.3. Depictions of Egyptian-influenced naked goddesses on scarabs. Bronze Age, Palestine.

order to cultivate the slopes signifies a major step forward. We also find many cisterns and silos in the new settlements, as well as voluminous clay jars (*pithoi*) for storage. All this points to agricultural methods that are anything but primitive; as regards both the use of resources (terraces, cisterns) and the storage of products (silos, *pithoi*), they are highly advanced.[34]

But even then, people did not live on olives, fruit, and wine alone. Grain remained, as before, the basic staff of life. It could be cultivated only in small quantities and in particular places within the new settlements, with two consequences. First, the new settlements had to trade with one another so that the grain grown in the hill country could be made available to all. And, second, because grain from the hills would not be sufficient for their own use, they had to be in commercial contact with the inhabitants of the old cities in order to exchange their products for the grain cultivated there.[35]

No matter what contrasts there may have been between the new settlements and the old cities, there was no contradiction regarding their fundamental economic situations; they were, rather, mutual enhancing.

But where did these new settlers come from?[36] There are many candidates for their origin, and we must insist from the outset that it is improbable that there will only be one place of origin. The fall of the Bronze Age cities did not mean that their inhabitants disappeared. It may well be that the new settlers included former inhabitants of those cities and their surrounding lands. Especially the ᶜApiru, who were in the land even before the collapse of the cities, could have scattered into the newly developing settlements.[37] But the majority of the new settlers may have come from (semi)nomadic backgrounds.[38] These pastoral nomads, who are to be seen as closely identified with the Shasu in the Egyptian texts,[39] often lived in a symbiotic relationship

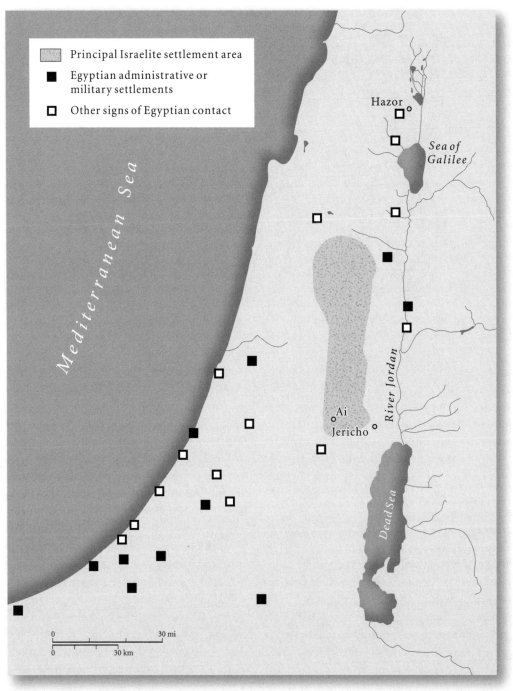

6.4. Map of Israelite settlement area.

with the cities and had to seek new ways of living when the cities fell. But we cannot exclude the possibility that there were immigrants from elsewhere who settled in the land for the first time.[40]

It is true that the archaeological sources, on which we have relied exclusively to this point, tell us nothing about the ethnic composition of the new settlers. We need to avoid any over-hasty conclusions. Since there was such a thing as "Israel" before the beginning of this new settlement, as attested by Merneptah's victory stele, and since around 1000, at the transition to Iron Age II, we again have certain evidence of "Israel," connecting the settlement with "Israel" is not altogether unfounded. From the Merneptah stele, we learn that this "Israel" was not ranked with the old city-states, but was part of the newly emerging small city structures. But that in turn should not be seen as a mutually exclusive contrast. The fact that there were both continually inhabited older cities and new foundations and resettlements of temporarily abandoned cities in Iron Age I, and that at the time of Israel's kings a distinction was made between Israelite and Canaanite cities,[41] can only mean that after a certain time even some city-dwellers considered themselves members of Israel.

More than this, however, is not clear. Whether, for example, all the new settlers could be immediately identified by that name, or whether there were a number of groups alongside one another and the name "Israel" was ultimately applied to all of them, remains an open question.[42] It likewise remains murky whether the new settlers thought of themselves as an ethnic unit in any way, or from what point in time that was true. Moreover, the role of possible immigrants in this process of the reshaping of a whole region's society can, in principle, receive no further clarification.[43]

The Beginnings of Israel as an Evolutionary Process

As was already emphasized at the beginning of this section, there is no other epoch in Israel's social history in which its shape was so much in flux. This is natural inasmuch as this was the epoch of Israel's beginnings. This reconstruction of Israel's origins contradicts the biblical picture as sketched in the book of Joshua, according to which a whole nation took possession, during a short military occupation, of a land that was previously inhabited by other nations.

That does not mean that the biblical texts yield no reliable historical recollections at all, but it is true that those appear only when one deconstructs the overall textual picture and evaluates the individual narrative elements on their own.

As regards the conditions in the land of Canaan, the biblical texts present a picture according to which "Canaan" is not a political unit, but is splintered into a great many kingdoms. In the conquest narrative, there is a "king of Jericho" (Josh 2:2-3), a "king of Ai," (Josh 8:1-2, 14, 23, 29), a "king of Jerusalem" (Josh 10:1, 3, 5, 23), and several more. In the narrative in Josh 10:1-27, the king of Jerusalem does not fight alone against the Israelites, but builds a coalition of five city kings, just as in Josh 11:1-15 the "king of Hazor" puts together a coalition of any number of rulers. This matches the Amarna letters, from which we learn of the establishment of such coalitions. So the texts can speak in summary fashion of "all the kings of the Amorites" and "all the kings of the Canaanites" (Josh 5:1; cf. 9:1) or of the "kings of Canaan" (Judg 5:19). The deuteronomistic lists of the Land's prior inhabitants (Gen 15:19-21; Exod 3:8; 23:23, and frequently), which represent a late collection of names of the most varied type and origin, also touch historical reality when they portray the previous population as ethnically diverse.

The biblical picture of Israel's becoming a nation is, as we can easily see from the texts, a combination of two histories of origins. One of these traces Israel back to a group of nomadic herders who entered the Land from the east. According to the other, Israel stems from a group of "Hebrews" who escaped from Egyptian slavery. As late as Hosea in the eighth century, these two origin narratives stand independently alongside each other (compare especially the parallel Jacob and Exodus traditions in Hosea 12).

In the first place, the biblical picture is interesting because it indicates that the later nation of Israel cannot be derived from a unilinear descent from one predecessor group. On the one hand, we have the tradition that the Israelites descended from a group of "Hebrews" who escaped from Egypt. According to Exod 1:11, they had been forced to build the supply cities "Pithom" and "Ramses" for the Pharaoh. This, of course, recalls the model letter from the time of Ramses II, cited above.[44] The connection between the papyrus and the text of Exod 1:11 also makes it understandable that the Hebrew equivalent ʿivri ("Hebrew") appears nowhere so frequently as in the narrative development of the theme of the sojourn in Egypt in Exodus 1–15 (Exod 1:15-16, 19; 2:6-7, 11, 13; 3:18; 5:3; 7:16; 9:1, 13; 10:3). The only comparable concentration of instances of this word is in the narrative of Joseph and his brothers, which as we know is also located in Egypt (Gen 39:14, 17; 40:15; 41:12; 43:32).[45]

Just as in the extra-Israelite sources the Shasu Bedouins are mentioned alongside the ʿApiru, so in the biblical picture of the early period we perceive the nomadic families of the ancestors alongside the "Hebrews." As the Egyptian witnesses show such nomadic herders being permitted to reside in Egypt in times of scarcity—without their being forced into slave labor like the ʿApiru—so it is said of the ancestral families that in times of famine they sought refuge in Egypt, and in such a way that there was not a thought given to the danger of being enslaved (Gen 12:10-20; 42-46; cf. 26:2).

Of course, a comparison of the Exodus and ancestral traditions on the one hand with the extra-biblical sources on the other reveals how artificial the construction of the final biblical text is, from a historical point of view. In the extra-biblical texts the Shasu and ʿApiru are always strictly separate entities. Thus, that nomads might flee to Egypt because of famine and there mutate into ʿApiru is historically next to impossible. Nevertheless, the necessary deconstruction of the overall biblical picture does not automatically condemn its individual elements as unhistorical. In this case, what this means is that, even if there was no such thing as an "ancestral period," an epoch preceding the sojourn in Egypt and the occupation of the Land,[46] that does not exclude the possibility that parts of later Israel stemmed from a milieu resembling the one depicted in the Genesis accounts.

According to the biblical picture, later Israel was fed from several sources. Besides the ʿApiru and the Shasu line, we have the indication that Israelite origins had something to do with the Arameans (Gen 11:10–32; 24; 29–31; Deut 26:5–9). The picture of a mixed heritage is altogether historically probable. According to the biblical picture, Israel's origins were in any case not autochthonous. The Bible presumes a clear sequence: First there were a number of different peoples living in the Land, and then Israel entered it as well. The historian must regard this portrayal as ambivalent. Against it stands, with great certainty, the mention of a group called "Israel" on Merneptah's stele, something that cannot be harmonized with the biblical picture of the people's coming together in Egypt and subsequently occupying the Land. On the other side is the texts' stubborn insistence on a non-autochthonous origin, which could scarcely have been manufactured out of thin air.[47] Finally, other peoples assert with equal stubbornness that they have always lived in the place where they now are—from the creation of the world onward. Certainly the claim to a particular territory is better founded on that kind of an assertion than if one were to say that one's people had moved there at some later time.

While the biblical narrative attempts to integrate the various traditions of Israel's origins into one continuing history, the theories of the so-called conquest of the Land that developed in the course of the twentieth century have sought to capture the "real" process in a single model, whether of military conquest,[48] gradual infiltration by pastoral nomads,[49] or intra-Canaanite revolution.[50] In the wake of the scholarly discussion of these three models, we can say that in any case the idea of a unified conquest of the Land by a people coming from outside it has been shown to be untenable.[51] Beyond that, all three models suffer by their monocausality. In reality it is rather unlikely that the process that can be called resettlement or occupation in this broad sense took place according to a single model in the different parts of the land and at different times between about 1200 and 1000 BCE.[52] And besides: from a social-historical point of view, such a process scarcely ever proceeds "according to plan," but rather is a multifaceted event to which, indeed, all the elements that are absolutized in the various models may contribute.[53]

Hence, it is inviting to describe Israel's coming-to-be in the Land as an evolutionary process.[54] It took place differently in different regions and at different times. What emerged in Iron Age I parallel to the dissolution of the system of the Canaanite city-states goes back to a blending, no longer subject to detailed historical reconstruction, of elements from the old city-state system, of nomadic herders and ʿApiru, but perhaps also of immigrants from the Aramean region. We have no direct evidence for the ethnic and religious identity of these people. But we do know that already at the end of the thirteenth century a population group "Israel" is mentioned on Merneptah's stele alongside the city-states, and there is epigraphical evidence of "Israel" from the ninth century onward. This assures us that what was happening in the twelfth and eleventh centuries outside the old city-states belongs, in any event, to a depiction of Israel's social history.

But how can we picture for ourselves the social form of this developing entity?

Structures of Kinship-Based Societies

Designation of Eras

Seldom can we so clearly recognize how much a social history description of past epochs is shaped by our own present-day experiences as in the attempt to name this era of Israelite history. Ordinarily we speak of the *pre-state period*.[55] This can be understood in a purely temporal sense, insofar as this epoch was, in any case, prior to the emergence of political states in Israel and Judah. But even then it is only relative, because in comparison with Egypt or the Canaanite city-states the emerging society was post-state or only incidentally possessed state-like characteristics. In principle every one of these descriptions presumes that statehood is the normal condition of society, and therefore the designation is made in terms of the absence of the primary characteristics of a state.

The difficulty is no less if we attempt to understand Israel in this epoch not in terms of its subsequent political statehood, but in contrast to contemporary Canaanite political forms. We then speak of *liberated Israel*,[56] call it an *acephalic society*,[57] and describe its forms of government as *regulated anarchy*.[58] But these conceptions of *pre-state* Israel are also oriented to the notions of *kephalē* (headship or govern-

ing authority) or *archē* (rule) and regard the absence of these as a defining characteristic.

Only a closer look at social structure, economic forms, and authority relationships will make it possible to examine and test the suggestions that have been made for understanding Israel's form in this epoch of its social history. I will use, as the most general category, the term *kinship-based society*.[59] This is intended to emphasize the contrast with Canaanite political organization. In chronological terms, I will mainly refer to the "pre-state period," fully aware both that this applies only to the internal history of the subgroup "Israel" within the larger social picture of Canaan, and that the concept itself suggests an orientation to political organization.

Biblically, the epoch is called the *time of the judges*, referring to a fixed time period

6.5. Drawings of bronze figures of Canaanite deities.

between the occupation of the Land and the beginnings of Israelite monarchy. This picture is not very helpful to scholarly reconstruction. It is true that the book of Judges, with its military savior figures and its accounts of the beginnings of political organization, does contain much material that can be evaluated in historical terms. But the overall picture of an epoch in which judges continually ruled the whole of Israel is much too clearly oriented to the later monarchy: it retrojects elements of central and constantly exercised rule into the pre-monarchic era.

State of the Sources

The above discussion indicates how meager the sources for the pre-state epoch are. The book of Judges itself presents not only the above-mentioned elements of central and continuing governance; it also portrays the epoch in such a way that it inevitably moves toward monarchy. Consequently, we cannot rely in any way on the chronology of the individual episodes. We may also feel certain that the texts of the book of Judges were formulated, at the earliest, in the royal era, so that, in any case, they reflect the image of the preceding epoch as crafted during the royal period. The extent to which historically reliable recollections were thus preserved must be tested in every individual case.

In the case of social structures, of course, later material may to some extent be considered reliable. That is, we will see that the kinship structures on which the preceding society was based remained constant, in principle, in subsequent epochs as well. This makes it possible for us to draw conclusions about what preceded, though with extreme caution because there were, obviously, some shifts taking place.

The biblical material is thus only usable to a very limited degree,[60] and of contemporary extra-biblical written sources there are none. This was not because there was nothing to report. Rather—besides the accident of archaeological findings, which must always be taken into account—the collapse of the old city-state system and the temporary weakness of the great Near Eastern empires led to the absence of these two sources of written culture that might otherwise have produced documents. Only after the creation of territorial states in the southern Levant and the advance of the Assyrians do we have—from the ninth century onward, and then with increasing frequency—a renewal of written sources.

Thus the archaeological findings remain our primary source. These must be interpreted by means of the methods of social history. Ethnology serves us also, as a heuristic aid. We must ask of the latter's descriptions and the theories constructed from them whether they furnish us with models that can help us to interpret the findings of archaeology and the critically examined biblical material.

The Social Structure of Kinship-Based Societies

In attempting to describe the social structure of kinship-based society, we can refer first of all to what was said earlier in this chapter about the Land's resettlement.[61] The most striking characteristic of the new settlements, in contrast both to the older Canaanite cities and the later ones contemporary with the Judahite and Israelite kingdoms is the absence of any fortifications or the associated towers, as well as of any monumental structures.[62] As a rule—the exceptions will be treated presently[63]—the houses in such settlements were about equal in size. We may conclude from this that the individual families that inhabited the houses and cultivated the surrounding fields did not live in a hierarchical society with superiors and subordinates, but in a more or less egalitarian relationship.

It is also striking that the new settlements were relatively small.[64] In individual cases that could mean that the inhabitants of such a settlement were related to one another. The clan and the settlement could have been identical. But we must also suppose that the people dwelling in such settlements—especially the somewhat larger ones—belonged to several different clans. In those cases, both kinship and neighborhood played a role in identity and social relationships.

Two texts that describe casting lots (Josh 7:14-18 and 1 Sam 10:18-21) present the following structure for the larger social entity "Israel" (whose existence as such is taken for granted): tribe (shevet), clan (mishpakhah or ʾelef), house (bayit), man (gever). In this structure, the family is the basic unit of society.[65] Since the Hebrew word bayit is extremely elastic (it can mean dwelling, family, dynasty, state, and other similar concepts), it is usually qualified as "father's house" (bet ʾav) or "my house" when seen from the perspective of the head of the family.[66] This type of designation presumes, for one thing, settlement, because otherwise the "house" would scarcely constitute a point of reference. It also shows that the family was defined by its male head.

It would, of course, be premature to automatically deduce a subordinate position for women in such a society from its patrilineal construction of genealogies. Ethnological observation of peoples that do not have a political organization tends rather to suggest gender symmetry. A simply structured, [67] primarily agricultural economy requires the cooperative work of both men and women (and children). In such conditions, planting gardens near the houses and working in the fields are part of the duties of married women with children, while we also encounter unmarried female shepherds in the texts (Gen 29:6-9; Exod 2:16). In general, the biblical narratives present the women of the pre-national period as very self-aware figures—think only of the matriarchs Sarah, Rebecca, Leah, and Rachel, or women like Deborah, Samson's mother, Ruth, or Hannah, who even make independent decisions about their husbands' sexuality (Gen 30:14-16) and the life choices of their children (1 Samuel 1).

While the family is defined in terms of its male head (while he is living), the case of the clan is different. Its kinship is established through an ancestor to whom all trace their lineage but who is no longer a real, living head of family. The more broadly branched are the relationships, the farther back in the past is the common ancestor to be sought, until he is lost in the mythical past.[68]

Above the clan, in the schema of Josh 7:14-18, stands the tribe. The existence of tribes cannot be established from archaeology. It is very difficult to define a tribe ethnologically. And even the biblical texts reveal a complex picture, although they clearly show the existence of tribes. The question is: what real significance did they have for social structures?[69]

We can conclude from this picture that the more distant the social structure from the day-to-day family unit, the less is its social significance. What follows as far as Israel is concerned? In the texts that speak of the pre-state period, it is clear that only the later layers of tradition think of Israel as a unified entity. Otherwise it is a matter of individual tribes or coalitions of tribes. This is true also for the Song of Deborah, in which ten tribes appear, seven of them participating in an anti-Canaanite coalition while three stand aside (Judg 5:14-18). Like the narratives about the time of the judges, the Song of Deborah presumes the existence of an entity called Israel, but its mention is reduced to the framing and introductory verses (Judg 5:2, 7–9, 22). Whether we attribute these verses to a subsequent redaction that assumes a later political situation[70] or place the whole song in the period of (early) national political existence[71]—in either case only the tribes appear as real, acting subjects in the period before the monarchy. But does that mean that "Israel" as a common term of reference is completely irrelevant?

The Unity of Kinship-Based Societies

The tribes appear to be the highest acting social unit. What connects them? First of all, it seems probable that whatever united them was symbolized by the name *Israel*. One thing in favor of this is the reference to something called *Israel* on Merneptah's stele. Even if we can say essentially nothing about its structure, it is the only social unit mentioned besides the three Canaanite cities. The second argument is closely related to this one. As soon as there is a state, there is also an entity called *Israel*. In light of the Merneptah stele, there is no reason to think that the naming of the new state as "Israel" was an invention of the tenth century. And third, the Song of Deborah, even if it did not originally contain the name *Israel*, shows the presumption of a social unit existing beyond and independently of an accidental gathering of tribes willing to act as a coalition. The fact that Gilead, Dan, and Asher are reproached for not taking part in the common struggle (Judg 5:17) presupposes that one should have been able to expect them to

participate. But that in turn implies a feeling on the part of all ten of the tribes mentioned in the song that they belong together, an idea that, taken together with the earlier Merneptah stele and the later name of the national state, can only be symbolized by the name *Israel*.

Certainly, whatever social reality was represented by this *Israel* can scarcely be reconstructed. In particular, we must guard against retrojecting later conceptions of the early period back into historical reality. So we should note that the Song of Deborah mentions not twelve, but only ten tribes, and those include two (Machir and Gilead) that appear in none of the lists of the later twelve-tribe system, while Judah, Simeon, Gad, Manasseh, and Levi, all members of the later system, are missing here. If we anticipate the conditions at the time of the state's establishment, with Judah and Israel standing alongside one another, everything seems to favor the idea that Judah was not originally part of this entity called *Israel*.[72]

The fragmentary, imperfect state of the sources counsels against applying sweeping analogies from societies outside Israel to pre-state Israel. Max Weber suggested that we should speak of a *confederation*.[73] Martin Noth took as his model the sacred tribal leagues of ancient Greece and Italy and spoke of an *amphictyony*.[74] But we can neither date the idea of a covenant in the sense of Weber's confederation back to the pre-state period nor can we demonstrate the existence of an amphictyony with a central cult in Martin Noth's sense. Neither analogy has proven sustainable.

In recent scholarship it has become customary to speak quite modestly: for example, of a "growing sense of belonging to the entity 'Israel,'" or a "sense of a common bond among the tribes,"[75] or still more restrictively: "The basis for common action can *only* have been the

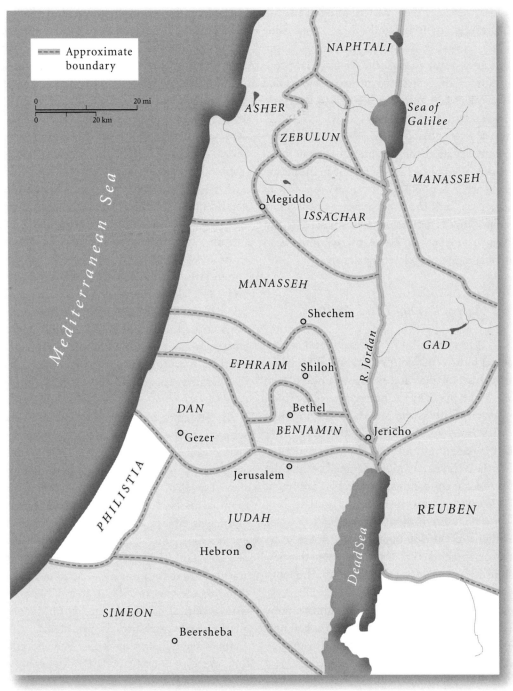

6.6. Map of the territory belonging to the twelve tribes of Israel corresponding to the tribal lists in Numbers 26 and Joshua. The list of Jacob's sons in Genesis 49 includes Joseph and Levi instead of Manasseh and Ephraim, however, and the much earlier list in Judges includes ten, not twelve tribes.

awareness of a common bond with social and religious roots."[76] The source of this awareness was primarily a sense of separateness. Rainer Neu writes: "I therefore suggest that we should understand 'Israel' in the pre-national period as a collective name that derived its meaning only from the contrast 'Israel = Not-XY,' that is, as a disassociation from the neighbors who were regarded as 'foreigners.'"[77]

It is probable that worship of the God Yhwh was originally associated with the awareness of a common bond within the group that understand itself as *Israel*. This need not mean that the worship of other deities was forbidden within family religion. But the role of Yhwh as Israel's national god, demonstrated by inscriptions in the monarchical period, such as the Mesha stele, indicates the likelihood that this god was already a symbolized the tribes' unity before that time. That does not mean, of course, that the worship of this god was the only unifying bond, in the sense of Norman Gottwald's *Tribes of Yahweh*; in particular, the idea of a conversion to Yhwh would seem to be an anachronism.[78]

But if the consciousness of a common bond did not necessarily manifest itself in political or religious institutions—as in the models of a confederation or amphictyony, which draw analogies from different historical epochs of European history—it must have had a material basis. In light of observations about the significance of family, clan, and tribe, recent suggestions draw on ethnological research that describes newer extra-European societies and concentrates not primarily on central governing structures but on kin relationships that hold the society together. Following research especially on African tribes and the theories built on it,[79] Frank Crüsemann has suggested that we call pre-state Israel a "segmented

society."[80] More precisely, Rainer Neu calls it a "segmented lineage society."[81]

This description, "segmented lineage society," is oriented to kin relationships and describes social organization both vertically and horizontally. Lineage indicates the vertical structure: all segments of society are organized by agnatic descent, that is, through the male line back to a common ancestor via his sons, their sons, and so forth. On the horizontal level, the society is organized in segments; all the segments that are related at the same distance to the same ancestor have equal rights, even though in the African societies studied the segments reveal enormous differences in size.[82]

If the unity of pre-state Israel is symbolized by the name *Israel*, it is primarily because in the genealogical system *Israel* is the name of the oldest common ancestor, from whom the genealogy begins to branch. The ancestors of the different tribes are regarded as his sons, the heads of clans and families as their descendants.[83]

This unity through genealogy can also be described as ethnic unity. That, of course, presumes the abandonment of concepts of ethnicity tied to common language and culture, common territory, or common race. It accords with the biblical text itself to define ethnicity, with Kathryn A. Kamp and Norman Yoffee, exclusively in terms of genealogy: "Sociologists and cultural anthropologists define an ethnic group as a number of individuals who see themselves 'as being alike by virtue of a common ancestry, real or fictitious, and who are so regarded by others.' . . ."[84]

Describing pre-state Israel as an ethnic unit in this genealogical sense is by no means intended to revive concepts that assume a dualistic contrast between Israel and Canaan and see Israel as a positive counter-image to a

Canaan regarded entirely in negative terms. Canaan was made up of multiple ethnic groups, and those groups that were becoming Israel were part of Canaan. But Israel was an independent and recognizable part of Canaan. More than that is not intended.[85]

The concept of a genealogically constituted ethnicity must not be thought of in static terms. While in the section on kinship-based societies we have put all the emphasis on the fact that this society consisted of a number of groups with different origins, and that its structure was continuously developing, that still does not contradict the concept we are proposing here.[86] For, on the one hand, we are completely in the dark about the point at which the various groups out of which *Israel* was formed began to consider themselves *sons of Israel*. On the other hand, membership

in the group was fluid. This is clear not only from the various and mutually deviating tribal systems, but also from the loose relationship to groups like the Kenites, who were regarded as a foreign people (Gen 15:19; Num 24:21), but at the same time were bound in friendship to the Israelites (1 Sam 15:6). Thus the Kenites could be then genealogically included as "sons of Hobab, Moses' father-in-law" (Judg 1:16; 4:11), until finally, in Chronicles, they are incorporated into the genealogy of Judah (1 Chr 2:55).[87]

Also calling a segmented linear society an egalitarian society[88] has sometimes brought on those advocating this idea the charge of being social romantics.[89] But it must be emphasized that in a segmented society "equality" refers only to the place of the segments that are at an equal distance from the same ancestor, in

Selected Tribal Lists in the Biblical Texts			
Genesis 49	**Numbers 26**	**Joshua**	**Judges 5**
Leah's offspring:	Reuben	Judah	Ephraim
Reuben	Simeon	Manasseh	Benjamin
Simeon	Gad	Ephraim	Machir
Levi	Judah	Reuben	Zebulon
Judah	Issachar	Gad	Issarhar
Zebulun	Zebulun	Benjamin	Reuben
Issachar	Manasseh	Simeon	Gilead
	Ephraim	Zebulun	Dan
Bilhah and Zilpah's offspring:	Benjamin	Issachar	Asher
Dan	Dan	Asher	Naphtali (10)
Gad	Asher	Naphtali	
Asher	Naphtali (12)	Dan (12)	
Naphtali			
Rachel's offspring:			
Joseph			
Benjamin (12)			

relationship to one another and with respect to their mutual status.[90] Nor does it mean that these individual segments (tribe, clan, or family) are equally large or equally strong economically, and nothing is being asserted about the equality of individuals.[91] So we may certainly accept Niels Peter Lemche's careful formulation: "Instead of speaking of egalitarian societies it would be more appropriate to speak of societies which are dominated by an egalitarian ideology."[92]

The concept of a segmented lineage society also makes it possible for us to interpret the few pieces of evidence we have for economic relationships in the society of pre-state Israel.

Economy

We need not waste many words explaining that the dominant economic system of pre-state Israel was farming, combined with animal husbandry on site. The same is true for all pre-modern societies and is attested by archaeology, because all the new settlements were based on the cultivation of the surrounding fields and gardens. The presence of bones also shows the existence of flocks, primarily smaller ruminants. The biblical picture of the so-called time of the judges likewise presumes the dominance of agricultural production.

However, there are also the statements in the Song of Deborah that Dan "abide[s] [as a foreigner] with the ships" or "serves in the ships" (instead of taking part in the battle) (Judg 5:17). This says that members of this tribe, which was settled in the north, apparently worked on board the ships of their neighbors, the Phoenicians. It fits with this that immediately afterward Asher is accused of sitting still on the seacoast. Those from Zebulon who take part in the battle are called

moshekhim beshevet sofer (v. 14), which literally means "hauling under the secretary's staff," and it is quite possible that this is an allusion to slave labor in the Canaanite cities.[93] In any case, in the sayings about the tribes in Genesis 49 the tribe of Issachar, which is closely related to Zebulon, is clearly called "a slave at forced labor" (v. 15).

In Iron Age I in Canaanite society, there were the inhabitants in the surviving cities and farmers in the available land. Additionally, there were those who served as slaves in Canaanite and Phoenician cities. Neither of these facts contradicts the insights derived from a general description of ethnicity. We may again cite Kathryn A. Kamp and Norman Yoffee: "Important in the analysis of ancient Western Asian social systems, the term 'ethnic group' allows for the existence of more than one type of social organization within the single bounded unit."[94] Thus there is no reason to doubt the picture, similar to the biblical legends, according to which pre-state Israel understood itself as a segmented society, the segments of which lived primarily, but not exclusively, from agriculture.

Leadership Structures

If we look at the small settlements created in the southern Levant's hill country during Iron Age I, each containing a few probably interrelated farming families, we will not expect to find elaborate governmental structures. The absence of the places and symbols of hierarchically organized rule, such as palaces and city gates, is indeed characteristic of these new structures. The inhabitants of such settlements probably settled their common business by means of what Europeans, accustomed to hierarchical structures involving commands and obedience, have denigrated as "empty talk." Quarrels would have been settled by direct confrontation, without the authorized intervention of a third party.[95]

But besides the small settlements there were also communities called cities. Among those from the pre-state period worth mentioning are Sukkoth and Penuel (Judg 8:4-21), Shechem (Judges 9), Gilead (probably to be understood as a city in Judges 11),[96] Gibeah (Judges 19–20), and Jabesh-Gilead (1 Samuel 11). Obviously all these texts were shaped at a later time and certainly they introduce later social conditions into the texts. All of them—and this is very striking for a point of view that posits a sharp opposition between "Israel" and "Canaan"!—leave the ethnicity of the inhabitants of these cities remarkably open. Thus the Shechemites in Judges 9 are decisively portrayed as non-Israelites (although Abimelech's rule, extending from Shechem [v. 22], is regarded as rule "over Israel"),[97] while the inhabitants of Jabesh-Gilead (1 Samuel 11) are definitively "Israelites." Thus it is by no means certain whether, from the point of view of these texts, Israelite and Canaanite cities exist separately side by side,[98] or whether they presume that there was a mixed population in individual cities.[99]

All this makes the question of governmental structures anything but simple. In general terms, it seems obvious that in a community of a certain size, one we can call a city, not all the inhabitants can be related as members of the same family. And in that case, common business, including conflicts, cannot be settled within the family. Rather, the families will have to appoint representatives. But these general reflections encounter the phenomenon that in these texts two entities appear and speak in public matters: namely, the men of a city (Judg 8:5, 8-9, and frequently) and the

elders (Judg 8:14, 16; 11:5, and frequently). Probably we should imagine the relationship of these two groups in such a way that the elders represent a selection from among all the men in the city. But in the texts, the relationship of these groups remains fluid; we cannot posit any sharp distinctions between them.[100]

The negative conclusions to be drawn from these observations can be expressed as follows: "There was no public central authority with the power to impose sanctions. This is a common feature of the settlements of Sukkoth, Gilead, and Gibeah during the period of the judges. The social arrangements in all these settlements were characterized by a narrow range of distinctions."[101] Positively stated: "In the premonarchical period the elders were the representatives of a particular place."[102] Using Max Weber's categories, we can call governance thus exercised "traditional authority."[103]

It remains questionable whether, beyond the exercise of authority in the family in the small settlements and the authority of the men and elders in the larger settlements, there was a form of traditional authority at the tribal level. The silence of the texts is rather eloquent. Occasionally the figure of the *nasi³* has been considered as representing a kind of tribal head.[104] In fact, in later texts a *nasi³* is often mentioned in connection with the organization of the people into tribes (Num 1:16; 2:3, 5, and frequently). But those are all very late texts. Moreover, *nasi³* is a very general title like English "lord, dignitary"; Ezekiel uses it for the king of Judah (Ezek 12:10; 19:1; 21:17; and frequently). There is no evidence that in the pre-state period there was an institutional office of headman or sheikh. There remains the possibility that, on the tribal level as in the cities, elders acted as representatives.

With the texts mentioned thus far from Judges (and 1 Samuel 11) we have, certainly, not yet gotten to heart of the narratives. Those, as we know, tell of "judges,"[105] called in Hebrew *shofetim.* The root *shpt,* however, means not merely "judge," but "rule" in general. And in fact the figures of the biblical judges are drawn as predecessors to the kings, inasmuch as there is a continuing succession of judges who, like the kings, both govern and lead in battle (the functions of royalty according to 1 Sam 8:20). Obviously this is a picture drawn entirely from the perspective of the monarchical period.

But within it another image is visible. In times of military crisis, leaders are chosen whose only task is to deal with the immediate situation. Their origins can be very different: Gideon comes from a minor family (Judg 6:15), Jephthah is introduced as "the son of a prostitute" (Judg 11:1), and Deborah (Judges 4–5) is a woman. They cannot force anyone to follow them, and their exercise of power is limited to the period of the crisis and its resolution. The field within which they exercise authority is very limited, and the "Israelitizing" in each case is easily recognized as redactional. The texts occasionally call them "savior" (*moshia^c*; Judg 3:9, 15; 12:3). It is emphasized in various ways that the divine "spirit" comes upon them (Judg 3:10; 6:34; 11:29; 13:25; 14:6, 19; 15:14; see also 1 Sam 11:6). Again with Max Weber, we could here speak of "charismatic authority."[106]

Social Stratification

The picture we have sketched thus far of the social conditions in the pre-state epoch is colorful enough. Besides the majority of tribes living an agrarian life, there were some that were in service to Canaanite or Phoenician cities. Some dwelt in small settlements and others in large settlements, called cities. And of course there were older and younger peo-ple, men and women, and stronger and weaker segments. But on the whole we have brought forward the picture of a fairly unified society out of which the states of Judah and Israel would emerge.

But the rise of these states would scarcely have been possible if the society we have sketched, on the model of a fundamentally egalitarian segmented linear society, had not revealed some fraying around the edges. Such fraying can be observed in both the upper and lower boundaries of society.

Archaeology gives us a first indication of this. Besides the little village-type settlements, there were structures that can be interpreted as large farmsteads.[107] They are isolated, contain one or more buildings, and are surrounded at a distance by a wall that apparently served, not for defense, but to hold animals. Within the biblical tradition, one is immediately reminded of the rich man Nabal in 1 Samuel 25. He is called "very rich" (literally "very big") and is supposed to have possessed some three thousand sheep and a thousand goats (v. 2), which were cared for by shepherds in his employ (vv. 7-8). He also hired shearers at the annual sheep-shearing (v. 11). His wife Abigail was in a position to go out to David with a handsome offer of produce, and she herself had people under her orders (vv. 18-19).[108]

What we are seeing here is a upward mobility. Like the powerfully typicized Nabal, Saul is also called a "big man," and it is possible that Judg 5:10 also belongs in this same context. That verse speaks of men who ride on white donkeys and sit on rich carpets. They could be interpreted as the beginnings of a developing stratum of the well-to-do.

Much more clearly than the upward development, the texts speak of a downward social fraying. In the nature of things, archaeological indicators are lacking here. But the texts are unmistakably clear. In two cases they tell how family conflicts lead to breakups. One is the case of Abimelech, who is the son of one of his father's concubines (Judg 8:31) and therefore comes into conflict with his (half-) brothers (9:1, 5). He is polemically called "son of a slave woman" (9:18). In the conflict Abimelech does not rely only on his mother's side of the family, but also on a group of men who are called "worthless and reckless fellows" (9:4). We do not learn where they come from.

The case of Jephthah is similar. His mother is called *ishah zonah* (Judg 11:1), which probably does not mean a professional prostitute, but simply an unmarried woman.[109] He is driven out by his half-brothers, the sons of his father's legitimate wife, so that he will not share in the inheritance (11:2). Jephthah gathers "outlaws" around him (11:3), and again nothing is said about where they come from.

Here we can be aided by a remark that is included in the story of David's rise but really belongs to the pre-national period; in it we are at the very beginning of the transition to an undeveloped national identity. According to 1 Sam 22:2, David gathers a group of men around him who are described in three terms: as "in distress," "in debt," and "discontented." Out of this we can reconstruct three reasons for their coming together, as described, to form a band: family conflicts as in the cases of Abimelech and Jephthah, economic difficulties, and perhaps as a third factor some crime (such as murder or accidental killing) that forces them to flee.

Thus the pre-state society in transition to statehood reveals itself as a structure with a broad center that forms the core of the segmented society and is so strong that we will have to call the newly created states of Israel and Judah segmented states. But the state was not formed from that core. Rather, we will see that a "big man" (Saul) attempts to form a state, but that fails, while another attempt (by David) to call on the outcasts of the old society is crowned with success.

7

Israel and Judah: From Early Statehood to Full Development

KEY POINTS

- Biblical account of the early monarchy
  - Early Iron Age I, Saul's monarchy in Benjamin and neighboring areas
  - After Saul's death in battle, Saul's rival David overthrew Saulides by killing Saul's son
  - David expanded rule to include all Israelites, local Canaanites, and neighboring peoples
- Maximalism/minimalism
  - Maximalism: biblical account historical
  - Minimalism: biblical account almost totally ahistorical
  - Preferred middle position: David ruled over all Israelites and integrated prior Canaanite territories into kingdom
- After Solomon's death, kingdom splits into Judah and Israel shortly after 930 B.C.
- Kingdoms of Israel and Judah both secondary constructed states
- Reasons for the monarchy's creation:
  - Need for a strong military leader (Judges and 1 Samuel)
  - Need for political order (Judges and 1 Samuel)
  - Development of city "elders"
  - Formation of armed bands
- Israelite monarchy understood as "chiefdoms"
  - Helps undermine idea of extended Israelite Davidic/Solomonic empire

- Fully developed states developed in Israel only in the ninth century, in Judah only in the eighth
- Development of the Israelite-Judahite state:
  - Pre-state period
  - Incomplete early state—Saul, early Davidic period
  - Typical early state—David's kingship
  - Fully developed state—ninth century Israel, eighth century Judah
- Resistance to the monarchy
  - Former Prophets criticize monarchy for not centralizing the cult
  - Latter Prophets criticize monarchy for not protecting society's poor and weak
  - The social nobility whose socioeconomic position is threatened
- Accommodating to the monarchy
  - Participation of the well-to-do in the state
  - Some members of lower class attained positions of authority
  - Little change for the lower classes
- Transition to the state
  - The family and clan remain basic structure of society
  - The monarchy-household economy—nonintervention in state economy
- Structure of the monarchical state
  - King and his court
  - Women in the royal family and the court—not equal to the men

- Royal officials
- Governor of the capital
- Provincial officials
- City elders
• The military-professional army and the muster
• Forced labor
• Payments
  - Produce delivered to the court
  - Taxes to meet tribute demanded by Assyria, Egypt, Babylon
  - Income from royal property to support the court and border fortresses
• The legal system
  - State officials now intervene in local affairs

- Codification of the law
• The religion of the Kingdom of Israel
  - YHWH worship symbolic of Israelite society's unity
  - Local and central or royal sanctuaries exist side by side—gifts given to both
  - Cult centralized under Josiah in the seventh century
  - Gift giving at the temple leads to a monetary economy and increased commerce
  - The northern kingdom understood itself in light of the exodus—a people freed from forced labor
• The northern kingdom marked by frequent dynastic changes

THE TRANSITION TO EXISTENCE AS A STATE at the end of the eleventh and beginning of the tenth century BCE marks the first point at which it becomes possible to write a history of events for the entity named *Israel*. Ruling figures appear. The states make war and conclude treaties. Existence as a state implies a growing need for written records, and as a consequence, the number of inscribed monuments increases.

At the same time, after the turn of the millennium, the world-political vacuum that had existed since the collapse of Egyptian dominance in Canaan during the transition from the Bronze to the Iron Age was gradually being filled.[1] Pharaoh Shishak's campaign at the end of the tenth century remains only an isolated episode, but from the ninth century onward the burgeoning Neo-Assyrian Empire appears on the Levant's political horizon, and in the eighth and seventh centuries Assyria dominated the region. It was succeeded, in the last third of the seventh century, by the Egyptians of the 26th Dynasty and the Neo-Babylonians. All this led to a richer stream of sources for the history of events in the Levant than had existed in the preceding centuries.

However, this improved state of the sources does not mean that the events, their scope, and their consequences are less disputed than was the case with questions concerning the pre-state society's structure. For this reason, it is necessary, before we investigate the social structure of Israel and Judah after their start as states, to sketch the course of events in each, so that I can be clear about my assumptions. The same is true of each of the succeeding epochs. This must and can, of course, only be a sketch because there is no space for a detailed discussion and because much of what can be said about social forms is relatively independent of the course of events.

From Initial Statehood to the Middle of the Eighth Century

Some time around the turn from the second to the first millennium BCE, there arose in the southern Levant the two states of Israel and Judah, which existed until the eighth and sixth centuries respectively. After some preliminary stages in Iron Age I, Saul established

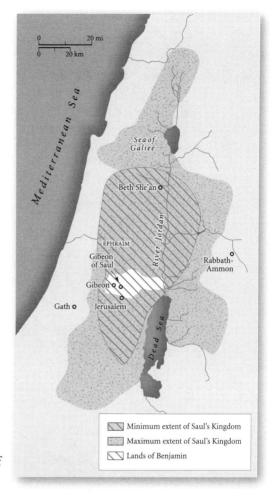

7.1. Map showing minimal and maximal extent of Saul's territory.

an initial monarchy extending over the tribal territory of Benjamin and some neighboring regions to the north and south.[2] In the beginning, this creation of a state was heartily supported, or at least indulged, by the Philistines (whose rule encompassed the coastal plain and extended far into the hill country and who were superior to the Israelites in every respect), because they saw Israel as a buffer against competitors to the east. Thus Saul's foundation of a state took place more or less under the watchful eyes of a Philistine military outpost (1 Sam 10:5; 13:3, 23; 14:1), and his first campaign was against the Ammonites east of the Jordan (1 Samuel 11).[3] But when Saul subsequently turned against the Philistines themselves, his rule quickly came to an end (1 Sam 13:1).[4]

The reason why Saul's kingdom did not last any longer, even though one of his sons (Ishbaal) succeeded him (2 Sam 2:8–9), was that a rival arose in the person of David, who established an independent sphere of influence in the region south of Benjamin. He succeeded in winning Saul's and Ishbaal's generals to his side and, by marrying Saul's daughter Michal, in establishing a claim to Saul's kingdom.[5] With the murder of Ishbaal (2 Samuel 4),

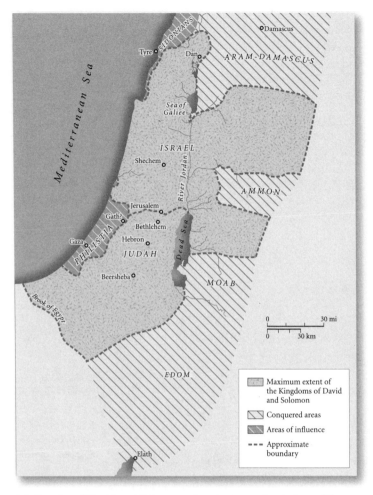

7.2. Empire of David and Solomon, showing a maximal view of the
United Kingdom. "Areas of influence" are states in treaty-relationship
with David.

David was able to assume power over the former sphere of Saul's rule as well (2 Samuel 5).

David now reigned over Judah, which probably at this point came together as an independent entity (a "tribe") for the first time, and over a few of the northern tribes as well. By winning over the old Jebusite city of Jerusalem (2 Sam 5:6-11),[6] he obtained a capital city independent of tribal territories, and from there he pursued the expansion of his own state's territory in three directions. First, he proceeded to incorporate the Israelite tribes in the north that had not previously been ruled by Saul. Next, he subdued and integrated the older Canaanite population groups that, due to the manner of Israelite settlement in the pre-state period, had not entirely disappeared. Finally, he turned to expanding his rule over neighboring peoples (2 Sam 5:17-25; 8; 10-12).

We cannot be absolutely certain about any of this today. The extremes in historical scholarship are marked on the one side by the acceptance of a Davidic-Solomonic empire extending from the borders of Egypt to the Lebanon and from the Mediterranean to the Euphrates (reflecting, for example, Josh 1:4),[7] and at the opposite extreme by the thesis that the existence of a united kingdom was entirely a later Jewish invention intended to make Judahite claims to the territory of the northern kingdom plausible after the latter's collapse.[8]

Neither of these extreme positions can be sustained. Against the maximalist position

it seems remarkable that—even if we do not make many demands on the archaeological and epigraphical evidence—an empire of the scope thus posited would have left no traces at all. Even the dating of building works in the north during the time of Solomon—Megiddo is the prime example—is suspect of resting on circular reasoning: because the Bible reports such building works (for Megiddo, see 1 Kgs 9:15) the archaeological findings are dated to the time of Solomon, which in turn serves as evidence for the reliability of the biblical tradition.[9] And the idea that such an empire could have been ruled from Jerusalem, which at

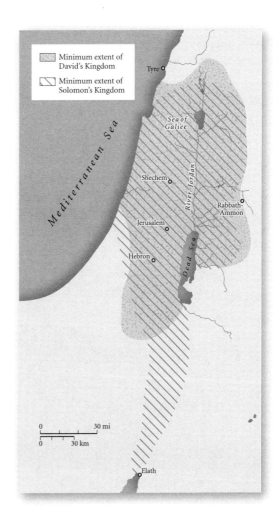

7.3. Minimal view of kingdoms of David and Solomon (according to J. Maxwell Miller).

the time was perhaps "no more than a typical highland village," does not exactly make the idea more plausible.[10]

On the other hand, the minimalist position, with its denial of any northern expansion on David's part, encounters nearly insurmountable difficulties in view of the biblical traditions. In particular, even the Saul tradition in 1 Samuel is thoroughly imbued with the idea of absolving David from any accusation that might have been raised against him by Saul's followers. There surely would have been no need for that if David had been a local chieftain who never even lifted a hand against Benjamin. There is also the tradition in the northern kingdom that its founding was an act of liberation from foreign domination, which is why the exodus tradition became the state religion of the North.[11] It is

scarcely possible to explain the construction of such a tradition in a later time when the exodus tradition had also been received in Judah as a matter of course—namely, in the period after the fall of the northern kingdom[12]—and in any case it violates Occam's Razor: hypotheses should be as simple as possible.

Hence a middle position seems more appropriate.[13] In this view one should accept that, under David, Judah did in fact expand northward, thereby uniting all the Israelite tribes, and in addition integrated territories of prior Canaanite settlement into the new state while subjecting neighboring peoples. The memory of this was then enhanced in the process of elevating the traditions about David and his successor, Solomon, into the notion of a great empire encompassing the entire Levant.

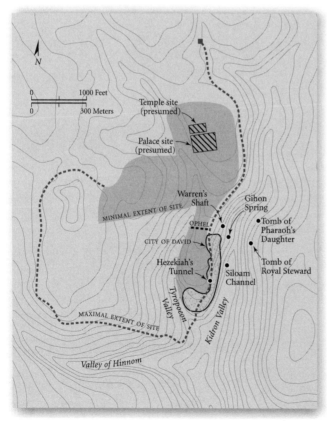

7.4. Plan of Iron Age Jerusalem and its stages of development.

After the death of David's successor, Solomon,[14] this empire broke apart in the period shortly after 930 BCE. Soon thereafter, Pharaoh Shishak I undertook a campaign in Palestine, some information about which is recorded in a list of names in Karnak.[15] Because the list contains no names from the territory of Judah and Jerusalem, the information in 1 Kgs 14:25-26 may be correct: we can conclude from it that Shishak was deterred from moving against Jerusalem by the offering of tribute.[16] The north, however, was threatened by the advancing army, as shown by the appearance of Pharaoh's name-cartouche on a stele fragment found in Megiddo.[17] However, Shishak's campaign remains a single episode that did not prevent the further development either of Israel or of Judah.

The period after the establishment of two independent kingdoms of Israel and Judah was marked by constant rivalry, with Israel the stronger and more developed entity. Especially from the time when the dynasty of Omri took power (beginning in about 880 BCE) and gave the northern kingdom its own capital city in Samaria (1 Kgs 16:24), Israel became a middle-level power, playing a significant role in the power-games of the Levantine states.

From the time when the Assyrian Empire began to expand westward after the middle of the ninth century, kings of Israel begin to appear in the inscriptional evidence. The first of these is Omri's son Ahab, called "Ahab of Israel" in an inscription of the Assyrian king Shalmaneser III and named as one of the members of an opposing coalition in the battle of Qarqar (853 B.C.E).[18] Here the name *Israel*, three and a half centuries after its first appearance on the stele of Pharaoh Merneptah at the end of the thirteenth century,[19] appears once again in an inscription, now clearly as the name of a state. Soon afterward (ca. 840) comes the stele of King Mesha, which mentions Omri, king of Israel, and his son, not named but presumably Ahab.[20] It is evident that the Omrides were highly significant for the Assyrians' recognition of the northern kingdom, since their name was associated with the state even after the dynasty had fallen. Thus the same Shalmaneser III who had recorded "Ahab of Israel" for posterity called Jehu, the man who put a bloody end to the Omride dynasty (ca. 841 BCE) "Jehu the son of (= dynastic heir of) Humri."[21] "Humri" or "Omri" continued to be used for Israel in other Assyrian inscriptions.[22]

Even though Israelites and Aramaeans appear at the battle of Qarqar in alliance with others against Assyria, the ninth and beginning of the eighth centuries were marked above all by sharp rivalry between Israel and the various Aramaic states, especially Damascus. This is the background for the inscription from the first half of the ninth century, found at Tell Dan, in which an Aramaean ruler reports that he killed "the king of Israel."[23]

It is true that it is not this reference on the Tell Dan stele, unsurprising after the Assyrian inscriptions and the Mesha stele, that has led to a flood of discussion, but rather the immediately succeeding letters *bytdwd* on the same stele.[24] This is probably to be understood as meaning nothing other than "house of David." As long as we had only fragment A with the letters *bytdwd*, the meaning was occasionally disputed: people tried to see *bytdwd* as a reference to a divine epithet, *dwd*,[25] or an otherwise unknown city name analogous to *Beth*el, *Beth* Shemesh,[26] or Ash*dod*.[27] But the discovery of fragment B, according to which the ruler in question most likely bore a name ending in *–yahu*, has made it nearly impossible to deny a connection to the "house of David" known from the Bible.[28]

Whereas the Aramaeans and the Israelites were still allies in the battle of Qarqar, on the fragmentary Tell Dan stele the rulers of Israel

7.5. The "Moabite Stone," set up ca. 830 BCE by King Mesha of Moab. The monument describes Mesha's conquest and annexation of Israelite territory. Photo © Erich Lessing/Art Resource, NY

7.6. Fragments of an Aramaic inscription on a victory monument set up by King Hazael of Damascus. The text contains the first mention of "the House of David" outside the Bible. Photo courtesy The Hebrew Union College.

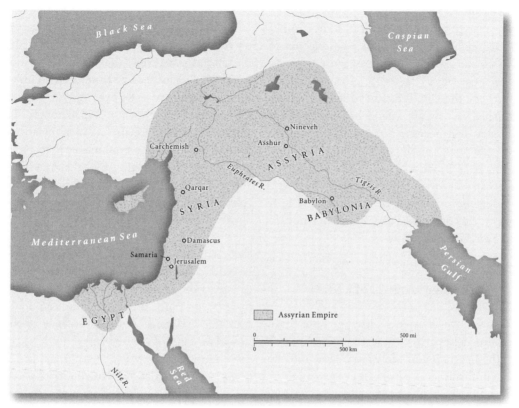

7.7. The Assyrian Empire.

and those from the house of David appear as common enemies of the Aramaeans. We should probably not take these as fixed relationships. Rather, the small and mid-sized states in the Syro-Palestinian land bridge would have changed alliances according to the current state of their interests.

Since Assyrian pressure toward the west became more and more intense from the eighth century onward, and the Aramaeans were the first ones affected by it, Aramaean pressure on Israel weakened correspondingly. Under Jeroboam II (787–747), the northern kingdom experienced a veritable blossoming of independence. But that epoch quickly ended with the campaigns of Tiglath-pileser III (745–727) and his successors. The attempt by the Ara-maeans and the Israelites to force Judah to join them in an anti-Assyrian coalition in the so-called Syro-Ephraimite War (734–732) was a failure, and the consequences for both states were profound. The Aramaean state of Damascus disappeared from the political map. The northern kingdom of Israel was diminished by successive Assyrian annexations until—after a whole series of *coups d'état* in the last ten years of its existence—it collapsed with the fall of Samaria in 722. The independent kingdom of Israel became four Assyrian provinces. Judah, which from this time onward was repeatedly mentioned by that name in Assyrian sources,[29] purchased its continued independence by voluntarily placing itself in vassalage to Assyria (2 Kings 16:5–10).

Naturally, the history of the royal period continues to the end of Judah at the beginning of the sixth century. But for a description of Israel's social history, it makes sense to break here at the end of the eighth century. For one thing, by the eighth century the early states of Israel and Judah, established in the tenth century, had become developed nations; we will illustrate this in what follows. Besides, an internal process began in the mid-eighth century that can be summarized as the development of an ancient class society. We will pursue this in the next chapter when we again take up the history of events.[30]

The Beginnings of a State

Having traveled rapidly through about three hundred years of history, let us now jump back to the beginning of the epoch. How did the states of Israel and Judah come into being?

In looking at the previous period, we saw that the earlier picture of an occupation of the Land that took place in a relatively short period of time is no longer sustainable. Instead, it is more appropriate to speak of Israel's becoming or establishment within its Canaanite environment. In contrast, the transition to statehood represents a more clearly marked division. However, it would be false here as well to follow the picture suggested by the Bible and to trace the origins of the monarchy to the will of a popular assembly in Ramah (so 1 Samuel 8). For one thing, there were a variety of attempts before states were really and firmly established, and for another, the society-altering consequences of existence as a state only appeared gradually in the wake of the monarchy's establishment.

For anthropological research, the transition from autonomous village communities to societies with central governments represents a deep cleft in human history. However, a distinction is made between primary and secondary state-construction. Primary construction of states is perceived when central governments develop for the first time, without influence from other, already-existing states in the environment of the society in question. In the nature of things there are few such instances, and they are restricted to ancient Mesopotamia, Egypt, India, China, and the Americas. Secondary state-construction is much more common; this takes place in an environment of already-existing states.

After what we have been saying, it is clear that the establishment of the states of Israel and Judah represents secondary state-construction, since in the southern Levant there were both autochthonous and long-standing city-states and the presence of the Egyptian empire. Nevertheless, neither of these forms of state was a direct precursor of the states formed by the Israelite tribes, and these did not follow those former models. But they were not without predecessors.

The fourteenth-century Amarna correspondence makes it evident that states had formed in the northern and southern hill country around Shechem and Jerusalem that clearly extended beyond the compass of the cities themselves. Both Labaya of Shechem and Abdi-Hepa of Jerusalem ruled over regional territorial states.[31] These two entities belong to the pre-history of the later states of Israel and Judah primarily because they were geographically located where the later states developed. Continuity of population in Jerusalem can only be traced to the time of its occupation by David. But in Shechem things are more complicated.

According to the tradition in Judges 9, there was an attempt to found a monarchical territorial state centered in Shechem.[32] Although the events related in the text cannot be dated exactly,[33] this is in any case a successor to Labaya's state.[34] A certain Abimelech erected a kingdom out of the settlement of Aruma that also included the territory of the city of Shechem as well as the settlement of Thebez in the neighborhood of Shechem. The text is remarkably ambiguous about the ethnic makeup of Shechem's population.[35] On the one hand it depicts the Shechemites as non-Israelites who pray to their Baal (vv. 4, 27, 46). Abimelech is said to be the son of an Israelite and a non-Israelite Shechemite woman (vv. 8, 31), and according to the text Abimelech makes use of that difference in establishing his rule (9:1–6; cf. v. 18). On the other hand, Abimelech is said to rule over Israel (vv. 22, 55). But even independently of these verses, which from a literary-critical point of view are certainly later, the tradition in the Abimelech episode in the book of Judges only makes sense if it is understood to be part of the pre-history of the later kingdom in Israel.[36]

In some sense comparable to Abimelech's ephemeral kingdom is the case of Jephthah, as described in Judges 11. The initial situation is at first different, namely a military crisis involving "Gilead."[37] In that sense, Jephthah is among the leaders who take action in such crisis situations, the biblical savior-figures.[38] But like Abimelech he seeks a lasting rule, though the title used is not "king" (Judg 9:6), but "head" (Judg 10:18; 11:8-11). As in the case of Abimelech, the "lords of Shechem" (9:2-3, 6) played the deciding role in his elevation, so in the case of Jephthah the "elders of Gilead" do the same (11:5-11). Like Abimelech, Jephthah has a mixed heritage (8:31 and 11:1-2, 7), and both are supported by a troop of "outlaws" (9:4; 11:3).

Both Abimelech and Jephthah exercise governance over a narrowly restricted geographical region, and both rule only temporarily. There is no dynasty-building. The first kingdom in Israel with greater endurance, including the beginnings of establishing a dynasty, and that extended over a somewhat broader territory, was that of Saul the Benjaminite.

Reasons for Establishing the Monarchy

The biblical tradition that retrospectively tells about the monarchy's establishment offers two lines of reasoning and one subjective motive for this deep historical caesura. One set of reasons relates to threats from outside. The cyclically recurring attacks by foreign peoples during the so-called time of the judges, according to this historical picture, are followed in 1 Samuel 4–7 by an account of struggles with the Philistines and in 1 Samuel 11 by a story of war with the Ammonites, at the successful conclusion of which Saul finally emerges as king.

According to the other line of reasoning, internal difficulties press for the establishment of a kingdom. The book of Judges closes in chapters 17–21 with a series of gruesome stories linked by the refrain that at that time there was as yet no king in Israel (Judg 17:6; 18:1; 19:1; 21:25). According to 1 Sam 2:11-17, 22-25, the Elide priests at the YHWH-sanctuary in Shiloh stole the sacrificial offerings and slept with the women "who served at the entrance to the tent of meeting" (v. 22). Even Samuel's sons, who were supposed to judge, did so only for bribes and so perverted justice (1 Sam 8:1-3). So, according to this arrangement of the text, there was pressure toward a political order. Finally, the two lines of thought are brought together on the lips of the Israelites in these words: "our king [will] govern us and go out before us and fight our battles" (1 Sam 8:20b). The subjective motive precedes this: "so that we also may be like other nations" (1 Sam 8:20a).

Probably, this multilayered picture comes closer to historical reality than the monocausal explanation attempted in "histories of Israel" until very recently, which made the establishment of the monarchy due solely to danger from the Philistines.[39] As is almost always the case in history, major upheavals do not have just *one* cause; they are *multicausal*. For the rise of a state in Israel and Judah, we may adduce the following factors.

As we have already seen above, besides the small settlements whose inhabitants all belonged to one extended family, there were also larger collections of dwellings ("cities") in which the members of various families lived together. In these, elders represented the individual families.[40] This does not mean that family structures were abolished. But the crossing of family boundaries and the institution of the elders created the preconditions for a form of governance that could ultimately be established entirely independently of family structures, as a state. As in the cases of Abimelech and Jephthah, so also in the establishment of David's kingdom elders would play an important role (2 Sam 5:3).

Another development in pre-state society is what I spoke of above as a "fraying downward."[41] This had two consequences. First, the appearance of armed bands shook public order and rendered it insecure. The narrative in 1 Samuel 25 gives a vivid picture of how such a band could lay claim to rule a particular territory by demanding protection money, threatening to kill those who did not do as they asked. On the other hand, such groups established a power base for building up a state government, as the examples of Abimelech, Jephthah, and David show.

Finally, although it was not the sole reason, external threat also played a role in the establishment of the kingship. As in the case of Jephthah, where temporary leadership turned into enduring rule, Saul was likewise elevated to the kingship after a victory over the Ammonites (1 Sam 11:15).[42]

With the subjective motive, the desire to be "like other nations," the biblical text also touches on historical reality. It is true that we cannot say of this as a verbally formulated motive that it already presumes historical reflection. But it is true that people did not have to invent statehood in Israel. It already existed in the environment. Israel's state-building was not primary, but secondary.[43]

That none of these factors alone was sufficient to provoke the establishment of kingship is clear from the very fact that there were repeated attempts—the rule of Abimelech, of Jephthah, and possibly others about which we know nothing, and in a certain sense the rule of Saul as well—that failed. David was the first one who succeeded in establishing an enduring dynasty.

"Early States"

In recent times it has occasionally been disputed that the first relatively stable kingdom in Israel, that of Saul, and the beginnings of David's rule represented state-building at all. On the basis of ethnologically grounded theories of development that insert the phase of *chiefdom* between pre-state and state epochs, people have called the reigns of Saul and the early phase of David's rule *chiefdoms*.[44] Later there were even attempts to expand this epoch of chiefdom very broadly, extending it for Israel into the ninth century, and for Judah even into the eighth.[45]

It must be considered that the theories originally taken as models were constructed with a view to primary state-building, and even then they were not undisputed among ethnologists. Mutually contradictory quotations[46] are quite representative for the current state of discussion.[47] An appeal to apparently clear and unmistakable "current sociological, cultural-anthropological, and ethnographic studies"[48] is thus impossible. It is necessary to construct sociological theories to describe the development at the time of the transition to monarchical rule, but without insisting on one particular theory.

A number of instances supporting the "chiefdom" theory that have been introduced into the discussion are of no value because they are not clear evidence of "chiefdom" or "state."[49] However, there are some examples that point rather clearly to state-building. We may mention, for example, the fact that Saul's son Ishbaal follows his father after Saul's death (2 Sam 2:8-9). Had Saul been a "chief," his defeat by the Philistines would have been a clear indication that his authority and charism were extinguished. It is quite improbable that, of all people, the son of a failed "chief" would have been called to succeed him, especially since the son had not been previously active in any way and subsequently proved rather ineffective. The calling of an incapable son as successor is a typical sign of a monarchical state. Likewise, the fact that he has to be gotten rid of by murder (2 Samuel 4)—a "chief" could simply be deposed—points in the same direction.

The traditions about David also show that from the beginning his goal was to establish a dynasty. Here the stele from Tell Dan, with its letters *bytdwd*, interpreted above as a reference to the "house of David,"[50] is of further help to us. It shows that the Aramaic author of the stele is aware of a communal entity he calls a "house," and that he calls after the dynastic founder "house of David." But that does not

point to something like a "chiefdom"; it indicates, rather, a dynastic state.

Above all, however, the "chiefdom" theories create the impression that early Israel and Judah could have existed as "chiefdoms" in an environment of states. If one correctly emphasizes nowadays how closely Israel was integrated into its Canaanite environment, it is difficult to postulate for it a centuries-long special existence in the middle of a sea of statehood, as the expanded form of the chiefdom thesis does.

In spite of this criticism, the chiefdom theory has made two contributions that should not be denied. First, it is part of a whole series of studies that have combined, both powerfully and justifiably, to destroy the picture of an extended Israelite empire under David and Solomon.[51] Its second contribution is that it shows that it was only in the ninth century (for Israel) and the eighth century (for Judah) that fully developed states emerged, with the kingship relating to a society that was steadily stratifying into an upper and lower class. But when the chiefdom thesis qualifies everything that preceded these fully developed states as "chiefdoms," it tosses out the baby with the bathwater.

This danger is avoided by another theory, likewise drawn from the socio-ethnological debate. Formulated primarily by Henry J. M. Claessen and Peter Skalnik, it speaks of "early states."[52] In this way the authors make it clear that they are interested in the form of society that exists between the pre-state period and the "fully developed or mature state."[53] This converges with even the expanded chiefdom theories: we can certainly speak of a fully developed state, with its principal criterion class differentiation within society beneath the state's apparatus, in Israel beginning with the ninth century, and in Judah beginning with the eighth century.

The transition from the pre-state period to the fully developed state took place in several stages. The "incomplete early state"[54] corresponds almost exactly to the situation under Saul and at the beginning of David's reign. The government contains only one full-time specialist, who is also a relative of the king (1 Sam 14:50-51). The king's tribe is the basis of his rule (1 Sam 22:7-8). Income consists of ad hoc offerings; the king has no means of sanction if these are refused (10:27), and the king himself still participates in agricultural production (11:5). This changes with the transition to the "typical early state,"[55] which closely corresponds to the picture sketched by tradition of the transition to David's kingship. The territorial principle now joins with ties of blood (2 Sam 2:4; 5:1-5, rule over Judah and Israel; 2 Sam 8:1-15, conquest of non-Israelite territories). The king's relatives move into the background of government (8:16-18; 20:23-26), and social stratification is so advanced that king and court no longer take part in production. Apparently, this condition prevailed into the ninth and eighth centuries, when the transition to the fully developed state began.

On the whole, the biblical depiction of history tends to accent the transitions between epochs quite sharply. It places a deep cleft between Moses and Joshua and causes what we see to be a gradual emergence of Israel in the Land to appear as a rapid conquest. Similarly, it marks the transition from the period of the judges to the monarchy very sharply by depicting it, in 1 Samuel 8–12, as an event concluded within a few weeks in a series of popular gatherings. Likewise, in its portrayal of a Davidic-Solomonic empire with a mighty court, magnificent buildings, and broad international relationships, especially under Solomon, it assumes that the state developed very quickly to its full maturity, whereas our

historical knowledge shows us that we need to imagine more of a gradual development of statehood leading to a full development only in the ninth and eighth centuries.

This picture attempts to do justice to the model of the early state, with its stages of development. Nevertheless, we must be clear that the decisive break was between the pre-state and state epochs—contrary to a trend, evident in some representatives of the chiefdom theories, to minimize that disruption, as James D. Martin describes: "There is . . . a fairly obvious trend . . . towards seeing the advent of statehood and monarchy in ancient Israel as a natural development, a historical continuum from the preceding period, as opposed to the widely accepted view of discontinuity in the nature of these two stages of social development."[56] This view is correct in seeing that the creation of stable states is not the work of a few weeks, but it minimizes the qualitative break between the epochs. That break is evident from the fact that all the efforts to develop centralized rule before Saul and David failed, whereas they were first successful under these leaders. But it is also clear from the emergence, after the establishment of early states that showed themselves likely to endure, of resistance to the monarchy.

Resistance to the Monarchy

If we assemble the factors that lead to monarchy and the changes that monarchy brings with it (described more fully below), it is not surprising that the establishment of a monarchy does not take place without friction.[57]

It is true that—as we might expect—such resistance cannot be proved if, in constructing our theories, we confine ourselves to the archaeological findings. We have to turn to the biblical texts. Here the difficulty in identifying resistance to the establishment of states lies in the fact that Judges and 1 Samuel only received their final redaction at a time when they were looking back at the history of the kingdoms of Israel and Judah after they had come to an end. Therefore we have to test in each individual case which statements are due to retrospective evaluation and which might contain older material. Besides linguistic analyses, which cannot be discussed in this study,[58] the question of social interests and the criteria for critique of the monarchy may be helpful to us in this case. In the later texts, we find two types of argumentation. One—found especially in texts of the later or writing prophets—criticizes the monarchy for not realizing the function claimed by its own royal ideology, namely protecting the poor and weak in society. The other strand of criticism, which dominates the final redaction of the deuteronomistic texts in the Former Prophets, criticizes the monarchy almost exclusively for its religious faults, which are in turn measured against Deuteronomy's laws for centralizing the cult.

Against these clearly visible lines of critique of the monarchy, a few texts that presuppose an entirely different context of conflict stand out. The fable of Jotham in Judg 9:7-15, obviously a secondary insertion in the narrative about Abimelech's failed kingship in Shechem, tells how the trees first offer the crown to the noble trees: the olive, the fig, and the vine. They all refuse because they are worthy enough in themselves and have no need to rule over others. So the bramble, the most worthless of bushes, takes over. Here, neither religious criteria are applied to the kingship nor is there a social critique "from below." It is the social nobility that reject monarchical rule, and it is the marginal elements that seek it.

Likewise, the so-called *law of the king* (1 Sam 8:10-17), placed on the lips of Samuel within the deuteronomistically shaped composition of 1 Samuel 8, in the context of the people's desire for a king, reveals a social constellation that does not recur in later texts. As in Jotham's fable, it is not the lower class that suffers the consequences of royal rule, but the well-to-do class of landowners. Their sons will be conscripted—but for leadership functions in the army (vv. 11–12). They will have to contribute part of their property (which is portrayed as ample, v. 14). The people envisioned by this text are themselves the slave owners (v. 16).

It was probably the same kind of well-to-do landowners that the brief note in 1 Sam 10:27 had in mind. Here we read that, after Saul was made king, some people refused to bring him a "present" because they doubted that he could "save" them. Saul passes over this in silence. Both things show that these opponents are not "little people": They are not in need of the "saving" or "help" they think of as coming from a king, and they can afford to refuse to follow him, without having to expect any serious sanctions.

1 Samuel 25 sketches a prototype of this class in the person of Nabal, whose name means "fool." He is wealthy (v. 2); he does not need the protection of David's people; he refuses to give any gifts to the future king (vv. 10-11). In the narrative's logic, he has to pay for this with his life (v. 38), and his wise widow will marry the coming king (v. 42). But as we know from 1 Sam 22:2, David's troop was recruited, among others, from people who had fled from wealthy people like Nabal because of their burdensome debts.

What all these texts have in common is that they lack any religious motivation for criticizing the monarchy. This makes it impossible to assign them to a later epoch as "deuterono-mistic."[59] At the same time they reveal a social constellation that is quite untypical of the later period but may well be explained by the radical change represented by the transition from a pre-state to a state society.[60] If we consider the beginnings of social differentiation, traces of which we thought we could perceive in the pre-state society,[61] we can understand that those who could call a considerable state of comfort their own would have had little interest in erecting a central authority. Their question to a king is, in fact: "What good will that do us?" (1 Sam 10:27). But those who had fallen through the cracks of the kinship-based society saw in the monarchy their one and only chance to achieve power for themselves; the story of David and his band is a good example of this. And the mass of independent farm families could expect from the monarchy at least a greater degree of external and internal security, so that they had no reason to resist.

This set of interests, shaky as a whole, is reflected not only in the texts discussed above, but also in the reports of various revolts against the first kings. Saul is confronted by David's group of mercenaries (beginning with 1 Samuel 22). David's son Absalom rises up against him (2 Samuel 15–18). The account of Absalom's revolt has incorporated accounts that suggest enduring opposition by follow-ers of Saul (2 Sam 16:5-15; 19:17-31). Under a certain Sheba, the northern tribes attempt to liberate themselves from David (2 Samuel 20). Under Solomon we have the account of a revolt by the Ephraimite Jeroboam (1 Kgs 11:26-28, 40). And finally, according to 1 Kings 12, under Solomon's successor Rehoboam, the northern tribes separated from the Davidides.

It is true that the story shows that none of these attempted revolts resulted in the restora-tion of pre-state conditions. And the resistance

of the well-to-do landowners against the new institution of the monarchy did not last long. Rather, they quickly accommodated them-selves and seized the opportunity to partici-pate in the new power, as Nabal's wife Abigail foreshadows in that story: it is foolish to resist the king, and it is wise to marry him. Since some of the lower class immediately attained positions of power, and since apparently at first very little changed for the mass of farming families,[62] the kingship quickly attained a high degree of stability.

Even though the monarchy, as a form of state, was not instantly created in its fullest development, so that the consequences of the change were only gradually apparent, the creation of states nevertheless represents an epochal break. In the next section, we will first consider the overall consequences, before we then turn to the different profiles of the north-ern and southern kingdoms.

Society and State under Monarchical Rule

With the establishment of the kingship under Saul and David, and thus the crucial and epochal step from a kinship-based society without a central state to statehood, we are faced with the question: what changes hap-pened in society in the stretch of land that con-tained the states of Israel and Judah, as a result of state creation? And how did the apparatus of the "early state," at first so rudimentary, begin to develop?

Perseverance of the Kinship-based Society

In the transition from a kinship-based to a state society, we can observe for the first time a phenomenon that will shape the ongoing social history of Israel: in the transition to the new epoch, essential elements of the preceding epoch were retained and were transformed only gradually and, to some extent, only externally.

Concretely, this means that the kinship-based society remained the basic structure, as before, with the apparatus of the state superimposed on it without, at first, introducing any profound changes. Families and clans remained the basic units of society. They remained essentially autonomous and self-sustaining; differences in size, which had begun to appear at the end of the pre-state period, did not yet lead to antagonistic conflicts. There is no indication of any fundamental changes in gender relationships, as far as the mass of the population is concerned; for the state hierarchies things were somewhat different.[63]

That the state apparatus at first lay like a thin layer on top of society is evident especially from the fact that there were no state interventions in the economy. This does not mean that the kings were not economically active. The royal economy was organized as a household economy, with the royal household headed by a "steward" (ʾasher ʿal-habbayit).[64] But the monarchy did not intervene in the economic activities of the populace.[65] In modern terms, we could say that the monarchy was active on the level of business, but not economics.[66]

The early state was characterized by a simple, twofold division. One the one side were the rulers, "a ruling elite of probably no more than two percent of the population,"[67] and on the other side were those ruled, the great mass of the people. For them, economic and social life at first continued just as in the time when there was no central government. This situation, in which on the one hand a state has been established, but on the other hand the pre-state

structures continue alongside and below the state structures, has been called a "tribe/state paradox."[68]

But even though the social base with its relationships defined by kinship endured after the establishment of the monarchy, the existence of a state did enable gradual change. Before we consider the state's particular activities, which ultimately helped to bring about a profound social transformation, we must first take a look at the state's apparatus itself.

The Apparatus of the State

Describing the apparatus of the royal state represents a twofold abstraction: first a spatial abstraction, and second, a temporal abstraction. Spatially, there is no essential distinction between the northern and northern kingdoms. A few differences will be given below.[69] Here we are interested in what they had in common. Temporally, we should certainly take for granted that the state apparatus also evolved, which the model of the early state in fact presumes. Still, what we want to show here is the new thing that entered social reality with the establishment of a state, even though all that was new need not have been immediately present, and may certainly have been subject to change.

It is a tautology to say that a monarchy is headed by a king. All the biblical accounts and narratives about the monarchical period presuppose that as a matter of course. The texts of the so-called royal ideology show what a powerful role can at least be attributed ideally to the monarch. According to these, the welfare of state and society depends on the person of the king, along with repulsing external enemies and to some degree even the fertility of nature (Pss. 2; 45; 72; and frequently).

7.8. Representations of kings and high-ranking Israelite officials appearing on seals.

Because in a sense the king embodies the state, the common storage jars used in the time of Hezekiah, at the end of the eighth century, were marked as state property with a stamp that read "belonging to the king" (*lmlk*).[70]

The king has a court. This consists of the members of his family, first of all the queen mother, then his wives, sons, and daughters (see the lists in 2 Kgs 24:12, 15; Jer 29:2). We have seals from sons, and from one daughter, with their names and the titles *bn hmlk*[71] and *bt hmlk*[72] respectively. The designation *son of the king* is also common in the Bible (1 Kgs 22:26; Jer 36:26;[73] 38:6; Zeph 1:8; 2 Chr 18:25; 28:7). The fact that kings' sons repeatedly exercise official functions does not make the *bn hmlk* a mere titular figure, of course—as is sometimes suggested—but only means "that in ancient

Israel one might give the sons born to the king certain administrative roles."[74]

The case of royal relatives illustrates how gender roles change in a hierarchical society. While there is something to be said for the suggestion that the kinship-based society manifested a certain gender symmetry[75] (and for the mass of the population probably nothing essential changed in that regard under the new social conditions), in the new social hierarchies relationships were asymmetrical. Individual women could assume higher positions. First to be mentioned is the influential role of the queen mother, as is attested in Judah (1 Kgs 2:19; 15:13 = 2 Chr 15:16; 2 Kgs 10:13; Jer 13:18; 29:2; and frequently). That the king's daughters also had their own seals reveals that they were exalted persons. But at the same time, hierarchical ordering meant being placed below and after, for despite all sorts of reverence in accord with the rules of protocol (1 Kgs 2:19), the king could also depose his own mother (1 Kgs 15:13). And it is uncertain whether the seal-bearing royal daughters really applied those seals in business or officially, since we have no such impressions from the seals. Finally, the sole case in which a woman herself became queen, Athaliah, is depicted by the biblical authors as a total catastrophe (2 Kings 11).[76]

But the royal court was not only composed of relatives. The seals with "NN *ᶜvd hmlk*" have the same structure as those with "NN *bn hmlk*."[77] Their owners thus describe themselves as the "slave" or "servant" of the king. As is shown by the use of seals, which were often works of art, and the frequent reference in the biblical texts to such *ᶜevadim* immediately surrounding the king (from 1 Sam 8:14-15 to 2 Kgs 24:12), these people were at the center of power. They bore no titles that would indicate their function, but were defined exclusively by their subjection to the king. This personal service is very clear in the seals that bear the king's proper name instead of *ᶜvd hmlk*. Attested in this form are "slaves" of kings Jeroboam II and Hoshea from the northern kingdom and Uzziah, Ahaz, and Hezekiah from the south.[78]

Along with the *ᶜevadim*, the biblical texts occasionally also mention *sarisim* (1 Sam 8:14-15; 2 Kgs 24:12), which could be translated "eunuch" or "courtier." They are closely tied to the court (2 Kgs 9:32; see also 2 Kgs 20:18 = Isa 39:7) and to the person of the king (1 Kgs 22:9 = 2 Chr 18:8; 2 Kgs 8:6). Zedekiah's *saris*, Ebed-melech (Jer 38:7, 10, 12; 39:16) was, as a foreigner (a Cushite), especially dependent on the king himself.

The royal officials were clearly distinguished from the members of the court who were characterized by their personal relationship with the king.[79] Their work was directed outward, even when they were top officials who were also involved in the central administration. And frequently their field of activity was expressed in a special title.

The top officials who made up the royal administration appear as a group and paradigmatically in the four lists of officials in 1 Sam 14:50; 2 Sam 8:16-18; 20:23-26; and 1 Kgs 4:2-6. The sequence and tendency of these lists reflects a very typical development in an early state. Saul had only one official, the commander of his army (1 Sam 14:50). The office of army commander was also preeminent under David, but was augmented by other civil and religious offices. Beginning with the second Davidic list, the office of "head of the forced labor" should be noted. The most important innovation under Solomon was a head of the royal palace, the "one set over the house" (*ᶜal-habbayit,* 1 Kgs 4:6).

Most of the official titles in the lists are found in both biblical and epigraphical evidence from the monarchical period. We will speak about the commanders of the armies and the ministers of forced labor below when dealing with the army and labor.[80] The only high office in the official lists that has not yet been epigraphically attested for Israel is the *mazkir,* who must have functioned as a kind of secretary or chancellor.[81] In the case of the office of scribe (*sofer*)[82], it is not altogether clear how high in the hierarchy an official with such a title should be ranked, since semantically the word, like the English "secretary," can be used either for subordinates or for executives. Certainly a high office is that of the *ʾasher ᶜal-habbayit,* the "one set over the house."[83] According to Isa 22:21-22, this office was almost like that of the king, and according to 2 Kgs 15:5 it was assumed by a royal son, who as *ᶜal-habbayit,* is regent for the ailing king. One holder of this office had himself memorialized in an inscription on a tomb in Silwan (Siloam), near Jerusalem.[84] The very ability to order such a private cave tomb for oneself points to the owner's high station; see also Isa 22:16.

The offices discussed here are those belonging directly to the royal court and the central government. Those who held these offices are collectively called "the high officials" (*sarim*) (1 Kgs 4:2; cf. 2 Kgs 24:12; Jer 29:2; 34:19; 36:12, 14, 19; 37:14–15; 38:4, 25, 27). When the Lachish ostracon no. 6[85] directly juxtaposes the "letter of the king" and the "letters of the officials" (as it does in lines 3–4), this shows that these high officials belong to the king's closest retinue.

But there were also officials who were not in the central administration and did not hold key positions. One special office was that of "governor of the city," "commander of the city," or "mayor," attested for both capitals, Samaria (1 Kgs 22:26; 2 Kgs 10:5) and Jerusalem (2 Kgs 23:8).[86] The epigraphical attestations on seals and seal impressions with the inscription *sr h^cr* (approximately "official of the city")[87] are striking, inasmuch as no personal name precedes the title, as is otherwise the case on officials' seals. These, then, are not the personal seals of high officials, but proper seals of office. The existence of a seal of office and the attestation of that office only in the capital cities indicate that this office stood at a midpoint between central and local administration.

In contrast, the prescript of a petition from Mesad Hashavyahu brings us into the provinces.[88] "May my lord the commandant hear the concern of his servant."[89] A harvester subject to forced labor had to address the responsible military and civil officers as *ʾdny hsr* (approximately "lord official"). The same form of address appears on an ostracon: a widow addresses an official.[90] The sequence *ʾdny sr* is

also found on an ostracon from Arad,[91] but it is so fragmentary that we cannot make out anything about the context of the address.

The view from below, characteristic of the petitions on the ostraca, also marks the form of speech in the socially critical texts of the prophets. The objects of their criticism are often "the officials" (Isa 1:23; 3:14; Jer 34:8-22; Ezek 22:27; Zeph 1:8-9; 3:3; using other terms, but certainly including officials are Jer 5:5; Mic 3:1, 9, 11). Except for Zeph 1:8-9 there is little likelihood that they are thinking in general of the highest ministers surrounding the king, because the actions of the officials who are being criticized have a direct effect on ordinary people. Occasionally they are mentioned in direct parallel to other civil persons who are also complicit in the oppression of the weak (Isa 3:14; Jer 34:8–22; Ezek 22:23–31). For the common people—and the prophets take this perspective as their own—these functionaries at the lower levels are those with whom the people have direct contact, and as such they appear as "the officials" (or "heads" or "leaders").

This is striking because the internal correspondence between officials, as attested by the ostraca from Arad and Lachish, paints a different picture. These functionaries at the lower and middle levels address each other only by name, without any use of titles. The hierarchical order is expressed either with "lord" and "slave" or "son" in the case of superiors and subordinates, or with "brother" between equals. Only the high officials are given a title (*sar*) in these letters (Lachish ostraca nos. 3 and 6).[92]

Overall, these statements about officials reveal a clear hierarchy. At the top is a leading officialdom surrounding the king. These people can be called summarily "the officials." Under them is a lower, middle set of offices in which people apparently knew each other so well that an address by name was sufficient for official correspondence. Nevertheless, from the people's point of view these, too, were "the officials," and in individual cases they were to be addressed as "my lord the *sar*."

When, in a vehement polemic, Isaiah (3:12-15) announces that YHWH is coming to enter into judgment "with the elders and princes [= officials] of his people" (v. 14), the text sets prior to the officials we have been discussing a second group, the elders.[93] What are they doing in a section about administration in the monarchical period?

We have already encountered elders in city governance structure in the pre-national period.[94] In fact, the office of elder is essentially tied to the city.[95] The elders appear in the period before the monarchy as representatives of their cities, and they retain that function in the state period, but are then likewise tied into the state's governmental system. They assume judicial, representative, notarial, and cultic functions in their respective cities.[96] The degree to which these functions are closely identified with the monarchy is shown in the narrative of the judicial execution of Naboth (1 Kings 21).[97] The laws in Deuteronomy present the same picture: state judges and overseers act in conjunction with the city elders, and the legal system functions only in that combination.[98]

In discussing the elders, we have already gone beyond the state's apparatus in the narrower sense of the royal court and its officials. It is evident that incorporating city elites into state administration had consequences for social relationships. Before we consider that subject, however, we must first take a look at the activities of the monarchical state, for it is not so much the mere existence of a state's apparatus, but above all its actions that influence social development.

Activities of the National State

According to 1 Sam 8:20, making war is among the central duties of the king. Therefore we will begin the description of the state's activities with the military.[99]

When war threatens a society without state organization, all those who are capable seize their weapons. Leadership of the troops falls to anyone who feels called to the role and whom the troops will follow. When the acute danger is past, the army dissolves. The leaders, too, as a rule have no ongoing governance function. But there are also armed groups, as both the frequent references to the ʿApiru in the second millennium[100] and biblical allusions to "outlaws" (Judg 9:4; 11:3) show. Anyone who sought ongoing rulership needed such a troop.

With the creation of the state, the simultaneous phenomena of armies summoned ad hoc and armed bands of outlaws gave way to a twofold structure of professional army and occasional muster. Of Saul, we read that he built up a standing army with his uncle Abner as "commander" (1 Sam 14:50-52). Things were different with David, inasmuch as he brought his own troop with him. After he managed to seize the kingship, they were transformed from a group of bandits into an official army.[101] The military commanders of the band became the most important ministers, as the official lists show (2 Sam 8:16; 20:23).

Nevertheless, the new state did not attempt to do without the armed strength of its population. It established the twofold force of the professional army and the muster. We can conclude from some accounts of wars that the small professional army assumed the dangerous tasks of acting as advance guard or storming walls, while the mustered men, certainly less well armed, were inserted in the climactic and concluding phases of the struggle (from the account of the war with the Ammonites, see esp. 2 Sam 11:1, 11, 14-17; 12:26-29, and from the account of an Israelite-Aramaean war, see 1 Kgs 20:14-20).[102]

Command of the troops was exercised by officers bearing the Hebrew title *sar*, from "commander of the army" (*sar[hats] tseva'* or similar terms; 1 Sam 14:50; 17:55; 2 Sam 2:8, etc.)[103] to the captains of smaller units. The Arad ostraca from the beginning of the sixth century[104] attest that in the late period of Judah simple soldiers could also be professionals. These ostraca refer to a troop of *Kittiyim*, that is, Greek mercenaries.[105] But their officers were also Judeans, as the names in the correspondence, which are almost all constructed with the element *-yahu*, attest. When war broke out, however, the entire male population was called to service, as the mention of the "secretary who was the commander of the army who mustered the people of the land" (2 Kgs 25:19 = Jer 52:25) shows; this is in connection with the second exile after the final conquest of Jerusalem. This confirms that the double structure of professional army and muster continued until the end of the monarchy.[106]

We can observe from the structure of military institutions, which in principle existed from the beginning of the monarchy until its end, how a gradual but profound revolution took place in spite of a certain continuity from the pre-state institutions. As before, the able men went to battle, but they now mostly supported the professional army. Formerly free fighters, they were now subject to levy and commanded by professional officers. Military might, which before the time of the state lay with those who were in a position to exercise it, was now a monopoly of the state.

Besides war, there were many community tasks for the state, especially building projects.

In the pre-state period, such undertakings may have been kept within narrow limits (road building, simple fortifications, local shrines). Naturally, with the founding of a state these activities took on quite different dimensions. In both the biblical and extra-biblical literature, we find countless passages in which kings are subjects of the verb *build* (*bnh*) (see the Mesha stele[107] as well as 1 Kgs 9:17–19; 12:25; and frequently). Archaeology also attests that the monarchical period in Israel and Judah was a time of active building. Human labor was needed for all aspects of building. Such labor was no longer locally self-organized but mandated by the state. It has become usual to characterize this with an expression from medieval feudalism, *socage*.[108] It is attested throughout the entire monarchical period, from the lists of David's and Solomon's officials (the minister of forced labor = *'al-hammas*, 2 Sam 20:24; 1 Kgs 4:6; see also 1 Kgs 5:28 [English: v. 14]; 12:18) to the seal impression of "Pelayahu '*sr 'l hms*" from the seventh century[109] to the prophetic accusations in Mic 3:10; Hab 2:12, and Jer 22:13-19.

From the beginning, the use of forced labor is presented as by no means conflict-free. Even the so-called law of the king in 1 Sam 8:10-17, dated backward by the deuteronomistic composition into the discussion about the creation of the kingship, warns that the king will take the sons and daughters of free persons for service.[110] Solomon's labor levy of the inhabitants of the north to work led ultimately, under his successor Rehoboam, to the secession of the northern tribes (1 Kgs 12). The accusations in Mic 3:10; Hab 2:12; and Jer 22:13-19 point to Judah in the late eighth and early sixth centuries. The ostracon of Mesad Hashavyahu[111] presents us with an epigraphical document from the late period of Judah[112] whose subject is publicly required labor. It is true that this is not about building, but harvesting, but it shows the broad field covered by the demand for labor among the state's activities.

In all these biblical and epigraphical texts it is important to see that they never question the institution of forced labor as such. In the exemplary depictions of the early period, the only disputed issue is the scope of the work to be demanded, as in the ostracon from Mesad Hashavyahu. Micah 3:10 and Hab 2:12 connect building works with the accusation of shedding blood, and the central point of the critique in Jer 22:13-19 is that the object to be built is an unnecessary royal luxury.

Besides demanding labor, the newly created state required payments.[113] In this regard the epigraphical and biblical evidence strongly suggests that the significance of the taxation system was narrower than and different from that of forced labor. This seems to contradict the oldest textual reference to a governmentally organized system of provision for the royal court in 1 Kgs 4:17-19.[114] According to that text, Solomon had twelve "officials" in twelve different regions in the north who were responsible for provisions for the court. But we can scarcely conclude from this that a thoroughly organized system of "provinces," "districts," or "regions"[115] existed because both the officials and the areas for which they are responsible are too differently described for us to be able to read any systemizing tendencies from this passage. Instead, the "officials" seem to be local personages who have influence "in" the places and regions mentioned.[116] They are to secure the loyalty of the local population for the king, and at the same time be the king's representatives in the locality. In two cases the individuals' particular loyalty is secured by marriage to the king's daughters (vv. 11, 15).[117] Probably their duty, besides political representation, consisted in the delivery of produce to

the court, though scarcely in the unrealistic form of a monthly rotating obligation like that suggested in v. 7. In any case, this was not a developed system of taxation.[118]

A tithe, as a regular tax or contribution, is only rarely mentioned in the Bible, and those references do not permit us to conclude that there was a uniform system.[119] Thus 1 Sam 8:15, 17 speaks of a royal tithe on agricultural produce, while Gen 28:22 and Amos 4:4 would lead us to believe there was a sacral tithe that, however, benefited the royal sanctuaries in the northern kingdom. Deuteronomy 12:6, 11, 17 then presumes such a tithe, to be paid to the central sanctuary, in the late period of Judah. Jerusalem likewise yields the only certain epigraphical evidence; an ostracon from the end of the eighth or beginning of the seventh century contains the numbers 200 and 18, which are associated with the process of tithing (*lᶜsr*).[120] Of course, the condition of the artifacts is such that we cannot tell whether the document is from the state or the temple administration. But it may be that no distinction was drawn between the two.[121]

In the late periods of both states, Israel and Judah, we also learn of a special tax that was raised in order to meet the tribute demands of the Assyrian and Egyptian overlords (2 Kgs 15:19-20 and 2 Kgs 23:35). But, despite the one-time character of this levy, since both states from the mid-eighth century onward were dependent almost without interruption on Assyria, and later, in the case of Judah, on Babylon and Egypt, and that dependence involved an annual payment of tribute,[122] we must at all times assume that the kings had major financial needs. Therefore, even without an uninterrupted chain of evidence, we may well conclude that "at the latest with dependence on Assyria and the obligation to make regular payments of tribute, a taxation system would have become inevitable in Judah as well."[123]

To maintain the apparatus of the state, not only the court and the civil officials but also and especially the army, the monarchical state needed an income. Besides personal services and a system of taxes, the scope of which is not very clear, the kings in Israel and Judah could rely on an economic sector of their own.[124]

Royal estates consisted in part of the family holdings of the kings (for Saul, see 1 Sam 9:1-2; 11:4-5; and frequently; for David, 1 Sam 16:11, 19; 17:15; and frequently; for David's son Absalom, 2 Sam 13:23). Added to this was territory gained by political actions, such as the city of Ziklag ("therefore Ziklag has belonged to the kings of Judah to this day," 1 Sam 27:6), or the city of Jerusalem, which was captured by David (the "city of David," 2 Sam 5:9). There was opportunity to purchase land as well (2 Sam 24:18-24 for David; 1 Kgs 16:24 for Omri; see also 1 Kgs 21:1-2). Kings might also take possession of the lands of people who were condemned for treason, as David seized the property of Saul's son Mephibosheth (2 Sam 16:1-4), and Ahab took Naboth's vineyard (1 Kings 21). Finally, we may consider the possibility that ownerless land automatically belonged to the king, as in Mephibosheth's case before he was discovered to be the owner (2 Samuel 9) and in the instance of the wealthy Shunamite woman who left the land during a famine (2 Kgs 8:1-6).

All these instances show that the kings had land, but they cannot show that they owned extensive "royal estates," the existence of which would have been responsible for the social crises beginning in the eighth century.[125] Besides, the notion of royal crown estates is handicapped in that it uses a concept drawn from medieval feudalism and is therefore inseparably associated with notions of

fiefdoms and vassalage.[126] But the texts suggest nothing of the sort, and so it is preferable to abandon the idea of royal crown estates altogether and instead to speak in neutral terms of royal property.

In addition to the biblical texts, epigraphical remains also point to the existence of royal lands. Martin Noth in particular[127] interpreted the Samaria ostraca from the second quarter of the eighth century as registering receipts from the supposed crown estates, but for the mass of the findings that can scarcely be the case.[128] Only those few ostraca that contain nothing but a note of origin "from vineyard X" and the description of the goods can be interpreted as indicating royal property.[129]

The case is different with the stamped jar handles bearing the inscription "property of the king (lmlk)."[130] There are a great number of them[131] half a century later in the northern kingdom—that is, in the last quarter of the eighth century during the reign of Hezekiah. All the storage jars thus marked come from the same pottery, or several located very close together.[132] The four places named in the stamps (Socho, Hebron, Ziph, or mmsht, all of which were probably located around the well-known town of Hebron) were royal property. They indicate the origin of the wine or oil that was then consumed in Jerusalem and in the fortified cities, where the overwhelming number of jar handles were found. The concentration in the fortresses is probably explained by Hezekiah's preparations for resistance to Assyria, which nearly ended in 701 with the conquest of Jerusalem.[133]

For epigraphical reasons, together with the high number of the regnal year of the unnamed king, the so-called fiscal bullae are quite certainly to be dated to the time of Josiah.[134] They confirm deliveries from various Judahite cities (Lachish, Gebim, Nezib,

Eltolad, and Arubbot) "to the king" (*lmlk*). It is not evident from the *bullae* whether we should think of these deliveries as coming from a general taxation system[135] or from royal property. But the fact that in comparison to the lists in Josh 15:18–19[136] only a few place names are mentioned speaks against interpreting these as referring to tax payments. Since a system of taxation must be applied universally, the places named on the fiscal *bullae,* like those on the *lmlk* stamps, may probably refer to royal property.

Finally, the ostraca found in the southern fortress of Arad bring us to the latest period of independent Judah.[137] These, together with the excavated storehouse, attest that the fortress was a collection and distribution point for large quantities of agricultural products. But where did they come from? Only ostracon 25 gives information on that score; it contains a list of three place names preceded by *min* ("from") and followed by a statement of the quantity of grain delivered.[138] These places could have been royal property, as in the *lmlk* stamps. But it is not impossible that the reference is to agricultural products from villages subject to taxation.

If we combine the information about economic activity with what we know about the kingdom, it can be regarded as certain that in Israel and Judah during the monarchy there was relevant royal property that served primarily to support the fortresses and the court itself. But on the whole we do not get the impression that the existence of royal property made any fundamental changes in the economic life of the country, because families and clans continued to hold property alongside that of the king. Royal property was organized as a "house" (*bayit*) headed by the (*ʾasher*) *ʿal-habbayit*.[139] This royal *bayit* was probably larger than that of the wealthiest residents

of the land, but alongside it the numerous "houses" of Israelite and Judahite families continued their existence. The royal economy remained a household economy or, in modern terms, a business economy. It did not develop into a national economy that regulated the economic life of the whole country.

Another field of state activity is the judicial function.[140] Here again, we find certain aspects of continuity with the pre-state society that then give way to far-reaching changes. In the case of the pre-state period, we can presume that cases of conflict were adjusted directly between the parties concerned. The result could be anything from negotiations and feuds to the application of force. Essentially, the outcome would depend on the relative strength of the parties. What is important is that probably, as a rule, there was no third-party arbiter.[141] In any case, in cities and towns we may suppose that elders exercised a mediating function. But even then we cannot assume that they were in a position to issue authoritative judgments, especially because their own interests always made them parties to the disputes themselves.

It is true that this constellation of judicial relationships did not fundamentally change because of the establishment of the monarchy, but it was pushed in a particular direction. The very existence of a king and powerful persons associated with him in the cities of the land (officers, officials) changed the justice system. We cannot imagine it any other way: in local disputes these powerful people would have been brought into the conflict. At least, the weaker party in each instance must have had a direct interest in such an intervention. Thus, there arose a form of judicial system in which those who had the power to bring judgment into effect also did the judging. In a small stronghold that could be the commandant, as the ostracon from Mesad Hashavyahu shows.[142] In larger settlements the elders gathered to deliberate and enter judgment, supported by state judges and secretaries. The degree to which royal authority could intervene directly in this system is shown by the narrative about Naboth's vineyard (1 Kings 21).[143] Obviously, this system was not equally well developed from the beginning and consistently in all places. But it can be presumed for the final period of the Judaic monarchy in the relationships that Deuteronomy intends to influence.

Of course, in discussing the role of the king and the power derived from him in actually issuing judgments, we have by no means touched the most important function of the monarchy with regard to the judicial system. Namely, as a counter to the increasing class divisions in Israelite and Judahite society, as evident from the eighth century onward, there was a move to codify law. We may suppose that the monarchy played a significant role in the process.[144]

The military establishment, mandated taxation and labor for the state, the development of a royal economic property, and the monarchy's influence on legal affairs are activities of the state activity whose development and evolution marks the shift from an early to a fully developed state. The more strongly the state intervened in these fields, the deeper its simultaneous influence on the population's social structures of the population. Once social distinctions began—and we saw traces of that at the very beginning of the monarchy—the state's demands for soldiers, laborers, and taxes served to intensify them: a powerful household can respond to these demands without being very much weakened, but for an already damaged household they can lead to ruin. At the same time, the existence of a professional army and state assumption of influence over judicial matters restricts the opportunities for the lower classes to escape the clutch of their creditors, as they were still able to do in David's time by forming bands.

Role of the Temple

Before we pursue the somewhat different developments in the states of Israel and Judah, let us take a brief look at the temple's social significance.[145] In the framework of a social history, such an examination can, of course, have only a narrow focus, concentrating on its economic significance and the immediate social consequences of its influence.

The symbolic meaning of religious establishments is much higher than their economic significance. Among the very few more-or-less solid criteria defining a state is the presence of a common ideology. The unity of a state was symbolized in pre-modern societies by the unity of its religion. The latter could be quite varied in itself and have different expressions on the different social levels of family, village, region, and state. The much-discussed question whether, during the monarchical period in Israel and Judah, the postulate of worship to YHWH alone already existed, or whether there was still a kind of polytheism, such as flourished throughout the Levant, and what role the various social classes played in all this is something that need not be discussed here. What is decisive is that the society as a whole, represented from the time of the state's establishment in the nation itself and in the figure of the king, symbolized its unity by the worship of YHWH. When the Moabite king plundered Israelite cities, he seized equipment belonging to YHWH and placed it before his state and national god Chemosh, as he records on his victory stele.[146]

But even the more economic significance of religious establishments, especially the temple, had first and foremost a deeply symbolic character. "No one shall appear before me empty-handed" (Exod 23:15; 34:20)—that is a basic demand of every religion, which in Israel is described as appearing "before the face of YHWH" (Deut 16:16). Worshipers bring the deity their gifts in the form of sacrifices, firstfruits, tithes and free-will offerings, which the deity accepts and rewards by bestowing fertility and blessing, which in turn evoke corresponding gifts from the worshiper: an endless circle of giving and reciprocating that keeps the world in motion.[147] The material reality to which this can be reduced, that people give part of what they have earned to a religious institution, does not exhaust the symbolic significance.

Gift-giving as a basic form of religious behavior is not linked to any particular type of society. Obviously there were sanctuaries even in the pre-state period, and gifts were brought to them. At the same time, the transition to statehood brought with it a change that ultimately led to completely different circumstances from those that existed before the state, because now there were royal sanctuaries in addition to the local ones: in Jerusalem for the south and in Bethel and Dan for the north. Gifts were brought to these royal sanctuaries, too. The tithe mentioned in Amos 4:4 and Gen 28:22 points to this in the case of Bethel (and Gilgal?).[148] We have a tradition that there was a collection chest in Jerusalem into which donations were placed (2 Kgs 12:5-17; 22:3-9).[149] Not only the priests, but also one of the king's scribes, had access to the contents of these chests (2 Kgs 12:11).

The gifts from visitors to the temple, together with royal "dedicated gifts" or "votive gifts"[150] (see 2 Sam 8:11-12; 1 Kgs 7:51; 15:15;

2 Kgs 12:19 [English: v. 18]), made up the temple treasure. From the many references to it in the books of Kings, we learn three things (1 Kgs 14:25-26; 15:18; 2 Kgs 12:19; 14:14; 16:8; 18:15; 24:13). First, the temple treasury was always distinguished from the state treasury. Second, the temple treasury is always mentioned first, which can probably be attributed to the deuteronomistic redactors' special interest in the temple. Third, it is always presumed that the king has access to both treasuries. The last point underscores how much, under royal rule, at least the central sanctuaries were tied into the state order.

At the end of the monarchy in Judah the relationship between local and central sanctuaries was reversed. While in the pre-state period there were only local sanctuaries, and during the whole monarchical period both existed side by side, under Josiah at the end of the seventh century the local sanctuaries were closed and the cult was centralized in Jerusalem (2 Kgs 23:5, 8-9, 15, 19-20; cf. Deuteronomy 12). We will not speak here of the religious-historical consequences of the cult's centralization.[151] But the event is also significant from the perspective of social history.

Centralization of the pilgrim feasts led to the problem that the foodstuffs brought as gifts and for purposes of sacrifice, especially cattle, had to be transported for very long distances, which was not practical. For that reason, the people were permitted to translate these things into silver in their home districts and use the money to repurchase calves, sheep, wine, and similar nonperishable items at the temple (Deut 14:25-26). It is obvious that in this way both internal commerce and the money economy took a huge upswing. On the one hand, the temple had to purchase, in the countryside, the goods that it would sell to the pilgrims. On the other hand,

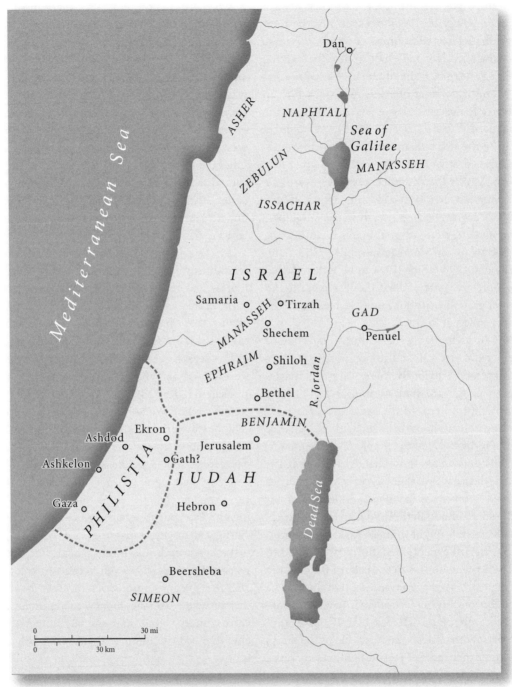

7.9. The Divided Kingdoms of Israel and Judah.

this commercial act did not take the form of an exchange of natural products, but involved silver, which thus quite clearly assumed a monetary function, even if it was not coined but had to be individually weighed (see the description in Jer 32:9–10 and the prohibition against having two kinds of weights in the same sack, Deut 25:13). That it was the temple, and indeed the state temple under royal control, where gifts that were originally in the form of natural products were transformed into money matches observations from other cultures.[152]

This reflection on the Josianic reform of the cult and its consequences for the economy brings us to the end of the monarchical period. But we must now go back to the beginning and sketch the specific profiles of the two states of Israel and Judah.

Profiles of Monarchy in Israel and Judah

The establishment of the monarchical state in Israel and Judah had fundamental consequences for the structures of both state and society in the two kingdoms; these were treated in the previous sections. But since developments did not run parallel in the two states,

either in time or in structures, we must at this point develop individual profiles of each.

Israel: Revolution, Overthrow, and Stability

It is not difficult to discern, beneath the deuteronomistic surface of the descriptions in the books of Samuel and Kings, two characteristics of the beginnings of the northern kingdom: it was the older of the two states, and, in its own self-perception, its origin was owed to a twofold impulse toward freedom.

Saul's kingdom, which can readily be perceived as a rule over Benjamin and neighboring territories, arose in connection with the struggle for freedom from the Philistines, who play a crucial role both in the stories of the Ark and in those about the rise and fall of Saul. They are depicted as supremely powerful. It is striking how often the stories show them speaking of the Israelites as "Hebrews" (1 Sam 4:6, 9; 13:19; 14:11; 29:3). This name appears only twice on the lips of someone not a Philistine (1 Sam 13:3, 7), and, once, we even encounter a group of Hebrews who only join Israel in the course of the conflict (1 Sam 14:21). This reflects a usage attested in the Amarna correspondence and other texts of the second millennium: ʿApiru are rebels against

7.10. Seal of Shema, a servant of Jeroboam. The lion is associated with Judah. Photo © Erich Lessing/Art Resource, NY.

the legitimate state authority; in times of conflict they may join one side or the other.[153]

No explicit links are given in 1 Samuel to the frequent allusions to "Hebrews" in the stories of the sojourn in Egypt and the Joseph novella.[154] This points to an early, independent tradition closely associated with the figure of Saul. It can be called a "founding legend of the nation-state Israel."[155]

Of course, there is a second founding legend alongside this one, reflected in 1 Kings 12. According to this narrative the northern kingdom arose out of a secession from the rule of the Davidides. Beneath the overpainting in the narrative, which makes the time of Solomon a golden age, we can discern that Solomon, resident in Jerusalem like his predecessor, David, was extending his rule over the north. In doing so, he subjected the north's population to forced labor, even though we can only speculate about its nature and extent. From 1 Kgs 5:27-31 [English vv. 13-17], one gets the impression that forced labor in the form of hard, physical work was universally expected of all Israelite men. A subtler image emerges from 1 Kgs 9:20-22, according to which the Israelite population were, instead, placed in leadership positions.[156] But the polemic in 1 Sam 8:10-17 shows that for a population living in freedom, both could be interpreted as "enslavement."[157]

According to 1 Kings 12, the conflict shifted to Solomon's son Rehoboam when power passed to him. However, even in previous struggles under the rule of David and Solomon,[158] the north's striving for independence was always at the root of the conflicts. David's son Absalom had already turned deliberately to "the men of Israel" (2 Sam 15:3, 6) in seeking to raise a rebellion. As he fled, David was reviled by a man from Saul's clan (2 Sam 16:5-14; 19:17-24). The Benjaminite Sheba

also attempted secession from David's rule, a movement that was put down by David's elite troops (2 Samuel 20). Under Solomon, then, the Ephraimite Jeroboam had to flee after attempting a revolt (1 Kgs 11:26-28, 40).

After Solomon's death, the northern tribes split off without resistance from the Davidides. Such a relatively unproblematic secession is not unusual in a state in its early stages, although—as the previous failed attempts show—it was not simply a matter of course. A separation without a consequent civil war, or something similar, is comparably easy because those holding central authority are supported by local groups and not by the interests of a whole class that stand in opposition to those of another class, as will be the case with fully developed states.[159] If local groups withdraw their loyalty from the center and are supported by their local population—to which they are not in class-determined opposition—separation from the central authority can scarcely be prevented.

From the perspective of social history, it is interesting that the secession of the northern tribes from the Davidides did not result in a dissolution of the state, but in a new kingdom. After the separation from the Davidides, Jeroboam the Ephraimite was made king (1 Kgs 12:20). Of course, it would be senseless to separate from Davidide rule only to establish the same type of kingdom, but with a different ruler at the top. Since the separation from the house of David meant that there were no more obligations to work on the building projects in Jerusalem, there was initially no reason for a comprehensive system of obligatory labor. The new kings of the northern kingdom at first shifted their residence from place to place—starting in Shechem, perhaps also in Penuel (1 Kgs 12:25), then in Tirzah (1 Kgs 14:17; 15:33; 16:6, 8-9, 15, 17, 23). We learn nothing about a building up of these cities, not because of a lack of sources, but because the step toward constructing a metropolis was not taken until Omri, who built Samaria about fifty years after the secession (1 Kgs 16:24).

The self-concept of the new kingdom in the north was programmatically expressed in its cultic polity. The two new royal sanctuaries in Bethel and Dan were expressly dedicated to the God of the Exodus (1 Kgs 12:26-33). The God of the new kingdom is the God who freed Israel from forced labor in Egypt. The exodus tradition remained typical of the northern kingdom throughout its existence (as is clear especially from its complete absence in the prophets of the northern kingdom, Isaiah and Micah), while in the south, the worship of YHWH in the state cult was linked to Zion theology. How closely the founding of the kingdom in an act of secession from the Davidides was linked to the exodus from Egyptian slavery is shown by the literary stylization in 1 Kings 12: Jeroboam appears as the new Moses who leads his people to freedom.[160]

Hence, just as the older Saul tradition can be called a "founding legend of the nation-state Israel,"[161] the exodus tradition has an equal right to be regarded as the "northern kingdom's myth of origins."[162] The answer to the question of the relationship of these two traditions of origin to one another may well be that the stylization of the exodus tradition associated with Jeroboam the Ephraimite presents us with the north's official state ideology. The Saul tradition, in contrast, is probably a special Benjaminite tradition. Since Benjamin always had a special affinity to Judah, it is entirely plausible that this Saul tradition was handed on independently in Benjamin, separate from the main Ephraimite line and at the same time a counterweight to genuine Judahite traditions.

In contrast to the stable Davidide rule in Judah, frequent changes of dynasty were

characteristic of the newly created kingdom in the north, which bore the name *Israel*.[163] In the half-century between the founding of the kingdom and Omri's ascent to power, we encounter six rulers (including Omri) and three coups. Omri was the first ruler who succeeded in founding a dynasty of at least four successive kings, but they ruled only about forty years. The last Omride, Joram, was overthrown in 845 in the comprehensive Jehu revolution (2 Kings 9-10). Jehu also extirpated the dynasty of his predecessors (2 Kgs 10:7, 11, 17). He founded a dynasty that remained in power for nearly a hundred years and encompassed five kings. After the end of the last Jehudide reign, that of Zechariah, in 747, the northern kingdom lasted only twenty-five more years. That quarter-century was marked by one coup after another, until, in 722, the northern kingdom fell and was divided into four Assyrian provinces.[164]

What is so striking about the numerous changes of dynasty is that in many cases they were initiated by the army, which thus achieved a prominent role in the northern kingdoms' monarchy. The social consequence of the frequent shifts in power was that it was not as easy for elites to establish themselves as in a stable monarchy. With every coup, the predecessor's family and followers (1 Kgs 16:11, "his kindred [and] his friends"). This made it almost impossible for an aristocracy of civil servants to be created, its members bound to the court over generations, such as we find later in Judah.[165] Among the people of the land as well, the constant danger of coups must have minimized any inclination to form very close ties to the reigning royal house. Israel lacked any kind of unconditional fidelity to the ruling dynasty on the part of the rural aristocracy, as was typical of the northern kingdom.[166]

But it would be wrong to try to make a virtue of the troubled instability of the northern

Kings of Judah and Israel

Judah		Israel	
Rehoboam	922–915	Jeroboam	922–901
Abijah	915–913		
Asa	913–873	Nadab	901–900
		Baasha	900–877
		Elah	877–876
		Zimri	876
		Omride Era	
		Omri	876–869
Jehoshaphat	873–849	Ahab	869–850
		Ahaziah	850–849
Jehoram	849–843	Jehoram	849–843
Ahaziah	843–842		
		Jehu Dynasty	
		Jehu	843–815
Athaliah	842–837		
Joash	837–800		
		Jehoahaz	815–802
Amaziah	800–783	Jehoash	802–786
Uzziah (Azariah)	783–742	Jeroboam II	786–746
		Assyrian Intervention	
Jotham	742–735	Zechariah	746–745
		Shallum	745
		Menahem	745–737
		Pekahiah	737–736
Ahaz	735–727 or 715	Pekah	736–732
		Hoshea	732–722
Hezekiah	727 or 715–687		
		Fall of Samaria	722
Manasseh	687–642		
Amon	642–640		
Josiah	640–609		
Jehoahaz	609		
Jehoiachim	609–598		
Jehoiachin	598–597		
First capture of Jerusalem by Babylonians	597		
Zedekiah	597–586		
Destruction of Jerusalem	586		

kingdom. It is not appropriate to interpret the constant shifts in power with the concept of a "charismatic kingship" and to assert of the first phase, before the founding of the Omride dynasty, that one could "call the kingdom of Israel, while its charismatic monarchy was still at this age of its development, a kingdom of revolution based on the will of God."[167] For apart from the fact that, except in the case of Jehu, religion played no part in the transfers of power—and Jehu himself was successful because he relied on military power—the monarchs of the northern kingdom made every effort to introduce stable conditions, even though they had less success at it than the Davidides in the smaller state of Judah. The fact that nearly every ruler was, at first, succeeded by his son shows that the dynastic principle was regarded as the norm.[168]

One important step toward establishing the first stable dynasty was the creation of a residence in Samaria. As a new foundation, it was directly dependent on the king and outside the claims of existing city centers and tribal territories. Certainly, we can scarcely construct a dualism between a "Samaritan city-state"[169] and the remaining state territory out of this. Nevertheless, the creation of a government metropolis was an important step toward a fully developed state.

Even though the territory of the northern kingdom was much larger than that of the southern kingdom, we have virtually no material that gives any account of its administrative divisions. If it is true that, as 1 Kgs 4:7-19 reports, under Solomon there was no "provincial system," but instead a network of dependent relationships between the court and local entities,[170] there is little reason why that would have continued after separation from the Davidides. The first half-century of the northern kingdom, with its frequent bloody shifts

in power, would in itself have not favored the continuation or new construction of such a network.

It is certainly no accident that it was first under the Omrides that, in addition to the building of a capital, we begin to see some division of administration. In 1 Kgs 20:14-15, 17, 19 we read of "district governors." The word for "district," *medinah,* comes from Aramaic, which is easily explained from the close contacts between the Omrides and the Aramaeans in peace and war. According to 1 Kings 20, these district governors had military duties. But because their title, *sarim,* could be used for both military and civil functions, and because in practice both spheres probably often overlapped, we may have here a first move toward an organized administration.[171]

On the whole, we can observe a clear stabilization of the power system in the northern kingdom with the advent of the Omride rulers, and it was not deflected by Jehu's coup. Beginning with the time of the Omrides, we can speak of a state that was on its way from early statehood to the status of a fully developed national state.[172] Characteristic of an early state is that one can separate society into two layers: rulers and ruled. A fully developed state is characterized by the fact that within it the "people" itself falls into classes with competing interests, and the government acts in relation to these competing interests. The transitional phase, as we can see it from the time of the Omrides onward, is apparent in that the monarchy is allied with parts of the local upper class, but one need not suppose that there are distinctions of class within the population, even though the transitional aspects leading toward a developed class society are fluid.[173]

The first indication that the monarchy was allying itself with parts of the local upper class are found in texts that, to some extent, can be only indirectly evaluated in terms of social relationships. This is true especially of the prophetic narratives about Elijah and Elisha, but also the account of Jehu's revolution. These texts are valuable insofar as they locate the actions they narrate within a milieu that can certainly be understood as reflecting social reality. We can add to them the Samaria ostraca as primary sources, though it is true that these present severe problems of interpretation.

From the Elisha tradition, we may mention the double narrative about the great Shunamite woman (2 Kgs 4:8-37; 8:1-6). This story not only presumes the establishment of an upper class, but also that this woman has direct access to the king. That this is more than the familiar fairy-tale motif according to which every man and every woman can meet the ruler face to face is evident from the story about the conflict over Naboth's vineyard (1 Kings 21). That narrative, too, shows the close connection between the upper class and the royal house. This is true, first of all, in the opening conflict over the vineyard—the classic constellation in an early state in which the interests of the monarchy collide most directly with the interests of the well-to-do free farmers.[174] It also affects the conflict's resolution. The royal house is supported by the "elders and nobles" of the city (1 Kgs 21:8), who carry out the judicial murder desired by the king without hesitation or question. The narrative shows that there were direct connections between members of the local upper classes and the royal house, and that the king could rely on a part of the city's elite in a local conflict.

The narrative of the conflict between Naboth and Ahab locates it during the reign of the Omrides. When Jehu rebels against them and resolves to extirpate the entire royal

family, he turns to the upper class in Samaria, where there are supposed to be seventy princes whom Jehu wants to eliminate. The leadership class is described in this connection in 2 Kgs 10:1, 5. It includes the rulers (sarim), the elders, and the guardians of Ahab's sons (vv. 1, 5), the steward of the palace, and the governor of the city (v. 5). The inclusion of the elders is interesting. Since Samaria was a new royal foundation, these were probably not representatives of long-settled clans in that place, but were elders from the land who resided at court. In terms of time, we are at the end of the first stable dynasty. Such stability was evidently the precondition for integrating parts of the rural population into the royal power apparatus. Incidentally, they willingly bow to the new power relationships and kill Ahab's progeny (2 Kgs 10:1-11).

The Samaria ostraca from the second quarter of the eighth century, which contain the names of shippers and recipients of goods, reveal a close relationship between members of the upper class and the royal court.[175] Analysis of the shippers' names and the names in the lists of recipients suggests the conclusion "that it was primarily a matter of personal relationships between recipient and sender, that is, deliveries to members of the elite who were resident in Samaria either temporarily or permanently, and who from time to time received small parts of their household needs from their properties belonging to them personally or to their families or clans and/or transferred to them by the crown."[176] In the nearly one hundred years of the Jehu dynasty, from which period the ostraca stem, it is entirely plausible that such an elite, closely connected with the court, could have established itself.

Finally, the critique of the prophet Amos shows how closely the elite was tied to the monarchy; his writing reflects conditions during the stable reign of Jeroboam II. Besides the social tensions, which we will return to below,[177] the prophet's words also criticize political oppression, and in doing so sketch a portrait of the upper class. Especially significant is the little collection of sayings against Samaria (Amos 3:9—4:3). According to these, such people reside in palace-like stongholds (3:10-11) in which they "store up violence and robbery," shorthand for wealth acquired through political oppression and economic exploitation. Their wealth is manifested in their ownership of winter houses and summer houses, "houses of ivory"—the prophet is probably thinking of ivory decorations and furniture ("beds of ivory," 6:4), which are also archaeologically attested in the great number of fittings that have been found[178]—or simply "many houses" (3:15). As a sign of wealth, these houses were not built of clay, but of hewn stones (5:11). There they held banquets and celebrated drunken feasts (2:8; 4:1; 6:4-6).

Of course, sayings like these are not objective social-critical descriptions of social conditions in Samaria in the eighth century; they are partisan polemic. But even partisan polemic can only fulfill its purpose if it does not invent the circumstances against which it polemicizes, though with one-sided exaggeration. At any rate, in retrospect the words of Amos appear to be a call to revolt against the king and the stability of the land (Amos 7:10). Even though the king is not named in the words that go back to Amos himself, the book of Amos reveals the situation of an upper class residing in Samaria and closely tied to the monarchy. At the end of nearly a century of rule by a single dynasty, such conditions can easily be imagined.

Only in Israel's last years, with renewed, constant shifts in power, were these conditions again destabilized. The murders of kings,

officers, and judges depicted in Hos 7:3-7 dramatically show the dissolution (probably the *sarim* in vv. 3 and 5 were military officers and the *shofetim* were civil functionaries). One of the rebels, Menahem, paid a tribute of a thousand talents of silver to Tiglath-pileser III of Assyria[179] "so that he might help him confirm his hold on the royal power" (2 Kgs 15:19). He collected the tribute by levying a poll tax on the free citizens (v. 20). Even though this is not spelled out in the texts, such events could only rupture the close connection between the monarchy and the land's leading classes, so that the elites began to fight one another in the successive coups.

Even the stable conditions of internal and external politics at the time of Jeroboam II, as reflected in the book of Amos, allow us to perceive that there was not much left of the impulse to liberation that had marked the beginning of the northern kingdom. This was all the more true of the confusions of the last quarter-century that form the background of the book of Hosea. Thus it is not surprising that in these two writings, going back to prophets who worked in the northern kingdom, the exodus tradition is taken up and, at the same time, is critically applied (Amos 2:10; 3:1-2; 9:7; Hos 8:13; 9:3; 11:1, 5; 12:10, 14; 13:4). The ideology of liberation as the northern kingdom's originating myth had been overtaken by real conditions.

Judah as a Participatory Monarchy

If we now turn our attention to Judah, we must go beyond the period extending into the eighth century that is the supposed scope of this chapter; it would make little sense to draw precise temporal distinctions within the text, since what we are looking for here is the basic profile. That does not mean, of course, that there was no development in Judah. We can even say with relative assurance that the development in little Judah took quite a bit longer than in Israel. While in the north the transition to a fully developed state can be discerned as early as the ninth century, it probably did not happen in the south until the eighth century.

Conditions in Judah were different from those in Israel in two respects. The first of these is the stability of the Davidic dynasty. The Aramaic author of the inscription at Tell Dan called the southern kingdom *bytdwd* ("house of David"),[180] and that designation continued valid until the end of the monarchy in 587/586 BCE. Despite all the crises experienced by the south as well as the north, there was never a dynastic change. The close alliance of the landed aristocracy with the royal house and the construction of an aristocracy of civil servants whose members served the royal house over generations, all of which we will discuss below, are easy to understand against this background.

Characteristic of Judah, besides the stability of its dynasty, was its weakness in foreign relationships. Even in the period of relative independence from the end of the tenth to the end of the eighth century, the kings of Judah repeatedly had to empty out the treasures of temple and palace to fend off enemies (1 Kgs 14:25-26; 15:18-20; 2 Kgs 12:19). Then Ahaz subjected himself to Assyria in order to avoid attack by the united Israelites and Aramaeans, and from then on all the kings of Judah were tributaries to the Assyrians and, after their collapse at the end of the seventh century, to the Egyptians and Babylonians. Every brief withdrawal of payment was met with even more brutal subjection by the great power of the moment.

The regular emptying of the state treasury, well attested epigraphically from the Assyrian period onward,[181] was only possible if the treasury was repeatedly refilled. From this we can surmise that serious burdens were laid on the people, despite the scarcity of source material on taxes and forced labor.[182] The desperation of the Judahite kings to obtain sources of funds is shown by Jehoshaphat's attempt (in the midninth century) to bring gold from east Africa by means of an expeditionary fleet. This failed miserably (1 Kgs 22:49).[183]

On the one hand, then, Judah's weakness in foreign affairs kept it behind the northern kingdom, from a purely material point of view. The development of national building projects as we see it in the northern kingdom from the ninth century and the rule of the Omride dynasty onward was apparent in the south only about a hundred years later, and artistic treasures like the Samaritan ivories are unknown in the south. On the other hand, Judah was for the same reason less affected by the foreign-political storms that swept through the Levant. By paying tribute to the Egyptians, the Aramaeans, the Assyrians, or the Babylonians, the little state found it relatively easy to maintain tranquility, because no great power was deprived of lucrative plunder on its account. That was certainly an objective basis for the stability of the Davidic dynasty.

But this alone cannot explain the dynastic stability. Rather, a more profound reason was that the Davidides succeeded in uniting themselves closely with the so-called "people of the land," the ʿam-haʾarets, and at the same time creating a civil-service aristocracy that, as an independent group, both participated in royal power and supported it. In every crisis situation, this constellation proved itself capable of sustaining the dynasty's continuance.

We first hear of an intervention by the ʿam-haʾarets, on the side of the Davidides with the fall of Queen Athaliah (2 Kings 11). From that point on, there is no crisis in the Davidide succession in which the ʿam-haʾarets do not intervene on the side of the dynasty. When Amaziah ascends the throne, we suspect their intervention only because he has to overcome a palace revolt (2 Kgs 12:21-22; 14:5). When Amaziah himself dies in a coup, it is explicitly "all the people of Judah" who make his son Azariah (Uzziah) king (2 Kgs 14:19-21). With these events we have arrived at the turn of the eighth to the seventh century. When Manasseh's son Amon dies in 639 as the result of a conspiracy, the ʿam-haʾarets make the eight-year-old Josiah his successor (2 Kgs 21:24). After Josiah's death in 609, the people of the land again take the initiative and make his son Jehoahaz king, passing over the older Jehoiakim (23:30-31, 36). The close tie between the royal house and the ʿam-haʾarets is shown, finally, by the fact that the punishments meted out by the Babylonians after the fall of Jerusalem are directed not only at the king and his family, but also "sixty men of the people of the land" are executed (2 Kgs 25:19-21 = Jer 52:25-27).

The Hebrew expression ʿam-haʾarets is semantically very broad.[184] It does not refer to the people as a statistical entity (that is, including women and children), but originally it did probably mean at least the male heads of free families. In this sense, when Uzziah is elevated to the throne the text speaks not of the "people of the land," but of "all the people of Judah" (2 Kgs 14:21). But with increasing social stratification, which will be described in more detail below, this group became more stratified as well. When Ezek 22:23-31, looking back to the fallen kingdom of Judah, names as those responsible for the catastrophe not

only kings,[185] priests, officials, and prophets, but also the ʿam-haʾarets, for having oppressed the needy, the poor, and the stranger (v. 29), it is clear that here ʿam-haʾarets does not mean the population as a whole, but its economically powerful upper class. The translation "landed aristocracy" is entirely appropriate in this case.

Semantically, these distinctions among the ʿam-haʾarets are evident in new expressions that would have been unthinkable before the social division of (Israelite and) Judahite society and are, in fact, not previously attested. Thus on the one hand in texts connected with the last years of Judah, we read of the ʾele-haʾarets ("the elite of the land"; 2 Kgs 24:15; Ezek 17:13). We would not go wrong if we were to see in these "the leading heads of the 'people of the land.'"[186] Contrasted with them are the ʿanwe-haʾarets, the needy, the humble, the poor of the land (Amos 8:4; Zeph 2:3), that is, the lower class, which has been distinguished from the ʿam-haʾarets at the lower end of the scale.

Both the information about the intervention of the ʿam-haʾarets in various quarrels over the succession and a look at the term's semantics show us that the ʿam-haʾarets is to be seen as an independent subject of power in the Judahite state that is, at the same time, closely connected to the Davidic royal house. One of the means of forming such bonds was evidently the Davidide marriage policy. We know one narrow but significant segment of this because the framing notes in the books of Kings mention the names of the mothers of the Judahite kings. In this information, what is striking first of all is that it reports only two instances of marriages to foreign princesses, one of them concerning Solomon (1 Kgs 3:1; 11:1-8)—though the historicity of this information may well be very doubtful, certainly as regards the number of wives—and the other relating to Joram, who married the Omride princess Athaliah (2 Kgs 8:26). All the other future mothers of successors to the throne, by contrast, come from Judahite families. If we include the places of their origin we have the following picture: Jerusalem is mentioned three times (2 Kgs 14:2; 15:2; 24:8), and once each for Beersheba (12:2 [English v. 1]), Jotbah (21:19), Bozkath (22:1); Libnah (23:31; 24:18), and Rumah (23:36). Thus in the five cases we know about, the princes' wives came from families of the land, and certainly not from the poor farmers, but from the families of the landed aristocracy, the ᶜam-haᵓarets.

Besides the ties of the royal house to the families of the landed aristocracy, there are also cases of marital ties to families of civil servants. Two of the local provincial "officials" on whom Solomon relied were married to royal daughters (1 Kgs 4:11, 15),[187] and Jehoiachim was married to a daughter of Elnathan of Jerusalem (2 Kgs 24:8), who at the time of Jehoiachim's rule was functioning as a high official (Jer 26:22; 36:12, 15); his father Achbor was a confidante of Josiah (2 Kgs 22:12, 14) and his son Konyahu may have occupied the office of commander-in-chief of the army in Zedekiah's time.[188]

With this last, we are confronted with the phenomenon of genuine civil-servant families who served the Davidide kings over generations. They constituted an aristocracy of officialdom that, alongside and together with the landed aristocracy, formed the support for the Davidide rulers. Such official families are attested for the late period of Judah, and there is every reason to believe that the need to constitute such an official aristocracy first occurred at the time of the transition to a fully developed state in the wake of the social crisis beginning in the eighth century.

The most important official family we can observe is that of Shaphan, who held the office of "secretary" under Josiah (2 Kgs 22:3, 8-10, 12, 14). We know of four of his sons who exercised important functions: Ahikam (2 Kgs 22:12, 14; Jer 26:24; see the seal in WSS, no. 431; HAE 2/2, no. 1.52), Gemariah (Jer 36:10, 12, 14, with the seal in WSS, no. 470; HAE 2/2, no. 3.28), Elasah (Jer 29:3), and Jaazaniah (Ezek 8:11). The third generation of the Shaphanides included Gedaliah, son of Ahikam (2 Kgs 25:22-25; Jer 39:14; 40:5-9, 11-16; 41:1-4, 6, 10, 16, 18; 43:6) and Micah, son of Gemariah (Jer 36:11, 13). If an impression of the inscription "Azaliahu ben Meshullam" (WSS, no. 90; HAE 2/2, no. 1.137) goes back to an authentic original, and if the owner of the seal was the father of Shaphan (2 Kgs 22:3), we might be able to trace this family through two additional generations. From what we know, other families had fewer branches. We may mention Hilkiah (2 Kgs 22:4, 8, 10, 12, 14; 23:4, 24) and his son Gemariah (Jer 29:3), in connection with the marriages of Achbor, already mentioned, with Elnathan's son and probably his son Konyahu, then Shelemiah (Jer 36:26) with his son Jehucal (Jer 37:3; 38:1) and his son Jehudi (Jer 36:14). Add to these the brothers Baruch ben Neriah ben Mahseiah (Jer 32:12-13, 16; 36:4-5, 8, 10, 13-19, 26-27, 32; 43:3, 6; 45:1-2, with WSS, no. 417; HAE 2/2, no. 2.30), and Seraiah ben Neriah ben Mahseiah (Jer 51:59, 61, with WSS, no. 390; HAE 2/2, no. 21.103).

Even if the identifications of names are not absolutely certain in every individual case, the overall picture is coherent. The king, in exercising his power, relied on the various branches of the civil servant families. When the throne changed hands it was apparently by no means a given that the high officials would change. Thus even in Jehoiachim's fifth year

(Jer 36:9) important Shaphanides occupied high offices of state, and at the same time they were engaged in concrete conflicts with the king (Jer 26:24; 36). On the other hand, the king had the last word. So none of the officials who, according to Jeremiah 36, were opposed to Jehoiachim were still in office in the final reign, that of Zedekiah (Jer 38:1). It appears that in the last years of Judah the Shaphanides withdrew entirely from active politics, in order then to be ready, with Gedaliah, to take over the leadership roles after the Babylonian conquest.

Such a high degree of independence on the part of the officials was only possible if they had their own economic base to rely on. And indeed, there are indications of just that. The priests Abiathar and Amaziah are explicitly said to have been the owners of their own estates (1 Kgs 2:26; Amos 7:17). Joab, the general of the army, also speaks of "my field" (2 Sam 14:31). The families whose sons the king would appoint as officials, according to the polemic in 1 Sam 8:11-17, were all landowners. Also, in Isa 22:15-22 the landless Shebna (v. 16) is deliberately contrasted to Eliakim, with his connections to his own apparently propertied family. The fact that the officials are attacked, in the prophets' social critique, because of their economic activities presupposes that they have lands of their own (Isa 3:12-15; Jer 5:26-28; 34:8-22). It was this base that afforded the high officials their relative independence of the king.[189]

Their landholdings brought the members of the civil-service aristocracy into close relationship with the ʿam-haʾarets, the landed aristocracy. There is every reason to believe that the higher officials were recruited from the noble families. How closely, in such cases, the exalted position of a member of a noble family was connected to the interests of that family as a whole is shown by Isa 22:15-22. In vv. 20-23 of this oracle, the installation of one Eliakim as ʾasher ʿal-habbayit ("master of the palace household)" is announced. The oracle ends with the words, "and he will become a throne of honor to his ancestral house" (v. 23), just as Joseph, according to Gen 45:13, is ready to make use of his "honor" as the highest official in Egypt on behalf of his family. This is taken as a matter of course. Only when the whole thing is overdone, when—as an addition to Isa 22:24-25 expresses it in a masterful piece of imagery—"the whole weight of his ancestral house" comes to hang on this one member of the family who has achieved high honor, will the peg and all the equipment that had been hanging from it give way and rip out of the wall.

We can call the form of rule that developed in Judah "participatory monarchy."[190] This ideal type can be delimited on two sides. The first would be a despotic or autocratic model of monarchy. That model did not succeed in Judah because there was a counterweight to the king's power and that of the court apparatus directly dependent on him, in the form of the civil-service aristocracy and the landed gentry. These latter, because of their landownership, had an independent economic base that lent them independence, but at the same time they were closely connected to the royal power, which they supported and in which they participated.[191]

The other ideal-typical counter-model would be an aristocracy in which the king is, at most, the highest representative of the nobility. Despite all the independence of the official class and the landed population, this cannot be attributed to Judah. The king was the final authority over his officials as well; he chose them and all their decisions had to be authorized by him. This undisputed highest position of the monarch is reflected not only in texts colored by royal ideology (Pss 2; 45; 72; and frequently); it also appears in list-style enumerations in the book of Jeremiah in which the king is always first (Jer 8:1: "The kings of Judah . . . its officials . . . the priests . . . the prophets . . . the inhabitants of Jerusalem"; 1:18; 2:26; 4:9; and others). Likewise, in the so-called "sermon to the leaders" in Ezek 22:25-29 the "princes" come first.[192] And in the Arad ostracon 24, from the end of the Judahite monarchy (beginning of the sixth century), a military order to the occupiers of Arad is emphasized by the writer of the letter with the words "and the word of the king lies with you, on your souls."[193]

It would be a complete misunderstanding if in speaking of a "participatory monarchy," we were to think of a constitutional monarchy in the modern sense, where the monarchy is reduced to the tasks of a representative democracy. We are close to such a misunderstanding when Shemaryahu Talmon speaks of a "participation of the people and its representatives."[194] Fohrer's distinction "between the Israelite popular kingship and the absolute kingship of the ancient Near East" could also be understood in that way. But in Judah it was *not* "the people" who participated in the king's power, but an upper class that stood in contrast to the mass of the people.

With these reflections on the landed and civil-service aristocracies in Judah, we are already in the midst of the developments that we now need to consider in detail. It appears that in both kingdoms, Israel and Judah, the early state was fully developed by the eighth century at the latest. The rulers were confronted by a society divided into classes. But with that we have reached a new epoch in the social history of Israel.

8

The Formation of an Ancient Class Society

THE HISTORY OF THE MONARCHY IN ISRAEL and Judah extends from the tenth century to the end of both states in the late eighth and early sixth centuries respectively. Therefore, especially in describing the monarchy's structures, we have been compelled to refer repeatedly to documents from the late period.

Nevertheless, within this four-hundred-year history, the eighth century represented a deep caesura that, from a social-historical point of view, opened a new epoch. It was only in the eighth century that the early form of the state gave way to a fully developed state. The crucial transition was not the evolution and increasing

8.1. Assyrian warriors with their spoil from the conquest of the
Israelite town of Lachish (701 BCE). Relief from the palace of
Sennacherib at Nineveh, Mesopotamia. British Museum,
London. Photo: © Erich Lessing/Art Resource, N.Y.

complexity of the at-first-rudimentary forms
of state apparatus and modest fields of state
activity. That was only the external aspect of
the process. What was decisive, in terms of
social history, was that the simple relationship
between rulers and ruled characteristic of the
early state gave way to a division of the ruled
into classes with opposing social interests.
The rulers were thus faced with the task of
positioning themselves over and against this
opposition.

Before we examine this process more
closely, we must once again briefly recapitulate
the history of events, continuing the history

initially presented above, of the period up to
the eighth century.[1]

The Political Background from the Eighth to the Sixth Century

The growth of fully developed states in Israel
and Judah falls broadly within the time period
of Assyria's increasing dominance in the
Levant. It is true that this dominance did not
directly cause the greater development of these
two states and the rise of a class society within
them, which at least in the north was evident

even before the major advances of the Assyrians, but it did act to strengthen those trends. In any case, the development in the north was soon interrupted, since after the capture of Samaria, it was integrated into the Assyrian empire. It was different in the south, which had freely submitted to Assyrian overlordship; there the evolution of the state and increased social stratification continued.

It is true that the Judahite king Hezekiah attempted to get free of Assyrian rule, but his effort failed, even though the siege of Jerusalem in 701 did not lead to its capture since Hezekiah paid a tribute and Sennacherib had other priorities (see 2 Kgs 18:13–14 and Sennacherib's report on his campaign).[2] The sequel was not only the devastation of the Judean lands but the unconditioned vassal status of Judah until the end of Assyrian rule in the last third of the seventh century.

The beginning of Josiah's reign in 639 BCE coincided with the beginning and rapid completion of the decline of Assyria's position of dominance in the Near Eastern world. This was connected to the rise of the Neo-Babylonians on the one side and the 26th Dynasty in Egypt on the other; these two entered into bitter rivalry for dominance and the Egyptians made a compact with the remaining Assyrian forces against the Babylonians. Judah and its tiny kingdom had to establish a new position within this constellation of power.

For the purpose of strengthening national unity, internal reforms were carried out in Josiah's reign with the effective cooperation of Shaphan, the highest civil official, and the High Priest Hilkiah. These reforms affected the cult, which was purified of non-Yahwistic elements and concentrated in Jerusalem. In addition, in response to a sharpening social critique, an internal social equalization was proposed. Both are reflected in the basic text of the Deuteronomic law in Deuteronomy 12–16, which underlies these measures.

Josiah's reform[3] is depicted in the account in 1 Kings as an epochal event comparable only to the reign of David. And that is how it has been treated, for a very long time, in the writing of Israel's history. A contrary idea has now been advanced, and this position has been pushed to the point of asserting that such a reform "never happened."[4] This confuses the frequent, legendary ornamentation of historical events with their actual creation. In particular, it ignores a characteristic of biblical depiction of profound changes: the nearly constant use of personalization and focusing, so that profound changes are ascribed to outstanding persons and concentrated within a very brief period of time, whereas in our historical judgment, they more probably occurred in multiple stages and involved a great many persons and groups. Outstanding examples of this are the occupation of the Land under Joshua, Samuel's creation of the state, or Ezra's promulgation of the Torah. A critical examination of the material on the Josianic reform points with a high degree of probability to efforts at purifying the cult[5] that were very likely connected with centralizing cultic worship in Jerusalem and its surroundings.[6]

Josiah's policies were thus able to take advantage of the weakness of Assyria, whose capital city, Nineveh, fell in 612. But when Josiah tried to extend his territory northward at the expense of the Assyrian provinces he ran afoul of Egyptian interests, and in 609 Pharaoh Neco II had him executed.[7]

The last years of Judah were marked by shifting control of the land between the great powers of Babylon and Egypt. The balance of power was decided at the battle of Carchemish in 605 in such a way that Egypt withdrew to its heartland. Judah now belonged to the

8.2. The "Black Obelisk" of Shalmaneser III. The monument depicts the submission of conquered kings to Assyria. Photo © Erich Lessing / Art Resource, NY.

8.3. This detail from the "Black Obelisk" depicts King Jehu (or his envoy) prostrating himself before Shalmaneser III. Photo © Erich Lessing/Art Resource, NY.

8.4. Detail from the "Black Obelisk" showing Israelite tribute bearers carrying items, which are described in the accompanying inscription.

Babylonian sphere of influence. Two attempts at revolt, in the futile hope of Egyptian support, led in 598/597 to an initial seizure of Jerusalem by the Babylonian, and a first group of exiles was taken away. When the last king of Judah, Zedekiah, again rose against his overlords, Jerusalem was taken after a long siege in 587/586, and this time it was destroyed. Again large numbers, especially from the upper classes, were sent into exile. The independent monarchy was at an end. Judah became part of the Babylonian provincial system.

Israel and Judah as an Ancient Class Society

If, in the case of an early state, one must start with the idea of a simple contrast between king and people, that is not the same as saying that the people are an amorphous mass in which all are equal. It says only that the differences in power, influence, and wealth have not yet reached a level at which one must speak of class-related differences or opposition. The difference, to put it simply, lies in whether there are richer and poorer farming units within a single region, or whether, instead, the poorer farmers are falling into debt slavery to the wealthier and are gradually losing their farms and lands.

Obviously the transition from one form of society to the other does not happen with lightning speed, and the evidence is correspondingly sparse. In addition, we are not talking about direct sources (such as business documents), but about narratives in legendary form about prophets, stories that look back to the prophets' activities. Nevertheless, these narratives presume a certain milieu. And since these are not the conditions that we can perceive with relative certainty in the eighth

century, they can be evaluated as sources for the time before that—with a certain degree of blurring that does not allow us to pinpoint events within a decade.

We may point in particular to three anecdotes from the prophetic narratives about Elisha. The one in 2 Kgs 4:1-7 describes a classic case of ruinous debt. A family has credit as long as the father is alive. But, after his death, the creditor sees the repayment of the loan as imperiled and seizes the children as security. The episode in 2 Kgs 6:1-7 brings us into the same milieu of Elisha's disciples. It also depicts an instance of borrowing. One of the prophet's disciples who has borrowed an iron axe knows that if he does not give it back he will have to offer something in its stead, and that will apparently mean that he must give up some other part of his possessions—which cannot be very great if he has to borrow an axe—or else offer his labor in exchange.

The counterimage to these two stories is the double narrative in 2 Kgs 4:8-37; 8:1-6. This is about a "great [wealthy] woman" (4:8). She is astonishingly ready to take the initiative: she suggests to her husband, and then carries through on her suggestion, that they should furnish an upstairs room in their house for Elisha, the man of God (4:9-10). We learn that her husband hires laborers for the harvest (v. 18). The woman herself commands the ne'arim, the household servants (v. 22), or "her na'ar" (v. 24). Later we learn that the woman lives in a foreign land for seven years during a famine. When she returns, she demands that the king, who had taken her "womanless" land for himself, give back "her house and her land" (8:3, 5), and in fact she receives "all that was hers" (v. 6).

All these stories take place in a environment in which the society is developing toward social division. There are poor people who must borrow and are threatened with debt slavery, and there are rich people who have at their disposal a large house, fields, and workers. It is obvious that this kind of stratification can lead to a direct conflict of interests. And in fact, beginning in the eighth century—for the northern kingdom that means near the end of its existence—we can say that a class society had developed.

Manifestations of Social Crisis

The first author in whose work we can detect a clear development toward an antagonistic society is the prophet Amos, who worked briefly in the northern kingdom at the end of Jeroboam II's reign in the mid-eighth century.[8] The book of Amos[9] reveals the picture of a society divided into two classes. Amos 2:6-8 lists a whole series of "social types" who appear as the victims of unnamed actors. These groups then reappear in 4:1; 5:10-12; 8:4-6. The cause of their misery seems to lie in their having been brought into indebtedness and in the rich bending the laws to their own favor. The sayings about "selling for silver" and "for a pair of sandals" (2:6) and about "garments taken in pledge" and "wine bought with fines they imposed" (2:8) point to the first of these causes, as does the image of a deliberate accumulation of debtors for the purpose of drawing people into one's power (8:4-6).[10] That in all this the legal system did not intervene to protect the weak, but instead was an additional tool of power in the hands of the strong is shown by the accusations about manipulating the laws in 2:7; 5:10-12; 6:12.

Those whose economic existence was thus threatened do not appear to have been the classic biblical oppressed persons; the book of Amos never speaks of widows and orphans. Rather, these are small farmers who are expected to hand over more and more, and who, when nothing more is to be had from them, fall into debt slavery. And the "girl" to whom, according to Amos 2:7, "father and son go in," is apparently a daughter already given into debt slavery and is sexually abused by her owners and overseers.

The upper class is accused not only of exploiting the lower class, but of unbridled luxury in architecture (3:10-11, 15; 5:11), furnishings (3:15; 6:4), and banqueting (2:8; 4:1; 6:4-6). Since they were closely attached to the power of the state, we have already referred to the upper class above when we spoke of the establishment of an elite in the northern kingdom.[11]

The crucial new element in the picture the book of Amos draws of conditions in the mid-eighth century in contrast to the Elisha narratives is this: whereas in the Elisha stories wealth and poverty exist alongside one another, so that the society is indeed stratified, with Amos wealth and poverty are seen in a cause and effect relationship. The wealthy are rich because they exploit the poor; the poor are impoverished because they are exploited by the rich. The simultaneous existence of rich and poor has become an antagonistic opposition.

Amos does not present any kind of social-scientific analysis, but rather a severe polemic that undergirds his ominous threats of destruction. This shows that we cannot read Amos's words in their transmitted form as simply reflecting mid-eighth century social realities in Israel. Still, it would be wrong to dismiss them as sheer fantasy: for one thing, because of the opposition to Amos's preaching by the religious authorities (who were also the state officials), which underlies the narrative in Amos 7:10-17 (though this last is, of course, theologically stylized to a high degree). In addition, we could scarcely understand how Amos's words would have been handed on by his disciples, and later also by tradents in the southern kingdom, if they lacked any kind of objective basis. We could compare the historical reality of Amos's social critique with modern polemics like "property is theft" or "silence gives consent"; neither saying describes reality in neutral terms, and at the same time they do point to real social problems.[12]

That social development in the south ran along similar lines to that in the north—though with a certain historical time lag—is shown by the sayings attributed to the two prophets of the southern kingdom, Isaiah and Micah.[13] The broad agreement in their pictures of social conditions, despite their different theological profiles, is evidence—beyond what has been said with regard to Amos—for the underlying historical reality of their accusations.

Central to the social criticism of these two prophets of the southern kingdom, who worked in the last third or fourth of the eighth century, is the concentration of property in the hands of a few (Isa 5:8; Mic 2:1-2). This is a dynamic process that has not yet come to completion. The old order, presented as the ideal, in which every household works its own inherited land independently, is being destroyed by indebtedness.[14] The result is the loss of property and freedom on the part of the former property owners. Micah explicitly points to women and children as the victims of this development (2:9-10). Differently from Amos and Micah, Isaiah also includes "widows and orphans" as the classic oppressed persons who have been deprived of their rights (Isa 1:21-26) and become the prey of others (10:1-2).

Both prophets also paint a clear picture of the upper class they are accusing. Isaiah 3:14-15 mentions elders and officials, thus pointing to an upper class composed of landed gentry and the official aristocracy, something we have seen was characteristic of Judah.[15] Likewise, the structure of the "Micah memoir" in Micah 1–3*[16] with its charges against the economically powerful in chapter two and the "heads and rulers" in chapter three paints the same picture. The fact that members of this upper class are also accused of luxurious living (Isa 5:11-12) rounds out the picture.

A long chronological gap yawns between Isaiah and Micah, prophets from the end of the eighth century, and the other prophets of the southern kingdom, Nahum, Zephaniah, Habakkuk, Jeremiah, and Ezekiel, all from the end of the seventh and beginning of the sixth centuries. A glance at these prophets, insofar as they express social criticism, shows that there had been no fundamental change in real social conditions. But the summary of Zephaniah's preaching in Zephaniah 1, which reflects the situation at the beginning of the last third of the seventh century, attests that the social circumstances between the early and late prophets are not entirely identical. Here there are new elements alongside the familiar ones. We recognize the reproaches directed against civil officials and the court on the one hand (Zeph 1:8), and against the wealthy landowners on the other (Zeph 1:12-13). What is new is the accusation that members of the court "dress themselves in foreign attire" and "leap over the threshold" (1:8-9), apparently aping fashions of the Assyrian overlords. New also is a social group that had not appeared heretofore, the traders and money-changers in Zeph 1:10-11. This reflects the move toward urbanization in Jerusalem, the result of the fall of the northern kingdom and the devastation of the Judean landholdings by Sennacherib's campaign in 701. The clearest sign of this is the building of a complete "new city" or "Second Quarter" in which, according to Zeph 1:10, the traders and money-changers have settled.[17]

With the increasing threats to Judah's very existence, becoming ever clearer after Josiah's death in 609 and with the wavering foreign policies of his successors, the prophetic accusations become steadily more general. In the dramatically structured composition of Jeremiah 2–6, Jeremiah[18] accuses the "great" (or "rich") in general terms, contrasting them with the "small" (or "poor") (5:1-6). In using the phrase "breaking the yoke," the text finds a concept for what we would today call "class divisions". The story of a temporary manumission of slaves in Jer 34:8-22 shows that the upper class still consists of landed aristocracy and officialdom ("all the officials and all the people," v. 10), who are contrasted to the "Hebrew slaves, male and female" (vv. 9-11).

Although Ezekiel was already in exile and was active after the fall of Jerusalem, he confirms the basic features of this picture. This is especially clear in his retrospective account of the causes of Judah's fall in Ezek 22:23-31.[19] Those he calls responsible are the rulers and their ideologues (princes, priests, officials, prophets, and ʿam-haʾarets), to whom are contrasted the widows, the needy, the poor, and the strangers, their victims. The parable of the shepherd (Ezekiel 34) is also based on contrasts between shepherds and flock (rulers and people), as well as between the strong and weak in the flock itself.

This description of the prevailing social conditions in Israel and Judah from the mid-eighth century until the fall of the respective states raises a whole series of questions: how does it happen that a society that reveals social inequalities becomes a society of social conflicts? How can we speak of the form of such a society in conceptual terms? And what role does the state itself play in this process of transformation? These are the questions we will address next.

Causes and Structures of an Ancient Class Society

The decisive factor in moving ancient farming societies toward being class societies was the institution of credit.[20] Biblical texts take it as a given that one of the fundamental contrasts in society is that between lenders and borrowers (for example, Isa 24:2; Jer 15:10). A proverb crystallizes the general opposition between rich and poor: "The rich rules over the poor, and the borrower is the slave of the lender" (Prov 22:7). This reveals in a striking way the difference between ancient Israelite society and a feudal or modern society in which wealth and poverty are determined by feudal landholding or the ownership of capital and the means of production on the one side and serfdom or the possession of nothing but one's ability to work on the other. The problem of indebtedness is not restricted to one era in Israel's history, for we can observe the contrast between poor and rich even in the pre-state period. The crucial change that led to the conditions evident from the eighth century onward is the transition from "normal" indebtedness to an irreversible debt overload.

In the "normal case" of necessity owing to illness or accident, bad harvests caused by pests or drought, or catastrophic events such as earthquakes or war, a farm family borrows food or seed in order to survive and be able to renew production. Later, what has been borrowed is repaid, and the social balance is restored. If this rhythm does not function because the need becomes perpetual, a mechanism is set in motion that ultimately brings about the ruin of the formerly self-sufficient farming economy. Deposits must be given for what is borrowed. If the loan, and the interest added to it, cannot be repaid, the deposit is retained by the creditor. Such deposits could be things or people, who in that event became debt slaves. When there are no more people to be handed over to debt slavery, the independent existence of the family is at an end.

People who have become slaves are subject to the power and at the disposal of their master (whether male or female). Such subjection extends far beyond compulsory labor; it includes control of the family's makeup (Exod 21:2-6), and in the case of women, of their sexuality (Genesis 16; Amos 2:7), and extends to harsh physical punishment (Exod 21:20-21, 26-27). There was also a practice of selling slaves to other owners, as slave contracts from Samaria attest even in the fourth century.[21] On the other hand, slaves were at least fed by their owners so that they would be able to work. For day laborers—who do not appear in the Book of the Covenant, but are first mentioned in Deut 24:14-15—not even that much is guaranteed; if they find no one who will pay for their labor they have no income. From there it is only a small step to beggary, which is mentioned for the first time in Ezek 18:7, 16.

Altogether, this development eroded the family as the basis of society. Men lost their property, the basis of the family economy; women and children could no longer be supported by it (Mic 2:1-2, 9-10). On the other side there were "great [wealthy] women," such as those we meet in the narratives about Abigail (1 Samuel 25) or the woman of Shunem (2 Kgs 4:8-37; 8:1-6), who had property and personal attendants at their disposal. The beginnings of class division affected men and women, even though in the process of impoverishment the women were the first victims (in the later text

of Neh 5:1-13 the position of daughters as the first persons to be given into slavery).

It need not be emphasized that such an all-too-brief ideal-typical description elides many differences. Here we are looking at common features. These include, for one thing, that the mechanism of heavy indebtedness, once set in motion, allows scarcely any to escape. In addition, we must see that the creditor had no interest at all in putting an end to the indebtedness, for as long as it existed the dependent family had to work for the creditor, either independently until the debt was paid, or as debt slaves (for this active interest of creditor's in indebtedness, see Amos 8:4-6; Jer 5:26-28). Moses Finley is surely correct in saying "that the profit from labor and relationships of solidarity, from a historical point of view, represent an older purpose of indebtedness than profit in the form of interest."[22]

The fundamental change observable from the eighth century onward, from the usual processes of debt and repayment to a permanent situation of heavy indebtedness—like the transition from the pre-state era to the state period—is not explained by a single cause, nor can we pinpoint a particular time when the transition from one condition to the other took place. Among the causes of the change was, first of all, the difference between stronger and weaker economies that began in the pre-state period. One factor that favored the advance of inequalities was the natural growth of the population. External events such as wars and their associated costs and—in case of defeat—the payment of tribute worked to drive social groups that were already unequal in economic strength even farther apart. At the same time, the existence of a state restricted the opportunity to escape the creditor's grasp by fleeing and joining an outlaw band. Add to that such contingent events as drought, pests, and earthquakes, any of which could bring an already unstable situation to total collapse. From the last third of the eighth century onward—that is, especially in the period that shaped Judah's development—the unending dependency on the neighboring great powers was also important. Nevertheless, this last could not have been the primary cause of social class-building, as the conditions depicted by Amos, even before the grip of Assyria expanded to engulf Israel and Judah, clearly show.

Out of this bundle of factors, there arose, around the middle of the eighth century in Israel and at the end of the same century in Judah, what we can call an ancient class society.

A variety of theoretical models have been proposed to describe this society.[23] An important scholarly conceptualization developed that revolved around the idea of interest capitalism, centering on the property rent demanded by the landowner. This was introduced to Old Testament scholarship by Oswald Loretz in 1975.[24] It was a very accurate description of the way the society of that time functioned, but what this concept did not encompass was social evolution in Israel and Judah. For, contrary to the picture Loretz drew of Israel's integration into the conditions prevailing throughout the Middle East,[25] the Old Testament texts reveal a dramatic transition from a relatively egalitarian society to a highly stratified one. Theoretical constructs that, while they ultimately go back to Karl Marx, represent independent developments in themselves take their starting point here. So it has been popular in Latin America to describe ancient Israel as a tributary system.[26] However, the tributary system, like the Marxist "Asiatic mode of production" that lies behind it, is, like interest capitalism, a stagnating system. Marx himself did not apply this model to Israel because he attributed the

"Asiatic mode of production," with its common property, to village societies that paid tribute to a landowner, whereas he saw "the Jews," like the Romans and Greeks, as having individual private landed property as their economic basis.[27] Against this background, Hans G. Kippenberg has described ancient Israel as an ancient class society, and I myself have accepted this terminology.[28] Unlike the idea of interest capitalism, which intends to integrate Israel "within the overall economic and social history of the Ancient Near East,"[29] the idea of an ancient class society emphasizes that the dynamic moment of "transformation of the archaic tribal society" observable in Greece, Italy, and Israel from the eighth century onward as a result of "indebtedness" has "great significance."[30]

Emphasizing this moment of transition underscores that, beginning with the eighth century in Israel and Judah, something new was developing, namely a class society with contrasting and opposing classes: the concept of class is here an economic one and relates to the ownership of the means of production.[31] As a result of heavy indebtedness, some farmers, who hitherto had been free because they owned their own land, became propertyless. Over against them were those who, because they owned land, were in a position to give more credit and thus ultimately to draw more and more people into economic dependency on them.

After the description we have given of the Israelite and Judahite states, it is clear that this developing upper class contained various elements of the elite classes. In Israel it would have included those who resided (temporarily?) at court and were supplied by their families with the produce of their lands, but also those who were attacked in Amos's social critique and who were certainly identical, at least in part, with those named in the Samaritan ostraca.[32] In Judah we should of course think of the ʿam-haʾarets and the official aristocracy, who were also sometimes attacked simultaneously by the prophets.[33] But what role did the state, and especially its embodiment, the king, play in all this?

In describing the monarchy as a type of state, we pointed out that certain obvious activities of a state, such as the requirement that people work on national building projects (forced labor), compulsory military service, or taxation, would necessarily have a divisive effect on a society that was already separated into poorer and wealthier groups. We have also named the state's very existence as a factor that made it more difficult to solve the problem of excessive debt through flight or the creation of outlaw bands.[34]

If the mere existence of a state is a factor that favors the development of a class society, though not the sole and causative factor (as shown by the fact that an antagonistically split society is clearly observable only about two hundred years after the creation of the monarchy), the development became irreversible when the monarchy allied itself with the emerging upper class. The fact that these circles were, at the outset, those who were least comfortable with the new institution of the monarchy and who were most likely to support resistance[35] against the state was not an enduring obstacle. Since the monarchy established itself quickly and was extremely stable, it made more sense for the well-to-do to unite with the power of the monarchical state instead of continuing to resist or merely standing aside. The picture we get of the northern kingdom, in part already in the ninth century but quite clearly in the eighth century, and of Judah from the eighth century until the end of its independence as a state ("participatory monarchy") shows how firm that alliance became.

It was through this alliance that the early state became a fully developed one. In contrast to the early state, with its simple structure of two classes, the rulers and the ruled, in the developed state the ruling class stood over against a society that was itself divided into classes. Henri Claessen and Peter Skalnik speak of "overtly antagonistic classes" or a "mature class society,"[36] whose existence was the precondition for the "mature" or "fully developed" state.

But in spite of the close alliance between the power of the monarchical state and the economic and social upper class, the function of the state was not exhausted in being "an organization for the protection of the possessing class against the non-possessing class," as Friedrich Engels first formulated it.[37]

Responses to the Crisis

The prophetic critique, which from the days of Amos in the mid-eighth century never fell silent, shows that the crisis-laden social development in Israel and Judah was not accepted without resistance. We may suppose that those who were directly affected by burdensome debt did not submit willingly to their fate, and that supposition is strengthened by prophetic social criticism, which repeatedly accuses the members of the upper class of violent acts. Nevertheless, we cannot perceive any organized movement of resistance, to say nothing of one with clearly defined goals, and the prophets can certainly not be seen as leaders of such movements or representatives of programs of social revolution.

But when the prophets show any sign of expecting a change in the situation through

8.5. Seals showing the influence of Egyptian religious motifs. Upper left: seal belonging to a minister of King Ahaz. Upper right and bottom: seals with imagery similar to Isaiah's vision in Isaiah 6.

political action, their hopes are directed to the king. Here we should first mention the fact that Isaiah and Micah offer almost no critique of the king. It is true that later prophets of the southern kingdom criticize the court's pursuit of luxury (Zeph 1:8-9; Jer 22:13-19; Ezek 22:25). But the origins of that criticism have nothing to do with the division of society into an upper and a lower class. And when Jeremiah calls for action on behalf of the lower class, he appeals to the "house of David" (Jer 21:12). Jeremiah 22:15-16 even expressly asserts that Josiah practiced "justice and righteousness" on behalf of the "poor and needy."

Such statements look to a self-concept of ancient Near Eastern monarchy reflected in their royal ideology. According to this ideology, kings act for the sake of "justice and righteousness" (2 Sam 8:15; 1 Kgs 10:9). The beneficiaries of such royal activity are the needy, who otherwise would never receive justice. The same idea is found applied from the ancient Babylonian king Hammurabi—who set up a law stele "so that the strong may not

oppress the weak, and to help the orphan and widow to receive justice"[38]—through Psalm 72 to some of the sayings about the king in the book of Proverbs (Prov 16:12; 20:28; 29:14).

With good reason this thought-world is called a royal *ideology*. For what, out of this royal self-image, was put into practice in individual cases was a different matter entirely. Nevertheless, the ideology had a basis in reality. It was founded on the fact that the monarchy, despite all its ties to the upper class, was not directly involved in social divisions. There had already been a kingship beforehand. Its existence was not originally linked to the upper class; in reality, it did not even emerge from it in the case of Judah. One could describe the same situation from the perspective of the lower class as well: those who found themselves in need and required credit could turn to a relative, a neighbor, or a well-to-do official, but not to the king or the royal court. So, in fact, the king really did stand outside the fundamental conflict between debtor and creditor.

8.6. Cylinder seal from Beth-Shean depicting El on his throne.

It was this objective basis that made it possible for the kings to intervene in social relationships. There are two instances of this in the biblical narratives. One is the making of the covenant under Josiah, narrated in 2 Kgs 23:1-3, which must have far-reaching social implications if, in fact, Deuteronomy or an early form of it was the basis for this episode. More of a single instance is King Zedekiah's intervention, according to Jer 34:8-22, in the last days of Judah, which led to a general manumission of slaves. In both cases, the initiative came from the king. In both cases, of course, the "people" (2 Kgs 23:3) or the members of the upper class (Jer 34:10) joined in. This shows that even when the king took the initiative he nevertheless needed the agreement of the upper class. The ideology according to which the king was the protector of the poor and the weak had to be mediated in terms of the Judahite reality of a participatory monarchy. It is evident how ephemeral the king's intervention was: soon after Josiah's death the social consequences of his reform vanished, and the manumission of slaves ordered by Zedekiah was quickly reversed.

Much more far-reaching than such selective interventions was the recording of laws in writing, which took place in the late monarchical period. Here our social-history description has to be restricted to hints, but it is at least possible, since some extensive studies of the history of law have been recently produced.[39] It is striking that biblical witnesses to written laws fall within the epoch in which the social crisis erupted (Hos 8:12; Isa 10:1; Jer 8:8-9). This is congruent with the external evidence, according to which written culture as a whole was little developed before the eighth century, but at that point took a visible upswing.[40] This in itself allows us to conclude that the production of written law was causally connected to social development, a conclusion supported by comparisons to other cultures.

It is striking that, in the biblical view, the king himself never appears as a lawgiver. This is a fundamental difference from the Mesopotamian cultures and it had far-reaching consequences for the significance of the Torah in Judaism. Nevertheless, without the monarchy the commitment of the law to written form, beginning in the eighth century, would have been unthinkable. Whether one thinks that the formulation of the corpora of the Book of the Covenant and Deuteronomy (in their monarchical-period form) is due to "circles learned in the law" or "the administrative upper class of educated officials,"[41] or to a "Jerusalem upper class,"[42] in any case a tie to the institution of the monarchy is a necessary presupposition.

What came into being in this fashion, under the protection of the supreme royal authority, was also highly relevant for social history. Both the Book of the Covenant and, emphatically,

Deuteronomy are devoted—though by no means exclusively and in isolation—to regulating social relations. Prominent in the Book of the Covenant are the rules for the institution of slavery (Exod 21:2-11, 20-21, 26-27), then the prohibition on interest and the law governing deposits (22:24-26), regulations for the judiciary (23:1-8), and social arrangements for having land remain fallow land, and for rest from labor on the seventh day (23:10-12). Most of this is taken up in Deuteronomy and given further development, but there is new material as well: in particular the forgiveness of debts, intended to happen every seven years (Deut 15:1-11), a social tax for the poor (14:22-29; 26:12), the prohibition on giving up runaway slaves (23:16-17), the commandment to pay hired laborers every day (24:14-15), and the great block of institutional laws (16:18—18:22)—though in the last case, it is heavily debated whether they belong to the monarchical period or to postmonarchical planns for a new beginning.[43]

The extent to which the social laws were revised in Josiah's time can only be a matter for speculation. However, the praise of Josiah as an exemplary, socially conscious ruler in Jer 22:15-16 may be an indication that something along those lines did happen. Still, the conditions after Josiah, as reflected in Jeremiah and Ezekiel, show that not much remained of the social impulse of the reform (whereas, apparently, the centralization of the cult, the other focus of the law, was generally accepted). Nevertheless, the process of writing the law in the Book of the Covenant and Deuteronomy had far-reaching consequences for the continued existence of the Jewish people after the end of the independent state. Precisely because these corpora were not directly linked to the person of the king, they could be handed on as a definitive basis for Jewish community even after the monarchy had ended. Of course, it was still a long time before they took on the form of a Torah binding on all.

9

Exiles and Their Consequences

AFTER ISRAEL AND JUDAH, FROM THE mid-eighth century onward, fell within the ancient Near Eastern great powers' spheres of influence, the people of both small states began to experience periods of exile. With the intervention of the Assyrians in the Syro-Ephraimite War in 732, the inhabitants of the northern kingdom's northern provinces were deported (2 Kgs 15:29).[1] The end of the northern kingdom in 722 was accompanied by the transport of large parts of the population to Assyria—Sargon II says that he conquered

27,280 people. A little later, in 701, Judah likewise suffered massive deportations. According to Sennacherib's account of his campaign there were 200,150 of these people,[2] a doubtful number merely on demographic grounds. But that is not the point. What is important is that it was a large number. And still more important is that, in contrast to the north, Judah did not cease to exist as a state, even though from then on it lived under Assyrian overlordship.

This situation remained stable for nearly a century and only changed when Assyrian rule collapsed, quite rapidly, at the end of the seventh century. Here we must first of all continue the history of events, following what we have already outlined above.[3]

From Nebuchadnezzar to Cyrus

After the brief interlude of Egyptian dominance under Neco II, which, cost Josiah his life in 609, the beginning of the period of Babylonian overlordship for Judah and the former territory of Israel can be dated to the year 605, when Nebuchadnezzar defeated the Egyptian armies at Carchemish. The Egyptians withdrew to their heartland and the Babylonians made vassals of the Levantine states, including Judah, now ruled by Jehoiachim (2 Kgs 24:1, 7).

But as early as 598, Jehoiachim attempted to again fall away from Babylon. His revolt, which ended with the surrender of Jerusalem under his son Jehoiachin—the father having died during the advance of the Babylonian army—inaugurated, in 597, the period of deportations to Babylon. For, despite the city's voluntary surrender, the young king Jehoiachin was exiled to Babylon, and with him parts of his court personnel and the upper class. There the members of the court were at first treated respectfully, as cuneiform tablets from the years around 592, with receipts for deliveries of oil to "Jehoiachin, king of Judah" and other people in his entourage, attest.[4] This deportation marks the beginning of the Babylonian exile (2 Kgs 24:10-16). In Jerusalem, Jehoiachin's uncle, Zedekiah, was installed as ruler by the Babylonians (2 Kgs 24:17) and bound to them by a vassal's oath (Ezek 17:1-21).[5]

When, just ten years later, Zedekiah also dared to revolt, Jerusalem was captured after enduring a long siege (587/586).[6] The king was thrown into prison, and again members of the court and the upper class, as well as skilled workers, were deported. The city of Jerusalem was destroyed, along with its temple. Judah's existence as an independent state came to an end (2 Kgs 25:1-21; Jer 39:1-10; 52:1-27). However, a Judean was installed as Babylon's governor: Gedaliah, son of Ahikam, the son of Shaphan, a member of one of the old families of the Judahite official aristocracy (2 Kgs 25:22; Jer 40:7).[7]

A further, that is, third deportation took place in the year 582, according to Jer 52:30. There is good reason to believe that the murder of Gedaliah by Judahite monarchists was the reason for this assassination. It is true that, according to 2 Kgs 25:25; Jer 41:1 this took place "in the seventh month." But that can scarcely have been the seventh month of the year of the conquest and destruction of Jerusalem, because in that case Gedaliah would have ruled for only two or three months, something that can scarcely be reconciled with the measures he adopted. Thus, we can suppose that Gedaliah's governorship lasted about four years.[8] After his murder, we have no historically datable information about the situation in the Land.

The next event that can be dated with certainty did not take place in the Land itself, but in Babylon. We learn from 2 Kgs 25:27 that in the year when the Babylonian king Evil-merodach ascended the throne in 562, Jehoiachin was released from prison and invited to the royal table. He must, therefore, in the intervening time have lost his previous honored status. We can only speculate that this happened in connection with Zedekiah's failed revolt or as a consequence of the Gedaliah's murder by an adherent of the Davidide house.[9]

The end of the Babylonian epoch came with the unresisted seizure of the city of Babylon by the Persian king, Cyrus II, in the year 539. Cyrus, who had already subjected the empire of the Medes as well as the whole of Asia Minor to the Aegean Islands, made himself king of Babylon, and in so doing inherited Babylon's rule over all the territory to the borders of Egypt.

If we divide the epochs in Israel's history during this period according to the dominant major power of the time, the Babylonian epoch clearly ended in 539. That, of course, did not mean that the Babylonian exile of the Jews ended at the same time, as stated in the so-called Edict of Cyrus as shaped in line with the theological biases of Chronicles would have it (Ezra 1:1-4; 2 Chr 36:22-23). The return from exile began only in 520.[10]

Judah under Babylonian Rule

Because the books of Jeremiah and Ezekiel, as well as Lamentations, contain a good deal of information relating to the time before and after the fall of Jerusalem, it is quite possible to sketch the consequences of that event for Judah's social structures. Several social structures can be distinguished, though of course in reality they were closely interwoven.

Structures of Governance

With the first deportation in 597, there began a unique kind of double structure: Judah had two kings, the banished Jehoiachin and Zedekiah, resident in Jerusalem. Since Jehoiachin was not deported alone, but took parts of his court with him (2 Kgs 24:12, 15)—as well as members of the upper class—we can speak of a real transfer of the court to Babylon, a sort of government in exile. Thus the Babylonian delivery receipts[11] mention not only Jehoiachin, but also his five sons, and they explicitly call Jehoiachin "king of Judah." In particular, those parts of the upper class who were already in exile continued to regard Jehoiachin as their king (see the book of Ezekiel, with its chronology dating from the date of Jehoiachin's deportation). In Judah itself, too, a part of the population looked forward to the rapid return of Jehoiachin to his former royal position, as shown by the prophecy of Hananiah that Jeremiah reports (Jer 28:4). The importance of this Davidide line for the future, despite the temporary arrest of Jehoiachin, only lifted in 562, is shown by the fact that after the Persians seized power a nephew of Jehoiachin, Zerubbabel (1 Chr 3:17-19) was one of the first prominent persons to reemerge in Jerusalem.[12]

Nevertheless, after Jehoiachin was deported, his uncle Zedekiah was immediately installed as king in Jerusalem, under Babylonian rule (2 Kgs 24:17). Although he was king in the full sense—as not only 2 Kgs 24:17 states with utter clarity, and as is presumed as such throughout by Jeremiah, but also as Ezek 17:11-21 presents the situation in interpreting the parable about the Judahite kingdom—in Jerusalem itself the continued existence of his rule, if not perhaps its legitimacy, was always in doubt. Thus Hananiah, in announcing the return of Jehoiachin to the throne in Jerusalem, seems to have received a thoroughly positive hearing (Jeremiah 28). For adherents of the deported king, Zedekiah was only a sort of temporary substitute for Jehoiachin.

The installation of Gedaliah as Babylonian governor, after the end of Zedekiah's kingship, marked the first time in nearly four hundred years when no Davidide held the highest position in Judah. So the Babylonians put an end to the rule of the royal house and yet, at the same time, did not completely break with the past, because they entrusted the direction of the province to a member of one of the official families that, at least since Josiah, had held the levers of power.

Gedaliah governed from Mizpah (2 Kgs 25:23; Jer 40:6, 8 10, and elsewhere). This could be related to the destruction of Jerusalem, but more probably it had symbolic significance. Because the rule of the Davidides was at an end, Jerusalem, its temple destroyed but its locale still the goal of pilgrimage (Jer 41:5), should no longer be the seat of provincial government.

We can learn scarcely anything about the structure of Gedaliah's government. It is quite clear that it was government under the direct orders of the Babylonians. Gedaliah himself "represent[s the people] before the Chaldeans who come to us" (Jer 40:10), and those beneath him "serve the king of Babylon" (2 Kgs 25:24; Jer 40:9). Therefore representatives of Babylon also remained at Gedaliah's seat of government in Mizpah (Jer 41:3). But Gedaliah also encouraged former officers and members of the army to remain in the Land (2 Kgs 25:23–24; Jer 40:7–9). We can gather from a passing remark in Jer 41:10 that there were also "king's daughters" around him: that is, members of the Davidide line who had remained in the Land. It was one such

Davidide, ultimately, who murdered Gedaliah (2 Kgs 25:25; Jer 41:1-2).

What happened in the Land after the murder of Gedaliah is outside our knowledge. It seems certain that the Babylonians did not again entrust governance of the province to a Judean, but instead took the matter into their own hands.

Property Relationships in the Land of Israel

Despite a good deal of information in various biblical texts, it is still difficult to determine how many people were taken away from Judah in the three deportations of 597, 587/86, and 582. It is certain that the later picture of a complete emptying of the Land is historically untenable. Probably the number of exiles lay between a fourth and, at the maximum, a third of the population.[13] It is also certain that those taken away were overwhelmingly members of the upper class plus those with special skills that could be applied in various ways in Babylon.

After the first deportation in 597, the situation was such that part of the upper class was sitting in exile in Babylon while another part remained in the Land. The resulting tension between the exiles and those that remained can be discerned from a quotation that Ezekiel, himself one of the exiles, places on the lips of those who remained in Jerusalem: "They have gone far from YHWH; to us this land is given for a possession" (Ezek 11:15; also 33:24). This seems to mean not only that those remaining behind have written off the exiles for the future, but also that they are taking possession of the landed property they left behind. At this level of events, the tension between those left behind and those in exile was thus confined to the propertied upper class.

This changed with the second deportation. Now another large portion of the upper class was exiled. The books of Kings say that the Babylonian officer who organized the deportation "left some of the poorest people of the land to be vinedressers and tillers of the soil" (2 Kgs 25:12; Jer 52:16; anachronistically, the same is said of the first deportation in 2 Kgs 24:14). This expression is also used in the account in the book of Jeremiah, which depicts the events surrounding Gedaliah's brief reign. There we read: "Nebuzaradan the captain of the guard left in the land of Judah some of the poor people who owned nothing, and gave them vineyards and fields at the same time" (Jer 39:10). This is not about a redistribution of property within the ownership class; it has the character of land reform.

In order to be able to measure the depth of this cleft from a social-historical point of view, one must recall that from the eighth century onward first the Israelite and then Judahite society had been marked by an accelerating tendency to concentrating landed property in the hands of only a few. Excessive debt that affected more and more people led to the loss of land and personal freedom; an increasingly smaller group of members of the landed aristocracy held the formerly free farmers in dependency and took possession of their land.[14] When Jer 34:8-22 presupposes that there was a large group of debt slaves in Jerusalem, these would seem to be such "poor people who owned nothing," those spoken of in Jer 39:10. Now they are given part of the property of those on whom they had become dependent through debt overload.[15]

With the seizure of power by the Babylonians and their agent, Gedaliah, refugees who had fled to neighboring lands to escape the circumstances of war also returned. With Gedaliah's permission they were allowed to settle in

Judah (Jer 40:11, 12a). It can be regarded as likely that they did not restrict themselves to what may have been their former property, but also cultivated land belonging to people who were now in exile.[16] The corresponding passage in Jeremiah 40 ends with the words "and they gathered wine and summer fruits in great abundance" (v. 12b). Given the Gedaliah-friendly tone of Jeremiah 39–40, this seems to say that land reform and the resettlement of refugees were not only an act of restorative justice, but were blessed with a rich harvest.

If we set alongside the portrait in Jeremiah 39 and 40 the picture we find in Lamentations, we could think we are in a different world. Lamentations bewails not only the general destruction, but also that food (Lam 1:11; 2:12; 4:4, 9), drink (4:4; 5:4), and firewood (5:4) are scarce and correspondingly overpriced. It is said that women are being raped (5:11) and all the traditional authorities are powerless (1:4, 6, 15, and frequently). While Jeremiah 39 and 40 try to awaken the impression of a hope-filled new beginning, Lamentations puts before our eyes an all-encompassing catastrophe from which there seems to be no escape.

A number of reasons can be given for this contradictory set of viewpoints. For one thing, Lamentations uses the language of a city lament, which is full of stock phrases; one cannot ask in each individual case how well they match with reality. In addition, it is possible that Lamentations addresses, at least in part, the time immediately after the conquest and destruction of Jerusalem, whereas two or three years later things may have looked quite different.[17] But the decisive factor may be that these two texts take different perspectives on the same events.

One example of this is Lam 5:2: "Our inheritance has been turned over to strangers, our homes to aliens." The lamenting "we" asserts, in the first part of the parallelism, that "strangers" have taken possession of the property. This could quite easily be the same procedure that is presented positively in Jer 39:10 as land reform. One social group sees Gedaliah's measures as a restoration of a just division of land while another regards the same action as despoliation. That now "the poor people who owned nothing" (Jer 39:10) have the upper hand looks to them like being ruled by "slaves" (Lam 5:8).[18]

However, at the same time, this group has a sharper eye for the events that are passed over in silence in the book of Jeremiah's Gedaliah-friendly depiction. For when it is lamented that "our houses" are being given to "aliens," this seems to emphasize an aspect of events neglected in Jeremiah 39–40. Both Babylonians and members of the neighboring nations would have enriched themselves from Judean property, and phenomena such as rising prices and uncertain conditions—of which unpunished rapes are the keenest expression—were certainly part of the reality of the times that are generally ignored in Jeremiah's picture of a flourishing period under Gedaliah.

We cannot trace the further development of conditions after Gedaliah's murder with any certainty. The conflicts then perceptible at the beginning of the Persian period, however, indicate that the basic constellation remained unchanged.[19] The period of Babylonian rule over Judah was a time in which those who had been able to concentrate large landholdings during the time of the monarchy lost them, in part or altogether. This land was taken by those who had formerly lost it to the well-to-do, but surely also by Babylonians and people from the neighboring nations. Thus the Judah of the Babylonian period did not, despite Gedaliah's reforms, represent a "classless society," especially since we do not know how things

developed after Gedaliah's murder. But it was marked by a shift in ownership relations that would fundamentally influence the conflict situation in the Persian period.

But first we must consider the conditions of life in exile.

Israel in Exile

The previous description has attempted to make clear that "exile" is not to be understood in the way that the biblical picture in Chronicles (2 Chr 36:20-21)—which lacks any parallel in its model in 2 Kings 25—would like us to think: that for seventy years the Land lay "desolate," because all of Israel had been led away into exile in Babylon.[20]

This picture is not only false because not all of Israel's population was led away into exile, but also because it depicts an end to the exilic epoch that did not happen. From the time of the deportations starting at the beginning of the sixth century, Israel has lived the double existence of a population partly resident in the Land and partly in diaspora outside the Land. In the two and a half millennia that have passed since that time, the quantitative and qualitative relationships between the two groups have frequently shifted, but even the historic point marked by the foundation of the modern state of Israel in the year 1948 did not put an end to the basic structure of this twofold existence. The consequence for the picture we are presenting here is that the subject of "exile" cannot remain limited to the approximately fifty years between the destruction of Jerusalem and the capture of Babylon by Cyrus; it must be taken up again in the context of treating the Persian and Hellenistic periods.[21]

Before I begin this description, I want to again briefly explain why I speak of "Israel" in the title of this section. In fact, only "Judah" was exiled in the deportations of the early sixth century. There were still some shattered remnants of the people of the northern kingdom who had been exiled in 732 and 722 (as also of the Judahite deportees from the year 701). This is indicated by Assyrian-style names of Jews, and Jewish names in Assyrian territory, belonging to people we can view as the descendants of people who had been deported by the Assyrians.[22] We can certainly speculate, too, that after the deportations there had been a joining together of Israelites and Judahites from the earlier Assyrian exiles in 732, 722, and 701.[23] But these individuals were not a politically relevant entity. This, however, led to the more frequent use of the ancient name

"Israel" by the Judeans to also describe themselves. Deutero-Isaiah, *the* prophet of the exile, who speaks so clearly of Judah, Jerusalem, and Zion, is also dominated by an address that parallels Jacob with Israel (Isa 40:27; 41:8, 14, and frequently). Judah, which until the end of the northern kingdom was at best the "little brother" of the northern tribes, becomes identical with Israel. And even when there is thought of a future "reunification," so that the existence of two entities, "Israel" and "Judah," is again in view (Jer 31:27, 31; Ezek 37:15-28; Hos 2:2),[24] there is no notion of reconstituting a particular "Israel" in the north, but instead of a unified Israel under Judahite dominance.[25] After the end of the separate states of Israel and Judah, "Israel" increasingly became the

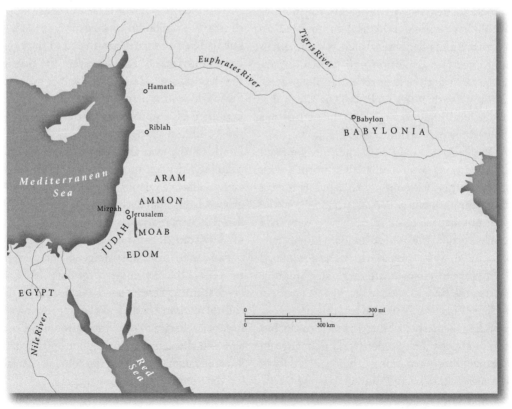

9.1. Babylon and Judah

ideal self-designation of both the exiles and the inhabitants of the territory of Judah and Samaria.

The Babylonian Exile

The writing attributed to the prophet Ezekiel—who as a priest and therefore a member of the upper class had already been sent into exile in 597—gives a narrow insight into the exiles' way of life. They lived in closed settlements. Ezekiel himself calls the place Tel-abib (Ezek 3:15). Some Neo-Babylonian business documents attest Jewish names in the region of Nippur and in Sippar.[26] Other names are known from the Persian era (Ezra 2:59; 8:17; Neh 7:61), though certainly we cannot be sure whether these places were settled by Jewish people in the Babylonian period, or not until the Persian era. The exiles could hold assemblies in the places where they lived. Their representatives were the elders, who are called "the elders of Judah" (Ezek 8:1), "the elders of Israel" (Ezek 14:1; 20:1, 3), or even "the elders among the exiles" (Jer 29:1). This indicates that the exiles enjoyed self-government, though it was probably restricted. When the Letter of Jeremiah (Jer 29:1-23) advises the exiles to establish themselves by building houses, planting gardens, and making marriages for their sons and daughters (Jer 29:5-6), it assumes the kind of life we can perceive behind the Ezekiel passages.

The Letter of Jeremiah also shows that there was regular contact between the exiles and those who remained in the homeland, at least in the time between the first and second deportations, that is, between 597 and 586. Thus Jeremiah 29 contains not only Jeremiah's letter but also one written from exile to the priests of the temple in Jerusalem (Jer 29:26-28). Jeremiah gives a member of an official delegation that traveled to Babylon during Zedekiah's reign an assignment: to carry out a symbolic action in Babylon (Jer 51:59-64). In turn, Ezekiel's symbolic actions and parables that warn of a revolt in Jerusalem during the time of Zedekiah only make sense if they were made known in Jerusalem also, and in a relatively short time.[27]

Unfortunately we have no information at all about the relationship between the exiles, living in their settlements, and King Jehoiachin, resident at the Babylonian court, and his retinue. That Jehoiachin, from the Babylonian receipts stemming from the 590s until the news of his release in the year 562 (2 Kgs 25:27-30) was titled "King of Judah" could indicate that he, although in exile, remained the formal head of the province.[28] At the same time, he could be considered the head of the exiled Judeans—of course, under the umbrella of Babylonian overlordship. But that is not explicit in the texts.[29]

Most significant for the ongoing social history of ancient Israel are the internal developments within the community of exiles. Until the end of the monarchical period, we must presume that the kinship-based structures that marked the pre-state society had been preserved in their essentials. This means that families, within the framework of larger clans, were the basic units of society, and that probably family and settlement structures were generally coextensive. It is true that those structures had been shaken by social developments and by the uninterrupted state of war beginning with the Syro-Ephraimite conflict, because people lost their property due to heavy indebtedness or had to abandon it because of military exigencies. But even Deuteronomy, which already presumes this shaky state of things, views the free landowner as the basis of society. And the official families, some of which we have been able to trace over generations,[30] show that at least in the upper class the family structures remained intact.

With the exile, this system lost its matter-of-fact hold on reality. The places where the exiles settled were certainly assigned to them for reasons of state. They probably had more the status of leaseholders than free landowners.[31] "Inheritance" as the basis of the kinship system vanished. (For the significance of the *nakhalah* as the basis of pre-exilic society, Deut 19:14; 1 Kgs 21:3; Mic 2:2; and frequently.) Moreover, members of different and unrelated families came together in the places of exile. The families were, in turn, sometimes ripped apart by exile; thus Ezek 24:21 speaks of exiles who had left their sons and daughters behind in Jerusalem.

All this did not mean that kinship relations as the basis of community unity entirely disappeared. On the contrary, with the loss of independent statehood, they were in some sense even more important. But they received a new form. In place of kinship relations that "everyone" knew and that were established primarily by a common place of residence and by inheritance, there was now a registration in lists. A first indication of this is Ezek 13:9, where certain prophets are threatened that "they shall not be . . . enrolled in the register of the house of Israel." The word *ketav* for "register" contains the root *ktv*, "write," which shows that this was a register maintained in writing. The same word reappears in Ezra 2:62 = Neh 7:64 and there refers to the "genealogical records" (see also the root *ktv* in Ezra 2:62; 8:1, 3; Neh 7:5, 64) in which all the Israelites in exile had to be recorded. Only those who can point to this registration belong to Israel; those who cannot are given separate treatment (Ezra 2:59–63 = Neh 7:61–65). Even if the lists in Ezra 2 and Nehemiah 7 derive from

the Persian period, Ezek 13:9 and the internal logic both show that the process itself must have developed, at the latest, when, after the second and third Babylonian deportations in 586 and 582, expectations for a rapid return had vanished.

The same backdating applies to the designation for extended families. In texts that, at the earliest, stem from the Persian period but reflect a practice that must have begun during the Babylonian era, these are called *bet ʾavot* = "house of the fathers" (Exod 12:3; 2 Chr 25:5; 35:12). This is the continuation of the older *bet ʾav*, "house of the father."[32] The heads of these extended families are called, with their full titles, *raʾshe bet ʾavot* (1 Chr 7:7) or *raʾshem levet ʾavot* (1 Chr 24:4), or usually, abbreviated, just *raʾshe (ha)ʾavot*, heads of the families (Num 36:1; Josh 19:51; Ezra 1:5; Neh 12:22; 1 Chr 8:6; and frequently).

This registration by extended family that developed during the Babylonian exile constituted the social basis that held the exiles together and preserved their identity. This, of course, could scarcely have succeeded if the exile community had not set up its central symbols of identity, namely male circumcision, keeping the Sabbath, and the food laws, and if, theologically speaking, there had not developed, within an almost overpowering religious and cultural climate in Babylon, the monotheistic confession of YHWH as the only God. This must be mentioned in any social history of Israel, though it cannot be explored in detail.

The Egyptian Exile

After Gedaliah's murder, the perpetrators of the deed fled, with a group of Jewish women and men, into Egypt. Because they took with them the prophet Jeremiah and the scribe Baruch ben Neriah, who worked closely with him, we have received some information about these events in Jeremiah 41–44, even though the texts were later given a deuteronomistic revision.[33]

It is important for our question about the Egyptian exile—and here, to begin with, about its first phase—that Jeremiah, according to 44:1, addressed himself to "all the Judeans living in the land of Egypt, at Migdol, at Tahpanhes, at Memphis, and in the land of Pathros." This listing shows that these people were to be found scattered throughout Egypt, for Migdol and Tahpanhes (= Daphne) lie in the Nile delta, Memphis lies south of the delta, and Pathros is a designation for Upper Egypt. The Hebrew participle used, *hayyoshevim*, "the dwellers," is apparently meant to indicate that these Jews had already been settled in these places continuously for a long time.

With the mention of "the land of Pathros," our attention is directed to the Jewish military colony settled at Elephantine in Upper Egypt. The documents we have from there come from the fifth century and must therefore be examined more closely in the chapter about the Persian period.[34] But it is explicitly said in the Elephantine papyri that the community's temple of Yahu was built before the conquest of Egypt by the Persian Cambyses in the year 525.[35] An immigration in the seventh or sixth century also corresponds to a common practice during the Saite (26th) dynasty (664–525), who encouraged the settlement of mercenaries and traders from throughout the eastern Mediterranean. Internal evidence suggest that the colony was established in the late period of the monarchy in Judah. The fact that, besides Yahu, the deities Ashim-Bethel and Anat-Bethel are mentioned[36] is more easily explained if the emigration to Elephantine took place early, in the seventh century. In that case the emigrants would have taken the form of YHWH religion they had practiced in their

homeland with them to Egypt and preserved it there, while it became obsolete in their homeland.[37] Likewise, the matter-of-fact way in which a temple was built outside Jerusalem is harder to imagine after Josiah's centralization of the cult than before; at any rate, the Babylonian exiles did not attempt to build a temple. Against the background of these reflections, then, a remark in the *Letter of Aristeas* 13[38] acquires more significance, even though that document is from the Hellenistic period. It says that a Pharaoh Psamtik—Psamtik I (664–610) or Psamtik II (595–589)—brought Jewish troops to fight against the king of the Ethiopians, which suggests an emigration during the monarchy.

But this gives us a quite different picture than in the case of the Babylonian exile. The latter came about as a result of forced deportations, while the Egyptian exile was a voluntary emigration. Large parts of the upper class, plus skilled workers, were exiled to Babylon, while those who went to Egypt were mainly soldiers and traders. The beginning of the Babylonian exile is clearly marked by the deportations beginning in 597, while the emigration to Egypt seems to have been a gradual process starting in the late monarchical period. Those exiled to Babylon saw themselves as persons forcibly carried away and hoping to return to their homes as soon as possible. Those who emigrated to Egypt fashioned an existence for themselves there and regarded Egypt as their new home. But Jer 44:1 shows that, even in Egypt, they maintained their Jewish identity.

As different as was the origin, so different was the further development of the Jewish groups in Babylon and Egypt. While the Babylonian exile dominated the development of Jewish society in the Persian period, the Egyptian exiles were marginal during that time. Their greatest period would come during the Hellenistic era.

10

Provincial Society under Persia

KEY POINTS

- 539: Cyrus overlord of Israel
- 331: Alexander the Great's conquest of the Persian Empire.
- Features of Persian imperial policy:
  - Partial local provincial autonomy
  - Efficient administration
  - Diverse cultures under a central government
- What was Israel in the Persian period?
  - The inhabitants of Judah and Samaria
  - Jews in surrounding provinces and in Egypt
  - The exiles.
- Important events:
  - 538: Permission to rebuild the temple
  - 520: Beginning of actual construction
  - 445: Nehemiah an official in Jerusalem
  - 398: Ezra an official in Jerusalem
  - 398–333: Almost no information about events in Judah and Samaria
- Society:
  - Alteration of family structure because of deportation
  - Basis of family structure now genealogical registration
  - Mixed marriages between Jews and non-Jews in Yehud
  - Sufferings and success of women
  - Class divisions
  - Similar conditions in Samaria
- Government:
  - Direct intervention of Persian government in provincial political life
  - Cooperation of the temple's high priest and the local governor
  - Other local officials: elders, nobles, provincial officials
  - Local governors with own courts and military forces
- The Second Temple:
  - Central sanctuary for Judah, Samaria, and the Diaspora
  - Priesthood part of local governmental structures
  - Economically important
  - Intimately related to the Persian state
  - Increased role of the high priest
- Ezra and the Torah
- Diaspora life:
  - Independent Jewish economic and social life in diaspora
  - Varied socioeconomic classes—from poor to rich
  - Strong sense of Jewish identity
- Yehud and Samaria as Persian-era provincial societies:
  - Provincial governors in both
  - Greater influence of temple in Yehud
  - Dynastic governorship, the Sanballat, in Samaria
  - Distinctive usages for "Jew," "Judahite," and "Israel"

IF WE TAKE OUR POINT OF ORIENTATION simply from the building and dedication of the temple in Jerusalem in the years 520–515, we can rightly call the era now beginning the Second Temple period. In that case, it must be extended to the Temple's destruction by the Romans in 70 CE. But since, as regards social history, the rule of the dominant power, be it Persian, Hellenistic, or, later, Roman has serious consequences for Israel's social organization, I prefer in this case to first isolate the Persian epoch from the larger Second Temple period.

From Cyrus to Alexander

The Achaemenid Cyrus II developed the Persian empire within two decades from a small state to a major power that ruled not only the Iranian highlands but all of Asia Minor to the Aegean coast. In the year 539, Cyrus entered Babylon without a fight, became king of Babylon and thus inherited all that Babylon possessed, to the borders of Egypt. With this, not only the Judeans living in exile in Babylon, but also the provinces that had been created since the Assyrian and neo-Babylonian eras in the territory of the previous states of Israel and Judah became subject to the king of Persia. Cyrus's son Cambyses succeeded in capturing Egypt in 525, but the attempt of his successor to subject the Greek city-states on the European mainland was less successful. Nevertheless, the Persian empire of the fifth century constituted a great power on a scale never known before, extending from the Indus to the Aegean and from the Caspian Sea to Upper Egypt.

However, this rule was not undisputed. Especially important in the Levant were revolts in Egypt and subsequently those of

the Persian general Megabyzos, who had put down the Egyptian revolt. These events in the mid-fifth century point to the regional instability in the southwestern part of the world empire. Then, in 404, Egypt separated itself altogether. It is true that it was reintegrated into the Persian empire for twenty years, but in 333, after the loss of the battle at Issos, Persian rule over Egypt and the Levant collapsed. With Alexander's entry into Babylon in 331 BCE, the two-hundred-year history of the Persian world empire was at an end.

It was not merely the extent of the Persian empire that caused it to introduce a qualitatively new stage in the history of the ancient world. In some fundamental features of imperial policy as well, the Persian empire stood apart from its predecessors. The first thing we must emphasize is the partial reversal of Assyria and Babylon's policy of deportation. A further expansion of this policy meant that the Persian empire granted partial autonomy to the peoples of their provinces, which applied primarily to cultural (which at that time meant, primarily, religious) affairs. The goal of this new policy was to bind the subjugated peoples to the Achaemenid royal house through loyalty.[1] The chief matter in hand was the collection of the imperial tax. For this purpose, the Persians built up an efficient administration seated in the provinces, a system introduced by the Assyrians and Babylonians. The most important innovation was the creation of satrapies as a middle level between the central government and the provinces. The Levant as a whole made up the satrapy of Trans-Euphrates. Thanks to a system of rapid communication, the "Persian Post," the central government could react quickly to developments in every part of the land. A secret service (the "eyes" or "ears of the king")[2] made

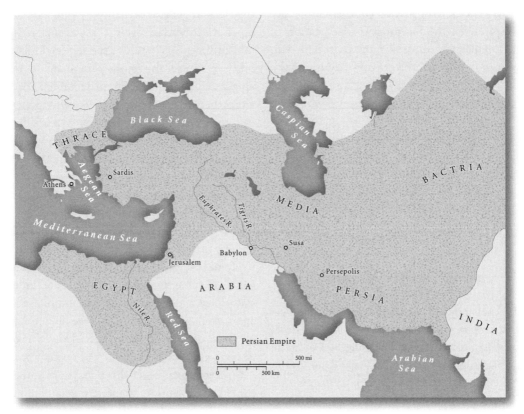

10.1. The Persian Empire.

sure that the government was given early information on all developments.

This Persian empire, which united a variety of local cultures under a unified government and administration, was the locus of the next phase of Israel's history. In the Persian period, the question of what the people of Israel is and who belongs to it becomes more and more acute. From a purely external point of view, we can distinguish various groups that could make a claim to belong; the most obvious of these was the claim of members of the Babylonian exile.[3] Next came the inhabitants of the provinces of Judah and Samaria, though their membership in the people Israel was by no means unquestioningly recognized by the exilic community. Finally, there were people in the surrounding provinces who could have understood themselves to be Jews or Israelites, as well as the members of the Egyptian diaspora. The Jews of Elephantine, for example, turned directly to Jerusalem in important religious matters, regarded themselves as Jews, and acknowledged Jerusalem as their center. All these entities must in some sense be included in the depiction of Israel's social history, even if both the state of the sources and historical influence focus on Judah and Jerusalem.

Two points stand out in the history of events in the Persian epoch. One is the early period, with the first group of returnees from exile, the building of the Second Temple in the years 520–515, and the constitution of a new form of common life in Judah. Another is the missions of Nehemiah, whom I place in the period between 445 and 433, and Ezra, whom I locate around 398.

After the Persians' seizure of the Babylonian empire they offered the exiles the opportunity to rebuild the temple in Jerusalem, with the Persian administration and the resident population responsible for the work. This would be the historical kernel of the so-called Edict of Cyrus of the year 538, the text of which is given in Aramaic in Ezra 6:3-5. A certain Sheshbazzar, who according to Ezra 5:14 had the title of *governor*, is entrusted with returning the temple's equipment and beginning the rebuilding. But building really began only in 520, in the reign of Darius I. From Haggai and Zechariah, who both produced propaganda for the building of the temple, we can conclude that the primary reason for the delay was economic need (Hag 1:2-11; 2:15-19; Zech 8:9-13). Only after the end of a struggle for the throne lasting a year and a half, when Darius was able to solidify his power, did a large group of exiles return to Judah in 520, led by Zerubbabel, an uncle of Jehoiachin, the next-to-last king of Judah (Ezra 2:2; for the genealogy, see 1 Chr 3:19). The central role of Zerubbabel, who like Sheshbazzar bore the title *governor* (Hag 1:1, 14), in the building of the temple indicates that it was primarily the members of the exile community who carried out the rebuilding. After five years of building activity, the sanctuary was dedicated in the year 515 (Ezra 6:15).

With the mention of Sheshbazzar and Zerubbabel, both of whom bore the title "governor,"[4] we have arrived at the disputed question whether Judah was from the beginning a separate province, or whether it was initially part of a larger province of Samaria and only became independent through the work of Nehemiah after the middle of the fifth century.

Albrecht Alt concluded the latter.[5] But because new epigraphical material has come to light since Alt gave reasons for his thesis in the year 1934, pointing to the existence of governors of an independent province of Judah even before Nehemiah, the biblical material that was the principal object of Alt's interpretation is also placed in a new light. Three named persons appear in the biblical texts bearing the title "governor" (*pekhah*): Sheshbazzar (Ezra 5:14); Zerubbabel (Hag 1:1, 14), and Nehemiah (Neh 5:14; 12:26), and there are another three allusions to governors without names given (Mal 1:8; Ezra 6:7; Neh 5:15). Add to these, as extra-biblical evidence, Elnathan, named on a seal impression, the governors Yeho'ezer and Ahzai, named on jar impressions, Yehezekiah, attested by a coin, and Bagohi, known from the Elephantine correspondence. Bahozi is the only one who bears a clearly Persian name.[6] Whether we can reconstruct from this evidence a seamless list of the governors of Judah[7] is not certain; it depends on the dating of the epigraphical evidence. But the multiplicity of names makes it rather improbable that Judah was a mere subprovince of Samaria until the middle of the fifth century.

On the other hand, "various witnesses" speak "for a change in status and political structure in Judah . . . beginning in the second half of the fifth century,"[8] so that Charles E. Carter divides the epoch into "Persian I" (538–ca. 450) and "Persian II" (450–332).[9] We may mention the building of fortresses from the mid-fifth century onward, which was connected to the Egyptian revolts and the Megabyzos insurrection,[10] and increased settlement of the land. Add to this that from this time onward, the number of seals increases markedly and there begins to be a coinage for the province Yehud (the Aramaic name that was becoming common). Thus we will have to modify Alt's position to the extent that, while Judah was not a "sub-province of Samaria," it is also "improbable politically that a fully established province of Judah existed before Nehemiah."[11]

It is undisputed that Samaria was an independent province from the start. But here, too, new findings make it possible to reevaluate the material previously already known from the Bible, Josephus, and the Elephantine papyri. We can see from this that the governorship over Samaria had lain since the middle of the fifth century in the hands of the Sanballat dynasty, and that there were a number of governors with that name. A hypothetical reconstruction, following that of Douglas M. Gropp, might look like this: Sanballat I—Delaiah—Sanballat II—Yaddua or Yeshua—Hananiah—Sanballat III.[12]

Overall, the material shows that the dualism of a northern kingdom of Israel and a southern kingdom of Judah, which shaped the history of the monarchical period, continued, after the destruction of these two independent states, in the provinces that succeeded them. From a political point of view, they remained separate entities, and their mutual relationship was marked by tension. Only in the middle of the fifth century, with the appearance of Nehemiah, did Judah emerge more clearly from the political shadow of Samaria.

Our description of the period up to Nehemiah has rested primarily on Ezra-Nehemiah (with additional information from the prophets Haggai and Zechariah); this will be all the more true for a depiction of the activities of Nehemiah and Ezra, because we have no other sources for them. For that reason, I must first give my opinion of the sources, even though I cannot give detailed reasons for it. On the whole, I accept the historical reliability of the so-called Nehemiah memoir in Nehemiah 1–7;

11–13*, even though Nehemiah's interests are all too evident in every line: for example, in his anti-Samaritan polemic or in the attacks on all the prophetic groups in Judea (Nehemiah 6).[13] I find historically reliable elements in the material about Ezra as well, even though one must certainly make distinctions at particular points.[14]

If we take the critically evaluated material from Ezra-Nehemiah as a basis, together with what we know of overall political developments, we have the following picture: after the Egyptian revolts and then Megabyzos the general's insurrection had been put down, by 448,[15] the central government's concern must have been to pacify its outlying lands extending to the borders of Egypt. Therefore Artaxerxes I, in the year 445 (the twentieth year of his reign, according to Neh 1:1; 2:1) permitted his Jewish cupbearer Nehemiah (Neh 1:11) to return to Jerusalem in order to stabilize the situation there.[16] Nehemiah has the city wall rebuilt (Neh 2:11—7:3), orders a one-time forgiveness of debts (Neh 5:1-13) and a *synoikismos,* that is, the forced settlement of rural dwellers inside the city so that it would not remain underpopulated (Neh 7:4; 11:1-2). Probably near the end of his activity—Neh 13:6 mentions the thirty-second year of Artaxerxes, that is, 433 BCE—Nehemiah carried out measures affecting the administration of the temple, the keeping of the Sabbath, and the regulation of marriage to non-Jewish women and men (Neh 13:4-31).

After the political situation in the province of Yehud had thus been stabilized, there followed, several decades later, a mission by a high Jewish official under orders from the Persian government.[17] In the year 398, Ezra was sent to Jerusalem to put a particular "law" (Ezra 7:26) into effect there, and to carry out internal reforms based on that law. We will deal below, in a separate section, with the question of what Ezra's promulgated law entailed, especially the question of what texts might have been identical with the law and whether the promulgation took place within imperially authorized, as was customary in the Persian empire.[18]

We have, for the most part, no information about events in Judah and Samaria during the fifty-five years between Ezra's mission in 398 and the victory of the Greek army over the Persians at Issus in 333, which is why those years are sometimes called "the dark century."[19]

Society and State in Judea and Samaria during the Persian Period

The social and political conditions during the Persian period reveal for the first time a general picture of what we may properly call the rule of Israel's social history: social institutions and organizations, once developed, do not disappear; they are developed further and thus simultaneously transformed. This is true for the kinship structures that, from the prestate era onward, formed the basis of society; it is true also of the state's organization, in which participatory elements from the monarchical period were transformed under the circumstances of a Persian-era provincial society; and it is true of the society's classist structure, which was not only retained through and beyond exile, but also further exacerbated by it.[20]

Family Structures under Threat

The deportations from the last third of the eighth century onward represented an extreme threat to the family as basis of society, not only because, due to external circumstances,

people were killed and families were torn apart, but above all because the fundamental connection between the family and its lands in the ancestral homeland was disrupted. The answer to this problem that was developed in Babylon was to decouple family and residence, and to bind the family's solidarity to a written registration in genealogical lists. The family remained the basis for society, but it now took on the form of a genealogically registered "father's house."[21] This structure was then retained in the province of Yehud. The bureaucratic regulation of family relationships, once developed, was retained even under the conditions imposed by a Persian-era provincial society.

The threat to the accepted nature of family solidarity was increased by the province of Yehud's settlement geography. That province was a tiny entity surrounded by non-Jewish provinces. Not all the Jews settled in Yehud, and not all the inhabitants of Yehud were Jews.[22] The consequence was mixed marriages (Mal 2:11; Ezra 9–10; Neh 13:23-27). Even if much of what is said of Nehemiah's and Ezra's supposed measures against mixed marriages is not historically accurate, it does indicate the problem's relevance. The fact that propagandistic or even bureaucratic measures were adopted in this area reveals how little the unity of the people was now taken for granted.

Likewise, the division of classes that had been proceeding in Israel and Judah since the eighth century disrupted family solidarity. The example of Neh 5:1-13 shows how the burden of indebtedness led to a situation in which daughters and sons of the family fell into debt slavery.[23] Beyond this, a whole series of texts shows how, under economic and social pressure, solidarity among neighbors and within the family was being shattered.[24] Micah 7:5-6 formulates it in drastic terms:

"Put no trust in a friend; have no confidence in a loved one; guard the doors of your mouth from her who lies in your embrace; for the son treats the father with contempt, the daughter rises up against her mother, the daughter-in-law against her mother-in-law; your enemies are members of your own household."

It is obvious that women are especially endangered by the collapse of solidary neighborhood and family structures, and this is attested by many biblical texts. According to Neh 5:5, daughters have already been handed over to slavery, while sons are only now coming under threat. Job 24:3 and 24:9 paint a vivid picture of how widows are being robbed of their oxen and even their infants. The slaves listed in the Samaritan papyri include women.[25]

Still it would be wrong to assume a tendency towards a deteriorating status of women in the Persian period. On the contrary: the loss of state sovereignty elevated the importance of family for the life, and often the survival, of individuals. This made women more important.[26] Even if we set aside the marriage contracts from Elephantine, with their generally egalitarian gender rules, because they are not products of the homeland, there remain some significant indicators. For example, the question of mixed marriages was so explosive precisely because, apparently, women had the right of inheritance, so that the property of Jewish families might fall into foreign hands through a woman's marrying outside the Land, or through the foreign wife of a Judahite man.[27] The polemic against mixed marriages is not, then, about misogyny, but about group identity. In addition, some information in Ezra-Nehemiah shows that women were by no means confined within their families. Thus under Nehemiah, a certain Shallum worked on the building of the wall of Jerusalem, together with his daughters

(Neh 3:12). In Neh 6:14, there is mention of a woman prophet, Noadiah, who was the leader of a whole group of prophets. Nehemiah 8:2-3 explicitly emphasizes that the popular assembly before which the Torah is read includes both men and women (also Ezra 10:1; Neh 10:29). There is also emphasis in Nehemiah 5 that women from among the people are taking part in the unrest described in 5:1. At the other end of the social scale, a woman owned a seal with the inscription "Shelomith, ʾamat of Elnathan the governor." This comes from the Persian period, even though its exact dating is disputed,[28] and was found together with a whole trove of *bullae,* including one from the governor himself and some with the name of the province, Yehud. This woman thus "held an important position in the administration of the province of Judah."[29]

In general, the development of the family reveals, on the one hand, the continuation of its basic function for Israelite society. The forced removal of its own royal house and the mixed settlement structures of the period actually increased the importance of the society's kinship organization, and it appears that this was not a detriment to the social position of women. The "post-state" epoch has been compared in this regard to the pre-state condition of kinship-based society.[30] On the other hand, this element of continuity was offset by a discontinuity from the ongoing intensification of class contrasts, which both threatened families and led, at the lower margin of society, to their decay.

Social Relations

The monarchical period, from the eighth century onward, had witnessed a society that was increasingly drifting apart. After the end of the northern kingdom, it is difficult to trace the history of the successor provinces in the Assyrian and neo-Babylonian empires, but we can scarcely suppose that the old tensions disappeared with the change in over-lordship. In Judah, the violent end brought special conditions in its wake. For one thing, the impoverished people took possession of the exiles' landed property, and, in the initial period, Gedaliah officially encouraged this. On the other hand, the banished upper class survived as a social group during the Babylonian exile, and they never surrendered their claim to the land.[31] The opportunity to return to Judah thus portended a conflict situation in continuity with the pre-exilic situation and, yet at the same time, contained elements of discontinuity.

An essential element of continuity lay at the heart of a divided society. All the elements of indebtedness, oppression, and impoverishment that can be observed in the late monarchical period are found also in the Persian era; the tendency to impoverishment appears to have increased. Thus Haggai and Zechariah name bad economic conditions as the reason for the tardiness in beginning to rebuild the temple. In drastic terms: "you that earn wages earn wages to put them into a bag with holes" (Hag 1:6). Even though general economic misery says nothing in particular about social relationships, the text shows that there were not only farming families, but day-laborers as well, that is, people without land who had to hire themselves out for wages.

If we add further texts that are in all probability to be dated to the Persian era, the picture becomes much sharper. Isaiah 58:6-7 lists prisoners, "the oppressed," "the hungry," "the poor," "the homeless," and "the naked"; this is a collection of all the elements of debt slavery (see also Isa 61:1-2) and destitution. The book of Malachi speaks of people "who oppress the

hired workers in their wages, the widow and the orphan . . . who thrust aside the alien" (Mal 3:5). Job 24 reveals in a devastating way the degree of degradation possible at society's lower margins. That chapter describes the life of destitute people reminiscent of present conditions in the Third World (Job 24:5-8).

Against the background of such a text, the conclusions of Ronny Reich and Eli Shukron about their excavations on the eastern slope of the old city of Jerusalem, which falls off to the Kidron Valley, are quite plausible.[32] They have found thick layers of trash that they interpret as household garbage. Even though the archaeological findings point to the Roman era, the references to the "Dung Gate" in Neh 2:13; 3:13-14; 12:31 attest that waste was already being deposited there in the Persian era. The same word here translated "dung" appears in 1 Sam 2:8 = Ps 113:7, where it is said that God "lifts the needy from the ash heap." Is that only metaphorical, or does it show, as Reich and Shukron posit,[33] that even then there were "dump people" who lived on the garbage of the rich?

While these last reflections have brought us to the lowest level of the social scale, what we learn from Nehemiah's time takes us to the core of society. Nehemiah 5:1-13 shows that in the mid-fifth century there was unrest because the farming population were threatened with excessive debt leading to the loss of their fields and houses and the enslavement of family members.[34] It is obvious that this is a portrayal of structural problems typical of ancient class societies.

However, a contingent event may have furnished an external impetus for unrest: namely, the building of Jerusalem's city walls.[35] According to the data in Neh 2:11 and 6:15, this took place between the middle of August and the beginning of October, that is, at the time for harvesting summer fruit, especially wine grapes and olives. Because Nehemiah was apprehensive of Samaritan threats and therefore demanded a rapid work pace, the project required practically the population's entire labor force. The workers' song cited in Neh 4:4 [English: v. 10] expresses how the people were being driven to the limits of their strength. And Neh 5:14-19 gives as his reason for going without his food allowance as governor "the heavy burden of labor on the people" (v. 18), which points in the same direction.

These immediate burdens caused by the building of the city wall indicate structural problems. The account even emphasizes that women participated in the protest (v. 1) as well as that daughters were the most threatened by impoverishment (v. 2, and especially v. 5). It speaks of people (v. 2) who have pledged their sons and daughters, but says nothing of real estate. These could be landless people, artisans, small merchants, or day-laborers. Then comes a group (v. 3) who have pledged fields, vineyards, and houses; these are probably farmers who are still free.[36] Finally, in vv. 4-5 the two are brought together. All these people are overburdened with debt. The reasons given for assuming debt are the necessity for credit simply for food consumption (v. 2), famine (v. 3), and the taxes to be paid to the Persian king (v. 4). We will speak of this last below,[37] but by now it must be clear that is a new reason for impoverishment, and one that does not appear in texts referring to the monarchic period.

Nevertheless, it is important to see that the rebellion in Neh 5:1-13 was not an anti-Persian uprising. The attacks are directed against "Jewish kin" (v. 1). Both the appeal of the protesters (v. 5) and Nehemiah's arguments for an immediate cancellation of debts (v. 8) are aimed at intra-ethnic solidarity. Nehemiah seems to be recalling a practice from the Babylonian exile,

when Jewish men and women who had been enslaved by foreigners were purchased and freed (v. 8). In a conclusion "from the easier to the more difficult," intended to defuse the explosive situation, Nehemiah applies this to intra-ethnic enslavement, which he condemns as still worse.

In speaking of the royal tax and the motif of intra-ethnic solidarity, we have acknowledged two elements that are not attested in the same form in the monarchical period. The third element of discontinuity is made still more obvious if we ask, "What is the composition of the upper class that profits from impoverishing most of the population"?

We may begin with the fact that it was primarily the members of the monarchical period's upper class who had to leave the Land during the various deportations. Dwelling in their several locations in Babylon, they did not descend into poverty,[38] and they maintained their consciousness of being legitimate—if not the only legitimate—heirs of Israelite and Judean traditions. Meanwhile, in the Land, some members of the former lower class had taken possession of the property of the exiles, and there, too, a new upper class had arisen, possibly made up primarily of non-Jewish elements.[39] This portended a twofold conflict in the Persian era: a struggle over land and over political and religious leadership.

However, reconstructing that conflict demands a highly critical reading of the texts, because in their present form in the principal sources, the books of Ezra and Nehemiah, they are presented exclusively from the point of view of the former exiles. They create the impression that the land, if not entirely empty, had at least been empty of real Judeans, and they obscure to the extent possible that there was any kind of intra-Judean conflict over the land. The texts construct a fundamental opposition between those returning from exile, the "children of the exile" (*bene haggolah*, Ezra 4:1, 3),[40] and those in opposition to the returnees from exile, the "neighboring peoples" or "peoples of the lands" (*ᶜamme haᵓaratsot*) (Ezra 3:3) or the "people of the land" (*ᶜam haᵓarets*) (4:4; see also Ezra 9:1-2, 11; 10:2, 11; Neh 10:29, 31). These are the ones who have not returned from exile: Jewish inhabitants of Judah, non-Jewish inhabitants, and Samaritans. Terminologically, they are all somehow associated with Gentiles.[41] Despite the conflict's ideological construction, the texts show that the exiles' elevated role is properly construed. In the simplest terms, we may say that in Persian-era Judah the returnees from the exile assumed the role of the upper class and that the social contrast between the upper and lower classes was at least partly equivalent to that between the returnees and those who had remained in the Land.[42]

The fact that the exiles and their descendants were able to implement their claim to the leadership role in the Land and to maintain their position that they were the legitimate heirs of Judah's monarchy was connected to their possessing the necessary material means. This is evident from the list of returnees' contributions to the about to be rebuilt temple (Neh 7:69-71).[43] The prophet Zechariah is also aware that the silver and gold he needs for a symbolic action (Zech 6:9-15) he can "collect" (v. 9) "from the exiles," that is, more precisely, from those who have returned from exile.

The tensions that must have resulted with the return of members of the former upper class are shown by an almost offhand remark in the list found in Ezra 2:1-67 = Neh 7:8-68. This seems to represent "a record of immigrants and settlers, perhaps of several different groups, over a considerable period of time, not a single mass return in the early years of Cyrus."[44] The crucial problem lurks behind the simple observation that the exiles returned "all

to their own towns" (Ezra 2:1 par. Neh 7:6). This shows that the exiles, or their descendants, maintained an awareness, even more than half a century later, of which was "their town." They take it for granted that they can return to their former properties, and there is no mention at all of the fact that in the meantime two or three generations of descendants of the former lower class have settled there. The early Persian era must have experienced a profound conflict over the question of the real ownership of the land.[45]

There are two more texts in which we find subtle traces of the conflict over the question of landownership.[46] In Zech 5:1-4 we find Zechariah's dream of a flying scroll, of which it is said: "This is the curse that goes out over the face of the whole land; for everyone who steals has—for a long time now!—gone unpunished, and everyone who swears falsely has—for a long time now!—gone unpunished." But now the curse is to go out in the name of God, "and it shall enter the house of the thief, and the house of anyone who swears falsely by my name; and it shall abide in that house and consume it. . . ." Apparently this is about claims to house ownership, obtained by false oaths; stealing is used as a rhetorical image. What remains unclear is whether it is those remaining in the land or the returnees who are solidifying their claims in this way. But because Zechariah otherwise, in advocating for the building of the temple, is on the side of the returnees from exile, and because the assertion is that the evildoers have gone too long unpunished, the dream may well mean that the well-established residents have lived far too long in houses that do not belong to them.[47]

A second text that can be interpreted in terms of the conflict over the land might be the law of Jubilee in Leviticus 25. It is certain that this law claims to be a generally valid rule. But the provision that after fifty years "you shall

return, every one of you, to your property"
(Lev 25:10) could also be concretely read to
mean that after the fifty years of the exile—
corresponding more or less to the period
between 587 and 537—lost property should
again fall to the returnees.[48]

The observation that there was a marked
contrast between those returning from exile
and the population still in the Land led Joel
Weinberg to the much-discussed thesis that
Persian-era Judah was organized in the form
of a "citizen-temple community."[49] Such a
"citizen-temple community"—a common phenomenon throughout the whole of the Middle
East, according to Weinberg—included not
only the whole population of a community,
but a group of privileged citizens organized
around the temple. In the beginnings of Yehud
this "community" would have consisted of
about 20 per cent of the resident population,
and after Nehemiah it would have grown to
about 70 per cent.[50]

The critique of Weinberg's thesis rests
essentially on three points:[51] (1) The assumption that throughout the Middle East there
was a multitude of "citizen-temple communities" is by no means proven, and even if there
were, a transfer of that concept to Yehud would
not be a matter of course. (2) Weinberg treats
the numbers in the books of Ezra and Nehemiah uncritically. In order to be able to posit
the existence of a separate community, he has
to work with very large numbers that cannot
be archaeologically verified. (3) All that the
texts are meant to show is that the temple
represented the symbolic unity of all in the
province of Yehud, just as Nehemiah and Ezra
acted on behalf of all those in the province.
Thus, despite many important observations
in Weinberg's work, as far as his basic thesis is
concerned the judgment must remain that "the
attitude that Ezra-Nehemiah takes toward the

temple can thus scarcely be harmonized with
the idea of a 'Jerusalem cultic community,' a
'Jerusalem temple-state,' or a 'citizen-temple
community.'"[52] What remains correct is the
initial observation, that there were manifest
conflicts of interest between those returning
from exile and the inhabitants of the Land.

No matter how much the fundamental
social conflict in the Persian era can thus be
described as a conflict between those who
had remained in the Land and those returning from exile, it can by no means be reduced
solely to that. For one thing, by far not all
those who returned from exile were members
of the upper class. When Nehemiah recalls
the purchase of Jewish male and female slaves
who had found themselves in the hands of
non-Jews (Neh 5:8), this must refer to events
in Babylon. Such freedmen and freedwomen,
who probably became dependent on their Jewish purchasers, would most probably have also
been among those returning. And besides,
there is no reason to presume that in the fifty
years since the beginning of the exile no new
upper class could have developed in the Land
itself. It is certain that this did happen in the
province of Samaria. The slaveholders in the
Samaritan papyri are not returnees from exile,
but they undoubtedly constituted the upper
class in that province.

This brings us to the northern part of the
region inhabited by Israelites: Samaria, for
which we have no further biblical evidence
after the northern kingdom's fall that would
permit conclusions about the social situation.
But the so-called Samaritan papyri attest epigraphically that the social conditions were
very similar to those in Judah.[53] These papyri
are contracts for the purchase of slaves, from
the period from 385 to 335, that is, the last fifty
years of the province before the Hellenistic
conquest. Almost all the actors—sellers and

buyers, female and male slaves—bear names containing the syllable *Yah*. The status of the slaves? Some of them may have been born in their owner's houses, but most of them probably succumbed to slavery in the usual way, through indebtedness. As the frequent "forever" in the contracts attests, however, it was only when they were sold that they entered the status of lifelong slavery.[54] In any case the contracts show that there was a typical ancient class society in Samaria as well, in which the dividing line ran between creditors and debtors, and in which slavery was as essential a component as is unemployment in a modern society based on the ownership of capital and employment for wages.

We may summarize: the fundamental structure of an ancient class society, as it developed from the eighth century onward in ancient Palestine, continued into the Persian era as well. The polarizing tendencies even increased, so that we must posit a growing impoverishment on the lower end of the social scale. But there were shifts in the composition of the social strata originally connected with the fact that it was primarily the Judean upper class who were exiled and that the returning exiles took over the leading roles in the Persian province of Yehud. In that province, members of the upper class and exilic returnees were practically identical. But the example of Samaria shows that this was a special development, and that an upper class could exist quite independently of the phenomenon of deportation.

State Structures in Judah and Samaria

That both Judah and Samaria were provinces within the Persian empire necessarily prescribed their political structures. Their head was thus the Persian king. Both belonged to the satrapy of Trans-Euphrates or Ebernari—"beyond the river," from the Persian central authority's point of view—and both were ruled by a Persian governor who, as a rule, was a local.[55]

Even if belonging to the Persian empire was a *de facto* given when the Persians seized power from the Babylonians, this historical seam nonetheless represented a crisis point, for as building began on the second temple, the Jewish prophets Haggai and Zechariah, who supported and advanced the building of the temple with their prophecies, also advanced ideas that could have been understood as threats to Persian overlordship. One of these was the notion that, through God's intervention, the temple would "soon" become the center of the world to which the nations would bring their wealth in tribute (cf. Hag 2:1-9; Zech 8:20-22). If we set alongside this the Persian concept of empire as recorded in the Behistun inscription of Darius I or in the programmatic images in Persepolis, the conceptual similarity is evident.[56]

If, as regards the expectations for the temple, we could think of religious ideas that can exist alongside one another—contrary to the rules of formal logic, any number of sanctuaries could be regarded as the center of the world—the contradiction to the political proclamations of Perisa is rendered still more acute.[57] When, in Hag 2:21-23, the Davidide Zerubbabel, whom the Persians had appointed governor for the rebuilding of the temple, is called the "signet ring" and YHWH's chosen one, then in the first place Jeremiah's rejection of Jehoiachin's kingship, also expressed in the image of a signet ring (Jer 22:24-27), is reversed. And the proclamation, in the same prophecy, that God will "overthrow the throne of kingdoms" and "destroy the strength of the kingdoms of the nations" is a tongue-lashing that puts the

Persians' dominant position up for grabs in the near future. Zechariah, who, following Jer 23:5-6, calls Zerubbabel a "branch" (Zech 3:8 6:12), goes one step farther by enacting a symbolic crowning, and a step backward by setting the high priest alongside the new Davidide king (Zech 6:9-15).

The high-flying hopes of these two prophets were not fulfilled. There was no restoration of the Davidic dynasty in Jerusalem, and the temple remained a Persian imperial sanctuary throughout the entire period. But the ongoing history shows that demonstrably, until the mid-fifth century, there were messianic movements in Jerusalem that were gladly taken up in polemical fashion in Samaria, and from which Nehemiah had to sharply distance himself (Neh 6:1-14).[58]

In fact, with the temple's dedication, the messianic dream of the restoration of an independent Davidide kingship as a contemporary, society-altering force had come to an end. The Persian overlordship remained undisputed until the Greek conquest and made its influence felt in various ways. Thus, for one thing, the Persian central government was able to exercise influence in the provinces through the appointment of governors and other important persons, as in the cases of Nehemiah and Ezra (Nehemiah 1–2; Ezra 7). In addition, it had the opportunity to intervene in events through written orders, as is also frequently depicted in the books of Ezra and Nehemiah.

However, Persian tax policy represented the closest link between the central government and the provinces. In connection with the social conflicts in the time of Nehemiah, we have already seen that the royal tax was given as one reason for the people's impoverishment (Neh 5:4).[59] According to Ezra 6:8, the same tax was not called "the king's tax" (*middat hammelek*), but "tributes of the province Beyond the River" (Aramaic *middat ʿavar naharah*). This points to the taxation system introduced, according to Herodotus (*Hist.* 3.89), under Darius I (522–486), in which each satrapy had to deliver a fixed annual sum to the central government. The absolute amount and the fact that it was to be delivered in precious metal show how severe the system was. It took no economic catastrophes into account, and in a region like Judah and Samaria, where there were no natural sources of silver, it required that all superfluous production be exhausted to purchase silver.[60]

This royal tribute was probably not all that was required of the population, for in Ezra 4:13, 20; 7:24 *middah/mindah* introduces two more kinds of taxes, namely *belo* and *halakh*. We can interpret these as income tax and wealth tax,[61] and by this means the element of the taxpayer's ability to pay was introduced alongside the royal tax. The state taxation was enhanced by a payment that directly supported the financing of the Persian governor's office (Neh 5:14-15; see also Mal 1:8). Then there was probably another, parallel system of taxes for the temple, but we will examine that in more detail below.[62]

Thus while the Persian central government massively intervened in the provinces' political life through its personnel policies, edicts, and demands for taxation, it seemed in turn to work on the principle that the various local authorities should be integrated into its system of government. For Judah, where the state of the sources is better, this yields quite a colorful picture, but the same is true in principle for Samaria, where the information is sparser.

As we already saw in connection with Haggai's and Zechariah's failed attempts to restore the Davidide dynasty, in Zech 6:9-15 the high priest has moved into an equal role alongside the Davidide king.[63] This has been called "the picture of a dyarchy of high priest and king."[64] The texts that retrospectively view the building of the temple do so in the way that the priest, Jeshua, and the governor, Zerubbabel, appear as acting together (Ezra 3:2, 8; 4:3; 5:2).[65]

If we move to the older textual level of the temple construction narrative in Ezra 1–6, we come upon a group called "the elders [of the Jews]" (Ezra 5:5, 9; 6:7-8, 14).[66] In what is said about the satrap Tattenai, who reviews and ultimately confirms the legitimacy of the building of the temple after 520, these elders are seen as those properly responsible. Only in 6:7 are "the governor of the Jews and the elders of the Jews" named together. This indicates that the Persians recognized the local authorities as a political factor to be taken seriously, alongside the governor they themselves had appointed—even when, as in the case of Zerubbabel, he was member of the last royal house in line to succeed to the throne.

The picture thus obtained is confirmed and at the same time further refined when we come to the Nehemiah traditions. Here there are frequent combinations in the form of lists, with three core elements: the "nobles" (khorim), the "provincial officials" (seganim), and the "rest [of the people]" or "the people" (in this sequence in Neh 2:16; 4:8, 13; 7:5).

In the case of the khorim, the "nobles," we should probably think of the same group who appear in Ezra 1–6 as "the elders [of the Jews]." When Neh 13:17 speaks of the "nobles of Judah," apparently both designations are combined. For the author of Ezra-Nehemiah, these same people are ultimately the "heads of the families [= fathers' houses]" (Ezra 1:5; 2:68; 3:12; and frequently). It is not just the various terminological designations that indicate that here the text is speaking of the province's economic and political leadership class, but also the information we can draw

from Neh 5:1-13. According to the latter, it is these nobles, together with the provincial officials, who have given credit in the form of gold and grain to the families that are becoming impoverished (v. 9), and who in exchange have obtained their fields, vineyards, olive groves, and houses (v. 10)—and probably also members of their families as debt slaves (v. 5). We also learn from Neh 6:17-19 that the members of the Judean upper class maintain close familial, personal, and political ties to the Samaritan upper class.

Another group who make frequent appearances, along with the "nobles" (khorim), and always in a subordinate place, are the "provincial officials" (seganim). In lexica and biblical translations they appear either as "prefects"[67] or (Luther) "councillors." This could be understood to mean—and was probably intended to mean—that they represented "the Jewish community."[68] But that role is already played by the "elders [of the Jews]" or the "nobles." Therefore the Einheitsübersetzung (the German "unified translation") and English translations like the NRSV are probably more accurate in using the word "official," though I would want to distinguish this from the sarim, the officials of the monarchical period, and so prefer the term "provincial officials."[69] That the seganim did in fact exercise an administrative function is confirmed by the Samaritan papyri from the fourth century.[70] Aramaic sgnʾ appears twice in the concluding formulae of the slave contracts (WDSP,10 and 10,10), and in other places it certainly should be inserted because of these texts' formulaic character. The segan always stands last, after the governor and a group of other named persons, in a listing of those before whom the contract was sealed or in whose sight some of its conditions have been fulfilled. This corresponds exactly to the sequence of "nobles" and "provincial officials" as persons who are assigned to and subordinate to the governor in the Judean texts. The final position of a *segan* in the papyri also leads us to conclude that he exercised a function similar to that of a secretary.

The Elephantine papyri confirms and makes more precise the picture we gain from the various biblical texts. Of special relevance is Papyrus TAD A4.7 from the year 407 BCE.[71] It mentions an earlier letter whose recipients reflect the province's political structures. That is, it was addressed to the governor and the high priest and his associates on the one hand, and to a certain Ostanes and the "nobles of Judah" (like Neh 13:17) on the other hand (11:17-18). This shows that the Persian governor—who is to be counted as part of the officialdom—relied on both the province's spiritual and secular elites. The fact that in the papyrus the priesthood are in the first position, whereas in the texts of the Nehemiah memoir they play practically no part at all, is related to the content of the particular texts. Nehemiah is concerned primarily with civil issues, whereas the Elephantine letter is about the Yahu temple on that island in the Nile.

In the lists from the Nehemiah tradition that were the starting point for this discussion the last place belongs to "the people." In general, they play no politically active role. We hear about real popular assemblies almost solely in connection with religious activities related to Ezra's mission. The term *qahal* is used for these; it can refer to the whole of the community without presuming that the community is assembled in one place (cf. Ezra 2:64 = Neh 7:66, and Neh 13:1).[72] Only in Neh 5:1-13 does it appear as if the popular assembly took a politically active role. This is especially interesting because to begin with there is a conflict between "the people and . . . their wives" and "their Jewish kin" (v. 1), the latter identical with the "nobles and provincial officials" (v. 7). Nehemiah turns first to them (v. 7a), but then he calls a "great assembly" (*qehillah gedolah*) "to deal with them" (v. 7b): that is, he makes the conflict public. He brings charges against the members of the upper class in front of the assembly; there he also declares that he himself is renouncing any claim to collect debts; and, finally, it is the assembly as a whole that sanctions the release from debt by its "Amen" (v. 13).

Of course we cannot really derive a "constitutional" role for the popular assembly in the province's political system from this incident. Rather, Nehemiah locates it within a current conflict by skillfully placing himself on the side of the people and, by means of public sanction, ties the members of the upper class into his own policy. In Greek terminology, one would certainly have been able to describe Nehemiah's actions as those of a "tyrant"—without the negative flavor the word later acquired. "In general, mobilizing the poor against the rich was a common method of tyrants, since their principal opponents, like Nehemiah's, were for the most part members of the established aristocracy."[73]

In summary, we may say in light of the system of rule in Judah and—as far as it can be reconstructed—in Samaria that it rested on unconditional loyalty to the Persian overlords but was strengthened by the fact that the local authorities were given a share of responsibility. The fact that the Persian governors in most cases were members of the local upper class[74] was both the basis and the expression of that balance. That provincial officials, subject to the governor, and noble members of the upper class appear as active in important decisions is likewise an expression of this balancing act. And that in Jerusalem, with its temple, the priesthood was tied into this constellation of power is nearly a matter of course.

If we look beyond Judah and Samaria, we can generalize still more: the Persian provinces in the Levant—Ashdod and Gaza as well as Judah and Samaria—almost had the character of small "states." They were ruled by a dynasty of governors—very clearly so in the case of Samaria[75]—most of them of local origin. They maintained little courts with a corresponding administration (Neh 5:14-18), had their own military troops (Neh 3:34 for Samaria, 4:1-17 for Yehud) and their own seals (*CWSS* 419 for Samaria), and in the second half of the Persian era they had the right to strike their own coins.[76] "Within this general political organization, the province of Judah did not differ basically from the others in Palestine. . . ."[77] Still, it should not be forgotten that this relative autonomy existed only within the framework of the Persian overlordship and for the sake of its security.[78]

What was apparently characteristic of the Persian epoch as regards family structures and social relationships, namely a mixture of continuity and discontinuity with the time of the monarchy, can be well attested for political structures as well. The way the governor relied on nobles and provincial officials had its closest parallel in what we have described above as the "participatory monarchy."[79] Here there is a clear instance of continuity. The discontinuity, in turn, lay on two levels. For one thing, the governor was not the sovereign of a state, even though a small one; he was the representative of a foreign overlord. Second, and the cause of this lay at least partly in the nature of foreign domination, the temple in Jerusalem and its priesthood played a much more important part in the political system than they had done in the time of the monarchy. Add to this that, with Ezra's reforms leading

into the fourth century, the implementation of the "Law" introduced an element into the Israelites' political system that, while it had its precursors in the codifications of laws begun during the monarchy,[80] now assumed a completely new function.

Temple and Torah

Israel in the Persian era presents a paradigmatic example of how closely religion was integrated into general social and political relationships in an ancient class society. The true starting point of the epoch was the building of the second temple in the years 520–515.[81] And there was a notable break in the year 398 with the mission of Ezra and the promulgation of a law that was to be valid for Jews in the province of Judah and in the satrapy of Trans-Euphrates.[82] Both events and their consequences, which extended far beyond the Persian epoch, must be included in any modern description of the history of religion in ancient Israel, but they are just as important for social history.

The Role of the Second Temple

What we saw to be true of family and social structures and political power relationships is true also of the central religious institution of Persian-era Judah: the second temple was in continuity with the first and yet was at the same time characterized by elements of discontinuity. Like the first temple, especially after Josiah's reform, it was the central sanctuary; its priesthood was, like that of its predecessor, incorporated in the structures of the state; and as a place to which the people brought their gifts it had important economic significance. But in all three of these points the second temple was significantly different from the first.

It was simply obvious, after Josiah's centralization of the cult, that the temple had to be rebuilt on the same site as its predecessor (Ezra 6:3). The continuity with the first temple this involved, however, posed the question: for whom, exactly, was this temple the central sanctuary? As long as the northern and southern kingdoms existed side by side, each had its own state sanctuaries.[83] After the fall of the northern kingdom, Bethel continued to function as a sanctuary (2 Kgs 17:28). Its altar was finally destroyed by Josiah in favor of the sole sanctuary in Jerusalem, which he was promoting (2 Kgs 23:15). It appears that Jerusalem was thereafter accepted as the central sanctuary even by Israelites who did not live in the territory of Judah (Jer 41:5). For the Persian era, there are some indications that the Samarian leadership was also religiously oriented to the temple in Jerusalem.[84] The biblical material is especially revealing here because the texts of Ezra and Nehemiah are saturated with anti-Samaritanism. It is all the more striking, then, that Samaria's interest in the Jerusalem temple is continually evident. Thus we hear, from the time when the rebuilding was beginning, that the Samaritans wanted to participate in the building work and the returned exiles refused to let them do so (Ezra 4:2-3). There were marriage relationships between the members of the upper classes of Samaria and Judah (Neh 6:18); some of these involved priestly families (Neh 13:28). One result of this was that the high Samaritan official Tobiah had an office of his own in the Jerusalem temple at the time of Nehemiah (Neh 13:4-9).

The Elephantine correspondence brings this dimly perceived picture from Ezra and Nehemiah into sharper focus.[85] When, in the year 407, the Jews of Elephantine sought support for the rebuilding of their temple, which Egyptian priests had destroyed, they appealed to the governors of both Judah and Samaria. Certainly, there seems to have been no dispute that the leadership lay in Jerusalem. This is evident from the fact that at first they wrote only to Jerusalem (TAD A 4.7:17–18), and only when they received no answer from there did they turn once again to the Persian governor in Jerusalem (the letter in TAD A 4.7) and simultaneously send a copy (TAD A 4.7:28) to Samaria. An answer was received from both governors; the Persian Bagohi, governor of Judah, is mentioned before the governor of Samaria, Delaiah (TAD A 4.9:1). Both approved the rebuilding, and so both together were regarded as those who represented the interests of Jews in cultic matters outside their own territory before the Persian authorities.

The mention of the Elephantine papyri brings us to the period shortly before the appearance of Ezra. Up to that time the temple was the religious center not only for Judah, but also for Samaria. It is true that in Nehemiah's time, there was an attempt to force the influence of the Samaritan upper class back out of the temple and to sever relations between the members of the upper classes of the two provinces (Neh 13:4-9, 28). But the role of the Jerusalem temple as the central sanctuary for all YHWH-believers was not fundamentally questioned. The members of the Diaspora were also included. Even the Jews of Elephantine, who had their own temple, did not consider themselves autonomous regarding questions about the correct celebration of the Passover. As the so-called Passover letter from the year 419 shows,[86] they received their answer from the Persian king, through official channels by way of the satrap for Egypt. However, in light of the material and sometimes linguistic similarities between the royal Passover edict and the order for the Passover in Exodus 12, it is unthinkable that the Persians would have decided an intra-Jewish religious matter without consulting the responsible Jewish authorities.[87] And as we already saw, the Jews of Elephantine turned to Jerusalem even regarding questions about their own temple.

If the temple and its priesthood were, in their spiritual function, the center for all YHWH-adherents in Judah, Samaria, and the Diaspora, they were at the same time an essential factor in the internal political constellation of the province of Judah as well.[88] We already saw how, in Zechariah's concept of a dyarchy and in the actual constellations of power in subsequent epochs, the priesthood was involved in the structures of Jewish power alongside representatives of the upper class.[89] Here the elements of continuity and discontinuity with the Israelite and Jewish monarchical period are clearly evident. For certainly the priests were involved in the political system during the monarchy; the priests of the state sanctuaries in Bethel and Jerusalem, in particular, were also royal officials. But as the king's officers they were also subject to his orders; they were, in fact, *only* the king's officials.

In the Persian era, however, the position of the Jerusalem priesthood was fundamentally different from that of the political authorities of the state. It is true that, in the domestic political system of the province, the Persian king's governor in some sense replaced the king of Judah. But because he represented a foreign ruler and in some cases might even be a Persian, the importance of the temple priesthood grew. It now embodied the elements of both national and religious identity, over against the Persians. In fact, the highest priest of the Jerusalem temple was not yet the sole political spokesman for the Jewish community, as he would be in the Hellenistic period.[90] But he was

also no longer merely one of the officers in the royal apparatus of officialdom. Together with the representatives of the laity, he stood alongside and opposite the Persian governor and his officials as the spokesman for the Jewish population. He went from being "the highest priest" (*kohen haro'sh*) (2 Kgs 25:18) to being "high priest" (*hakkohen haggadol*) (Hag 1:1; Zech 3:1; 6:11).[91] As the embodiment of a national religious identity over against a foreign power, the high priest even took on certain royal features. While before the exile, anointing was the honor reserved for the king (cf. 1 Sam 15:1, 17; 16:3; and frequently), who therefore bore the title "anointed one" (*meshiakh*) (1 Sam 12:3; 24:7, 11, and frequently), so now the high priest became the "anointed priest" (*hakkohen hammasheakh*) (Lev 4:3, 5, 16, and frequently). It is not surprising, then, that from the Persian era onward it is possible to reconstruct a list of high priests,[92] whereas in the monarchical period there was a list of the kings of Israel and Judah, but only sporadic and sparse information about the names of the highest priests.

During the Persian era, in addition to the religious position of the temple as cultic center for all Israelites and the domestic political role of its priesthood within the power structures of the Persian province of Yehud, the temple's economic significance also increased. The precondition for this was the cultic centralization at the end of the monarchical period, as a result of which all religious donations and taxes, at least for the province of Yehud, were funneled to Jerusalem; this also encouraged a trade in goods throughout the Land.[93] In addition, reflection on the historical experience of exile brought forth theological currents that further underscored the central position of the temple. These can only be briefly indicated here.[94] Most important was the concentration of worship at the one great altar in the priests' court, with lesser altars reserved for private worship that involved the laity in cultic actions, as well as the emphasis on the idea of cultic acts of atonement, all of which led to an increase in cultic routines. Whereas in the monarchical period the state temple was primarily at the service of the state cult, the second temple was increasingly a people's temple that attracted all worship acts to itself.

The elevated position of the second temple meant that the population had to contribute a great deal more to the support of the temple than had been the case in the monarchical era. Every sacrificial act required that portions be set aside for the priests (Lev 7:8, 33-36; 10:14-15, and frequently). Added to these were other gifts to the priests (Num 18:12-16; Neh 10:36-38). In addition, the official cult—apart from a contribution from the state treasury that will be discussed immediately below— had to be financed by the population. Besides this there was a temple tax, which according to Exod 30:11-16 was a half-shekel per year and according to Neh 10:33-34 was a third of a shekel. This was explicitly designated not for the priests' needs, but for acquiring what was needed for the sacrifices. Families also had to take turns delivering wood (Neh 10:35; 13:31). Beyond this, Mal 3:8-10 and Neh 13:12 also mention a tithe for the temple. Finally, there were free-will offerings that, no matter how freely presented, were like today's collections: one really had to give.

In light of all these burdens, it is not surprising to hear that people sought ways to avoid them. Thus Malachi speaks (1:8) of priests allowing the sacrifice of blind, lame, and sick animals that were brought to them by those responsible for the procurement (see also v. 13). In 1:14 we read that a blemished animal has been brought in fulfillment of a vow. And from 3:8-10 we can draw the conclusion that

tithes and taxes were not paid in full. Since 1:8 makes a comparison with gifts to the governor, in which case such tricks are not even attempted, Malachi is illustrating what a heavy burden of taxation the population as a whole has been subjected to.[95]

If, by means of cultic activities and taxes, the population was much more tightly connected to the temple than it had been in the monarchical period, the sanctuary still did not lose its character as a state temple; now, however, it was a Persian state sanctuary. It was built at the command of the Persians, it was partly financed by them (Ezra 6:3-4, 8-9; 7:21-23), and prayers had to be offered in it for the Persian king and his sons (Ezra 6:10).[96] There are some indications that the temple, in its function as state sanctuary, was also the place where the various taxes to be paid to the state treasury were collected and handed on to the satrapy or the central government.[97] Besides analogies from other parts of the Persian empire, we should here point especially to the allusion to the *yotser* in Zech 11:13, which despite the literal translation "potter"[98] probably does not refer only to a simple craftsperson, but to "a comparatively high-ranking official."[99] His task, in service to the Persians, is to melt the silver that has been received at the temple and forward it in this new form. The fact that Nehemiah as a matter of course, in his function as the Persian governor, can intervene in internal matters of temple administration (Neh 13:4-9, 10-13)[100] shows how closely the temple was tied into the Persian governmental system.

On the whole, it may be said of the role of the temple and its priesthood in the Persian period that, as was the case throughout the ancient world, it was a part of the social fabric and the political power system. But inasmuch as that fabric was altered in contrast to what it had been in the Israelite and Judahite monarchical era, the temple's role also shifted. The temple and the priesthood gained in importance in two ways. For one thing, they acquired particular identifying features of the national monarchy: the high priest was in some sense the successor to the king. And, as part of the local elites on which the governor relied together with the "elders" or "nobles," they participated directly in exercising governmental authority within the province.

The double weight of secular and spiritual authority, of the interests of the laity and the priests, that resulted from this power shift— and all of it under the umbrella of Persian overlordship—would also be a crucial factor in the process of the promulgation of the Torah under Ezra, which we will examine next.

Ezra's Promulgation of the Torah

Besides the building of the temple, which makes up the content of Ezra 1–6, and the mission of Nehemiah, described in the so-called Nehemiah memoir,[101] the account of Ezra's mission (which for the reasons given above[102] I believe to have come after that of Nehemiah) constitutes the third focus of the books of Ezra-Nehemiah. Even though this account encompasses Ezra 7–10 and, in any case, Nehemiah 8, because of its social-historical relevance I will restrict my remarks to the Aramaic text of Ezra 7:12-26, the account of a letter from King Artaxerxes to Ezra ordering the promulgation of a "law." The variously disputed question of its historical reliability[103] is, at any rate, "not of decisive consequence" since "even a fictional document . . ." may "introduce real institutions."[104] Nevertheless, it may well be possible to discern the historical kernel within the redacted letter of Artaxerxes in vv. 14, 25-26.[105]

In the king's letter—also called Artaxerxes' *firman*, using the technical Persian term— Ezra is commissioned to travel from Babylon to Jerusalem, taking with him funds from the Diaspora to be used to complete certain matters regarding the temple, and finally to organize the Land's legal situation. This last, which is addressed directly in Ezra 7:25-26, is what interests us here. It is prepared for by Ezra's being titled "scribe of the law of the God of heaven" (v. 12). This shows that Ezra is an official of the Persian administration whose portfolio is the "law of the God of heaven." The Passover letter, sent from the Persian king to the Jews at Elephantine twenty years before Ezra's appearance, shows that there must, in fact, have been an institution in the Persian government that was familiar with Jewish religious affairs.[106]

Ezra now received orders from the central government to appoint "judges who may judge all the people in the province Beyond the River who know the laws of your God; and you shall teach those who do not know them" (v. 25). Finally, those who do not obey the law are threatened with punishment (v. 26). The decree is thus for all the YHWH-believers in the satrapy of Trans-Euphrates, although, as the possibly secondary v. 14 rightly notes, it is primarily "Yehud and Jerusalem" that are meant.[107] Thus the law is regarded as known in principle; what is new is not the law as such, but the authority with which it is endowed. At the same time, the decree also takes cognizance of those who "do not know" it and who must be "taught." This can, of course, probably mean only that the extent of this law, on the one hand, is not clearly delimited, and on the other hand that not all its parts are generally known.[108]

This law is not only called "the law of the God of heaven" (v. 12), but also, in v. 26, it is said to be both "the law of your God" and "the law of the king." If we read the "and," Aramaic *waw,* that links the two phrases as copulative (treating the phrases as separate units), we are talking about two laws: one would be the Jewish law in the narrower sense, the other the tax laws and Ezra's commission, both emanating from the Persian king.[109] But since the rest of the text speaks only of one law, the *waw* can also be understood as explicative (a straightforward, clearly understood term, phrase, or statement). It would then mean: "the law of your God, namely [or: that is] the law of the king." According to the text, the "law of the God of heaven," which is valid for all who believe in YHWH, is simultaneously to be regarded as Persian state law.[110]

Adopting the latter opinion, some have drawn an analogy with other cases and described the process by which local laws were authorized by the Persian empire as valid imperial laws within the territory in question, that is, as simultaneously "the law of the king," as "imperial authorization."[111] However, the information about such cases is very widely distributed and concerns quite different cases. It is questionable whether one can conclude from this sparse information to a general institution of imperial authorization in the Persian empire.[112] The question need not be decided here, however, for Artaxerxes' *firman* in Ezra 7:12-26 itself does not speak of an "imperial authorization" as a legal institution, but of a particular set of events. So even if one maintains some doubt about the existence of this kind of legal institution, that does not dismiss the concrete case in question.

The "law of the God of heaven" that, as "law of the king" or in addition to it was put into effect in Yehud and Jerusalem and at the same time was declared binding on YHWH-believers in the satrapy of Trans-Euphrates was most probably the whole of the Pentateuch, which does not exclude the possibility that the then-existing form of the text was later expanded.[113] In any case, this was the view of the final redactor of Ezra-Nehemiah. But above all, this best explains the authoritative position of the Torah in Judaism, as well as the fact that the Samaritans, after their separation,[114] adopted the Torah, and only the Torah, as the basis for their community.

With the promulgation of the Pentateuch as "the law of the God of heaven," Judaism, after the loss of its own monarchy and state—and for many, their land as well—obtained a further element of identity alongside the cult. In the long run it would acquire greater significance than the cult as well. Therefore the Samaritans, after they had built their own temple, remained united with Judaism in acknowledging the Torah. Above all, after the temple was destroyed in the Roman era and the people were again driven from their Land, Judaism was able to survive, not only in the absence of its state anchor, but even without a cultic center.

However, it would be wrong to trace the Torah's ability to secure Judaism's identity exclusively to a single event such as the promulgation of the Law by Ezra. It was, rather, the result of a process extending over a long period of time.

The Process by which Torah Became Law

Ezra's promulgation of the Torah was neither the starting point for the Torah's becoming law nor the end. It was an important intermediate step, neither more nor less. The process itself began with the codifications of law in the monarchical period[115] and was completed in the Hellenistic era when authors like Jesus

Sirach, Philo of Alexandria, or Flavius Josephus presupposed as a given that the "laws of the fathers" or the "Torah of Moses" were the fundamental documents of Jewish existence. But what was the character of what I am calling "the Torah's becoming law"?

There is a consensus about the law codices of the ancient Near East within whose legal tradition the law of the Israelites visibly stands. It is formulated by Frank Crüsemann: "This was . . . not anything like positive law. Rather, what we have are documents resulting from legal scholarship that are . . . primarily . . . the product of theoretical work."[116] At the same time, this does not mean that there was no relationship between the legal codices and law as practiced. Inasmuch as in the Hebrew Bible "the Law . . . (was) directly attributed to the deity and not to a king . . . it took on . . . features of positive law, with an insistence that it be carried out," as Eckart Otto formulates it; he sees this "process of transformation of Judaic law" as beginning "in the Book of the Covenant, shortly before the exile,"[117] even though we have no external evidence with which to test the extent to which the directives in the Book of the Covenant or Deuteronomy were in fact obeyed.

From the Persian era, then, we have for the first time a document in our hands that shows how close the legal text and the law lay in practice. This is the Passover letter from Elephantine.[118] The Passover practice that is there declared to the Jews of Elephantine as in accordance with the law, promulgated at the command of the Persian king through the satrap of Egypt, corresponds in part, even in its wording, to the Passover regulations in Exod 12:1-20. The letter begins with the words: "In this year, the fifth year of King Darius, it was made known by the king to Arsham [the satrap of Egypt]. . . ." This would mean that it

originated about twenty years before Ezra's appearance, according to the time scheme I have presented. In that case, everything favors the supposition that the king, in writing his response to the Jews of Elephantine, is relying on just such a figure as Ezra who is telling him, on the basis of the "law of the God of heaven," how he should decide this matter.

With the Samaritan papyri, which were written in the years between 385 and 335, we arrive at a period later than Ezra. At first glance, their content might call the promulgation of the Torah under Ezra into question because it entirely contradicts the rules in the relevant laws. According to those laws either there can be no such thing as intra-Jewish slavery such as exists in most of the cases in these papyri (Leviticus 25), or it must be limited to six years (Exodus 21; Deuteronomy 15). Even if the slave, after six years, freely chooses to remain with the master "forever," as provided for in Exod 21:5-6 and Deut 15:16-17, he or she apparently cannot be sold to another "forever," as happens in the papyri. The incompatibility of the papyri with the provisions of the Torah cannot be relativized, either, by saying that in individual cases so-called "home-born" slaves (Gen 15:12-13, 23, 27; Jer 2:14) could be sold, for the majority of the slaves being sold here were debt slaves. The contradiction is all the more obvious in that all the documents were sealed before the governor, and some of them before a group of witnesses and the provincial officials, so that one cannot simply regard the slaveholders in these contracts as "sinners" who obey no law.[119]

But it would be too simple to deny, because of the papyri, that the promulgation of the Torah under Ezra actually took place. Even if the Torah's slave laws, on the evidence of the papyri, were not applied in fourth-century Samaria, it is a fact that Samaria, in separating from the Jews,[120] adopted the five books of Moses, and those books alone, as its law. Ezra 7:25-26 itself presumes that the ordinances of the Torah were not known everywhere and to the fullest extent at the time of Ezra's mission. If they were then declared binding in Jerusalem, that does not mean that the upper class and the leadership in Samaria immediately adopted them for their own territory. The Torah's formal proclamation under Ezra did not mean that the ordinances of the Torah were put into effect in every place and at every time with the same degree of force. Rather, that event represents nothing more and nothing less than an important step in a long process.[121]

That we should not imagine Ezra's putting the Torah into effect as an absolute turning point, but as one step in a longer process, seems also to be attested by a document recorded in Nehemiah 10, which contains the community's acceptance of responsibility for carrying out certain central Torah ordinances. It is loosely integrated into the literary context. It does not conform to the account of the reading of the Torah in Nehemiah 8–9, because what would be the purpose of commitment to a few core principles after the whole Torah, from beginning to end, had been read out loud in a comprehensible form over seven immediately preceding days (Neh 8:1-8)? But the text does not fit within the Nehemiah memoir either, since the latter presumes always that Nehemiah is an active mover of events, whereas in Neh 10:2 he is simply mentioned as one who signed the document, something that can be attributed quite easily to the final redaction. Thus a good many things point to the conclusion that the self-obligation, the oath sworn, in Nehemiah 10 comes from the period after Nehemiah and Ezra, perhaps even as late as the Hellenistic epoch.[122]

The agreement presented in vv. 31-40 represents a selection from ordinances drawn from all the *corpora* of the Pentateuch. In particular, it regulates numerous cultic questions, or rather the material provisions for worship (vv. 33-40). Only one ordinance is drawn from the social laws in the narrower sense: "and we will forego the crops of the seventh year and the execution of every debt" (v. 32b; English v. 31b). This is important in two ways for the question of how we should imagine the consequences of proclaiming the Torah as law. For one thing, we find here for the first time something like legal interpretation,[123] in that the sabbatical year of release in Deuteronomy 15 is adopted, while at the same time the jubilee year every half-century, from Leviticus 25, is left out of account.[124] Second, the restriction to the year of release excludes certain other social laws, including the ordinances regarding slavery. That, however, corresponds exactly to the situation we find also in the papyri from Samaria. Apparently promulgating the Torah did not mean that everything was rearranged at the same time and with the same intensity.[125]

With its restored temple, Jerusalem, the capital city of the province of Yehud, became the center not only of the province, but also for Judaism in the Diaspora, independently of the question whether there were other cultic centers—as there certainly was in Elephantine. Alongside it stood the province of Samaria, in which one group of the population were YHWH-believers who were also religiously oriented to the temple in Jerusalem, but which was politically separate from Yehud. With Ezra's promulgation of the Torah, Israel achieved a second center that was not bound to a single place. According to Ezra 7, the Torah was, in fact, brought from Babylon by Ezra. In spite of that, it received its authority in Jerusalem. This unusual tension between Jerusalem and Yehud as the undisputed center, a strong province of Samaria, and a Diaspora oriented to the center in Jerusalem is characteristic for Israel in the Persian era.

Before we attempt to bring all the elements together in a single picture we must first take a look at the situation in the Diaspora.

Life in the Diaspora

The "period of the exile," which began long before the destruction of Jerusalem in 586,[126] did not end when the Persians assumed power in 539. Both the Babylonian and the Egyptian Diasporas continued, and their significance would only increase through and beyond the period covered by the writings of the Old Testament, which is the subject of this study. But the course of the Diaspora's development was very different in the two regions.

Babylonian Judaism

No matter how dominant the returnees from exile were in the Land itself, by no means did the whole of the exiled population, or even a majority of it, return. For not only was it possible for the descendants of Jewish exiles to follow political careers in the Persian empire—Nehemiah, for example, was the royal cup-bearer (Neh 1:11) and Ezra was a kind of secretary of state for Jewish religious affairs (Ezra 7:12)—they also achieved a certain degree of wealth. Even though the source value of the textual material needs to be evaluated with discrimination regarding its details, the general impression that members of the exile community were in a position to support their homeland with considerable material contributions seems to be accurate (Ezra 1:6;

2:68-70 = Neh 7:69-71; Ezra 7:16; 8:24-30, 33-34). For the Jewish historian Josephus, later, the comfortable state of those in the Diaspora, which he portrays as a general condition, explained the fact, constantly glimpsed in the sources, that by no means all the Jews returned to their homeland. "Yet did many of them stay at Babylon, as not willing to leave their possessions" (*Ant.* 11.1.3).

Besides the biblical instances and Josephus, there is an interesting epigraphical witness that the Diaspora Jews—or at least some of them—were economically well integrated in Babylon and that as a group they by no means represented an impoverished lower class. These are the files of the banking and trading concern of Murashu and Sons, located in Nippur, from the time of the Persian kings Artaxerxes I and Darius II, or more precisely the years 435–403: generally speaking, the years of Nehemiah and Ezra. We see from these cuneiform documents that a certain portion of the banking house's business was involved with partners who quite clearly bore Hebrew names.[127]

Of course, it would be wrong to create the impression that all Diaspora Jews were rich people. Care is required in using the biblical sources because, in the interests of the claims of those returning exiles to be the dominant force in the homeland, they deliberately paint the picture of a Babylonian Diaspora more than willing to make large donations. And the businesses working with the house of Murashu were more of the "middle-class" type. "Like their neighbours, most of the Jews in the Nippur rural area were engaged in agriculture as holders and tenants of small and middle-sized fiefs."[128] But we should point especially to Neh 5:8, according to which there were certainly also Diaspora Jews who were so impoverished that they had fallen into debt slavery to non-Jewish creditors.

These brief bits of information show that the two possible extremes did not exist. Neither was the exiled population so integrated into its Babylonian environment that it lost its Jewish identity, nor did all the exiles return to the homeland. What came into existence was a Judaism with two poles (the Babylonian Diaspora and the Jews in the homeland), though the central position of the Land and Jerusalem was always acknowledged. This was expressed both in religious questions and in the constant possibility of return and in material support from the Diaspora.

The Egyptian Diaspora

For us, the Diaspora in Egypt in the Persian era is almost exclusively the colony at Elephantine, which collapsed soon after 400 as a result of the Egyptian revolts against the Persians beginning in 404.[129] It is true that there may have been Jewish life in other places—compare the numbers in Jer 44:1, and consider the fact that we find a blooming Diaspora later in the Hellenistic period—but we have no further information about it. As different as the Egyptian Diaspora was from the Babylonian, both in its origins and in its type, the two were alike in two respects: an independent economic and social life was developed in a foreign land, and at the same time Jewish identity was retained and concretely expressed in that the Land, and especially Jerusalem, were acknowledged as cultural reference points.

That the Jewish population on the Nile island of Elephantine, at the southern border of the country, assumed a respectable economic position is shown not only by the fact that they were able to afford their own temple,

but also from the papyri to which we owe our knowledge of this military colony. Besides the temple archive, these papyri consist of three family archives (Jedaniah, *TAD* A 4.1–10, and Porten, *Elephantine Papyri in English*, 125-51; Mibtahiah, *TAD* B 2.1–11, and Porten, *Elephantine Papyri in English*, 152–201; Ananiah, *TAD* B 3.1–13, and Porten, *Elephantine Papyri in English*, 202–54). They contain contracts for real estate transactions and wills, marriages, and slave sales, reflecting the activity of an upper class that may have constituted about a fifth of the Jewish population of the colony, which in total is estimated at about three thousand people.[130] In light of the large number of the documents, it is probably no accident that there is no mention of Jewish slaves, either men or women. We could conclude from this that there was a certain level of prosperity among the Jewish population, linked perhaps to the effort not to permit any intra-ethnic slavery (Lev 25:39-46).[131]

There are many expressions of the fact that the Jewish inhabitants of Elephantine, female and male, really had a *Jewish* identity. They call themselves "Jewish women" and "Jewish men" in their documents (*TAD* A 3.8:12; A 4.1:1, 10, and frequently) and thus distinguish themselves from "Aramaeans," although, like the latter, they used Aramaic as their language.[132] Their temple was dedicated to the God Yahu. Even if there were other divinities as well,[133] the fact that in given names only, –*yahu* (a suffix meaning "God") was used as a theophoric element (names like Jedaniah, Mibtahiah, Ananiah)[134] shows that Yahu was the principal god. And finally, in important questions recourse was had to Jerusalem and Samaria, especially the petition for political support for rebuilding the temple on the Nile island and the question about the right way to celebrate the Passover.[135]

Even if the colony in Elephantine collapsed before the end of the Persian period, it confirms the picture of a Judaism that, while it had its center in Jerusalem, knew also of independent groups in Babylon and Egypt. These latter in no way regarded themselves as existing only temporarily in foreign lands; they had settled down to a long-term existence in their respective environments, even though that proved impossible for the Jews of Elephantine.

How should we describe this unique form of Judaism in the Persian era?

Yehud, Samaria, Israel: A Provincial Society in the Persian Period

The description of Israel's social conditions in the Persian era sketched thus far shows that, while some elements of previous epochs were retained—kinship structures as the basis of society, the class conflicts that overlaid and threatened those structures, individual parts of the system of governance—on the whole something new had come into being, something that requires a new conceptual description of this society. Such attempts have, in fact, been made repeatedly since antiquity.

For Flavius Josephus, Israel had preserved since Moses the constitution of a theocracy (Josephus, *Ag. Ap.*2.164–65). For him, divine rule was made concrete in rule by the priests.[136] What is right about that conception is that, if not since Moses, at least from the time of the exile, in light of the absence of a national ruling monarch, the priesthood took on a more important function in the political system and for the nation's identity than was the case in the time of the independent kingdoms. Nevertheless, in the Persian era, in view of the strong lay element of the "nobles" and the Persian power apparatus, exercised in the provinces

mainly through locals, there can be no talk of priestly governance. We will have to examine below the extent to which Josephus' description is accurate for the Hellenistic period.[137]

Lacking the content description of a theocracy, as in Josephus, the description of the Persian era as a time of restoration—see, for example, Peter Ackroyd's title, "The Persian Period. Restoration in Judah,"[138] and many more such[139]—one-sidedly stresses the element of continuity with the monarchical period. What is problematic about this is that the monarchy was *not* restored, either in Judah or in Samaria,[140] and that the temple, for which one could really use this expression with some accuracy in view of its rebuilding, experienced a notable shift in the significance of its sociopolitical function.

The first scholarly attempt in recent times to establish a conceptual scheme for looking at Persian-era Judah in its social shape goes back to Max Weber. The definition in his study of "ancient Judaism" has remained normative for a long time: "The Jewish people were *a purely religious community group*."[141] Here Weber introduces into sociology a conceptual construct whose basis went back in Old Testament scholarship to the work of Julius Wellhausen. The latter saw the exile as the dividing point between "ancient Israel," which was "a people all its own," and "Judaism," which should be called a "religious community"; between the two lay the "distance of two different worlds."[142]

The description of a "religious community group" was meant to express the idea that belonging to this community was a matter of free choice and rested on a religious confession.[143] This does recognize something important. Whereas in the monarchical period, belonging to the people of Israel or Judah naturally occurred from descent and place of

Persian Provinces, Including
Yehud, in the Satrapy of
Beyond the River

- - - - Provincial boundaries

0   30 Miles

N

Sidon

Damascus

DAMASCUS

River Leontes

Tyre

Lake Huleh

ACHZIB

Hazor

KARNAIM

Karnaim

Acco

*Sea of
Galilee*

HAURAN

Mediterranean Sea

GALILEE

River Yarmuk

Dor

Beth-
Shan

Pella

GILEAD

DOR

Samaria

River Jabbok

SAMARIA

River Jordan

Joppa

Ono

Bethel

Rabbath-Ammon

Lod

Mizpah

Jericho

AMMON

Gezer

YEHUD

Heshbon

Ashdod

Jerusalem

ASHDOD

Keilah

Ashkelon

Beth-Zur

Lachish

Hebron

River Arnon

Gaza

En-Gedi

*Dead
Sea*

MOAB

Raphia

Beersheba

IDUMEA
(EDOMITES)

Wadi Zered

NOTE: The names in caps are names of
provinces or independent city-states

10.2. Persian provinces, including Yehud, in the Satrapy of Beyond the River.

residence, this was changed by the deportations. In the Diaspora, people had to confess their Judaism deliberately, which is why the confessional symbols of male circumcision, keeping the Sabbath, and food laws then became essential for building identity. In addition, the movements of peoples that had been undertaken since the Assyrian period added to the problem that individuals joined the people Israel by their own decision and free will, and opinions about how closed (Deut 23:2-9) or open (Isa 56:3-7) the community should be began to differ.[144]

Nevertheless, this does not justify speaking, with Weber, of a *purely* religious community group." The efforts from Josephus to Max Weber have been to emphasize the special character of Israel in the ancient world, and what has been found to be special is Israel's religion. As correct as this may be from the perspective of the history of religions, it is problematic to try to conclude directly from particular religious ideas to a social form of "theocracy" or a "purely religious community group." Instead, I propose that we choose a designation that contains as few pre-formed ideas as possible; the term that suggests itself is "Persian-era provincial society."[145] It was a *provincial* society insofar as it had no independent government but was led by a governor under orders from the central imperial government.[146] Since Yehud and Samaria were two separate provinces, it would be more accurate to say that these were two provincial societies with discernibly different individual profiles. Thus, for Yehud the temple in Jerusalem, as the sole sanctuary, was more influential than for Samaria, where we may suppose there were other sanctuaries besides the one in Jerusalem. For Samaria, on the other hand, it was characteristic that governance of the province lay for

a long time in the hands of a single dynasty, that of Sanballat.

Incidentally, these different characters were typical of the Persian era, since the empire did not attempt uniformity, but incorporated local structures within its system of rule. We have already spoken above about the character of the Persian provinces as a kind of "small states," though under strict Persian overlordship.[147] With Christiane Karrer we may say: "Rather, within the framing conditions of Achaemenid rule the different shaping of individual political units, oriented to their own local traditions, was tolerated."[148] Because Judah and Samaria, as Persian-era provincial societies, were not fundamentally different in their social organization from other provinces of the Persian era, they were able to pursue their own religious paths. But those may not be taken as the starting point for understanding their social character.

Add to this that what can be summarized under the name *Israel* did not cover both provincial societies, Yehud and Samaria, and was not simply identical with them (or one of them). For apart from the fact that members of other peoples, worshiping other gods, lived in both provinces, there was also a strong Diaspora in Persian-ruled Babylon and Egypt, which counted itself as part of Israel and manifested that identity in the worship of YHWH as its God (or, in Elephantine, its principal god).

Here, though, we encounter a semantic problem, and behind it lurks a serious material question. In Babylon the exiles who had come from Judah were, naturally, called "Judahites," ("Jews"), both by the Babylonians[149] and apparently by themselves, as we can conclude from the Nehemiah memorial (which will be discussed further below). We find an ethnic designation for these people in Hebrew and Aramaic that is unfamiliar to older texts:

yehudim, "Jews." As a result of the exile, "Jews" are no longer just the inhabitants of the land of Judah, whom the texts always call "people of Judah" (1 Sam 17:52; 2 Sam 2:4; 1 Kgs 1:9, and in the singular Judg 15:10; 1 Sam 11:8; 15:4; and frequently elsewhere), which can be reproduced in English as "Judeans." "Jews" are all those who understand themselves as descendants of the old Judeans, whether they live in or outside the Land. Even the Jewish inhabitants of Egyptian Elephantine called themselves that, as their documents prove.[150]

The old designation as "Judeans" had two sets of contrasting opposites, less often between the inhabitants of the countryside in contrast to those in the capital city, Jerusalem (2 Kgs 23:2; Isa 5:3; Jer 4:3; and frequently), and more often between the Judahite south and Israel in the north (1 Sam 11:8; 17:52; 2 Sam 19:42; and frequently). The first no longer exists for the expression "Jews." The second, however, continued even in the Persian period in contrast to Samaria. It appears in the Aramaic documents in which the leadership of Samaria denounce the Jews in Jerusalem (Ezra 4:12), and elsewhere in the Aramaic portions of Ezra 1–6. "Jews" also always describes the people of Yehud as distinct from those of Samaria (Ezra 4:23; 5:1, 5; 6:7-8, 14). The designation "Jews" then becomes characteristic of the Nehemiah memorial.[151] Here also it is used pointedly in contrast to Samaria (Neh 3:33-34; 6:6; each time placed on the lips of the Samaritan Sanballat), but then likewise as a general self-description (Neh 1:2; 2:16; 4:6; 5:1, 8, 17; 13:23).

The problem associated with the term "Jews" is apparent if we ask how it relates to the term "Israel."[152] If we juxtapose Neh 1:2 and 2:10, "the Jews" (1:2) are identical with the "people of Israel" (2:10). But alongside this there is also a more comprehensive use of "Israel" in the finished book Ezra-Nehemiah.[153] It appears especially in the religious-cultic context (Ezra 3:11; 7:10, 11; and frequently). Thus there is repeated reference to "the God of Israel" (Ezra 1:3; 3:2; 4:1; and frequently); a "God of Judah" would be utterly unthinkable. When, according to Ezra 6:17, twelve sacrifices for the twelve tribes of Israel are presented at the dedication of the temple, it is evident that "Israel" is more, in this concept, than the inhabitants of the province of Yehud. The members of this "Israel" are thought of as genealogically related; they are "children of Israel" (Ezra 3:1; 6:16, 21; and frequently). By contrast, the "children of Judah" (NRSV "Judahites") in Neh 11:4, 24-25 are members of the tribe of Judah as opposed to the Benjaminites; that is, they are *not* "Jews" in the comprehensive sense that the Nehemiah memorial otherwise assumes.

The tension between the designation as Jews, which in any case excludes the inhabitants of Samaria, and as Israel, which is open, is not resolved in the texts. The reason for this lies in the facts themselves. From a Judahite perspective, there is room for a broader concept of Israel according to which the returned exiles, those who remained in the Land and now join with them, and those still in exile all belong to Israel. This is the concept of Ezra-Nehemiah as a whole.[154] The YHWH-believing inhabitants of Samaria do not belong if they do not accept the leadership claims of the returned exiles. But the Samaritans themselves insist, even after their final separation from Judah, which took place only in the Hellenistic era,[155] that they are "Israel."

Such an "Israel" is an ideal, and here that means it is a religious entity. It can certainly be conceived as genealogical in nature. It is the "children of Israel," according to their twelve tribes, who make up this entity. But, differently from what Max Weber supposed, that does not mean the establishment of a "purely religious community group." Rather, the inhabitants of Yehud together with the Jews of the Diaspora and—according to their own self-understanding—the YHWH-believing population of Samaria made up this ideal Israel. It was held together by genealogical ties, but socially it became a reality in Yehud and Samaria, as two provincial societies that were thoroughly political in their structures.

11

The Jewish Ethnos *in the Hellenistic Age*

KEY POINTS

- Events in the Hellenistic Age:
  - 331: Yehud and Samaria under Alexander the Great's rule
  - 302–200: Ptolemaic rule
  - Five "Syrian wars"
  - 200–141: Seleucid rule
  - 190/189: Exploitation of Palestine by Antiochus III begins.
  - 170-168: Antiochus Epiphanes conquers Jerusalem during sixth Syrian War.
  - Sanctuary next to temple dedicated to Zeus
  - 168: Antiochus outlaws Jewish religion.
  - 167: Judas Maccabeus revolts.
  - 164: Peace treaty
  - 141: Start of the Hasmonean dynasty
  - 63: Seizure of Palestine by the Romans
- The family:
  - Family = basic social structure
  - Clan = social position
  - Endogamous marriage the norm
  - Patriarchal family the ideal
  - Family increasingly weakened
  - Escalating trend toward impoverishment
- Increased social stratification
  - Upper-class use of slaves
  - Development of a monetary economy and conspicuous consumption
  - Increased importance of noble families
  - Three great families: Tobiades, Oniades, Maccabees
- Almsgiving
- Government:
  - Hellenized Near East
  - Greek the lingua franca
  - Centralized rule
  - High priest most important official
  - Jerusalem a Hellenistic *polis*
- The Maccabeans
- The many forms of "Israel"

THERE CAN BE NO FIXED DETERMINATION of which epoch should end a description of Israel's history—including its social history. If we take our starting point as "Israel" in the widest possible sense, its history should, in principle, extend into the present era.[1] Any other decision can only be made on pragmatic grounds.[2] And if we take as the foremost pragmatic reason the time period covered by the Old Testament writings,[3] the Hellenistic epoch must not be treated as a "prospect" or "epilogue,"[4] but as an essential part. For the Hebrew Bible contains the books of Daniel and Qoheleth, which very certainly come from the Hellenistic period, and probably both the Prophets and the Writings in the canon were only completed in that era. Moreover, the Greek writings found in the Old Testament were all written in the Hellenistic epoch. Since both Daniel and the books of the Maccabees extend their accounts into the second century BCE, that must also serve as a pragmatic endpoint for describing Israel's social history.

But first, as always, we need to take a brief look at the history of events.

From Alexander the Great to the Hasmoneans

The history of events in the epochs dominated by the Hellenists in the Near East is clearly structured as a whole, even though sometimes confusing in detail. Anyone who wants an impression of the constant back and forth between the Ptolemies and the Seleucids, the two imperial powers that were of crucial importance for the territory of Israel, needs only to read Daniel 11; treaties and broken treaties, diplomatic marriages and military campaigns are so interwoven that there is almost no way of understanding events without a scorecard.[5] We find a similarly complicated situation when we try to examine the familial relationships in the major families of greatest importance in Jerusalem.[6] But for the purposes of social history such details are of little significance, and so we can be content here to describe the historical evolution of the basic social structures.

The eastern campaign of the Macedonian Alexander the Great, which accomplished its breakthrough in the battle at Issos in 333 BCE, reached its goal when Alexander entered Babylon in 331. The major cities of the Persian empire fell to Alexander without a fight, and he was able to extend his empire as far as India. What the Persians had not succeeded in doing in the fifth century, namely tying their eastern empire to the Greek West, Alexander now accomplished in his advance from the west. But Alexander died in Babylon in 323.

In the wars of the *diadochoi* (successors) in the years 321–302, Alexander's generals fought over his legacy. The unified world empire collapsed. Two empires were established in the East, and these would be the crucial factors in Judaism's future history. In Egypt, with its new capital of Alexandria, founded by Alexander

himself in 331, the Ptolemies came to power, and throughout the third century they exercised control over Palestine. In Syria and Mesopotamia arose the empire of the Seleucids, also with a new capital at Antioch, and in the second century they replaced the Ptolemies as rulers of the southern Levant.

The period of Ptolemaic rule in the third century was an era of political stability and economic prosperity. However, Ptolemaic leadership was never undisputed, so that in the course of the century there were a total of five "Syrian wars" between the Ptolemies and the Seleucids. These contesting constellations of power were reflected in Jerusalem in a struggle between pro-Ptolemaic and pro-Seleucid factions. With their decisive victory in the battle of Paneion, on the southern slope of Mount Hermon, in the year 200, dominance of Palestine shifted to the Seleucids.

At first, the politics of the Seleucid victors were Jerusalem-friendly, but that quickly changed. Antiochus III suffered a severe defeat by Rome in 190/189 and fell into serious financial difficulties, which drove him to more rapaciously exploit his subject peoples. In Jerusalem, the conflicts between the pro-Ptolemaic and the pro-Seleucid factions grew sharper.

In the sixth Syrian War (170–168 BCE), the Seleucid Antiochus Epiphanes captured Jerusalem, and to secure his control he built the Acra there as a military fortress. Its non-Jewish occupying forces naturally had the right to exercise their religion, and they did so right next door to the temple. In the eyes of Torah-observant Jews this desecrated their sanctuary. In this escalating situation, the High Priest Menelaus and the king went a major step further: the temple of YHWH was dedicated to Zeus Olympios; that is, YHWH, the "God of heaven" (Ezra 7:12) was identified

Dates in the Hellenistic Period (BCE)	
336–323	Campaigns of Alexander the Great
320–198	Judea rules by Ptolemies of Egypt
198–164	Judea conquered by Seleucides of Syria
175–164	Antiochus IV Epiphanes
175–168	Hellenistic reform in Jerusalem
168–167	Profanation of temple; Maccabean revolt
164	Rededication of temple by Judas Maccabeus
164–63	Judea independent under Hasmoneans (descendants of the Maccabees)
63	Conquest of Jerusalem by Pompey, Roman general

with the heavenly Baal of Syro-Canaanite religion and the Zeus of the Greek cult. Within the sanctuary itself, an object was placed on the altar of sacrifice that in the eyes of traditional Jews appeared as "an abomination that desolates" (Dan 9:27; 11:31; 12:11; 1 Macc 1:54). In the year 168, in order to exterminate the roots of opposition to the Seleucids and the high priest Menelaus, who was cooperating with them, the Jewish religion was outlawed and non-Jewish cultic practices were ordered to be introduced (1 Macc 1:44-50; 2 Macc 6:1-11).[7]

With that, the cup overflowed. In 167, there was a revolt led by Judas Maccabeus that brought surprising military successes. In 165 Jerusalem and the temple were reconquered and the Acra, where the pagan occupiers were entrenched, was besieged. Although in 164, the Seleucid troops were close to reconquering the Temple Mount, troubles in other parts of the empire led them to abandon the campaign. A peace treaty was reached with the Maccabees. The temple was rededicated and the ancient privileges were guaranteed. Still, the formal Seleucid overlordship was demonstrated by the Seleucid troops who remained in the Acra.

However, this fragile balance of power did not last long. After a change of Seleucid rulers, the Maccabees' revolutionary movement flared up again. In the wake of internal Seleucid quarrels over the throne, the Maccabee Jonathan was able, in 152, to achieve the office of high priest. After his murder, his brother Simon entered upon the office. In 141, he conquered the Acra in Jerusalem, the symbol of Seleucid presence in the city (1 Macc 13:49-52). A year later he had himself installed as high priest by a popular assembly, and no longer by the king. That act meant liberation from Seleucid rule. The Maccabees' revolutionary movement gave birth to the dynasty of the Hasmoneans—so called from the name of one of their ancestors.[8]

Even Simon's murder in 134 did not put an end to their rule; instead, Simon's son John Hyrcanus I, in the course of a thirty-year reign (134–104), was able to extend and stabilize the kingdom. But it was his son and successor Aristobulus I (104–103) who first assumed the title of king. Internal quarrels led to the intervention of the Romans, who seized political power in the land in the year 63 BCE and limited John Hyrcanus II to the office of high priest.

Changes in Society and State

It is characteristic of ancient Israel's social history that the basic structure of social relationships, once created, are maintained while their concrete manifestations continue to change. In general terms, we may distinguish three levels of social relationships, each changing at a different rate of speed. At the base are familial and kinship relationships; these change only very slowly. The class character of the society, which had clearly emerged by the middle of the monarchical period, also remained stable, but the composition of the upper class, in particular, reveals clear changes from the monarchical period through that of the Persian-era provincial society to the Jewish *ethnos* of the Hellenistic epoch. In view of the history of events and the comparatively frequent overturn of the highest governing authorities, it is almost a given that the most obvious changes are to be expected at the level of state structures.

The Family between Ideal and Reality

From the time of Israel's pre-state beginnings, family and kinship relations were the basis of the society. That did not change in the epochs shaped by Hellenism. In the second century, Jesus Sirach warns students of wisdom to maintain the family household by treating all its members well, and sketches the ideal picture of a patriarchal family (Sir 7:18-36). Other parts of this wisdom book develop individual aspects of the family ideal: thus, in 3:1-16 the honor due to father and mother, in 4:1-10 care for the poor, in 9:1-9 a warning against infidelity in marriage, in 30:1-13 the raising and education of sons, in 33:25-33 how to deal with slaves, in 36:20-28 the praise of a clever

and virtuous wife, and in 42:9-14 the way to bring up daughters. When, in 1 Maccabees, the priest Mattathias is addressed as one who is "supported by sons and brothers" (2:17) this shows how the stability and strength not only of the family, but also of the clan determines their social position.[9]

Two Jewish narratives from the Hellenistic era, Judith and Tobit, are practically structured in terms of the family ideal (in Judith, that of widowhood). Tobit also reveals shifts in specific aspects of family life in contrast to earlier epochs, since the family story in this short narrative is situated in the Diaspora. There it is especially important to marry within one's own people (Tob 4:12-13), so that ultimately the goal of the whole narrative is that the couple, Tobias and Sara, who dwell far apart, should come together. Endogamy, or intra-ethnic marriage, discussed earlier regarding mixed marriages in the Land itself during the Persian provincial society period, became the ideal for Diaspora Judaism (see Gen 24:3-4, 37-38; 27:46-28:9).

It is obvious that in this question—as we could already surmise in the Persian era[10]—religious and material grounds were closely allied, since marriage to a non-Jew meant not only that two cults had to be combined in one family, but also that, through inheritance, the property of a Jewish family could fall into foreign hands. The importance of this issue is also clear in the Tobit narrative, where the marriage story is explicitly about the issue of inheritance (Tob 3:15; 6:12).

It is true that both Jesus Sirach and the Tobit narrative present the patriarchal family, with the husband as master of the household and also its public representative, and the wife restricted to the sphere of the house, as the ideal.[11] But both texts allow us to perceive that this ideal is threatened. If we consider additional sources, we see that the weakening of family structures, something already observable in the Persian era,[12] increased sharply in the Hellenistic period. There was danger, of course, not to the family itself, but certainly to the husband's dominance within it, when he was unable to provide food for the family. So, after Tobit's blinding, his wife Hanna must work for pay, receiving money and occasionally food in return, which in turn causes the disabled patriarch to ask suspicious questions (Tob 2:11-14). What the Tobit narrative intimates in its portrayal of the husband,[13] the Wisdom teacher summarizes in a single sentence: "There is wrath and impudence and great disgrace when a wife supports her husband" (Sir 25:22).

Indirectly, Tobit and Jesus Sirach show that only part of the Jewish population was able to realize the ideal of the patriarchal household. Both texts also indicate that one part of the pious patriarch's role was to give alms. They thus take into account that there were hungry and naked people who relied on gifts of food and clothing (Tob 1:17), that there were poor and desperate people who had to live from the alms they received (Sir 4:1-10; 7:10, 32-33; 35:1-2). These were people who had no family structure to rely on. It is very likely that, as always, widows and orphans were among these particularly endangered persons (cf. the explicit mention of them in Sir 4:10).

We have already encountered hungry and naked people in Ezek 18:7, 16 and Isa 58:7, that is, before the Hellenistic period, and therefore we must assume that already in the Persian era there was a clear trend toward impoverishment.[14] Still, we must reckon with an escalation of that trend in the Hellenistic period, for while the region of Yehud and Samaria remained shielded from wars during the two centuries of Persian overlordship, the period

after Alexander's conquest was one of unending warfare. And war means the massive destruction of families. It is reported of Ptolemy I that, after conquering Jerusalem by force, he had Jews deported to Egypt.[15] The meaning of a lost war is expressed in exemplary fashion by a letter from distressed Israelites in the land east of the Jordan to Judas Maccabeus: ". . . all our kindred who were in the land of Tob have been killed; the enemy have captured their wives and children and goods . . ." (1 Macc 5:13). When there was a defeat, even the surviving men were taken into slavery, and only occasionally, when a peace treaty was made later, were those made captive in war released (thus 1 Macc 9:70-72). The text becomes especially dramatic when it describes how the slave dealers traveled with the hostile armies in order to purchase the prisoners (1 Macc 3:41), when in fact the profit from the sale of men and women captured in war is even presented as the goal of the war itself (2 Macc 8:10-11).

Certainly the consequences of the numerous wars influenced individual families differently, depending on their social standing. Poor widows, orphans, and the destitute poor were recruited from the families of the common people. Those who, according to Neh 5:1-13,[16] were on the edge of misery, or those who, according to the Samaritan papyri, had already descended into slavery,[17] were in extreme danger of falling utterly short of all social safety nets when dramatic external influences intervened. It was different for the great families which, though they were affected by external conflicts, on the whole were able to retain their power and even to make economic advances.

Further Intensification of Social Contrasts

The class society that was already developing in the eighth century continued through the

Persian epoch and into Hellenism, just as we would expect. The fact that Sir 7:20-21 counts slaves as part of a patriarchal family as a matter of course, and takes for granted a society divided into poor and rich (Sir 33:25-33; 34:24-27),[18] that Qoheleth makes the contrast between oppressed and oppressors (4:1) and the oppression of the poor (5:7) the object of his considerations and so presumes the opposition between slave workers and the wealthy (5:11) is sufficient evidence of this. That in the Greco-Roman world slavery was much more common than in the Near East, and that with the hellenization of the Near East corresponding attitudes found a home among the eastern upper classes likewise contributed to a sharpening of the contrast.[19]

But what interests us here is not this continuity, which is to be expected, but the social shifts within the upper class. The first striking change is politico-economic in nature. That is, Hellenism was associated with a notable expansion of the money economy. After the introduction of coins, in the Persian era, and the initial minting of a local coinage toward the end of that era, the number of coins in circulation continually increased—not always steadily, but at varying rates of speed.[20]

What is most significant, however, is not this quantitative increase, but the qualitative leap it effected. Qoheleth summarizes the essence of it: "The lover of money will not be satisfied with money" (Qoh 5:10). This expresses in an aphorism the fact that there is no natural measure of satiety in the possession of money. With objects for use or display, the possession of which was formerly the measure of wealth, there are natural upper limits beyond which further accumulation no longer makes sense. Money, on the other hand, because of the abstract value it embodies, is of its very nature without limit.

Traces of the significance of the money economy are everywhere to be found. In the Hellenistic period we hear for the first time that a Jewish family in Alexandria has deposited part of its fortune to be managed and disbursed according to instructions by someone under orders—someone, that is, who acts in the style of "Ptolemaic 'high finance'" (Josephus, *Ant.* 12.200–201).[21] Now the temple was also being used as a deposit bank for the wealthy, who placed their money there for safekeeping (2 Macc 3:11, 15, 22; 4 Macc 4:7). Demands for tribute were a prime factor in international relations (2 Macc 8:10). Seleucid heirs to the throne promised or demanded gigantic sums (1 Macc 10:40; 13:16). Those anticipating elevation to the office of high priest in Jerusalem competed in raising the price of bribes given to the Seleucids (2 Macc 4:23-25).

The second shift in the upper class was the increased importance of the great families. Of course, the existence of important families was not a new phenomenon; toward the end of the monarchical period we could already observe the presence of influential dynasties of officials.[22] In the Persian era in Samaria, the governorship was held tightly by the family of the Sanballatides.[23] Closely associated with them was a certain Tobiah, always called an Ammonite in the Nehemiah memoir and counted among Nehemiah's enemies (Neh 2:10, 19; 4:1; 6:1-14, 17-19; 13:4-9). The family of the Tobiades, who had great influence in the Ptolemaic and Seleucid periods, is probably traceable to him.[24] From the Zenon papyri, between 261 and 252 BCE, we learn that a Tobiah was the commander of a Ptolemaic kleruchy in the Ammanitis.[25] Josephus has an account of his son Joseph and descendants resting on a novelistic narrative about the family.[26] In the second half of the third century, he inherited the *prostasia,* the official representative of the Jewish *ethnos* before the Ptolemaic administration and the office of general agent for taxes.[27] The banking activities in Alexandria mentioned above, and depositing money in the temple at Jerusalem, are traceable to members of the Tobiade family.

Their principal rivals were the Oniades, whose position of power was the office of high priest, which as a rule incorporated the *prostasia*.[28] During the entire Hellenistic period, until the Maccabean revolt, the office of high priest was handed down through the ranks of this family. Menelaus became the first non-Oniade to hold the office, after having seized it (2 Macc 4:23-29), probably relying on the support of the rival Tobiades, and soon thereafter the Maccabean revolt broke out; it put an end to the influence of both families.

At the same time, with the Maccabees a new family dynasty enters the picture. It was true of the Maccabees as of all the great families: they were "supported by sons and brothers" (1 Macc 2:17).[29] We may simply mention, in addition, that sons and brothers were also the weak point of such families. So it was repeatedly the sons of prominent people who had to be given up as hostages (1 Macc 9:53; 10:6, 9; 11:62; 13:16); certainly they did not always come back alive. And brothers (and other close relatives) appear in all the great families as rivals and cause divisions that, on the whole, weakened the power of their families (1 Macc 16:11-17; 2 Macc 4:7-10; Josephus, *Ant.* 12.200–222).

The Institutionalization of Almsgiving

The six Syrian wars in the third century and the first third of the second century, and then above all the Maccabean struggles in the middle third of the second century led, because of all the killing and deportations into slavery, to repeated, acute food supply problems for the survivors. If it is true that once, after a victory, shares of the spoils were distributed to widows and orphans, as 2 Macc 8:28, 30 reports, that was but a temporary solution.

Such occasional aid could not be sufficient because the disruption of the family structures, the traditional social safety net,[30] was not restricted to events in war, but became permanent. Since there were well-to-do families after the fact as well as before, it seems appropriate to draw a balance. What had been attested since Ezek 18:7, 16 as a demand on the righteous, that they give bread to the hungry and clothe the naked, now became stereotypical. It was part of the pious ideal to give alms (Sir 7:10, 32-33; 16:14; 17:22; 29:12; 35:4; 40:17; Tob 1:17; 4:7-8, 15; 12:8).[31]

Of course, giving alms is a form of social support that intensifies and prolongs the poor's dependence on rich donors. In addition, the poor person's receiving alms depends on his or her fate, just as it lies with the arbitrary choice of the wealthy whether they give alms or not. This is probably the reason why the idea arose in Hellenistic Judaism that the institution of alms should be withdrawn, at least in part, from the direct donor-recipient relationships and that a fund should be established at the temple into which the well-to-do could make deposits and from which widows and orphans could be cared for. That is probably how we should understand the phrase in 2 Macc 3:10 that speaks of "deposits belonging to widows and orphans" (and not, as it is often interpreted, deposits made by widows and orphans themselves).[32] Thus the temple, besides being a place of refuge for those overburdened with debt (1 Macc 10:43), derived from its old role as a place of asylum—something that was generally acknowledged in antiquity—became a place for socially supported charitable action.

In the previous section we had to refer repeatedly to certain unique features of the Hellenistic system of governance that formed the frame for social developments in Judaism in that epoch. We must now examine those more closely.

Hellenistic Structures of Government

Since the eighth century, the region of the southern Levant had been subjected to a number of foreign rulers. To that extent, the replacement of the Persian overlordship by that of the Hellenists at the end of the fourth century was nothing new. However, the concrete form and cultural consequences of these new rulers distinguish Hellenistic overlordship very clearly from its predecessors. Even before distinguishing the different structures of the Ptolemaic and Seleucid exercise of power, and without regard to the special developments of interest to Judah, we can list a number of characteristics.

The Macedonian conquest of the east led to a great empire far surpassing that of the Persians in extent. While Assyrians, Egyptians, Babylonians, and Persians retained a base in their respective homelands and exercised their world rule from there, Alexander's successors established their empires in the very heart of the regions they ruled. Moreover, an active economic exchange and Greek settlement in the newly conquered lands—with the Greek cities, as *polis,* retaining an independent political structure—led to a genuine Hellenization of the Near East. This was strikingly evident in the architecture, in which Greek forms dominated (alongside a quasi-historical revival of local building traditions). It was most obvious in the dominance of the Greek language, which replaced Aramaic as the *lingua franca* of diplomacy and trade and also gained an increasing dominance in literature. Most significant for religious development were the tendencies to a homogenization of the religious cosmos. This was accomplished by identifying local divinities according to their functions and characteristics (for example, Baal = Zeus) and then led to a delocalizing of cults, which then expanded throughout the *oikoumenē,* the civilized (that is, Hellenized) world—the Isis mysteries, the Mithras cult, Christianity—so that ultimately the Hellenization of the East turned back on the West in the form of orientalization.

Despite the Greek presence in the East, obviously the long-settled local peoples remained in place. The Greeks called them *ethnoi.* Belonging to an *ethnos* bestowed a certain legal status. Around the turn of the era, the geographer Strabo described the situation this way: Syria was inhabited by Coele-Syrians, Syrians, and Phoenicians, and "mixed" with them were the *ethnoi* of the Judeans, Idumeans, Gazans, and Azotans.[33] In this sense, documents contained in the books of the Maccabees speak of the "*ethnos* of the Jews" (1 Macc 8:23, 27; 13:36; see also, 2 Macc 11:25).

Hellenism brought an economic and cultural flowering to the East, and local elites also succeeded in participating. But others—and there is every reason to believe that they speak for the mass of the people—experienced it as the most brutal form of foreign rule thus far. According to the vision of Dan 7:2-7, the fourth beast from the sea, symbolizing Greek rule, surpassed its three predecessors in its hideousness. And for the Egyptian Oracle of the Potter, the period of Hellenism was the time when "the sun was darkened."[34]

Against the background of this general line of development, however, the concrete governmental structures of the Ptolemaic and

Seleucid empires were differently applied to the Jewish people.

The Ptolemaic Kingdom and Central Administration

The most striking difference between Ptolemaic rule and that of the Persians was that the central weight of political decision-making was shifted from the province to the capital. The province of Syria and Phoenicia was administered directly from Alexandria by the *dioikētēs,* a kind of minister of economics and finance.[35] Within the larger province there were smaller units, hyparchies and toparchies, whose size corresponded approximately to the Persian provinces and districts. For the region that interests us, these were Judea, Samaria, Galilee, Idumea, and Ashdod. Within the hyparchies, which were inhabited by the local *ethnoi,* lay the Greek colonies with their *polis* status as well as newly established, special status royal domains.

This structure of government had a number of consequences for social conditions within the Jewish population. The shift of power to the center accorded still greater weight to the office of the high priest. If it could be said that in the Persian era "in post-exilic Judah the 'second man' after the *pachah* ["governor"] was the high priest,"[36] now, with no governor resident on site, he took the first place. He assumed the *prostasia,* the representation of the Jewish *ethnos,* before the Ptolemies.[37] Since the high priestly office was inherited, at the latest since the Persian era, it took on features of the pre-exilic Judahite monarchy.[38] It is no wonder that there were bitter struggles for possession of this important office (Josephus, *Ant.* 12.237–41; 2 Macc 4:7-10, 23-29; 5:5-10; and frequently).

The shifting power relationships in Judea can be clearly discerned in the prescripts to official letters. While in the Persian era, the Jews of Elephantine addressed their letter to Judea's Persian governor and, under him, the high priest with his priestly colleagues and Ostanes and the Jewish nobility,[39] now an official Jewish letter to Sparta is sent by the following: "The high priest Jonathan, the senate (*gerousia*) of the nation (*ethnos*), the priests, and the rest of the Jewish people (*dēmos*)" (1 Macc 12:6). The comparison shows that in the Hellenistic period the high priest had the position that had been occupied by the governor in the Persian era; from being the head of the college of priests, he has become the primary representative for the Jewish community.

Otherwise, however, the leadership structure remained amazingly stable. Under the high priest stood the two representatives of the laity and the priesthood. However, it is not entirely clear whether these were always two distinct bodies, since occasionally the listing of the Jewish authorities gives only the elders (1 Macc 13:36) or *gerousia* (2 Macc 1:10; 11:27), without mention of a college of priests, which could permit the conclusion that the priesthood supported its interests as part of the *gerousia.*[40] But since in other places the elders or *gerousia* and the priesthood are both listed (1 Macc 7:33; 11:23; 12:6; 14:20; Josephus, *Ant.* 12.142, 166), we must suppose that for a long period, at any rate, two bodies existed alongside one another.[41] Only in the Roman era, then, did the Sanhedrin become the highest organ, with priesthood and laity both represented in it.

Last in the lists stood the "people." They are called "the (remaining) *dēmos* of the Jews" (1 Macc 12:6; 14:20; 15:17), and once also "the *ethnos* of the Jews" (1 Macc 13:36). But nothing speaks of an active political role for the popular assembly, so we may suppose that the practical insignificance of the people's assembly, already observable in the Persian era,[42] continued in the Hellenistic epoch.[43]

If the advancement of the high priestly office followed a trend already established in the Persian epoch, tax farming represented a new institution that would have profound consequences for the social and political fabric.[44] From the Tobiade novel Josephus inserts into his *Antiquities*,[45] we see graphically how a member of the Jewish upper class purchases the collectorship and so attains wealth and power, until he takes the right of the *prostasia* from the Oniades.[46]

Even if the members of the Jewish upper class, whether Oniades or Tobiades, presented their activity as a blessing for the Jewish people (Josephus, *Ant.* 12.224–226), their collaboration with the Ptolemies meant, practically speaking, participating in exploiting the population. The explosive force of this development, however, revealed itself only after the mastery of Judah passed from the Ptolemies to the Seleucids.

The Seleucids and the Establishment of Jerusalem as a Polis

The transition from Ptolemaic to Seleucid rule did not represent a sharp cleft in the internal Jewish fabric. There were, of course, deep differences within the upper class that expressed themselves in bribery and murder, with multiple overlaps between the various factions (pro-Ptolemaic and pro-Seleucid) and families (Oniades and Tobiades). But it is not out of line to see a need for accommodation to the new Hellenistic framework of circumstances as the common interest of the upper class.

When, in 175 BCE, the Oniade Jason obtained the high priesthood (by payment of an eye-popping amount as a bribe to the new king Antiochus IV Epiphanes; 2 Macc 4:8), he obtained for Jerusalem the right to transform itself into a *polis*, with the same rights as the city of Antioch (2 Macc 4:9).[47] With this, Jerusalem emerged from the little-regarded status of an oriental *ethnos* to assume the privileged position of a Hellenistic *polis*. The citizens of this *polis* became equal members of the political leadership class of the Seleucid empire.

In obtaining a *polis* constitution for Jerusalem, the Hellenists were pursuing their goal of tearing down the barriers and hindrances that separated them from their non-Jewish environment. Food prohibitions obstructed the table fellowship without which contracts could not be made. The law against mixed marriages prevented the marital alliances by which great families were linked together. And the prohibition of commerce on the Sabbath was a direct attack on economic interests. If all that were eliminated, the Jewish upper class could integrate itself seamlessly into the fabric of Hellenistic society.[48]

But the price was high, for in fact the *polis* constitution delegitimized the Torah's socio-ethical demands. Apart from all its individual provisions, its core was the idea of a unified people in which all, because of descent from a common ancestral line (Abraham, Isaac, and Jacob), were brothers and sisters—from the slave woman or slave man to the king (Deut 15:12 with 17:15, 20). Even if that ideal was never a reality, the abandonment of it as a norm meant the open acknowledgment of a class society in which a few could participate in power while the mass of the people were subordinated to them. This division was strikingly evident in the fact that membership in the *polis* was no longer established genealogically,

11.1. Tetradrachma of Antiochus IV Epiphanes (175–163 BCE), Seleucid king of Syria who, by his persecution in Judea, provoked the Maccabean revolt (167 BCE). Israel Museum (IDAM), Jerusalem. Photo © Erich Lessing/Art Resource, N.Y.

but through enrollment in a list of citizens (2 Macc 4:9), even though it was not clear how one obtained the right to be enrolled. But the erection of a gymnasium, with its associated *ephēbeion* (theater structure), in Jerusalem (1 Macc 1:14; 2 Macc 4:9, 12), pointed to the deliberate establishment of a Hellenistically oriented elite.

The consequence of these efforts was civil war and civil unrest in Jerusalem, in which people from outside the city joined in rejecting the temple leadership (2 Macc 4:39-40). At the same time, the various factions within the upper class staged bloody conflicts (2 Macc 5:5-7). Antiochus IV's prohibition of the Jewish religion and introduction of non-Jewish cultic acts was the last straw. Open revolt broke out.

From the Maccabees to the Hasmoneans

The Maccabean revolt, which began in the year 167, had numerous religious and political aspects that cannot be treated here. In the framework of social history it must suffice to sketch a few lines of development.

The revolt was sustained by the rural population together with people who had fled to the countryside from Jerusalem (1 Macc 2:29–31, 43; 2 Macc 5:17). It was led by members of a lesser priestly family resident in Modein, in the hill country northwest of Jerusalem and called "Maccabees" (probably "hammer") after Judas's *nom de guerre* (1 Macc 2:1–6). They succeeded in bringing ideological unity to the revolutionary movement and leading it to military success by the application of guerrilla tactics.

In terms of its social basis and goals the Maccabean revolt was a conservative movement directed against the modernization of society within the framework of Hellenistically influenced ideas. In the eyes of the revolutionaries their opponents were those who "have forsaken the law/abandoned the holy covenant" (1 Macc 1:11, 15, 52), while they themselves held fast to the "religion of their ancestors" and the "covenant of our ancestors" (1 Macc 2:19–20). Equivalent to that contrast was that the opponents wanted to "make a covenant with the Gentiles around us" and to "observe the ordinances of the Gentiles" (1 Macc 1:11, 13), while the revolutionaries did not regard it as a negative accusation that they had "separated from" the Gentiles (1 Macc 1:11).

However, the contrast between keeping the old versus modernizing, or separating from the Gentiles versus uniting with them, remained empty of content. What gave the revolt its power was that the traditional and non-Greek was also understood as what was good for the lower classes of the nation.[49] This is evident from the fact that the Maccabean revolt's own self-concept incorporated the ancient ideals of *mishpat* and *tsedaqa,* with their content of social equality, which from this point of view had been betrayed by the Hellenists (1 Macc 2:29; cf. the hymn to Simon Maccabeus in 1 Macc 14:6–15). With this view, the popular assembly gained a new weight.[50] At the beginnings of the struggle it was the sole organ, together with the Maccabean leaders and the fighters, that could approve decisions (1 Macc 4:59; 5:16). Ultimately the popular character of the revolution was also evident from the fact that the traditional priesthood, which was suspected of being too friendly to Hellenism, was deposed. The Maccabees themselves came from a rural priestly clan. And for the rededication of the temple after the (preliminary) conclusion of peace with the Seleucids in the year 163 priests were expressly chosen who were considered faithful to the Torah (1 Macc 4:42).

It is important for the question of the social basis of the Maccabean revolt that besides the rural population, those who had fled from Jerusalem, and the Maccabees as leaders, there is mention of another group that played an independent role throughout: the so-called Hasideans (1 Macc 2:42). When the revolt broke out

in 167 they joined the Maccabees, but after the first, successful phase leading to the rededication of the temple, they were prepared in 162 to recognize Alcimus as high priest. He, however, perpetrated a genuine bloodbath among their ranks (1 Macc 7:12–18), probably because he saw them as the crucial support of the Maccabean movement (2 Macc 14:6). We will examine this group in more detail later, because in them we can recognize the phenomenon of an organized and visible distinction and separation within the one Israel.[51] This much, however, must be said at this point: The Hasideans were a religious movement that assumed its own organizational form. The fact that they appear as an important internal political factor in dealings with the high priest and the Seleucid generals (1 Macc 7:12–13) shows that they were by no means apolitical or marginalized in the eyes of the rulers.

The Maccabean revolutionary movement was part of a comprehensive resistance to the Hellenization of the East extending from Egypt through Judah and into Persia.[52] This resistance movement combined religious, economic, and political motives; because in each case the national and religious identity was at stake, however, in the nature of things there was no alliance among the oppositional movements. Among oriental resistance movements, the Judaic was one of the most successful because it succeeded in mobilizing the rural population together with dissatisfied parts of the population of the city of Jerusalem, because it had in the Maccabees a political and military leadership that was skillful in exploiting the weaknesses of the Seleucids, and because in the Hasideans, at least in the initial phase, it had the support of an intellectual group that gave the struggle a "theological legitimacy" and "religious language."[53]

And yet, despite its external success, the Maccabean revolt ultimately failed, not externally but from within, inasmuch as the Maccabean rulers accommodated themselves to the Hellenistic type. An initial turning point occurred in 152 with the naming of Jonathan as high priest. Now the leaders of the revolt themselves possessed the highest office in Jewish society. After the murder of Jonathan the people transferred the dignity of high priest to his brother Simon; with this the Jewish people replaced the Seleucid king, who had appointed Jonathan, as the highest authority (1 Macc 14:25–48).[54] The extent to which Hellenistic practices with regard to authority shaped these relationships is evident from the attempt of Simon's son-in-law Ptolemy to attain power by murdering the high priest and two of his sons (1 Macc 16:11–17). With the rule of Simon's son John Hyrcanus I (134–104), and then finally under his successor Aristobulus I (104–103), the anti-Hellenistic revolutionary movement became, once and for all, a Hellenized oriental kingdom. Consequently, Aristobulus assumed the title of king (Josephus, *Ant.* 13.301). If we were to apply the label of "theocracy" to an epoch of post-exilic Judaism at all,[55] it would best fit the epoch of the Hasmoneans.[56] In that case "theocracy" would *not* mean "rule by priests," but the identification of the offices of king and high priest.

The Many Forms of "Israel"

The documents of the Hellenistic period continually speak of the "Jewish people" or "the nation of the Jews" (1 Macc 8:23, 25, 27, and frequently elsewhere),[57] or simply of "the Jews" (1 Macc 8:31; 10:23, 29, and frequently). These expressions have their roots as early as the Persian era[58] and reflect the correct legal

terminology. Alongside them we still find references to "Israel," designating the ideal religious unit, since of course the "people called by your name" is Israel (Sir 36:17), and naturally the service of the priests is done for the "whole congregation of Israel" (Sir 50:13, 20). Likewise, Antiochus's religio-political measures were not directed at the legal unit of the "nation of the Jews," but against the religious entity "Israel" (1 Macc 1:20, 25, 30, and frequently elsewhere).

The problem of the identity of "Israel" that thus arises, however, takes on a new dimension, for besides the problem that had existed since the monarchical period, namely the relationships between North and South, Israel and Judah, Samaria and Jerusalem, and the enduring tension, since the exile, between the Israel in the Land and that in the dispersion, other distinctions were now added, as a consequence of which solid groups arose to dispute their claims to the right to be called "Israel." But since these developments were only partially important for social history and also touched the Old Testament writings only to a limited extent, we can content ourselves here with a brief sketch.

The separate development of Samaria

The tensions between Samaria and Jerusalem that marked the Persian era continued in the Hellenistic epoch.[59] The building of a temple on Gerizim probably happened at the very beginning of this era.[60] There is a good probability that its priesthood came from Jerusalem and had left the temple there because of internal disagreements.[61] Thus it is clear that it was the God of Israel who was worshiped on Gerizim also, and it is very questionable whether the notion of "schism"[62] can rightly be applied to this event, since it presupposes an overarching organization from which the "heretics" could separate, conditions that elude the social form of Israel in the Hellenistic period. We should note that, in addition to the temple in Jerusalem and that on Gerizim, there were other YHWH sanctuaries, namely, in the fifth century the one in Elephantine, then the temple built by the Tobiade Hyrcanus east of the Jordan around 200 BCE,[63] and finally the one built in Egyptian Leontopolis by Onias IV around the middle of the second century.[64] They were all thought to be sanctuaries of the God of Israel.

That the tensions between North and South stemming from the monarchical period continued and intensified is one side of the development. Symptomatic is Jesus Sirach's rejection of the "foolish people that live in Schechem" (Sir 50:25–26).[65] Parts of Samaria were conquered in the Maccabean revolt and placed under the rule of Jerusalem (1 Macc 10:38; 11:34). From that time on the mutual polemic grew louder, as is especially evident from Josephus (*Ant.* 9.288–291). But the other side is that the inhabitants of the land of Samaria understood themselves to be Israelites.[66] They kept the Torah;[67] indeed, for them the five books of Moses constituted the whole of sacred scripture. In their own interpretation they were anything but a branch that split off from Judah, but rather the legitimate heirs of the Israel from which, in the pre-state period, Judah had split away.[68] Likewise, the Jewish polemic that attempts to shove the Samaritans into a Gentile corner does not quite compute. There is, for example, a significant formulation in 1 Macc 3:10, according to which the army of the Seleucids includes "Gentiles" and people "from Samaria" who fight "against Israel." "Israel" here means only "Judah." But the people from Samaria are not simply identi-

cal with the Gentiles, either; they have to be named in addition. And according to 2 Macc 6:2 the desecration of YHWH's temple by Antiochus Epiphanes affects not only Jerusalem, but also the temple on Gerizim, which indirectly confirms that, even from the viewpoint of this source, the God of Israel is worshiped on Gerizim.

If we do not, as is usual in Jewish and Christian versions of the "history of Israel," unreflectingly take the side of the—historically speaking—unequally influential Jewish way, we must maintain that "Israel" in the Hellenistic period was embodied not only by the Jewish community around the Jerusalem temple, but also by the Samaritans, whose temple stood on Gerizim. However, and to this extent the common view from the Jewish perspective is correct, even then the importance of Jerusalem was unequally great. The following distinctions, for which the central position of Jerusalem is unquestioned, show that.

The Hellenistic Diaspora

What began with the exiles of the eighth to sixth centuries was transformed in the Persian era, and finally and more definitively in the Hellenistic period, into the Jewish Diaspora, which extended into large parts of the ancient world. In contrast to exile, as a forced collective deportation, diaspora meant a dispersion, originally attributable to external compulsion, but extended for economic, political, and personal reasons. Certainly to speak of a Diaspora presupposes a constitutive awareness of Jewish identity, with Jerusalem and the land of Judah as essentially the center in which, however, the dispersed people did *not* live. Without that awareness we would have to speak of assimilation, to the point of loss of the original identity.[69]

While the exiles in the Babylonian period first directed people to particular places within Babylonian territory, in the Seleucid empire the Diaspora spread to different centers. The Tobit narrative illustrates—in a fictional milieu of the late eighth century—how Jewish families lived far apart in cities of the eastern empire by locating the protagonists in Assyrian Nineveh and in Rages and Ecbatana in Media.[70] In other places, and not in a fictional context, the presence of a Jewish community is attested in one of the newly founded Hellenistic centers, the Seleucid metropolis of Antioch (2 Macc 4:36).

The Egyptian Diaspora, attested since the late monarchical period and created by a variety of circumstances,[71] enjoyed a powerful development in the Hellenistic epoch. In particular, the Jewish community in the newly founded capital city of Alexandria had great political, economic, cultural, and religious significance for all Judaism. The close political and economic ties to Alexandria, which during the third century was the proximate capital and administrative center for Jerusalem and Judah, was already illustrated by the role of the Tobiades, who were deeply involved in political and financial matters in Alexandria.[72] However, it would be a distortion of reality if one were to conclude from the Tobiades and a few other wealthy families to the overall social condition of Jews in Ptolemaic Egypt. The abundant papyrus material, in fact, yields a different picture: ". . . the majority of the Jewish people in Egypt was not rich and had no connexion with trade or money-lending."[73] "Jews served and worked everywhere, in every branch of the economic life of the country, as soldiers and policemen, tax-farmers and state officials, as tillers of the soil, artisans, and merchants."[74]

The transfer of rule over Jerusalem to the Seleucids by no means put an end to the significance of the Egyptian Diaspora. There is a great deal of documentation to show the importance of second-century Alexandria, the center of Jewish life, for the development of the entity that regarded itself ideally as Israel. We may mention the translation of the Wisdom writing of Jesus Sirach into Greek, two letters to "the Jews in Egypt" placed at the beginning of Second Maccabees (2 Macc 1:1–19; 1:11–2:18), the so-called *Letter of Aristeas*, which gives a legendary account of the origins of the Greek translation of sacred scripture,[75] and of course the translation of the whole Bible, the Septuagint. The fact that in this way Greek thought entered into Israel can be illustrated from the Septuagint itself and is later obvious in the work of such authors as Philo of Alexandria or Flavius Josephus.

As dispersed as the Jewish Diaspora was in the Hellenistic era, it clearly always maintained its identity as a *Jewish* community. This identity was, on the one hand, sustained by its spiritual center, the Torah of Moses. Its central symbols—from the time of the exile onward[76]—were male circumcision, the Sabbath, and the food laws. The sometimes intense discussions of these symbols—for circumcision, cf. 1 Macc 1:15, 60–61, for the Sabbath 1 Macc 2:31–41, and for the food laws 1 Macc 1:62–63—indicate only their significance for supplying identity. There is a simple but very impressive business papyrus from the third century from Egyptian Fayûm. It contains a numbered list of deliveries of bricks for a building belonging to the *dioikētēs* Apollonius, that is, the highest imperial official. For every day around a thousand bricks are noted. But under "7" the entry reads: "Sabbath."[77]

The second "center" that preserved the identity of the Diaspora was Jerusalem.[78] If we consider only the state of things in the Land, in the Persian and Hellenistic periods Samaria had a position quite comparable to that of Judah and Jerusalem. It was above all the Diaspora that made the superior religious weight of Jerusalem into an absolute monopoly, beside which Samaria shrank to the dimensions of a local phenomenon.

The Multiplicity of the One Israel

Alongside the diverging paths of Jerusalem and Samaria, and together with the tense relationship between the spiritual-religious center at Jerusalem and the Diaspora, there is visible in the Hellenistic era a third process of differentiation whose beginnings can be traced to the Persian period. Attempts have been made to describe it with phrases such as party building or sect building.[79] Both terms are problematic, the first because it makes us think of political groups and the second because it presupposes an orthodoxy that did not exist at this period.

Nevertheless, these terms are attempts to grasp real phenomena that require explanation. Let us begin in the field of social differentiation. This commenced in the monarchical period and was increasingly intense after the Persian era. What is striking in later texts, especially in individual psalms and in the prophets, is the contrast between entities that appear as fixed groups. In Isa 29:19–21 these are the needy and poor on the one hand and the tyrants, scoffers, evildoers, and lawbreakers on the other. Zephaniah 3:11–12 contrasts the humble and the lowly with the exultant proud. In Psalm 12 the needy and the poor are at the opposite pole from the wicked. In other texts the poor appear as "the meek of the earth" (ᶜanwe haᵓaretz; Isa 11:4; Amos 8:4; Zeph 2:3; Job 24:4), an expression that could make us think of a defined group. Likewise, the lament that the "godly" (Ps 12:2) have perished, or that the "devout" are taken away (Isa 57:1) can suggest fixed entities. The latter expressions ultimately lead to the observation that in the field of sayings about the poor we also encounter formulations that qualify these poor in religiously positive terms, for example as those "who fear YHWH" or "who seek YHWH" (Ps 34:10–11).

Whereas in previous scholarship it had been concluded that there was a genuine "party" of the poor,[80] recently it has become more common to speak somewhat reticently of a "piety of the poor," that, however, can be socially located in "lower-class circles."[81] That, too, has been disputed.[82] What is correct here is the indication that terms describing "poverty" could also be used by people who were not materially poor, in the sense of a religious self-description. Nevertheless, it would be too sweeping an argument to reverse everything by completely spiritualizing every contrast between poor and wicked, or all group designations of the poor and the devout, robbing them of all material content. We must maintain that the hardening of social oppositions from the Persian period onward had led to the rise of a consciousness in the poorer classes of the population in which the self-description "poor" was used in a positive sense. When that was linked to a religious self-concept of being especially close to God it contained at least the kernel of a socio-religiously motivated separateness.

When the word "devout," from the Hebrew root *chsd,* appears alongside "poor" (Isa 57:1; Ps 12:2; cf. also 1 Sam 2:9; Mic 7:2; Ps 31:24, and elsewhere), it leads us directly to the "group of the Hasideans" (*synagōgē; Hasidaiōn,* from

Hebrew *chasidim*), whom we met in connection with the Maccabean revolt.[83] What little we can learn of them shows them to have been primarily a religious movement. The name *chasidim*, i.e., "devout," or "faithful," is a religious designation. The characterization of them as loyal to the Torah (1 Macc 2:42) points in the same direction. In addition, we can take with confidence from the references to them that the Hasideans represented a defined group, a *synagōgē*. In 1 Macc 7:12–13 it is probable that the Hasideans are to be seen as either identical to or a subgroup of the "group of scribes" (*synagōgē*; *grammateōn*). We cannot gain any ultimate certainty about the social position of the Hasideans. Their political activity at the highest level shows, in any case, that they were not a "lower-class circle," even though by their designation as "devout" they are rendered terminologically close to the piety of the poor. Whether the reverse is possible, that the Hasideans should be identified as "the core of the devout *upper class*"[84] seems questionable. We must rather think, if we are using modern sociological categories, not of their identity, but instead of their social function; this consists in giving a "social group" its "homogeneity and awareness of its proper function."[85]

What is crucial for our question regarding differentiation within the one body of Israel is that with the "group of the Hasideans" in the second century we can for the first time recognize a defined group that is characterized primarily by its religious attitude. It has an independent form of organization, a sustaining social group; it engages itself programmatically for a particular religious interest; and it acts independently in religio-political affairs. At the same time the three references to the group all maintain that its members are "of Israel" (1 Macc 2:42), "among the Israelites" (1 Macc 7:12), or "of the Jews" (2 Macc 14:6).

The one large entity, Israel, is made concrete in a group that is different from others and yet, together with them, constitutes the ideal Israel.

There has been much discussion of the question to what extent the Hasideans are identical with the "wise" in Daniel 11–12. Of them it is said that they "give understanding to many" or "lead many to righteousness" (Dan 11:33, 35; 12:3, 10).[86] Like the Hasideans in the books of the Maccabees, they are in opposition to the Hellenistic tendencies of their time ("those who violate the covenant" in Dan 11:32), and they sympathize with the Maccabean revolt, which, however, they see as only "a little help" (Dan 11:34). If we suppose that Daniel 11–12 was composed at the time of the Maccabean revolt, whereas the books of the Maccabees are already looking back at it from a distance, we can understand the Hasideans as "successors"[87] to those "wise" who were the custodians of the Daniel tradition.

What is visible in the constellation of Daniel 11–12 and then, retrospectively, in the description in the books of the Maccabees, will shape the subsequent epoch of Judaism, namely the creation of well-established movements that also constitute themselves as defined organizations, but without surrendering their claim to be "Israel." In a social history of Israel restricted to the period of the Old Testament writings it is enough simply to list these. We can see the independence of such groups in the cases of the Essenes, the Pharisees, and the Sadducees. The Essenes and the Pharisees may represent distinct groups within the movement that was still a single entity at the beginning of the second century, the Hasideans,[88] whereas the Sadducees were the successors to the priestly group who at that time reveal a close alliance with Hellenism.

Besides such entities that can be perceived as groups in themselves, we find in the Hellenistic and later Roman epochs a multitude of religious movements that were probably always only partly identical with particular groups. These extend from the Torah-oriented piety reflected, for example, in Psalm 119, through the philosophy of a Qoheleth, to apocalyptic movements that found a place in the Old Testament canon, above all in Daniel. We can scarcely expect to find sharp distinctions among the various paths.

In naming these last groups and movements, we have already passed beyond the time period covered by the writings of the Old Testament, especially the Bible written in Hebrew. But there is plenty of evidence that the roots of such separate movements reach back into the Old Testament. We have already pointed to group designations surrounding the "piety of the poor." Conflicts with regard to the temple, which led to clear and manifest divisions, are indicated by passages like Isa 66:5, which speaks of "brothers" [NRSV: "your own people] who "hate you and reject you." And the prehistory of the division into Essenes, Pharisees, and Sadducees certainly includes the tension-filled history of the priests and Levites at the beginning of the Second Temple era.[89]

Despite all these differences, enmities, and mutual condemnations, we must not forget that all these groups and movements always identified themselves with Israel. To that extent the internal distinctions were no different from the geographically definable developments in Samaria, on the one hand, and in the Diaspora on the other. These, too, were developments within the ideal entity "Israel." Later, early Christianity would arise as a movement within Israel, even though very quickly, with its claim to be "the true Israel," it would take its place.

But that is a story that begins beyond the limits of the Old Testament writings.

Conclusion

ON THE BASIS OF OUR SELF-IMPOSED limitation, to restrict our study to the period covered by the Old Testament writings, our consideration of Hellenism brings us to the end of our journey through ancient Israel's social history. All that remains is a look backward and a look forward.

The look backward addresses a twofold question: first, whether we have been able to observe continuing features in Israel's social history that transcend epochs; second, the problem of identifying the entity called "Israel," the issue we addressed at the very beginning. But now to the first question!

Trans-epochal Features of Israel's Social History

In fact, our examination of Israel's social history has revealed continuing, epoch-transcending features. The first observation comes from comparing the biblical depiction of events with historical sources contemporary to the period discussed in the biblical text. The biblical view of events is characterized by a twofold tendency: it sharply delineates epochs, and it personalizes the transitions between epochs. This is true even of the period that can no longer be historically verified in any way. The ancestral period is supposed to have begun with Abraham's migration. The beginnings of the people in Egypt constitute the next major division. The transition from the wilderness wandering to the entry into the Land is associated with the transition from Moses to Joshua. Samuel establishes the kingship in the shortest possible time. In the late monarchical period, Josiah carries out a far-reaching reform. Cyrus's edict ends the exile, which had begun with the destruction of Jerusalem. Finally, Ezra promulgates the Torah in a solemn act, and from then on the Torah is in force for the Jewish community.

From a modern historical view, in contrast, the transitions between historical time periods are generally fluid, and individual persons play only a subordinate role. The development of Israel as a nation is a complicated process extending over some two centuries. Taking possession of the Land, in the proper sense, is only *one* phenomenon in this process. The monarchy does, of course, begin at a particular time, but it develops over about two hundred years into a mature state. At the same time there begins a process of class division that never ends. Exiles begin as early as the eighth century, and life in the Diaspora by no means ends with Cyrus. Even the promulgation of the Torah, while it may have had an important fixed point in the work of Ezra, was on the whole a process that required a long period of time. And in all these transitions we observe that as a rule there was not just *one* cause behind the change; epochal changes tend to be multi-causal in nature.

Still, it would be wrong to use these observations to negate dividing historical epochs according to social phenomenoa. In fact, the periods of Israel's origins, statehood, the rise of a class society, the exiles, the Persian-era provincial society, and the Hellenistic *ethnos*, which underlie social historical description from material remains, can indeed be sharply separated from each other. What in turn makes that separation permeable, however, leads us directly to another observation.

It is typical of Israel's social history that social structures and institutions, once created, tend to be retained, while at the same time changing their basic form. If I call the first epoch in Israel's social history a kinship-based society, that does not mean that in its subsequent forms kinship no longer constituted the basis of social relationships. Israel's kinship-based society only changed its form and was overlaid and altered by other social institutions and developments—the state, the widening divisions between classes, existence in foreign lands or under foreign rule. It is true that Israel's own monarchy was restricted to a single epoch, but certain forms of the participatory monarchy established in Judah were retained in an altered form in the Persian and Hellenistic periods. The conflict between the Israelite north and the Judahite south persisted into the Hellenistic epoch. The development into a class society continued without interruption from the eighth century onward. The forced exiles beginning in the eighth century led to Israel's existence in the Diaspora, something that continues even today. And the Torah, created in a long process, became, once it was generally accepted, Israel's unifying bond understood not only genealogically, but also religiously, that is as a religion as we conceive of one today.

This phenomenon of continuity through change is one of the conditions for the persistence of Israel's identity through time. But not all elements were equally important for maintaining the consciousness of its self identity.

Israel's Identity

Let me recall once more at this point the words of Philip Davies: "The modern 'British' are not the Britons of the Roman period, and mostly not descended from them. . . ."[1] He is using discontinuities to dispute the identity of "Israel" in general. But a glance beyond the object of historical description shows that the exclusive contrast between identity and discontinuity that Davies posits does not exist. The human body remains identical with itself, even though all its cells are replaced within a certain time period. A human being remains herself or himself even if her or his character, way of life, appearance, and customary dress are altered. And likewise there is a continuity between the Britons, if not of the Roman, then certainly of the Victorian era and those of today, even though these are not the same people. The fact of change alone is not yet an argument against identity.

The examples show that living historical existence always has two sides, identity and change. If we look at the social history of Israel in the time period we have examined, three principal marks of identity can be named: a genealogically construed sense of belonging, expressed in the name "Israel"; worship of the God YHWH, who is believed to have bound himself to this people; and finally the possession of the Land, the importance of which was apparent precisely at the point when it was no longer the routine expectation that all the people of Israel lived there. None of these characteristics remained unchanged in the course of the centuries, and their effectiveness in establishing identity may well have been different in the individual epochs. But there was no epoch in which they were not present in some form or other.

Noteworthy and by no means a matter of course was that existence as a state was not among Israel's continuing characteristics. Even if the desire to be an independent state never altogether vanished from the time of the monarchy onward, and was even realized at the end of the Hellenistic epoch, nevertheless Israel did not lose its identity even under the conditions of exile and foreign rule.

But there is another side to identity-in-change that developed increasingly throughout the social history of Israel. For the same characteristics that constitute the identity of a social entity can also cause separation and evoke centrifugal tendencies. In the life of Israel and Judah as neighbors from the monarchical period onward, in the social divisions that can be observed in the eighth century, in the conflicts and divisive ideological trends and groupings of the Persian and Hellenistic eras, the question was always: who, exactly, belongs to Israel? It is precisely in the struggle over identity that there can be denials of belonging or schisms and divisions. Israel's social history is marked by those as well.

Prospect: The Theological Relevance of Social History

At the beginning of this study I defined social history as a subdiscipline of history. As such it has an essential tie to theology, because in Jewish and Christian understanding theology speaks of a God who is self-revealed in historical acts.[2] On this general level, I considered it indisputable that social history is the necessary precondition for a biblical theology, just as philology is essential for understanding the texts.

But just as philology as such is not a theological discipline, the same is true for social history. It is theological inasmuch as it enters into the hermeneutical processes by which we understand the biblical texts. And here it is my conviction that biblical texts cannot be adequately understood theologically if one is ignorant of the social environment, more precisely the social world of those who produced them and were the first to receive them. Of course, this is true of different texts to varying degrees, and naturally it is not the only condition for understanding. But it is indispensable.

Obviously for this purpose the sketch of a reconstruction of social epochs such as I have given here is not adequate. In my view, two essential additions are needed. The first would be a history of institutions. At the beginning, I emphasized that a description of social history according to epochs, such as I present here, is not in conflict with a description in terms of institutions. I also indicated that there are such descriptions extending into the present. Certainly, in the future I can only imagine a really well-grounded history of institutions as a broadly conceived interdisciplinary work. It would have to include all the socially relevant constructs in the social and economic fields, the political and the governmental realms, as well as in religion, both in their internal structures and in their respective historical developments.

The second addition that gives immediate theological relevance to a social history oriented to epochs would consist in a pursuit of individual key words from their social background through their symbolic meaning to their theological application. Thus a word like "house" would be viewed in terms of the material shapes of housing as revealed by archaeology, then the symbolic use of the term for family, dynasty, or state, to "my Father's house in which there are many mansions" (John 14:2). The material compass of key words like "slave, servant" or "king" can be easily imagined, but shorter entries are also possible. At the present time there are a great many scholars at work on such a lexicon, and unlike the social history presented here, it is meant to include both the Old and New Testaments.[3]

I would say that the social history of Israel I have presented here has fulfilled its purpose if it is viewed as a frame or background. It is a frame in which the usual "history of Israel" can be inserted, especially the history of events, literary history, and religious history. And it can furnish the background for a description of Israel's institutions and serve as a social-historical grounding of the big and little words of the biblical writings that, without being given a social foundation, are in danger of becoming ideology rather than unfolding their liberating power.

Abbreviations

Collections of Primary Sources

AHI   Davies, Graham I., ed. *Ancient Hebrew Inscriptions: Corpus and Concordance.* Cambridge: Cambridge University Press, 1991.

ANEP   Pritchard, James Bennett, and W. F. Albright. *The Ancient Near East: An Anthology of Texts and Pictures.* 2 vols. Princeton: Princeton University Press, 1975.

ANESTP   Pritchard, James Bennett, ed. *The Ancient Near East: Supplementary Texts and Pictures Relating to the Old Testament.* Princeton: Princeton University Press, 1969.

ANET   Pritchard, James Bennett, ed. *Ancient Near Eastern Texts Relating to the Old Testament.* 2 vols. Princeton: Princeton University Press, 1955.

Arnold and Beyer   Arnold, Bill T. and Bryan E. Beyer. *Readings from the Ancient Near East: Primary Sources for Old Testament Study.* Encountering Biblical Studies. Grand Rapids: Baker Academic, 2002.

Beyerlin   Beyerlin, Walter, ed. *Near Eastern Religious Texts Relating to the Old Testament.* Trans. John Bowden. Philadelphia: Westminster, 1978. (Second German ed., *Religionsgeschichtliches Textbuch zum Alten Testament.* GAT 1. Göttingen: Vandenhoeck & Ruprecht, 1985.)

COS   Hallo, William W., ed. *The Context of Scripture.* Vol. 1, *Canonical Compositions from the Biblical World.* Vol. 2, *Monumental Inscriptions from the Biblical World.* Leiden: Brill, 1997, 2000.

CPJ   Tcherikover, Viktor A., and Alexander Fuks. *Corpus Papyrorum Judaicarum.* Vol. 1. Cambridge: Harvard University Press, 1957.

CWSS   Avigad, Nahman, and Benjamin Sass. *Corpus of West Semitic Stamp Seals.* Jerusalem: Hebrew University et al., 1997.

Deutsch   Robert Deutsch, ed. *Messages from the Past: Hebrew Bullae from the Time of Isaiah through the Destruction of the First Temple.* Tel Aviv: Archaeological Center Publications, 1999.

HAE   Renz, Johannes, and Wolfgang Röllig. *Handbuch der Althebräischen Epigraphik. Die Althebräischen Inschriften.* 3 vols. Darmstadt: Wissenschaftliche Buchgesellschaft, 1995–2003.

Jaroś   Jaroś, Karl. *Hundert Inschriften aus Kanaan und Israel. Für den Hebräischunterricht bearbeitet.*

	Fribourg: Universitätsverlag, 1982.
KAI	Donner, Herbert, and Wolfgang Röllig. *Kanaanäische und aramäische Inschriften*. Vol. 1. 5th ed. Wiesbaden: Harrassowitz, 2002. Vols. 2 and 3. Wiesbaden: Harrassowitz, 1964. English: Walter E. Aufrecht, ed. *A Synoptic Concordance of Aramaic Inscriptions (according to H. Donner & W. Roellig)*. Programming by John C. Hurd. International Concordance Library 1. Missoula: Scholars, 1975.
Matthews and Benjamin	Matthews, Victor Harold, and Don C. Benjamin. *Old Testament Parallels Laws and Stories from the Ancient Near East*. New York: Paulist, 2006. Also on CD-ROM; New York: Paulist, 2000; ISBN 0-8091-8278-5.
OTP	*Old Testament Pseudepigrapha*. Edited by James Charlesworth. 2 vols. Garden City: Doubleday, 1985.
TAD	Porten, Bezalel, and Ada Yardeni, eds. *Textbook of Aramaic Documents from Ancient Egypt*. Vol. 1. *Letters*. Vol. 2. *Contracts*. Jerusalem: Hebrew University, 1986–1989.
Textbook	Gibson, John C. L. *Textbook of Syrian Semitic Inscriptions*. Vol. 1. *Hebrew and Moabite Inscriptions*. Oxford: Clarendon, 1971.
Walton	Walton, John H. *Ancient Israelite Literature in Its Cultural Context: A Survey of Parallels between Biblical and Ancient Near Eastern Texts*. Library of Biblical Interpretation. Grand Rapids: Zondervan, 1998.

Secondary Literature

AASF	Annales Academiae scientiarum fennicae
ÄAT	Ägypten und Altes Testament
AAWGPHK	Abhandlungen der Akademie der Wissenschaften in Göttingen, Philologisch-Historische Klasse
ADPV	Abhandlungen des Deutschen Palästinavereins
AES	*Archives Européennes de Sociologie*
AO	Der alte Orient
AOAT	Alter Orient und Altes Testament
ASORDS	American Schools of Oriental Research Dissertation Series
ATD	Das Alte Testament Deutsch
AzTh	Arbeiten zur Theologie
BA	*Biblical Archaeologist*
BASOR	*Bulletin of the American Schools of Oriental Research*
BBB	Bonner biblische Beiträge
BBET	Beiträge zu biblische Exegese und Theologie
BE	*Biblische Enzyklopädie*
BEATAJ	Beiträge zur Erforschung des Alten Testaments und des antiken Judentum
BEvT	Beiträge zur evangelischen Theologie
Bib	*Biblica*
BibInt	*Biblical Interpretation*
BHT	Beiträge zur Historischen Theologie
BK	Biblischer Kommentar
BK	*Bibel und Kirche*
BN	*Biblische Notizen*
BTAVO	Beihefte zum Tübinger Atlas der Vorderen Orients
BTZ	*Berliner Theologische Zeitschrift*
BWANT	Beiträge zur Wissenschaft vom Alten und Neuen Testament
BZ	*Biblische Zeitschrift*

BZAW	Beihefte zurZeitschrift für die alttestamentliche Wissenschaft	JSOTSup	Journal for the Study of the Old Testament Supplement Series
CBQ	Catholic Biblical Quarterly		
CHJ	Cambridge History of Judaism. Edited by W. D. Davies and Louis Finkelstein. 4 vols. to date. Cambridge: Cambridge University Press, 1984–.	JTS	Journal of Theological Studies
		Jud	Judaica
		KAANT	Kleine Arbeiten zum Alten und Neuen Testament
ConBOT	Coniectanea biblica: Old Tesament Series	KBL	Koehler, L. and W. Baumgartner, Lexicon in Veteris Testamenti libros. 2d. ed. Leiden: Brill, 1958.
DJD	Discoveries in the Judean Desert		
		KD	Kerygma und Dogma
DOMA	Documenta et monumenta Orientis antiqui	KT	Kaiser-Taschenbücher
		LAPO	Littératures anciennes du Proche-Orient
EHS Theologie	Europäische Hochschulschriften Theologie		
		Lemaire	Lemaire, André. Inscriptions hébraïques. I. Les ostraca. Paris: Cerf, 1977.
EvT	Evangelische Theologie		
EXUZ	Exegese in unserer Zeit: kontextuelle Bibelinterpretation aus lateinamerikanischer und feministischer Sicht	MÄS	Münchner ägyptologische Studien
		MIOF	Mitteilungen des Instituts für Orientforschung
FAT	Forschungen zum Alten Testament	MWG	Max Weber Gesamtausgabe. Edited by Edith Hanke, and Thomas Kroll. Tübingen: Mohr Siebeck, 2005.
FB	Forschung zur Bibel		
FRLANT	Forschungen zur Religion und Literatur des Alten und Neuen Testaments		
		NEA	Near Eastern Archaeology
		NechtB	Neue Echter Bibel
FTS	Frankfurter theologische Studien	NSKAT	Neuer Stuttgarter Kommentar Altes Testament
GAT	Grundrisse zum Alten Testament	OBO	Orbius biblicus et orientalis
		OTL	Old Testament Library
GTA	Göttinger theologische Arbeiten	OTS	Old Testament Studies
		RB	Revue biblique
HBS	Herders biblische Studien	RevQ	Revue de Qumran
HSM	Harvard Semitic Monographs	RGG⁴	Religion in Geschichte und Gegenwart. Edited by Hans Dieter Betz et al. 8 vols. 4th ed. Tübingen: Mohr Siebeck, 1998–.
HTKAT	Herders theologischer Kommentar zum Alten Testament		
HTR	Harvard Theological Review		
HUCA	Hebrew Union College Annual		
IEJ	Israel Exploration Journal	SBLMS	Society of Biblical Literature Monograph Series
JBL	Journal of Biblical Literature		
JNES	Journal of Near Eastern Studies	SBLDS	Society of Biblical Literature Dissertation Series
JZR	Jewish Quarterly Revies		
JSOT	Journal for the Study of the Old Testament	SBLStBL	Society of Biblical Literature Studies in Biblical Literature

SBB	Stuttgarter biblische Beiträge
SBS	Stuttgarter Bibelstudien
Sem	*Semitica*
SGKAO	Schriften zur Geschichte und Kultur des alten Orients
SHCANE	Studies in the History and Culture of the Ancient Near East
SJOT	*Scandinavian Journal of the Old Testament*
Smelik	Smelik, Klaas A. D. *Historische Dokumente aus dem alten Israel.* Göttingen: Vandenhoeck & Ruprecht, 1987.
SSN	Studia Semitica Neerlandica
STW	Suhrkamp Taschenbuch Wissenschaft
SUNT	Studien zur Umwelt des Neuen Testaments
SWBA	Social World of Biblical Antiquity
TA	*Tel Aviv*
TB	Theologische Bücherei: Neudrucke und Berichte aus dem 20. Jahrhundert
ThB	Theologische Bücherei
ThZS	Theologische Zeitschrift Sonderband
TGI	Galling, Kurt, ed. *Textbuch zur Geschichte Israels.* 3d ed. Tübingen: Mohr, 1979.
TRE	*Theologische Realenzyklpädie.* Edited by Gerhard Krause and Gerhard Müller. Berlin: de Gruyter, 1977–.
TUAT	Kaiser, Otto, ed. *Texte aus der Umwelt des Alten Testaments.* Gütersloh: Gütersloher, 1982–2001.
UF	*Ugarit-Forschungen*
UTB	Uni-Taschenbücher
VF	*Verkündigung und Forschung*
VT	*Vetus Testamentum*
VTSup	Supplements to Vetus Testamentum

VWGTH	Veröffentlichungen der Wissenschaftlichen Gesellschaft für Theologie
WD	*Wort und Dienstag*
WdF	Wege der Forschung
WMANT	Wissenschaftliche Monographien zum Alten und Neuen Testaments
WUNT	Wissenschaftliche Untersuchungen zum Neuen Testament
ZABR	*Zeitschrift für Altorientalische und Biblische Rechtsgeschichte*
ZAW	*Zeitschrift für die alttestamentliche Wissenschaft*
ZDPV	*Zeitschrift des deutschen Palästina-Vereins*
ZEE	*Zeitschrfit für evangelische Ethik*

Ancient Literature

Augustine *City*	*The City of God.* Vol. 2. Trans. W. M. Green. LCL. Cambridge: Harvard University Press, 1963; repr. 1978.
Diodorus Siculus	*Diodorus of Sicily.* Vol. 12. Trans. R. R. Walton. LCL. Cambridge: Harvard University Press, 1967.
Herodotus *Hist.*	*The Persian Wars.* Trans. A. D. Godley. LCL. Cambridge: Harvard University Press, 1920; repr. 1990.
Josephus *Ant.*	*Jewish Antiquities*: Vol. 8. Books 9–11. Trans. Ralph Marcus. LCL. Cambridge: Harvard University Press, 1937, repr. 1987.
	Vol. 9. Books 12–13. Trans. Ralph Marcus. LCL. Cambridge: Harvard University Press, 1943; repr. 1998.
	Volume 13. Book 20. Trans. Louis H. Feldman. LCL. Cam-

Josephus *J. W.* bridge: Harvard University Press, 1965, repr. 1981.

Josephus *J. W.* *The Jewish War.* Vol. 1. Trans. H. St. J. Thackeray. LCL. Cambridge: Harvard University Press, 1926; repr. 1999.

Josephus *Ag. Ap.* *Against Apion.* In *The Life. Against Apion.* Trans. H. St. J. Thackeray. LCL. New York: Putnam, 1926.

Strabo *The Geography of Strabo.* Vol. 7. Trans. H. L. Jones. LCL. Cambridge: Harvard University Press, 1930, repr.

Xenophon *Cyr.* *Cyropaedia.* In *Xenophon.* Vol. 5. Trans. W. Miller. LCL. Cambridge: Harvard University Press, 1961.

Notes

1. The Social History Method

1. See Eckart Otto, "Sozialgeschichte Israels. Probleme und Perspektiven. Ein Diskussionspapier," *BN* 15 (1981): 87–92.

2. Willy Schottroff, "Thesen zur Aktualität und theologischen Bedeutung sozialgeschichtlicher Bibelauslegung im Kontext christlicher Sozialethik" in *Gerechtigkeit lernen. Beiträge zur biblischen Sozialgeschichte* (ThB 94; Gütersloh: Kaiser/Gütersloher, 1999; original German essay, 1987), 1–4, esp. 2.

3. Ibid.

4. Ibid.

5. Some reflections on the subject will be found in the final section of this book.

6. Fernand Braudel, *On History* (trans. Sarah Matthews; Chicago: University of Chicago Press, 1992), 38, 53n21.

7. Marvin L. Chaney, "Systemic Study of the Israelite Monarchy," in Norman K. Gottwald, ed., *Social Scientific Criticism of the Hebrew Bible and its Social World: The Israelite Monarchy. Semeia* 37 (1986), 53–76, at 58 uses the concept of a "systemic watershed" for such epochal divisions.

8. Braudel, ibid.

9. The translators of the work of Roland de Vaux originally entitled *Les institutions de l'Ancien Testament* (2 vols; Paris: Cerf, 1958–60) attempted to do it justice by calling it *Das Alte Testament und seine Lebensordnungen [The Old Testament and its Ways of Life]* (2d ed.; 2 vols.; Freiburg: Herder, 1964–66]). However, the notion of *Lebensordnung* ["way of life"] includes a normative element, subject to a theological anthropology, that is foreign to the sociological concept of institutions. The title of the English translation, *Ancient Israel: Its Life and Institutions* (trans. John McHugh; New York: McGraw-Hill, 1961; repr., Biblical Resource Series; Grand Rapids: Eerdmans, 1997), is closer to the original French usage.

10. Erhard S. Gerstenberger, *Theologies in the Old Testament* (trans. John Bowden; Minneapolis: Fortress Press, 2002), 21–25.

11. Benzinger, *Hebräische Archäologie* (3d ed.; Leipzig: Eduard Pfeiffer, 1927), 5–8.

12. Ibid., 1.

13. Ibid.

14. Rudolf Kittel, *Geschichte des Volkes Israel* (2 vols.; 5th–6th eds.; Stuttgart: Kohlhammer, 1909–29; Gotha: F. A. Perthes, 1923–25).

15. Alfred Bertholet, *Kulturgeschichte Israels* (Göttingen: Vandenhoeck & Ruprecht, 1919).

16. Johannes Pedersen, *Israel: Its Life and Culture* (4 vols; London: Oxford University Press 1926–1940; repr. with additions, 1959).

17. Ibid., 99–259.

18. Salo Wittmayer Baron, *A Social and Religious History of the Jews*, vol. 1, *To the Beginning of the Christian Era* (2d ed.; New York: Columbia University Press, 1952).

19. De Vaux, *Ancient Israel*.

20. Frants Buhl, *Die socialen Verhältnisse der Israeliten* (Berlin: Reuther & Reichard, 1899), "Vorwart," n.p.

21. Paul Volz, *Die biblischen Altertümer* (Calw: Vereinsbuchhandlung, 1914; repr., Wiesbaden: Fournier, 1989), iii–iv.

22. Peter Welten, "Ansätze sozialgeschichtlicher Betrachtungsweise des Alten Tetaments im 20. Jahrhundert," *BTZ* 6 (1989): 207–21, quoting 212.

23. As a more recent example, see Victor H. Matthews and Don C. Benjamin, *Social World of Ancient Israel 1250–587 B.C.E.* (2d ed.; Peabody: Hendrickson, 1995).

24. Willy Schottroff, "The study of the social reality of ancient Israel has thus far not advanced beyond the status of an auxiliary historical science" ("Soziologie und Altes Testament," *VF* 19, no. 2 [1974]: 46–66, quoting 47).

25. Max Weber, *Ancient Judaism* (trans. and ed. Hans H. Gerth and Don Martindale; New York: Free, 1952). From among the many sources on Max Weber, see only Siegfried Kreuzer, "Max Weber, George Mendenhall und das sogenannte Revolutionsmodell für die 'Landnahme' Israels," in *Altes Testament: Forschung und Wirkung. Festschrift für Henning Graf Reventlow* (ed. Peter Mommer and Winfried Thiel; Frankfurt: Peter Lang, 1994), 238–305; Eckart Otto, "Hat Max Webers Religionssoziologie des antiken Judentums Bedeutung für eine Theologie des Alten Testaments?" *ZAW* 94 (1982): 187–203; idem, *Max Webers Studien des Antiken Judentums. Historische Grundlegung einer Theorie der Moderne* (Tübingen: Mohr Siebeck, 2002); Christa Schäfer-Lichtenberger, *Stadt und Eidgenossenschaft im Alten Testament. Eine Auseinandersetzung mit Max Webers Studie "Das antike Judentum"* (BZAW 156; Berlin: Walter de Gruyter, 1983); and Shemaryahu Talmon, "The Emergence of Jewish Sectarianism in the Early Second Temple Period," in *King, Cult and Calendar in Ancient Israel: Collected Studies* (Leiden: Brill, 1986), 165–201.

26. Max Weber, *Die Wirtschaftsethik der Weltreligionen. Das antike Judentum. Schriften und Reden 1911–1920* (MWG 1/21; Tübingen: Mohr Siebeck, 2005), 234–40.

27. Ibid., 241.

28. Ibid., 244.

29. Ibid., 316.

30. Ibid., 347.

31. Ibid., 357.

32. Ibid., 360.

33. Ibid., 381.

34. Ibid.

35. Ibid., 382.

36. Ibid., 241.

37. For an early critique of Weber's thesis, cf. Julius Guttmann, "Max Webers Soziologie des antiken Judentums," in *Max Webers Studie über das antike Judentum. Interpretation und Kritik* (ed. Wolfgang Schluchter; STW 340; Frankfurt: Suhrkamp, 1981; original German essay, 1925), 289–326, esp. 321; and see the extensive discussion by Werner J. Cahnman, "Der Pariah und der Fremde: Eine begriffliche Klärung," *AES* 15 (1974): 166–77.

38. For the first of these, see Martin Noth, *Das System der zwölf Stämme Israels* (BWANT 52; Darmstadt: Wissenschaftliche Buchgesellschaft, 1930), and, for the last, the essays in Albrecht Alt's *Kleine Schriften zur Geschichte des Volkes Israel* (3 vols.; Munich: Beck, 1964–68) that deal with social relationships in Israel.

39. Schottroff, "Soziologie und Altes Testament," 54.

40. Antonin Causse, *Du groupe éthnique à la communauté religieuse. Le problème sociologique de la religion d'Israël* (Paris: Alcan, 1937), dedication to "le maître des études sur la *mentalité primitive*."

41. Ibid., 9n1: Weber "n'a pas suffisamment tenu compte de la structure primitive de la mentalité, de l'organisation sociale d'Israël."

42. Ibid., 9 (". . . le problème essentiel . . . est . . . de savoir comment s'est fait le passage de cette mentalité primitive, prélogique et grégaire . . . à des conceptions éthiques, rationelles et individualistes plus évoluées. Dans les pages qui vont suivre, j'ai essayé de marquer certains aspects de ce passage . . .").

43. Ibid., 183.

44. Ibid., 236, 301.

45. Ibid., parts I and II.

46. Peter Welten, "Ansätze sozialgeschichtlicher Betrachtungsweise des Alten Tetaments im 20. Jahrhundert," *BTZ* 6 (1989): 207–21, quoting 213.

47. In Israel (to fill out the map of focal points for the study of the Hebrew Bible) the traditions to which scholars felt most closely tied often depended on the origins of the scholars themselves.

48. Welten speaks correctly of "a forgetfulness in the recent history of scholarship" as regards the "beginnings of the social-historical method of studying the Old Testament in the twentieth century" ("Ansätze sozialgeschichtlicher Betrachtungsweise," 207).

49. Johan de Wit, *Leerlingen van de armen. Een onderzoek naar de betekenis van de Latijnamerikaanse volkse lezing van de bijbel in de hermeneutische ontwerpen en exegetische praktijk van C. Mesters, J. S. Croatto en M. Schwantes* (Ph.D. diss., Amsterdam, 1991), 25.

50. Gustavo Gutiérrez, *A Theology of Liberation: History, Politics, and Salvation* (trans. and ed. Sister Caridad Inda and John Eagleson; Maryknoll: Orbis, 1973).

51. See Welten, "Ansätze sozialgeschichtlicher Betrachtungsweise," 208; and for Latin America, the brief and instructive summary in Haroldo Reimer, *Richtet auf das Recht! Studien zur Botschaft des Amos* (SBS 149; Stuttgart: Katholisches Bibelwerk, 1992), 11–17.

52. Reimer, *Richtet auf das Recht!*, 13.

53. From the many titles, let me only mention Klaus Koch, "Die Entstehung der sozialen Kritik bei den Propheten," in *Spuren des hebräischen Denkens. Beiträge zur alttestamentlichen Theologie. Gesammelte Aufsätze 1* (Neukirchen-Vluyn: Neukirchener Verlag, 1991; original German essay, 1971), 146–66; Gunther Wanke, "Zu Grundlagen und Absicht prophetischer Sozialkritik," *KD* 18 (1972): 2–17; Marlene Fendler, "Zur Sozialkritik des Amos. Versuch einer wirtschafts- und sozialgeschichtlichen Interpretation alttestamentlicher Texte," *EvT* 33 (1973): 32–53; Fritz Stolz, "Aspekte religiöser und sozialer Ordnung im alten Israel," *ZEE* 17 (1973) 145–59; Oswald Loretz, "Die prophetische Kritik des Rentenkapitalismus. Grundlagen-Probleme der Prophetenforschung," *UF* 7 (1975): 271–78; and Svend Holm-Nielsen, "Die Sozialkritik der Propheten," in *Denkender Glaube. Festschrift: Carl Heinz Ratschow zur Vollendung seines 65. Lebensjahres am 22. Juli 1976 gewidmet von Kollegen, Schülern u. Freunden* (ed. Otto Kaiser; Berlin: Walter de Gruyter, 1976), 7–23. The list is not complete and breaks off in the mid-1970s.

54. A typical statement is Holm-Nielsen's summary: "The prophets were not subversives or revolutionaries in the Marxist sense, and so no one should use their preaching for the purpose of supporting a Marxist view of society" ("Die Sozialkritik der Propheten," 22).

55. Here, let me only mention Hans-Joachim Kraus, "Die prophetische Botschaft gegen das soziale Unrecht Israels," *EvT* 15 (1955) 295–307; and Albrecht Alt, "Der Anteil des Königtums an der sozialen Entwicklung in den Reichen Israel und Juda," in *Kleine Schriften zur Geschichte des Volkes Israel* (Munich: Beck, 1968; original German essay, 1955), 3:348–72; and Herbert Donner, "Die soziale Botschaft der Propheten im Lichte der Gesellschaftsordnung in Israel" [1963], in *Das Prophetenverständnis in der deutschsprachigen Forschung seit Heinrich Ewald* (ed. Peter H. A. Neumann; WdF 307; Darmstadt: Wissenschaftliche Buchgesellschaft, 1979; original German essay, 1963), 493–514.

56. C. H. J. de Geus, *The Tribes of Israel: An Investigation into Some of the Presuppositions of Martin Noth's Amphictyony Hypothesis* (SSN 18; Assen: Van Gorcum, 1976); Christiane Schäfer-Lichtenberger, *Stadt und Eidgenossenschaft im Alten Testament. Eine Auseinandersetzung mit Max Webers Studie "Das antike Judentum"* (BZAW 156; Berlin: Walter de Gruyter, 1983).

57. Wolfgang Schluchter, ed., *Max Webers Studie über das antike Judentum. Interpretation und Kritik* (STW 340; Frankfurt: Suhrkamp, 1981); and idem, ed. *Max Webers Sicht des antiken Christentums. Interpretation und Kritik* (STW 548; Frankfurt: Suhrkamp, 1985).

58. Frank Crüsemann, *Der Widerstand gegen das Königtum. Die antiköniglichen Tete des Alten Testaments und der Kampf un dem frühen israelitischen Staat* (WMANT 49; Neukirchen-Vluyn: Neukirchener Verlag, 1978); Rainer Neu, *Von der Anarchie zum Staat. Entwicklungsgeschichte Israels vom Nomadentum zur Monarcie im Spiegel der Ethnosoziologie* (Neukirchen-Vluyn: Neukirchener Verlag, 1992).

59. Loretz, "Die prophetische Kritik des Rentenkapitalismus"; and Hans G. Kippenberg, "Die Typik

antiker Entwicklung," in *Seminar: Die Entstehung der antiken Klassengesellschaft* (ed. Hans G. Kippenberg; STW 130; Frankfurt: Surhkamp, 1977), 9–61. For discussion, see Rainer Kessler, "Frühkapitalismus, Rentenkapitalismus, Tributarismus, antike Klassengesellschaft. Theorien zur Gesellschaft des alten Israel," *EvT* 54 (1994): 413–27.

60. Joel Weinberg, *The Citizen-Temple Community* (JSOTSup 151; Sheffield: JSOT Press, 1992).

61. Anti-Marxist advocates sometimes see this differently, but their position cannot be sustained. Compare Loretz's suspicion that in newer discussions the prophets are seen "in terms of their influence, e.g., on Karl Marx as cofounders of modern socialism" with the footnote that is supposed to support this: "See, e.g., the mostly vague allusions in the literature" ("Die prophetische Kritik des Rentenkapitalismus," 272).

62. M. Lurje, *Studien zur Geschichte der wirtschaftlichen und sozialen Verhältnisse im israelitisch-jüdischen Reiche von der Einwanderung in Kanaan bis zum babylonischen Exil* (BZAW 45; Gießen: A. Töpelmann, 1927). In an initial reaction, Walter Baumgartner, then teaching in Marburg, explicitly greeted the work: "The standpoint here generally expressed is as much justified and subjective as any other modern one, and its one-sidedness is not hard to prove. The only question is whether its very one-sidedness does not serve to advance our understanding of the Old Testament in that it sees some things that previously were not, nor not adequately, perceived" (review of M. Lurje, *Studien zur Geschichte der wirtschaftlichen und sozialen Verhältnisse im iraelitisch-jüdischen Reiche*, *TLZ* 52 [1927], 315–16, quoting 316). Forty years later nothing remains of such openness in Hans-Joachim Kraus's judgment: "In Old Testament scholarship this book, which attempts with flimsy arguments to 'prove' the existence of capitalism in the period of the judges, and builds its historical picture of economic antagonism on that 'proof,' is quite rightly treated as an 'outsider' not worthy of discussion" ("Die Anfänge der religionssoziologischen Forschungen in der alttestamentlichen Wissenschaft. Eine forschungsgeschichtliche Orientierung," in *Biblisch-theologische Aufsätze*

[Neukirchen-Vluyn: Neukirchener Verlag, 1972], 296–310, quoting 298).

63. Frank S. Frick, *The Formation of the State in Ancient Israel: A Survey of Models and Theories* (SWBA 4; Sheffield: Almond Press, 1985); and Rainer Kessler, *Staat und Gesellschaft im vorexilischen Juda. Vom 8. Jahrhundert bis zum Exil* (VTSup 47; Leiden: Brill, 1992).

64. Udo Rüterswörden, *Die Beamten der israelitischen Königszeit. Eine Studie zu sar und vergleichbaren Begriffen* (BWANT 117; Stuttgart: Kohlhammer, 1985); and Christoph Bultmann, *Der Fremde im antiken Juda. Eine Untersuchung zum sozialen Typenbegriff <ger> und seinem Bedeutungswandel in der alttestamentlichen Gesetzgebung* (FRLANT 153; Göttingen: Vandenhoeck & Ruprecht, 1992).

65. Gunther Fleischer, *Von Menschenverkäufern, Baschankühen und Rechtsverkehrern. Die Sozialkritik des Amos-Buches in historisch-kritischer, sozialgeschichtlicher und archäologischer Perspektive* (BBB 74; Frankfurt: Athenaeum, 1989); and José Luis Sicre, *"Con los pobres de la tierra." La justicia social en los profetas de Israel* (Madrid: Ediciones Christiandad, 1984).

66. Niels Peter Lemche, *Ancient Israel. A New History of Israelite Society* (Sheffield: JSOT Press, 1988).

67. Rainer Albertz, *A History of Israelite Religion in the Old Testament Period* (2 vols.; OTL; Louisville: Westminster John Knox, 1994); and Gerstenberger, *Theologies in the Old Testament*.

68. Paula McNutt, *Reconstructing the Society of Ancient Israel* (Library of Ancient Israel; Louisville: Westminster John Knox, 1999); Norman K. Gottwald, *The Politics of Ancient Israel* (Library of Ancient Israel; Louisville: Westminster John Knox, 2001).

69. J. David Pleins, *The Social Visions of the Hebrew Bible: A Theological Introduction* (Louisville: Westminster John Knox, 2001).

2. Environment as Living Space

1. *"La longue duree."* Fernand Braudel, *On History* (trans. Sarah Matthews; Chicago: University of Chicago Press, 1982), 38, 53n21.

2. I am using the designation "Canaan" along-side others such as Israel (Syro-)Palestine, or the Levant; for "the Land and its names" see Wolfgang Zwickel, *Einführung in die biblische Landes- und Altertumskunde* (Darmstadt: Wissenschaftliche Buchgesellschaft, 2002), 16–22.

3. See below, ch. 6, 46–50.

4. On this see below, ch. 7, 72–73.

5. For the "rhythm of the history of Syria and Palestine in antiquity," see the fundamental essay under that title by Albrecht Alt, "Der Rhythmus der Geschichte Syriens und Palästinas im Altertum," *Kleine Schriften Schriften zur Geschichte des Volkes Israel*. 3 vols. Munich: Beck. 3:1–19 [1944] (1968).

3. Material Remains

1. For this discussion see, by way of example, Ernest Axel Knauf, "From History to Interpretation," in Diana V. Edelman, ed., *The Fabric of History. Text, Artifact and Israel's Past* (JSOTSup 127; Sheffield: JSOT Press, 1991), 26–64, esp. 46–55; and the critical notes and suggestions by Christoph Uehlinger (1995): "Gab es eine joschianische Kultreform? Plädoyer für ein begründetes Minimum," in *Jeremia und die "deuteronomistische Bewegung"* (ed. Walter Groß; BBB 98; Weinheim: Beltz Athenaeum, 1995), 57–89, esp. 59–60. See also Herbert Niehr, "Some Aspects of Working with the Textual Sources," in *Can a "History of Israel" Be Written?* (ed. Lester L. Grabbe; JSOTSup 245; Sheffield: Sheffield Academic, 1997), 156–65.

2. Uehlinger, "Gab es eine joschianische Kultreform?" 60.

3. Knauf, "From History to Interpretation," 47n1.

4. I am thus associating myself with Joachim Schaper's judgment (*Priester und Leviten im achämenidischen Juda. Studien zur Kult- und Sozialgeschichte Israels in persischer Zeit* [FAT 31; Tübingen: Mohr Siebeck, 2000]); he believes "that the distinction between primary and secondary sources . . . cannot be entirely dismissed" (21), but is fully convinced that the distinction is "deceptive" if "it presumes a value judgment and hierarchizing of the sources" (19).

5. For a discussion of the relationship between archaeological and literary sources cf. the essays in the collected volume edited by Diana V. Edelman, ed., *The Fabric of History: Text, Artifact and Israel's Past* (JSOTSup 127; Sheffield: JSOT Press, 1991). Cf. also Keith W. Whitelam "Recreating the History of Israel," *JSOT* 35 (1986), 45–70.

6. On this question see Frank Crüsemann, "Alttestamentliche Exegese und Archäologie. Erwägungen angesichts des gegenwärtigen Methodenstreits in der Archäologie Palästinas," *ZAW* 91, 177–93; Jan Kees de Geus, "Die Gesellschaftskritik der Propheten und die Archäologie," *ZDPV* 98 (1982), 50–57.

7. See, for example, Israel Finkelstein, *The Land of Ephraim Survey 1980–1987: Preliminary Report* (Tel Aviv: Institute of Archaeology of Tel Aviv University, 1988–89), 15–16, 117–83; idem, *The Archaeology of the Israelite Settlement* (Jerusalem: Israel Exploration Society, 1988), 121–204; for discussion see *BASOR* 277/278 (1990), including the summary essay by William G. Dever, "Of Myths and Methods," 121–30.

8. This obvious truth is ignored in annoying fashion by the German translation of Israel Finkelstein and Neil A. Silberman, *The Bible Unearthed: Archaeology's New Vision of Ancient Israel and the Origin of its Sacred Texts* (New York: Free, 2001), which renders the English subtitle as "Die archäologische Wahrheit über die Bibel" [the archaeological truth about the Bible].

9. Adam Zertal, "An Early Iron Age Cultic Site on Mount Ebal: Excavation Seasons 1982–1987. Preliminary Report," *TA* 13–14, (1986–87), 104–65.

10. Volkmar Fritz, *Die Entstehung Israels im 12. und 11. Jahrhundert v. Chr.* (BE 2; Stuttgart: Kohlhammer, 1996), 88.

11. For the question of the dating of the monumental structures in the north see the references below, 202–3n9.

12. Roland de Vaux, *Ancient Israel: Its Life and Institutions* (trans. John McHugh; New York: McGraw-Hill, 1961; repr., The Biblical Resource

Series; Grand Rapids: Eerdmans, 1997), 72; the above discussion is based on the original French second edition, *Les institutions de l'Ancien Testament* (2 vols.; Paris: Cerf: 1964–66), 122; cf. the most recent presentation by Janne J. Nurmi, *Die Ethik unter dem Druck des Alltags. Die Impuse der gesellschaftlichen Änderungen und Situation zu der sozialkritischen Prophetie in Juda im 8. Jh. v. Chr.* (Åbo, Finland: Åbo Akademis, 2004), 226–27.

13. Abraham Faust, "Differences in Family Structure Between Cities and Villages in Iron Age II," *TA* 26 (1999): 233–52. See also the complex analysis by Gunter Fleischer, *Von Menschenverkäufern, Baschankühen und Rechtsverkehrern. Die Sozialkritik des Amos-Buches in historisch-kritischer, sozialgeschichtlicher und archäologischer Perspektive* (BBB 74; Frankfurt: Athenaeum, 1989), 391–94.

14. Part of the deciphered material is available in translations; the texts presented there were chosen with a view to the Old Testament traditions. Let me mention here especially *ANET, ANESTP, ANEP,* Arnold and Beyer, Beyerlin, *COS, TGI, TUAT,* Matthews and Benjamin, and Walton.

15. See below, in the introductory remarks beginning Part Two, 37–38.

16. Original texts, with translations, can be found primarily in *KAI, HAE,* and *CWSS.* There are translations in *Textbook,* Smelik, and *AHI.*

17. For the ostraca from Samaria see ch. 7, 91–97, below, and for the ostraca from Arad and Lachish see ch. 7, 97–102, and 88–91.

18. Cf. Nahman Avigad, *Hebrew Bullae from the Time of Jeremiah: Remnants of a Burnt Archive* (Jerusalem: Israel Exploration Society, 1986), esp. the plates on 15, 17; and the corresponding description on 18–19.

19. *CWSS.*

20. *HAE* 2.2, 81. See also Deutsch.

21. J. Maxwell Miller, "Is it Possible to Write a History of Israel without Relying on the Hebrew Bible?" in *The Fabric of History: Text, Artifact and Israel's Past* (ed. Diana V. Edelman; JSOTSup 127; Sheffield: JSOT Press, 1991), 93–102.

22. On this see the overview in Schaper, *Priester und Leviten im achämenidischen Juda,* 153–61.

4. The Texts of the Hebrew Bible

1. See chapter 3, 26–27, above.

2. This is how Rolf Rendtorff begins his *The Canonical Hebrew Bible: A Theology of the Old Testament* (trans. David E. Orton; Tools for Biblical Study 7; Leiden: Deo, 2005), 1.

3. Philip R. Davies (1995) 13: "All story is fiction, and that must include historiography." For Davies, however, it follows that the very attempt to give a historiographical assessment of literary texts is a "betrayal" both of literature and of the writing of history (17). We can join Hans M. Barstad ("The Strange Fear of the Bible," 1998) in describing this attitude as "bibliophobia."

4. On the separate world of fictional narrative, see David J. A. Clines "Story and Poem: The Old Testament as Literature and as Scripture," *Int* 34 (1980): 115–27, repr., *On the Way to the Postmodern: Old Testament Essays 1967-1998* (JSOTSup 292; Sheffield: Sheffield Academic Press, 1998), 1:225-39; David M. Gunn and Danna Nolan Fewell, *Narrative in the Hebrew Bible* (The Oxford Bible Series; New York: Oxford University Press, 1993), 1–11; David Rhoads, Joanna Dewey, and Donald Michie, *Mark as Story: An Introduction to the Narrative of a Gospel* (2d ed.; Minneapolis: Fortress Press, 1999), 4–5; and, for advanced discussion, Antoine Compagnon, *Literature, Theory, and Common Sense* (trans. Carol Cosman; Princeton: Princeton University Press, 2004), 78–82.

5. For a discussion see the essays in Lester L. Grabbe, ed., *Can a "History of Israel" Be Written?* (JSOTSup 245; Sheffield: Sheffield Academic, 1997); and V. Philips Long, "How Reliable are Biblical Reports? Repeating Lester Grabbe's Comparative Experiment," *VT* 52 (2002): 367–84.

6. Niels Peter Lemche, "Is it Still Possible to Write a History of Ancient Israel?" *JSOT* 8 (1994): 165–90, esp. 169, 171–72, 190.

7. Ibid., 187.

8. For a critique of Lemche cf. also Stig Norin, "Response to Lemche, 'Ist es noch möglich die Geschichte des alten Israels zu schreiben?'" *SJOT* 8 (1994): 191–97.

9. For the Amarna correspondence see below, chapter 6, 41–44.

10. This is to be maintained against Israel Finkelstein, "The Campaign of Shoshenq I to Palestine. A Guide to the 10th Century B.C.E. Polity," *ZDPV* 118 (2002): 109–35. He posits that ". . . a memory of an invasion of an Egyptian army was transmitted orally and was recorded in the late 9th century B.C.E. . . ." (112). His argument is circular: Because in his opinion written records originated in Judah only with the fully developed state structure of the late ninth century, there could be no written document from the tenth century, which is why the Shishak notice in the Bible could only have been handed down orally.

11. Fergus Millar offers an excellent example and discussion of deriving sociocultural data from ancient literature when he analyzes the early second century Roman author Apuleius's novel *Metamorphoses* (also known as *The Golden Ass*), "The World of the Golden Ass," *JRS* 71 (1981): 63–75.

12. For the distinction between events and circumstances in historical reconstruction see Siegfried Kreuzer's notes, "'War Saul auch unter den Philistern?' Die Anfänge des Königtums in Israel," *ZAW* 113 (2001): 56–73, at 56–57.

13. Helmut Seiffert, *Einführung in die Wissenschaftstheorie*, vol. 2, *Geisteswissenschaftliche Methoden: Phänomenologie—Hermeneutik und historische Methode—Dialektik* (Beck'sche Schwarze Reihe 61; Munich: Beck, 1970), 61–64.

14. See above, chapter 3, 22–23.

15. So, for example, Otto Kaiser, *Das Buch des Propheten Jesaja. Kapitel 1–12* (5th ed.; ATD 17; Göttingen: Vandenhoeck & Ruprecht, 1981), 84, on Isa 3:12; 105, on Isa 5:8; Robert P. Carroll, *Jeremiah: A Commentary* (London: SCM, 1986), 189, on Jer 5:26-28. In this regard, Christoph Levin, "The Poor in the Old Testament. Some Observations," in idem, *Fortschreibungen. Gesammelte Studien zum Alten Testament* (BZAW 316; Berlin: Walter de Gruyter, (2003), 322–38, quoting 331, goes farthest: in a first step he declares all mentions of the poor in the texts of the pre-exilic prophets secondary (likewise the appearance of the poor in legal texts). Then he asserts: "To assume that real

historical circumstances were behind this is an irrefutable presumption." Finally, his search for these "historical conditions" yields a quick result: "And in fact the account in Nehemiah 5:1–13 is evidence that at that time there was a real agricultural crisis . . ." (331).

16. J. Maxwell Miller, "Is it Possible to Write a History of Israel without Relying on the Hebrew Bible?" *The Fabric of History. Text, Artifact and Israel's Past* (ed. Diana V. Edelman; JSOTSup 127; Sheffield: JSOT Press, 1991): 93–102.

17. Such an integrated treatment of all the available sources is fundamentally different from the apologetic or polemical question whether extra-biblical sources "confirm" or "refute" the biblical text; cf. the excellent observations in Norman K. Gottwald, *The Politics of Ancient Israel* (Library of Ancient Israel; Louisville: Westminster John Knox, 2001), 185.

5. In Search of Analogies

1. See below, chapter 7, 74–76.

2. See above, introduction, 1.

3. Ibid.

4. See above, introduction, 1–3.

5. There are numerous examples in Christian Sigrist and Rainer Neu, eds., *Ethnologische Texte zum Alten Testament* (2 vols.; Neukirchen-Vluyn: Neukirchener, 1989–97).

6. On this see below, chapter 6, 55–59.

7. Frants Buhl, *Die socialen Verhältnisse der Israeliten* (Berlin: Reuther & Reichard, 1899), 28; Paul Volz, *Die biblischen Altertümer* [Calw, Germany: Verlag der Vereinsbuchhandlung, 1914; repr., Wiesbaden: Fournier, 1989), 332; Roland de Vaux, *Ancient Israel: Its Life and Institutions* (trans. John McHugh; New York: McGraw-Hill, 1961; repr., Biblical Resource Series; Grand Rapids: Eerdmans, 1997),19–23, 24–38.

8. Thus de Vaux, *Ancient Israel,* 24–25, 37–38.

9. For the significance of sociology for social history, Gary A. Herion, "The Impact of Modern and Social Science Assumptions on the Reconstruction of Israelite History," *JSOT* 34 (1986): 3–33; Niels

Peter Lemche, "On Sociology and the History of Israel. A Reply to Eckhart Otto—and some Further Considerations," *BN* 21 (1983): 48–58; Andrew D. H. Mayes, "Sociology and the Old Testament," in *The World of Ancient Israel: Sociological, Anthropological and Political Perspectives* (ed. Ronald E. Clements; Cambridge and New York: Cambridge University Press, 1989), 39–36; Eckhart Otto, "Historisches Geschehen—Überlieferung—Erklärungsmodell. Sozialhistorische Grundsatz- und Einzelprobleme in der Geschichtsschreibung des frühen Israel—Eine Antwort auf N. P. Lemches Beitrag zur Diskussion um eine Sozialgeschichte Israels," *BN* 23 (1984): 63–80; John W. Rogerson, "The Use of Sociology in Old Testament Studies," in *Congress Volume Salamanca 1983* (ed. John A. Emerton; VTSup 36; Leiden: Brill, 1985), 245–56; Christa Schäfer-Lichtenberger, "Zur Funktion der Soziologie im Studium des Alten Testaments," in *Congress Volume Oslo 1998* (ed. André Lemaire and Magne Sæbø; VTSup 80; Leiden and New York: Brill, (2000), 179–202.

10. See the relevant work of Udo Rüterswörden, *Die Beamten der israelitischen Königszeit. Eine Studie zu śr und vergleichbaren Begriffen* (BWANT 117; Stuttgart: Kohlhammer, 1985).

Part 2. The Epochs of Israel's Social History

1. The designation of the northern kingdom alone as "Israel" also appears in witnesses of non-Israelite provenance from the ninth century onward: on this, see below, chapter 7, 72–73. For "Israel" on the stele of the Pharaoh Merenptah at the end of the thirteenth century see below chapter 6, 45–46.

2. Philip R. Davies, *In Search of "Ancient Israel"* (2d ed.; JSOTSup 148; Sheffield: Sheffield Academic, 1995), 48, lists ten different ways of using the word "Israel."

3. See the section "Die Erzväter," in Herbert Donner, *Geschichte des Volkes Israel und seiner Nachbarn in Grundzügen* (GAT 4/1; 3d ed.; Göttingen: Vandenhoeck & Ruprecht, 2000)

1:84–97; and in the chapter on "Die Vorgeschichte Israels," 82. Cf. also, Abraham Malamat, "The Proto-History of Israel: A Study in Method," in *The Word of the Lord Shall Go Forth. Festschrift for David Noel Freedman* (ed. Carol L. Meyers and M. O'Connor; Winona Lake: Eisenbrauns), 303–13; for further discussion about Malamat's position see chapter 6, n46.

4. Niels Peter Lemche, *Prelude to Israel's Past: Background and Beginnings of Israelite History and Identity* (trans. E. F. Maniscalco; Peabody: Hendrickson, 1998).

5. Ibid., 73.

6. Thus, after a number of predecessors, J. Alberto Soggin, *Einführung in die Geschichte Israels und Judas. Von den Ursprüngen bis zum Aufstand Bar Kochbas* (Darmstadt: Wissenschaftliche Buchgesellschaft, 1991), 29; Dirk Kinet, *Geschichte Israels* (NEchtB; Ergänzungsband zum Alten Testament 2; Würzburg: Echter Verlag, 2001) also takes this as his starting-point by dividing the whole history of ancient Israel into only two epochs: "A. The Process of Becoming a Nation (1200–1000 B.C.E.)" and "B. The Kingdoms of Israel and Judah (1000–331 B.C.E.)."

7. Soggin, *Einführung in die Geschichte Israels und Judas*, 30.

8. For the authors for whom the real "history" begins with the kingship there is another problematic idea in the background, namely that the "history" of humanity or of a people only really begins when they form a political state.

9. For discussion, see below, chapter 6, 44–45. All the dates in Egyptian history up to the middle of the first millennium BCE, as translated into the chronology of the Julian-Gregorian calendar, are somewhat uncertain. In what follows, I will adopt Jürgen von Beckerath's chronology and orthography of the pharaonic names, *Chronologie des pharaonischen Ägypten. Die Zeitbestimmung der ägyptischen Geschichte von der Vorzeit bis 332 v. Chr.* (MÄS 46; Mainz: P. von Zabern, 1997).

10. Thus Philip R. Davies, "The Society of Biblical Israel," in *Second Temple Studies 2: Temple and Community in the Persian Period* (ed. Tamara C. Eskenazi and Kent H. Richards; JSOTSup 175;

Sheffield: JSOT Press, 1994), 22–33; also idem, *In Search of "Ancient Israel"*; and Keith W. Whitelam, *The Invention of Ancient Israel: The Silencing of Palestinian History* (London: Routledge, 1995).

11. Note Whitelam's intention "to free the past realities that are ancient Palestine . . . from the domination of an imagined past imposed upon it by the discourse of biblical studies" (*Invention of Ancient Israel*, 36).

12. On this, cf., ibid., 7–8; and the sharp polemic of William G. Dever against the adoption of Whitelam's work in certain Palestinian circles: "Their 'Palestine' is *Judenfrei*" ("Archaeology, Ideology, and the Quest for an 'Ancient' or 'Biblical' Israel," *NEA* 61 [1998]: 39–52, quoting 50).

6. Israel's Origins as a Kinship-Based Society

1. See below, chapter 7, 72–73. For the Bronze Age city-state system in Syro-Palestine, see the summary by Manfred Weippert, *Die Landnahme der israelitischen Stämme in der neueren wissenschaftlichen Diskussion. Ein kritischer Bericht* (FRLANT 92; Göttingen: Vandenhoeck & Ruprecht, 1967), 16–24.

2. See the text, translation, and discussion in Elmar Edel, "Die Stelen Amenophis' II. aus Karnak und Memphis mit dem Bericht über die asiatischen Feldzüge des Königs," *ZDPV* 69 (1953): 97–169, the text is on 113–36; and Barbara Cumming, *Egyptian Historical Records of the Later Eighteenth Dynasty* (Warminster, England: Aris & Phillips, 1982–84), 28-36; *COS* 2:19–23.

3. For the phenomenon of nomadism, see Horst Klengel, *Zwischen Zelt und Palast. Die begegnung von Nomaden und Seßhaften im alten Vorderasien* (Vienna: Schroll, 1972); Ernst Axel Knauf, *Die Umwelt des Alten Testaments* (Neuer Stuttgarter Kommentar, Altes Testament 29; Stuttgart: Katholisches Bibelwerk, 1994), 28–71; Michael B. Rowton, "Urban Autonomy in a Nomadic Environment," *JNES* 32 (1973): 201–15; idem, "Dimorphic Structure and the Problem of the *'Apirû-'Ibrîm*," *JNES* 35 (1976): 13–20; idem, "Dimorphic Struc-

ture and the Parasocial Element," *JNES* 36 (1977): 181–89; Jorge Silva Castillo, ed., *Nomads and Sedentary People* (Mexico City: El Colegio de México, 1981); Thomas Staubli, *Das Image der Nomaden im Alten Israel und in der Ikonographie seiner sesshaften Nachbarn* (OBO 107; Fribourg: Universitätsverlag, 1991).

4. On this see Staubli, *Das Image der Nomaden*, 184–99.

5. For references to nomads in Mari, see esp. Jean-Robert Kupper, *Les nomades en Mésopotamie au temps des rois de Mari* (Paris: Belles Lettres, 1957); and Weippert, *Die Landnahme der israelitischen Stämme*, 106–23.

6. Staubli, *Das Image der Nomaden*, 15–16: "So any systematic classification of ancient Near Eastern nomadism fails, because there was no system of nomadism in the ancient Near East."

7. Rowton, "Urban Autonomy in a Nomadic Environment"; idem, "Dimorphic Structure and the Problem of the *'Apirû-'Ibrîm*,"; and idem, "Dimorphic Structure and the Parasocial Element".

8. For example, Rowton, "Urban Autonomy in a Nomadic Environment", 202.

9. Ibid.

10. So Niels Peter Lemche, *Early Israel: Anthropological and Historical Studies on the Israelite Society Before the Monarchy* (VTSUP 37; Leiden: Brill, 1985), 198.

11. Redrawn in Helga Weippert, *Palästina in vorhellenistischer Zeit* (Handbuch der Archäologie 2/1; Munich: Beck, 1988), 213; and Thomas Staubli, *Das Image der Nomaden im Alten Israel*, plate 15b.

12. *TGI* no. 16. For Egyptian descriptions of Shasu in general, see Staubli, ibid., 20–66.

13. From the wealth of literature, cf. Jean Bottéro, ed, *Le problème des Ḫapiru à la 4ᵉ Rencontre Assyriologique Internationale.* (Cahiers de la Société Asiatique 12; Paris: Imprimerie Nationale 1954); Herbert Donner, *Geschichte des Volkes Israel und seiner Nachbarn in Grundzügen,* part 1, *Von den Anfängen bis zur Staatenbildungszeit* (3rd ed.; GAT 4/1; Göttingen: Vandenhoeck & Ruprecht, 2000), 80–82; Helmut Engel, *Die Vorfahren Israels in Ägypten. Forschungsgeschichtlicher Überblock über*

die Darstellungen seit Richard Lepsius (1849) (FTS 27; Frankfurt: Knecht, 1979), 179–82; Klaus Koch, "Die Hebräer vom Auszug aus Ägypten bis zum Großreich Davids," *VT* 19 (1969): 37–81; Niels Peter Lemche, *Prelude to Israel's Past: Background and Beginnings of Israelite History and Identity* (trans. E. F. Maniscalco; Peabody: Hendrickson, 1998; German original, 1996), 137–48; Oswald Loretz, *Habiru—Hebräer. Eine soziolinguistische Studie über die Herkunft des Gentilizismus ʿibrî vom Appellativum habiru* (BZAW 160; Berlin: Walter de Gruyter, 1984); Rowton, "Dimorphic Structure and the Problem of the ʿApirû-ʿIbrîm"; Roland de Vaux, "Le problème des Hapiru après quinze années," *JNES* 27 (1968): 221–28; Manfred Weippert, *Die Landnahme der israelitischen Stämme in der neueren wissenschaftlichen Diskussion. Ein kritischer Bericht* (FRLANT 92; Göttingen: Vandenhoeck & Ruprecht, 1967), 66–102.

14. Jean Bottéro, speaks of a "third force" ("troisième force"), ("Les Habiru, les Nomades et les Sédentaires," in *Nomads and Sedentary People* [ed. Jorge Silva Castillo; Mexico City: El Colegio de México, 1981], 89–107, quoting 89).

15. For the biblical instances, see esp. Koch, "Die Hebräer vom Auszug aus Ägypten"; and Loretz, *Habiru—Hebräer*.

16. On this see Engel, *Die Vorfahren Israels in Ägypten*, 287–90; Koch, ibid., 67–68; and Manfred Weippert, *Die Landnahme der israelitischen Stämme*, 90–94.

17. *TGI*, no. 12, p. 35; cf. also Bottéro, *Le problème des Ḫapiru*, 169–70.

18. See the text and translation in Gerhard Fecht, "Die Israelstele, Gestalt und Aussage," in *Fontes atque Pontes: eine Festgabe für Hellmut Brunner* (ed. Manfred Görg; ÄAT 5; Wiesbaden: in Kommission by O. Harrassowitz, 1983), 106–38, at 107–20; Erik Hornung, "Die Israelstele des Merenptah," in *Fontes atque Pontes: eine Festgabe für Hellmut Brunner* (ed. Manfred Görg; ÄAT 5; Wiesbaden: in Kommission by O. Harrassowitz, 1983), 106–38; *TUAT* 1: 544–52; and *Context* 2: 40–41. Because the word "Israel" appears in this closing hymn, the whole stele is sometimes referred to as the "Israel stele." That certainly emphasizes

the significance of the document for study of the history of Israel, but such a designation has nothing to do with the stele's contents. From the wealth of literature, let me simply point to John J. Bimson, "Merneptah's Israel and Recent Theories of Israelite Origins," *JSOT* 49 (1991): 3–29; Helmut Engel, "Die Siegesstele des Merenptah. Kritischer Überblick über die verschiedenen Versuche historischer Auswertung des Schlußabschnitts," *Bib* 60 (1979): 373–99; Fecht, ibid., 106–38; Volkmar Fritz, *Die Entstehung Israels im 12. und 11. Jahrhundert v. Chr.* (BE 2; Stuttgart: Kohlhammer, 1996), 73–75; Michael G. Hasel, "The Structure of the Final Hymnic-Poetic Unit on the Merenptah Stela," *ZAW* 116 (2004): 75–81; Hornung, ibid.; Anson F. Rainey, "Israel in Merneptah's Inscription and Reliefs," *IEJ* 51 (2001): 57–75; and Donald B. Redford, "The Ashkelon Relief at Karnak and the Israel Stela," *IEJ* 36 (1986): 188–200.

19. Hasel, "Structure of the Final Hymnic-Poetic Unit," 80–81, concludes from the determinative that "… Israel is designated as a socioethnic entity …".

20. See the important evidence in Rainey, ibid., for the word's metaphorical usage.

21. Bimson, "Merneptah's Israel and Recent Theories," 24, concludes from the fact that Merneptah's stele mentions "Israel" before the process of repopulation of the land was well advanced in the 12th century: "Before the beginning of the Iron Age Israel must have been chiefly a semi-nomadic people".

22. Fritz, *Die Entstehung Israels*, 74.

23. Redford, who compares Merneptah's stele with the Ashkelon relief in Karnak from the time of Seti I (1290–1279/78) and Ramses II (1279–1213), observes that all the names on the relief are also on the stele, but at the place where the relief has "Shasu," the stele has "Israel." "All the names in the poem appear in the relief sequence except for Israel. Thus the ethnic group depicted and named 'Shasu' by the scribes of Seti I and Ramses II at the beginning of the thirteenth century B.C.E. was known to the poet of Merneptah two generations later as 'Israel'" ("The Ashkelon Relief," 199–200).

24. Bimson, "Merneptah's Israel and Recent Theories," 23: "this long silence obviously does not mean that Israel had ceased to exist in the interim." Cf. Thomas L. Thompson, *Early History of the Israelite People. From the Written and Archaeological Sources* (SHANE 4; Leiden: Brill, 1992), 274–76, 310–311; and Philip R. Davies, *In Search of "Ancient Israel"* (2nd ed.; JSOTSup 148; Sheffield: Sheffield Academic, 1995), 58–60, for whom there is no continuity. In my opinion Davies' examples prove the contrary of what he wants to show. Certainly, "the modern 'British' are not the Britons of the Roman period, and mostly not descended from them . . ." (59). But does that mean that the Celtic Britons have no part in a "history of Great Britain"? It is only consistent with such positions that Keith W. Whitelam, "The Identity of Early Israel: The Realignment and Transformation of Late Bronze-Iron Age Palestine," *JSOT* 63 (1994): 57–87, demands that the expression "Israel" and the search for an "early Israel" should be abandoned, at least "for the time being" (76). For a critique of "minimalism" and for the continuity of the name "Israel," see Hartmut N. Rösel, "The Emergence of Ancient Israel—Some Related Problems," *BN* 114/115 (2002): 151–60.

25. Herbert Donner, *Geschichte des Volkes Israel und seiner Nachbarn in Grundzügen*, part 1, *Von den Anfängen bis zur Staatenbildungszeit* (3rd ed.; GAT 4/1; Göttingen: Vandenhoeck & Ruprecht, 2000), 48.

26. Niels Peter Lemche, *Prelude to Israel's Past: Background and Beginnings of Israelite History and Identity* (trans E. F. Maniscalco; Peabody: Hendrickson, 1998; German original, 1996), 145.

27. So Volkmar Fritz, *Die Entstehung Israels im 12. und 11. Jahrhundert v. Chr.* (BE 2; Stuttgart: Kohlhammer, 1996), 67; Lemche, ibid., 148.

28. Lemche, ibid., 150. For the events as a whole, see also J. Alberto Soggin, "Ancient Israel: An Attempt at a Social and Economic Analysis of the Available Data," in *Text and Context: Old Testament and Semitic Studies for F. C. Fensham* (ed. Walter T. Claassen; JSOTSup 48; Sheffield: JSOT, 1988), 201–208; Hayim Tadmor, "The Decline of Empires in Western Asia ca. 1200 B.C.E.," in

Symposia Celebrating the Seventy-fifth Anniversary of the Founding of the American Schools of Oriental Research (1900–1975) (ed. Frank M. Cross; Cambridge, Mass.: American Schools of Oriental Research, 1979), 1–14.

29. See the summary in Fritz, *Die Entstehung Israels*, 69.

30. Thomas L. Thompson, *Early History of the Israelite People: From the Written and Archaeological Sources* (SHANE 4; Leiden: Brill, 1994), 263–74 rightly suggests we should be cautious about dramatizing the "whirlwind advance of the sea peoples" and "mass migrations," as was previously so popular. Cf. also Robert Drews, *The End of the Bronze Age: Changes in Warfare and the Catastrophe ca. 1200 B.C.* (Princeton: Princeton University Press, 1993), whose own explanation, however, is one-sided in its military-political emphasis.

31. So Fritz, *Die Entstehung Israels*, 67.

32. For these examples see ibid., 69–70. For the Canaanite cities, see also Rivka Gonen, "Urban Canaan in the Late Bronze Period," *BASOR* 253 (1984): 61–73.

33. For the Negeb, see.Volkmar Fritz "Erwägungen zur Siedlungsgeschichte des Negeb in der eisen-I-Zeit (1200–1000 v. Chr.) im Lichte der Ausgrabungen auf der Hirbet-el-Mšaš," *ZDPV* 91 (1975): 30–45; and Lars Eric Axelsson, *The Lord Rose up from Seir. Studies in the History and Traditions of the Negev and Southern Judah* (ConBOT 25; Stockholm: Almqvist & Wiksell, 1987). Of course, not all the new settlements arose at the same time; on this, see Israel Finkelstein, *The Archaeology of the Israelite Settlement* (Jerusalem: Israel Exploration Society, 1988), 324–30. The process was different in different regions within the land as well, as Dieter Vieweger, "Überlegungen zur Landnahme israelitischer Stämme unter besonderer Berücksichtigung der galiläischen Berglandgebiete," *ZDPV* 109 (1993): 20–36, illustrates for the Galilean hill country in contrast to the Negeb. For Galilee, see also Zwi Gal, *Lower Galilee During the Iron Age* (ASORDS 8; Winona Lake: Eisenbrauns, 1992). For the events in the different regions of the land, see the various essays in Israel Finkelstein and Nadav Na'aman, *From Nomadism to Monarchy:*

Archaeological and Historical Aspects of Early Israel (Washington, D.C.: Biblical Archaeology Society, 1994); and for the lands east of the Jordan, see Siegfried Mittmann, *Beiträge zur Siedlungs- und Territorialgeschichte des nördlichen Ostjordanlandes* (ADPV; Wiesbaden: Harrassowitz, 1970).

34. For the agricultural conditions in general see above, chapter 2, 15–17. For the geography of settlement, see also the references in Israel Finkelstein, *The Archaeology of the Israelite Settlement*, esp. 324–35; idem, *The Land of Ephraim Survey 1980–1987: Preliminary Report* (Tel Aviv: Institute of Archaeology of Tel Aviv University, 1988–89): 15–16, 117–83; and idem, 1989. For the preconditions for agriculture, see David C. Hopkins, *The Highlands of Canaan. Agricultural Life in the Early Iron Age* (SWBA 3; Decatur: Almond, 1985); and Oded Borowski, *Agriculture in Iron Age Israel* (Winona Lake: Eisenbrauns, 1987).

35. Janne J. Nurmi, *Die Ethik unter dem Druck des Alltags. Die Impulse der gesellschaftlichen Änderungen und Situation zu der sozialkritischen Prophetie in Juda im 8. Jh. v. Chr.* (Åbo: Åbo Akademis, 2004), 82: "Specialization made trade among the settlements necessary, since the new settlements had to import grain from the lower-lying plains."

36. On this, see Finkelstein, *The Archaeology of the Israelite Settlement*, 336–48.

37. Cf. Hartmut N. Rösel, *Israel in Kanaan. Zum Problem der Entstehung Israels* (BEATAJ 11; Frankfurt: Peter Lang, 1992), 59: "The Israelite society did not originate with the Habiru of the Late Bronze Age, although it is quite true that Habiru were also present in Israel."

38. Finkelstein, *The Archaeology of the Israelite Settlement*, 337: " . . . the people settling in the hill country in the Iron I period, or at least most of them, came from a pastoralist background."

39. Rösel, *Israel in Kanaan*, 62: "Another group who may have been important for the origins of Israel were the Shasu"; after examining the evidence, Rösel concludes "that the Shasu are of the greatest importance for the origins of Israel, more important than many other groups" (65).

40. Fritz, *Die Entstehung Israels*, 92 questions this last possibility on the grounds that "the mate-

rial culture is clearly in the Canaanite tradition." In my opinion, this does not altogether exclude the possibility of the existence of immigrants, but it does establish that they could not have been the dominant element in the new settlements. Finkelstein, *The Archaeology of the Israelite Settlement*, 348: "Along with most other scholars, we accept that there must be a kernel of historical veracity in the deeply rooted biblical tradition concerning the origin of Israel in Egypt. . . . Certain elements among the settlers may well have come from outside the country . . . and a portion of the new population might have even come from a desert background."

41. See Christa Schäfer-Lichtenberger, *Stadt und Eidgenossenschaft im Alten Testament. Eine Auseinandersetzung mit Max Webers Studie "Das antike Judentum"* (BZAW 156; Berlin: Walter de Gruyter, 1983), 195-322.

42. Here Finkelstein's suggestion that we disengage the question of ethnicity from that of the people's self-identification seems to me to make sense: ". . . an Israelite during the Iron I period was anyone whose descendants . . . described themselves as Israelites. . . . Thus even a person who may have considered himself a Hivite, Gibeonite, Kenizzite, etc., in the early twelfth century, but whose descendants in the same village a few generations later thought of themselves as Israelites, will . . . be considered here as an Israelite" (*The Archaeology of the Israelite Settlement*, 27–28). Cf. also Vieweger's definition: "In what follows, 'Israelite' and 'Israelites' will describe those groups, clans, and tribes who (or whose descendants) lived at the time of the establishment of the monarchy under David and Solomon as the Israelite population in the newly constituted kingdom of Israel/Judah" ("Überlegungen zur Landnahme," 20n1).

43. For the question of ethnicity see also 55–59, below.

44. See above, 41–44. Niels Peter Lemche, sees in Exod 1:11 and this papyrus indications "that can be most concretely connected to an Israelite sojourn in Egypt," but adds that "even these . . . can be used only with the greatest caution," (*Prelude to Israel's Past: Background and Beginnings of Israelite History*

and Identity (trans. E. F. Maniscalco; Peabody: Hendrickson, 1998], 62–65, quoting 63). His own suggestion that we should see the note in Exod 1:11 as a backward projection from a later period must, of course, operate on the basis of pure speculation: "At that time (in the Saitic epoch) Pharaoh Necco may have used Israelite prisoners of war, after his campaign in the year 609 . . . for his building works. If this theory is not entirely satisfying, other possibilities may be considered . . ." (63).

45. For the occurrences in Exodus 1–15 and in the Joseph story, see Rainer Kessler, *Die Ägyptenbilder der Hebräischen Bibel. Ein Beitrag zur neueren Monotheismusdebatte* (SBS 197; Stuttgart: Katholisches Bibelwerk, 2002), 110, 143. The third block of text where the word "Hebrew" appears frequently is the Philistine stories in 1 Samuel; see below, chapter 7, 91–97.

46. Cf. Lemche's rhetorical question: "Was there ever an ancestral period?" (*Prelude to Israel's Past*, 34). See also Kathryn A. Kamp and, Norman Yoffee, "Ethnicity in Ancient Western Asia During the Early Second Millennium B.C.: Archaeological Assessments and Ethnoarchaeological Prospectives," *BASOR* 237 (1980): 85–99. In contrast, Abraham Malamat, following the traditional viewpoint oriented to the Bible, holds to the existence of an ancestral era as part of Israel's "proto-history," positing that memories going back centuries were reduced to three generations in the biblical account by a process of "telescoping" ("The Proto-History of Israel: A Study in Method," in *The Word of the Lord Shall Go Forth. Festschrift for David Noel Freedman* (ed. Carol L. Meyers and M. O'Connor; Winona Lake: Eisenbrauns, 303–313, at 307). Unfortunately, Malamat does not explain how a cultural memory that would have transmitted such memories in a pre-literate period might have functioned.

47. Moshe Weinfeld points to the parallel settlement of the coastal plain by the equally nonautochthonous Sea Peoples, "Historical Facts Behind the Israelite Settlement Pattern," *VT* 38 (1988): 324–32.

48. William F. Albright, "The Israelite Conquest of Canaan in the Light of Archaeology,"

BASOR 74 (1939): 11–23; Manfred Weippert (*Die Landnahme der israelitischen Stämme in der neueren wissenschaftlichen Diskussion. Ein kritischer Bericht* [FRLANT 92. Göttingen: Vandenhoeck & Ruprecht ,1967], 51) calls this model the "archaeological solution"; Volkmar Fritz ("Die Landnahme der israelitischen Stämme in Kanaan," *ZDPV* 106 [1990]: 63–77) speaks of an "invasion hypothesis." For a description and critique, see also Helmut Engel, *Die Vorfahren Israels in Ägypten. Forschungsgeschichtlicher Überblock über die Darstellungen seit Richard Lepsius (1849)* (FTS 27; Frankfurt: Knecht, 1979) 135–46; and Volkmar Fritz, "Conquest or Settlement? The Early Iron Age in Palestine," *BA* 50 (1987): 84–100.

49. Albrecht Alt, "The Settlement of the Israelites in Palestine," in *Essays on Old Testament History and Religion* (trans. R. A. Wilson; Garden City: Doubleday, 1967; original German essay, 1925), 133–69; idem, "Erwägungen über die Landnahme der Israeliten in Palästina," *Kleine Schriften zur Geschichte des Volkes Israel* (3 vols.; Munich: Beck, 1968; original German essay, 1939), 1:126–75; Martin Noth, *Geschichte Israels* (9th ed.; Göttingen: Vandenhoeck & Ruprecht, 1981), 67–82. For a description and critique, cf. Engel, *Die Vorfahren Israels in Ägypten*, 146–51.

50. George Mendenhall, "The Hebrew Conquest of Palestine," *BA* 25 (1962): 66–87 = *BARev* 3 (1970): 100–120; Norman K. Gottwald, "Domain Assumptions and Social Models in the Study of Premonarchic Israel," in *Congress Volume Edinburgh 1974* (VTSUP 28; Leiden: Brill, 1975), 89–100; idem, *The Tribes of Yahweh. A Sociology of the Religion of Liberated Israel 1250–1050 B.C.E.* (Maryknoll: Orbis, 1979); and idem, "The Israelite Settlement as a Social Revolutionary Movement," in *Biblical Archaeology Today: Proceedings of the International Congress on Biblical Archaeology, Jerusalem, April 1984* (Jerusalem: Israel Exploration Society, 1985), 34–46.

51. Even the few demonstrable cases of destruction by military action do nothing to prove that it was "Israelites," and they alone, who could have done it; see Weippert, *Die Landnahme der israelitischen Stämme*, 125: "The proof would be simpler if

the conquerors had left their victory steles behind on the ruins of the Late Bronze Age Canaanite cities."

52. Cf. Siegfried Herrmann, "Basic Factors of Israelite Settlement in Canaan," in *Biblical Archaeology Toda: Proceedings of the International Congress on Biblical Archaeology, Jerusalem, April 1984* (Jerusalem: Israel Exploration Society, 1985), 47–53, quoting 48, on the three models: "One of the first mistakes made . . . is the generalization of one model, and the assumption that the settlement process was characterized by the same presuppositions and conditions in every region."

53. See Robert B. Coote, *Early Israel: A New Horizon* (Minneapolis: Fortress Press, 1990), 1–2: "It is now clear that there was no conquest of highland Palestine by outside invaders as told in the Bible, no infiltration of disparate nomads into the Palestine hills to merge gradually in a tribal league as proposed by Alt and Noth, and no peasant revolution as proposed by Mendenhall and Gottwald. These views as such no longer apply, although ingredients of all three rightly continue to play an important role in the understanding of early Israel."

54. Cf. the concept of "emergence" in Baruch Halpern, *The Emergence of Israel in Canaan* (SBLMS 29; Chico: Scholars, 1983); Robert B. Coote and Keith W. Whitelam, "The Emergence of Israel: Social Transformation and State Formation Following the Decline in Late Bronze Age Trade," in *Social Scientific Criticism of the Hebrew Bible and its Social World: The Israelite Monarchy. Semeia 37* (1986): 107–47; Robert B. Coote and Keith W. Whitelam, *The Emergence of Early Israel in Historical Perspective* (SWBA 5; Sheffield: Almond, 1987); or "emergence" [*Entstehung*] in Volkmar Fritz, *Die Entstehung Israels im 12. und 11. Jahrhundert v. Chr.* (BE 2; Stuttgart: Kohlhammer, 1996); cf. also Niels Peter Lemche, *Early Israel: Anthropological and Historical Studies on the Israelite Society Before the Monarchy* (VTSUP 37; Leiden: Brill, 1985): 411–35.

55. Thus Winfried Thiel, *Die soziale Entwicklung Israels in vorstaatlicher Zeit* (2nd ed.; Neukirchen-Vluyn: Neukirchener, 1985).

56. Note Norman Gottwald's subtitle, *The Tribes of Yahweh. A Sociology of the Religion of Liberated Israel 1250–1050 B.C.E.* (Maryknoll: Orbis, 1979).

57. Frank Crüsemann, *Der Widerstand gegen das Königtum. Die antiköniglichen Tete des Alten Testaments und der Kampf un dem frühen israelitischen Staat* (WMANT 49; Neukirchen-Vluyn: Neukirchener Verlag, 1978), 203.

58. See the title of Rainer Neu's work, *Von der Anarchie zum Staat. Entwicklungsgeschichte Israels vom Nomadentum zur Monarcie im Spiegel der Ethnosoziologie* (Neukirchen-Vluyn: Neukirchener, 1992).

59. Christa Schäfer-Lichtenberger, "Zur Funktion der Soziologie im Studium des Alten Testaments," in *Congress Volume Oslo 1998* (ed. André Lemaire and Magne Sæbø; VTSUP 80; Leiden: Brill, 179–202, 2000), 186 speaks of a "community life organized by kinship."

60. For J. Alberto Soggin, "the texts that speak of 'Israel' in the pre-royal period . . . are for the most part qualitatively unsuited for giving us a historical picture of the development of Israel and Judah as peoples and nations" ("Probleme einer Vor- und Frühgeschichte Israels," *ZAW* 100 [1988]: suppl. 255–67, quoting 261). This accurate description of the state of the biblical sources, however, can scarcely support the conclusion: "Therefore my description of Israel's pre- and early history begins with the kingdom of David and Solomon" (259). For Soggin's position, see also above, at the beginning of this chapter.

61. See 45–49, above.

62. Israel Finkelstein, *The Archaeology of the Israelite Settlement* (Jerusalem: Israel Exploration Society, 1988), 30.

63. See below, 61–62.

64. Finkelstein, *The Archaeology of the Israelite Settlement*, 30.

65. On the family, see Shunya Bendor, *The Social Structure of Ancient Israel: The Institution of the Family (beit 'ab) from the Settlement to the End of the Monarchy* (Jerusalem Biblical Studies 7; Jerusalem: Simor, 1996); Georg Fohrer, "Die Familiengemeinschaft," in *Studien zu alttestamentlichen*

Texten und Themen (BZAW 155; Berlin: Walter de Gruyter, 1981), 161–71; Carol L. Meyers, *Discovering Eve: Ancient Israelite Women in Context* (New York: Oxford University Press, 1988); Leo G. Perdue et al., *Families in Ancient Israel* (Louisville: Westminster John Knox, 1997).

66. Bendor, *Social Structure of Ancient Israel*, 54–56, points to the slippery state of the language.

67. See below, 59–61.

68. Norman K. Gottwald, *The Tribes of Yahweh. A Sociology of the Religion of Liberated Israel 1250–1050 B.C.E.* (Maryknoll: Orbis, 1979), 334: "Only the extended family . . . could in fact trace its lineage to a known common ancestor. At all other levels the kinship links were fictitiously projected by means of mythical or assumed patrilineal ancestry."

69. For the ethnological and biblical problem of the category "tribe," see James D. Martin, "Israel as a Tribal Society," in *The World of Ancient Israel: Sociological, Anthropological and Political Perspectives* (ed. Ronald E. Clements; Cambridge: Cambridge University Press, 95–117 (1989). Because the category is so problematic, I have avoided describing pre-state Israel as a "tribal society" (as does, for example, Niels Peter Lemche, *Ancient Israel: A New History of Israelite Society* [Sheffield: JSOT Press, 1988], 88).

70. So Volkmar Fritz, *Die Entstehung Israels im 12. und 11. Jahrhundert v. Chr.* (BE 2; Stuttgart: Kohlhammer, 1996), 121–22, 179–84.

71. So Rainer Neu, *Von der Anarchie zum Staat. Entwicklungsgeschichte Israels vom Nomadentum zur Monarcie im Spiegel der Ethnosoziologie* (Neukirchen-Vluyn: Neukirchener, 1992), 165–67.

72. In his extensive analysis of the "all-Israelite tradition" and the "Israelite historical tradition", Niels Peter Lemche, comes to the conclusion that ". . . on no account were the basic preconditions present for the emergence of the concept of Israel as a unity before the period of the monarchy Furthermore, on no account could this concept of a united Israel have resulted in pan-Israelite historical writing before the time of the Exile" (*Early Israel: Anthropological and Historical Studies on the Israelite Society Before the Monarchy* [VTSUP 37; Leiden: Brill, 1985], 291–305, 306–85, quoting 384). However, Lemche also sees that the Merneptah stele suggests "that the Israel in question was a tribal society," "a coalition of tribes" (430). The only thing newly added in the monarchical period is the tribe of Judah and its integration into the overall picture of Israel.

73. Max Weber, *Die Wirtschaftsethik der Weltreligionen. Das antike Judentum. Schriften und Reden 1911–1920* (ed. Eckart Otto with the cooperation of Julia Offermann; MWG 1/21; Tübingen: Mohr, 2005); cf. Christa Schäfer-Lichtenberger, *Stadt und Eidgenossenschaft im Alten Testament. Eine Auseinandersetzung mit Max Webers Studie "Das antike Judentum"* (BZAW 156; Berlin: Walter de Gruyter, 1983).

74. Martin Noth, *Das System der zwölf Stämme Israels* (BWA(N)T 52; Darmstadt: Wissenschaftliche Buchgesellschaft, 1930); cf. C. H. J. de Geus. *The Tribes of Israel: An Investigation into Some of the Presuppositions of Martin Noth's Amphictyony Hypothesis* (SSN 18; Assen: Van Gorcum, 1976); Otto Bächli, *Amphiktyonie im Alten Testament. Forschungsgeschichtliche Studie zur Hypothese von Martn Noth* (ThZS 6; Basel: Friedrich Reinhardt, 1977).

75. Siegfried Herrmann, *A History of Israel in Old Testament Times* (trans. John Bowden; rev. and enl. ed., 2nd ed., Philadelphia: Fortress Press, 1981; German original 1980), 157; Winfried Thiel, *Die soziale Entwicklung Israels in vorstaatlicher Zeit* (2nd ed.; Neukirchen-Vluyn: Neukirchener, 1985), 136–37. Of course, both still assume that this consciousness led to some kind of tribal covenant.

76. Fritz, 12, my emphasis.

77. Rainer Neu, "'Israel' vor der Entstehung des Königtums," *BZ* n.s. 30 (1986): 204–21, quoting 215.

78. Jacob Milgrom, "Religious Conversion and the Revolt Model for the Formation of Israel," *JBL* 101 (1982): 169–76, points this out.

79. On this see, Christian Sigrist, *Regulierte Anarchie: Unters. zum Fehlen u. zur Entstehung polit. Herrschaft in segmentären Gesellschaften Afrikas* (Olten: Walter, 1979); and idem, "Segmentäre

Gesellschaft," in *Ethnologische Texte I. Vor- und Frühgeschichte Israels* (ed. Christian Sigrist and Rainer Neu; Neukirchen-Vluyn: Neukirchener, 1989), 106–22. But for a critique of this model, see David Fiensy, "Using the Nuer Culture of Africa in Understanding the Old Testament: An Evaluation," *JSOT* 38 (1987): 73–83, esp. 76–80.

80. Frank Crüsemann, *Der Widerstand gegen das Königtum. Die antiköniglichen Tete des Alten Testaments und der Kampf un dem frühen israelitischen Staat* (WMANT 49; Neukirchen-Vluyn: Neukirchener. 1978), 194–222. See similar suggestions by Norman K. Gottwald, *The Tribes of Yahweh: A Sociology of the Religion of Liberated Israel 1250–1050 B.C.E.* (Maryknoll: Orbis, 1979), esp. 293–341; and Robert R. Wilson, *Genealogy and History in the Biblical World* (Yale Near Eastern Researches 7; New Haven: Yale University Press, 1977), esp. 18–37; neither of whom reference Sigrist.

81. Rainer Neu, *Von der Anarchie zum Staat. Entwicklungsgeschichte Israels vom Nomadentum zur Monarcie im Spiegel der Ethnosoziologie* (Neukirchen-Vluyn: Neukirchener, 1992), 179–89.

82. An illustrative example is Paul Bohanan's description of the African Tiv ("Die Wanderung und Ausdehnung der Tiv," in *Ethnologische Texte zum Alten Testament*, vol. 1, *Vor- und Frühgeschichte Israels* [ed. Christian Sigrist and Rainer Neu; Neukirchen-Vluyn: Neukirchener,1989], 86–105).

83. John W. Rogerson, "Was Early Israel a Segmentary Society?" *JSOT* 36 (1986): 17–26, at 18, disputes that the later state of Israel arose out of a lineage society. Rather, he sees the pre-state society as an association of different chiefdoms and the creation of the state as the dominance "of one chiefdom over the others." However, such "chiefdoms" are not attested in pre-state Israel; see 60–61 below. Moreover, it needs to be shown how the consciousness of a common bond arose out of the association of competing authorities. For a critique of other chiefdom concepts, see below, chapter 7, 74–76.

84. Kathryn A. Kamp and Norman Yoffee, "Ethnicity in Ancient Western Asia During the Early Second Millennium B.C.: Archaeological Assessments and Ethnoarchaeological Prospectives," *BASOR* 237 (1980): 85–99, quoting 88. For the category of ethnicity see also Mark G. Brett, "Israel's Indigenous Origins: Cultural Hybridity and the Formation of Israelite Ethnicity," *BibInt* 11 (2003): 400–412.

85. For a critique of a Canaan-Israel dualism see Thomas L. Thompson, *Early History of the Israelite People: From the Written and Archaeological Sources* (SHANE 4; Leiden: Brill, 1992) 310–16; and cf. also Hartmut N. Rösel: ". . . it is important . . . that this Israel, though it lived 'in the land of Canaan' (= Palestine), was nevertheless separate from Canaan, that is, from the . . . Canaanite cities. According to the witness of the Merneptah stele, too, Israel was an independent entity that cannot simply be equated with Canaan" (*Israel in Kanaan. Zum Problem der Entstehung Israels* [BEATAJ 11; Frankfurt: Peter Lang, [1992], 52).

86. Certainly, such a static concept scarcely would apply to modern notions of ethnicity, either. The French people, for example, are made up of the descendants of Celtic, Roman, Frankish, Norman, and marginally of Basque and Alemannic and other groups, and they continue to be altered by immigration.

87. On this see Sara Japhet, *1 Chronik* (HTKAT; Freiburg: Herder, 2002), 116–17; and above, 54–55, for reflections on the new settlers' ethnic identity. The title of Antonin Causse's classic *Du groupe éthnique à la communauté religieuse* ("From the ethnic group to the religious community"; see chapter 1, 2–4, above) is thus misleading in two ways. First of all, the ethnic group is not the beginning; it is in itself the result of a dynamic process. Second, the process does not conclude by transforming ethnic groups into a different kind of entity.

88. See the definition of a segmented society in Gottwald, *The Tribes of Yahweh*, 322: "Segmented tribes are composed of two or more primary segments which are structurally and functionally equivalent and also politically equal."

89. So Ernst Axel Knauf, *Die Umwelt des Alten Testaments* (NSK-AT 29; Stuttgart: Katholisches Bibelwerk, 1994), 69.

90. In this regard, note that in the quotation from Gottwald, *The Tribes of Yahweh*, 322 (cited above), it is clearly the segments that are equal.

91. See Crüsemann's remark: "Nor are all the members equal in the abstract" (*Der Widerstand gegen das Königtum*, 206).

92. Lemche, *Early Israel*, 223.

93. This is Jürgen Kegler's interpretation, "Debora—Erwägungen zur politischen Funktion einer Frau in einer patriarchalistischen Gesellschaft," in *Traditionen der Befreiung. Sozialgeschichtliche Bibelauslegungen 2: Frauen in der Bibel* (ed. Willi Schottroff and Wolfgang Stegemann; Munich: Kaiser, 1980), 37–59, esp. 49–50.

94. Kathryn A. Kamp and Norman Yoffee: "Ethnicity in Ancient Western Asia During the Early Second Millennium B.C.: Archaeological Assessments and Ethnoarchaeological Prospectives," *BASOR* 237 (1980): 85–99, quoting 88.

95. On this see Frank Crüsemann, *The Torah: Theology and Social History of Old Testament Law* (trans. Allan W. Mahnke; Minneapolis: Fortress Press, 1996; German original 1992), 80–95.

96. For the question whether Gilead in Judges 11 is a territory, as is usually thought, or a city, as probably intended in 2 Sam 24:6; Hos 6:8; 12:12, see Christa Schäfer-Lichtenberger, *Stadt und Eidgenossenschaft im Alten Testament. Eine Auseinandersetzung mit Max Webers Studie "Das antike Judentum"* (BZAW 156; Berlin: Walter de Gruyter, 1983), 255–56; Rainer Neu, *Von der Anarchie zum Staat. Entwicklungsgeschichte Israels vom Nomadentum zur Monarcie im Spiegel der Ethnosoziologie* (Neukirchen-Vluyn: Neukirchener, 1992), 169–70.

97. For this question see also chapter 7, 72–73, below.

98. It is assumed by Schäfer-Lichtenberger, *Stadt und Eidgenossenschaft im Alten Testament*, 196 "that purely Israelite settlements can be distinguished from other settlements of Canaanite origin." For an attempt at archaeological identification of Israelite settlements, see Israel Finkelstein, *The Archaeology of the Israelite Settlement* (Jerusalem: Israel Exploration Society, 1988), 27–33.

99. Finkelstein, ibid., 11, posits this, for example, in the case of Shechem: "The Iron I inhabitants there were apparently mixed, that is, composed of different ethnic elements...."

100. The *sarem*, sometimes mentioned as actors alongside the elders and the men (Judg 8:6, 14; 9:30; 10:18), are a backward projection from the monarchical period; see Schäfer-Lichtenberger, *Stadt und Eidgenossenschaft im Alten Testament*, 253.

101. Ibid., 275.

102. Ibid., 242. This is not undermined by Volker Wagner's study, "Beobachtungen am Amt der Ältesten im alttestamentlichen Israel," *ZAW* 114 (2002): 391–411, 560–76. Wagner correctly shows that the office of elder essentially belongs to the monarchical period (396–403; see below, chapter 7, 88–91). Because that office, as Wagner also emphasizes, was particularly associated with cities (403–11), "its beginnings in the pre-national period" (409) are presumed to be found where, in the pre-national period, there were already cities.

103. For the typology of authority in Weber, see Max Weber, *Economy and Society: An Outline of Interpretive Sociology* (ed. Günther Roth and Claus Wittich; trans. Ephraim Fischoff et al.; Berkeley: University of California Press, 1978, 5th ed. German original, 1972), 122–76.

104. Schäfer-Lichtenberger, *Stadt und Eidgenossenschaft im Alten Testament*, 356–67.

105. On this see, Abraham Malamat, "Charismatische Führung im Buch der Richter," in *Max Webers Studie über das antike Judentum. Interpretation und Kritik* (ed. Wolfgang Schluchter; STW 340; Frankfurt: Suhrkamp, 1981), 110–33; Herbert Niehr, *Herrschen und Richten. Die Wurzel špṭ im Alten Orient und im Alten Testament* (FB 54; Würzburg: Echter Verlag, (1986); Ze'ev Weisman, "Charismatic Leaders in the Era of the Judges," *ZAW* 89 (1977): 399–411.

106. For the biblical figures of the judges as the expression of charismatic authority, see Max Weber, *Die Wirtschaftsethik der Weltreligionen. Das antike Judentum. Schriften und Reden 1911–1920* (MWG 1/21; Tübingen: Mohr, 2005), 297–98.

For a discussion see Malamat, ibid.; Neu, *Von der Anarchie zum Staat*, 221–23; and Weisman, ibid.

107. Volmar Fritz, *Die Entstehung Israels im 12. und 11. Jahrhundert v. Chr.* (BE 2; Stuttgart: Kohlhammer, 1996), 83–84, pls. 8 and 9, and also p. 92.

108. On 1 Samuel 25, see Thomas Staubli, *Das Image der Nomaden im Alten Israel und in der Ikonographie seiner sesshaften Nachbarn* (OBO 107; Fribourg: Universitätsverlag; Göttingen: Vandenhoeck & Ruprecht, 1991), 238–44.

109. Hannelis Shulte, "Beobachtungen zum Begriff der *Zônâ* im alten Testament," *ZAW* 104 (1992): 255–62; Corinna Friedl, *Polygynie in Mesopotamien und Israel. Sozialgeschichtliche Analyse polygyner Beziehungen anhand rechtlicher texte aus dem 2. und 1. Jahrtausend v. Chr.* (AOAT 277; Münster: Ugarit, 2000), 168–70.

7. Israel and Judah

1. See above, chapter 2.

2. For the expansion of the region of Saul's rule see Walter Dietrich and Stefan Münger, "Die Herrschaft Sauls und der Norden Israels," in *Saxa loquentur. Studien zur Archäologie Palästinas/Israels. Festschrift für Volkmar Fritz* (ed. Cornelis G. den Hertog, Ulrich Hübner, and Stefan Münger; AOAT 302; Münster: Ugarit, 2003), 39–59.

3. In this view I am following Siegfried Kreuzer: "Saul's rule thus arose under the eyes of the Philistines" ("'War Saul auch unter den Philistern?' Die Anfänge des Königtums in Israel," *ZAW* 113 [2001]: 56–73; quoting 71). See now similarly Georg Hentschel, *Saul. Schuld, Reue und Tragik eines "Gesalbten"* (Biblische Gestalten 7; Leipzig: Evangelische Verlagsanstalt, 2003), 22–24. For Saul's (and David's) dependence on the Philistines and their tense relationship with them, see also Ernst Axel Knauf, "Saul, David, and the Philistines: From Geography to History," *BN* 109 (2001): 15–18.

4. It is possible that the difficult number "two years" in 1 Sam 13:1 does not describe the whole length of Saul's reign, which from the circum-

stances themselves would be too brief, but only the remaining time of his reign after the outbreak of open conflict with the Philistines; see Siegfried Kreuzer, "'Saul war noch zwei Jahre König . . . .'" Textgeschichtliche, literarische und historische Beobachtungen zu 1 Sam 13,1," *BZ* n.s. 40 (1996): 263–70.

5. The idea that he was already previously married to Michal (1 Samuel 18) is a redactional narrative elaboration for the purpose of underscoring David's claims; on this, see Christa Schäfer-Lichtenberger, *Stadt und Eidgenossenschaft im Alten Testament. Eine Auseinandersetzung mit Max Webers Studie "Das antike Judentum"* (BZAW 156; Berlin: de Gruyter, 2003). The same is true of his supposed friendship with Saul's son Jonathan, who as much as lays the kingship at David's feet. Even if David's career really did begin at Saul's court, the traditions to that effect in 1 Samuel 16–31 are so highly developed in the direction of Davidic propaganda that nothing historically reliable can be reconstructed from them.

6. Whether this took place through military action, as the Bible suggests, or in peaceful fashion, as Schäfer-Lichtenberger, ibid., 385–90 proposes, can remain moot here.

7. Herbert Donner, 220: "David's empire," *Geschichte des Volkes Israel und seiner Nachbarn in Grundzügen*, part 1, *Von den Anfängen bis zur Staatenbildungszeit* (GAT 4/1; 3rd ed.; Göttingen: Vandenhoeck & Ruprecht, 2000); also Walter Dietrich, *Die frühe Königszeit in Israel. 10. Jahrhundert v. Chr.* (BE 3; Stuttgart: Kohlhammer, 1997), 148–201.

8. Philip R. Davies: ". . . we are unable to include in our reconstruction any kingdom uniting the territories of Israel and Judah," (*In Search of "Ancient Israel"* [2nd ed.; JSOTSup 148; Sheffield: Sheffield Academic Press, 1995], 65).

9. The archaeological literature on the dating of the "Solomonic" architecture is legion. As examples for an early dating, see Israel Finkelstein, "The Archaeology of the United Monarchy: An Alternative View," *Levant* 28 (1996): 177–87; for a defense of the traditional view see Baruch Halpern, "The Gate of Megiddo and the Debate on

the 10th Century," in *Congress Volume Oslo 1998* (ed. André Lemaire and Magne Sæbø; VTSup 80; Leiden: Brill, 2000), 79–121. For the debate over high chronology (HC = early dating of the archaeological findings) and low chronology (LC), cf. Steven M. Ortiz, "Methodological Comments on the *Low Chronology:* A Reply to Ernst Axel Knauf," *BN* 111 (2002): 34–39; and the critical evaluation of Israel Finkelstein's work by Raz Kletter, "Chronology and United Monarchy. A Methodological Review," *ZDPV* 120 (2004): 13–54. He comes to the tentative conclusion: "Hence, LC is possible, though it is not superior to the HC" (44).

10. The quotation is from Israel Finkelstein and Neil A. Silberman, *The Bible Unearthed: Archaeology's New Vision of Ancient Israel and the Origin of its Sacred Texts* (New York: Free, 2001), 142. Baruch Halpern, "The Construction of the Davidic State: An Exercise in Historiography," in *The Origins of the Ancient Israelite States* (ed. Volkmar Fritz and Philip R. Davies; JSOTSup 228; Sheffield: Sheffield Academic Press, 1996), 44–75, at 72–74, however, points out that capitals in that period were almost nothing else but centers of government and therefore could, in fact, be relatively small.

11. On this, see below, 91–97.

12. For the development of the Exodus from a northern Israelite tradition to one adopted by all Israel, see Rainer Kessler, *Die Ägyptenbilder der Hebräischen Bibel. Ein Beitrag zur neueren Monotheismusdebatte* (SBS 197; Stuttgart: Katholisches Bibelwerk, 2002), esp. 91–115.

13. On this, see Lester L. Grabbe, who, after an overview of scholarship designed to establish his position, concludes: "neither the 'minimalists' nor the 'maximalists' will win" ("Writing Israel's History at the End of the Twentieth Century," in *Congress Volume Oslo 1998* [ed. André Lemaire and Magne Sæbø; VTSup 80; Leiden: Brill, 2000], 203–18, quoting 215).

14. Lowell K. Handy, ed., *The Age of Solomon. Scholarship at the Turn of the Millennium* (SHCANE 11; Leiden: Brill, 1997).

15. For Shishak's campaign see Gösta Ahlström, "Pharao Shoshenq's campaign to Pales-

tine," in *History and Traditions of Early Israel. Studies Presented to Eduard Nielsen* (ed. André Lemaire and Benedikt Otzen; VTSup 50; Leiden: Brill, 1993), 1–16; Paul S. Ash, *David, Solomon and Egypt. A Reassessment* (JSOTSup 297; Sheffield: Sheffield Academic, 1999), esp. 50–56; Frank Clancy, "Shishak/Shoshenq's Travels," *JSOT* 86 (1999): 3–23; Israel Finkelstein, "The Campaign of Shoshenq I to Palestine. A Guide to the Tenth Century B.C.E. Polity," *ZDPV* 118 (2002): 109–35; and Bernd Ulrich Schipper, *Israel und Ägypten in der Königszeit. Die kulturellen Kontakte von Salomo bis zum Fall Jerusalems* (OBO 170; Fribourg: Universitätsverlag, 1999), esp. 119–32.

16. Israel Finkelstein calls it "a deal between the Jerusalem entity and Shishak" (ibid., 124).

17. David Ussishkin, "Note on Megiddo, Gezer, Ashdod, and tel Batash in the Tenth to Ninth Centuries B.C.," *BASOR* 277/278 (1990): 71–91, esp. 71–74.

18. *TGI* no. 19; *COS* 2:261–64.

19. See above, chapter 6, 44–45.

20. *KAI* no. 181; *TGI* no. 21; *TUAT* 1:646–50; *COS* 2:137–38. For the historical reliability of the stele—against Thompson's dismissal of it ("Problems of Genre and Historicity with Palestine's Inscriptions," in *Congress Volume Oslo 1998* [ed. André Lemaire and Magne Sæbø; VTSUP 80; Leiden: Brill, 2000], 321–26)—see John A. Emerton, "The Values of the Moabite Stone as an Historical Source," *VT* 52 (2002): 483–92.

21. *TGI* no. 20; *COS* 2:266–70.

22. Cf. *TGI* nos. 22, 26, 27; *COS* 2:276–77, 286–89, 291–92, 298.

23. First publication in Avraham Biran and Joseph Naveh (1993): "An Aramaic Stele Fragment from Tel Dan," *KEJ* 43 (1993): 81–98; and idem, "A New Fragment," *IEJ* 45 (1995): 1–18. Cf. *COS* 2:161–62.

24. The multitudinous literature in the ten years since the discovery of the first fragments is discussed by George Athas, *The Tel Dan Inscription: A Reappraisal and a New Interpretation* (JSOTSup 360; Copenhagen International Seminar 12; Sheffield: Sheffield Academic, 2003).

25. Ernst Axel Knauf, Albert de Pury, and Thomas Römer, "*Bayt Dawid ou *Bayt Dod? Une relecture de la nouvelle inscription de Tel Dan," *BN* 72 (1994) : 60–69; Reinhard Lehmann and Marcus Reichel, "DOD und ASIMA in Tell Dan," *BN* 77 (1995): 29–31.

26. Cf. Ehud Ben Zvi, "On the Reading 'byt-dwd' in the Aramaic Stele from Tel Dan," *JSOT* 64 (1994): 25–32; Frederick H. Cryer, "On the Recently Discovered 'House of David' Inscription," *SJOT* 8 (1994): 3–20; and Niels Peter Lemche and Thomas L. Thompson, "Did Biran Kill David? The Bible in the Light of Archaeology," *JSOT* 64 (1994): 3–22.

27. The comparison with Ashdod is, of course, untenable, because that name is composed of the root *shdd** with preformative aleph; see Frank Moore Cross and David Noel Freedman, "The Name of Ashdod," *BASOR* 175 (1964): 48–50.

28. So also Ernst Axel Knauf, "Das 'Haus Davids' in der alt-aramäischen Inschrift vom Tel Dan," *BK* 51 (1996): 9–10. See overall the extended discussion in Walter Dietrich, *Die frühe Königszeit in Israel. 10. Jahrhundert v. Chr.* (BE 3; Stuttgart: Kohlhammer, 1997), 136–41.

29. *TGI* nos. 23, 28, 39; *COS* 2:289–90, 302–303, 304–305.

30. See chapter 8 below.

31. See Jørgen A. Knudtzon, *Die El-Amarna-Tafeln* (Leipzig: J. C. Hinrichs, 1915), for Labaya's letters (nos. 252–54), and Abdi-Hepa's (nos. 285–290), as well as the letter of Shuwardata mentioning both of them (no. 280), and a letter (no. 250) that speaks of the sons of Labaya. Letters nos. 286 and 289 are also in *TUAT* 1:512–16.

32. From the literature on Judges 9, see Thomas A. Boogaart, "Stone for Stone: Retribution in the Story of Abimelech and Schechem," *JSOT* 32 (1985): 45–56; Edward F. Campbell Jr., "Judges 9 and Biblical Archaeology," in *The Word of the Lord Shall Go Forth. Essays in Honor of David Noel Freedman* (ed. Carol L. Meyers and M. O'Connor; Winona Lake: Eisenbrauns, 1983), 263–71; Volkmar Fritz, "Abimelech und Sichem in Jdc. IX," *VT* 32 (1982): 129–44; Christoph Levin, "Das vorstaatliche Israel," in *Fortschreibungen. Gesammelte Stu-*

dien zum Alten Testament (BZAW 316; Berlin: de Gruyter, 2003), 142–57; Hanoch Reviv, "The Government of Shechem in the El-Amarna Period and in the Days of Abimelech," *IEJ* 16 (1966): 252–57; Hartmut N. Rösel, "Überlegungen zu 'Abimelech und Sichem in Jdc. IX,'" *VT* 33 (1983): 500–503; Herbert Schmid, "Die Herrschaft Abimelechs (Jdc 9)," *Jud* 26 (1970): 1–11; J. Alberto Soggin, "Bemerkungen zur alttestamentlichen Topographie Sichems mit besonderem Bezug auf Jdc. 9," *ZDPV* 83 (1967): 183–98; Ernst Würthwein, "Abimelech und der Untergang Sichems—Studien zu Jdc. 9," in *Studien zum Deuteronomistischen Geschichtswerk* (BZAW 227; Berlin: de Gruyter, 1994), 12–28.

33. Volkmar Fritz dates the Abimelech tradition to the time of the Israelite monarchy, "since Shechem was not populated at all between about 1150 and 975" (*Die Entstehung Israels im 12. und 11. Jahrhundert v. Chr.* [BE 2; Stuttgart: Kohlhammer, 1996], 43–45, quoting 44). Consequently, for him the narrative is "without any historical value" (idem, "Abimelech und Sichem in Jdc. IX," 143). For the problematic literary premises of Fritz's analysis, see, for example, Boogaart, "Stone for Stone"; and Campbell, "Judges 9 and Biblical Archaeology". And it is questionable whether one can draw such broad consequences from the archaeological findings as Fritz does; cf. Levin, "Das vorstaatliche Israel," 155: "The difficulties in making a clear determination about early-Iron-Age Shechem from archaeology are of little weight in light of the literary attestation."

34. For the parallels between the rules of Labaya and Abimelech, see Reviv, "The Government of Shechem," 252–57.

35. Cf. Soggin's evaluation of the episode related in Judges 9: "It is important also because of the ethnic situation it depicts: a peaceful living together of an autochthonous Israelite and Canaanite population, though that life was not without its conflicts" ("Bemerkungen zur alttestamentlichen Topographie Sichems," 184). We should recall here the quotation regarding Shechem by Israel Finkelstein: "the Iron I inhabitants there were apparently mixed, that is, composed of different

ethnic elements. . . ." (*The Archaeology of the Israelite Settlement*, 81).

36. In light of attempts to find in the Abimelech tradition a secondary "Israelitizing" of an originally Canaanite narrative—see, for example, the opinion of Würthwein, "Abimelech und der Untergang Sichems," 22, that "Abimelech [belongs] to Canaanite and not to Israelite history"—Schmid rightly asks: "But why should a bum like that be made an Israelite?" ("Die Herrschaft Abimelechs, 2n3). Levin, "Das vorstaatliche Israel," esp. 153–56, emphasizes strongly that the tradition about Abimelech and his failed attempt to establish a state in Shechem is part of the pre-history of Israelite nation-building. Of course, whether the devaluing of all the rest of the traditions about the time before Saul and David has to go along with this, as Levin proposes, is a different matter entirely.

37. Whether this is about the territory or, more probably here, the city of Gilead is not relevant to the question of governmental structures; for this problem, see chapter 6, 59–61, above.

38. Ibid.

39. See for example, Herbert Donner: "But if it is true that the building of an Israelite nation-state did not arise as a matter of necessity out of the forms of life in the pre-national tribes, external forces must have been at work . . . the threat came from the Philistines" (*Geschichte des Volkes Israel und seiner Nachbarn in Grundzügen*, part 1, *Von den Anfängen bis zur Staatenbildungszeit* [3rd ed.; GAT 4/1; Göttingen: Vandenhoeck & Ruprecht, 2000], 197).

40. See chapter 6, 59–61, above.

41. See chapter 6, 61–62, above.

42. Siegfried Kreuzer, "'War Saul auch unter den Philistern?' Die Anfänge des Königtums in Israel," *ZAW* 113 (2001): 56–73, correctly stresses that Saul did not emerge as king from a battle with the Philistines.

43. Norman K. Gottwald, *The Politics of Ancient Israel* (Library of Ancient Israel; Louisville: Westminster John Knox, 2001), 120, rightly emphasizes that recognizing the secondary character of Israelite state-construction does not permit any conclu-

sions about the degree to which Israel took over concrete state institutions from its surroundings.

44. So, after the beginning with James W. Flanagan, "Chiefs in Israel," *JSOT* 20 (1981): 47–73; likewise Frank S. Frick, for example, *The Formation of the State in Ancient Israel: A Survey of Models and Theories* (SWBA 4; Sheffield: Almond, 1985); and Walter Dietrich, "Staat/Staatsphilosophie I. Altes Testament," *TRE* 23 (2001): 4–8. Cf. also the concept of "patronage society" in Niels Peter Lemche, "From Patronage Society to Patronage Society," in *The Origins of the Ancient Israelite States* (ed. Volkmar Fritz and Philip R. Davies; JSOTSup 228; Sheffield: Sheffield Academic, 1996), 106–20.

45. So Ernst Axel Knauf, "From History to Interpretation," in *The Fabric of History: Text, Artifact and Israel's Past* (ed. Diana V. Edelman; JSOTSup 127; Sheffield: JSOT Press, 1991), 26–64; and Hermann Michael Niemann, *Herrschaft, Königtum und Staat. Skizzen zur soziokulturellen Entwicklung im monarchischen Israel* (FAT 6: Tübingen: Mohr, 1993). For discussion of the chiefdom theories, see Rainer Kessler, "Chiefdom oder Staat? Zur Sozialgeschichte der frühen Monarchie," in *Freiheit und Recht. Festschrift für Frank Crüsemann zum 65. Geburtstag* (ed. Christhof Hardmeier, Rainer Kessler, and Andreas Ruwe; Gütersloh: Kaiser/Gütersloher, 2003), 121–40.

46. Aidan W. Southall ("Zum Begriff des segmentären Staates. Das Beispiel der Alur," [1953] in *Ethnologische Texte zum Alten Testament*, vol. 2, *Die Entstehung des Königtums* [Neukirchen-Vluyn: Neukirchener, 1997], 67–92, quoting 76), who calls the "chiefs of the early period" the "precursors of the kingship"; against Pierre Clastres ("Die Gesellschaft gegen den Staat [1976]," in *Ethnologische Texte zum Alten Testament*, vol. 2, *Die Entstehung des Königtums* [ed. Christian Sigrist and Rainer Neu, Neukirchen-Vluyn: Neukirchener, 1997], 47–60, quoting 52–53): " . . . the figure of the . . . 'chief' . . . is by no means the model for a future despot. The apparatus of the state in general can certainly not be derived from primitive chiefdom."

47. Thus Joyce Marcus and Gary M. Feinman summarize the debate at a conference on "Archaic Studies": "One source of disagreement was over such terms as 'chiefdom' and 'state,' which archaeologists have borrowed from ethnology and political science" ("Introduction," in *Archaic States* [ed. Gary M. Feinman and Joyce Marcus; Santa Fe: School of American Research Press, 1998], 5). Cf. also in Norman Yoffee concerning the problematizing of neo-evolutionary theories and the plea for a closer look at individual cases, *Myths of the Archaic State: Evolution of the Earliest Cities, States, and Civilizations* (Cambridge: Cambridge University Press, 2005).

48. Niemann, *Herrschaft, Königtum und Staat*, 282.

49. Thus Niemann qualifies an example of his extensive chiefdom thesis with "(*big man, chief, king*" (ibid., 129n600), thus showing that the features of early governance he is citing do *not* distinguish clearly between "chiefdom" and state. As regards the field of archaeology, we must note that everything here depends on the interpretation of the findings; Christa Schäfer-Lichtenberger: "In my opinion, it is not up to archaeology to decide an essentially theoretic debate, whose course until now has demonstrated only that the so-called hard facts are determined by the discussants' perspectives" ("Sociological and Biblical Views of the Early State," in *The Origins of the Ancient Israelite States* [ed. Volkmar Fritz and Philip R. Davies; JSOTSup 228; Sheffield: Sheffield Academic, 1996], 78–105, quoting 82).

50. See 64–72, above.

51. For Solomon, let me mention only the collection edited by Handy, *The Age of Solomon*.

52. For reference to these two authors, see Rainer Kessler, *Staat und Gesellschaft im vorexilischen Juda. Vom 8. Jahrhundert bis zum Exil.* [VTSup 47]; Leiden: Brill, 1992), esp. 157–60; and Christa Schäfer-Lichtenberger, "Sociological and Biblical Views of the Early State," in *The Origins of the Ancient Israelite States* (ed. Volkmar Fritz and Philip R. Davies; JSOTSup 228; Sheffield: Sheffield Academic, 1996), 78–105. See also the review by Frank S. Frick, "Social Science Methods and

Theories of Significance for the Study of the Israelite Monarchy: A Critical Review Essay," *Semeia* 37 (1986): 9–52, esp. 17–26. In contrast, Raz Kletter, "Pots and Polities: Material Remains of Late Iron Age Judah in Relation to its Political Borders," *BASOR* 314 (2004): 19–54, calls for abandoning not only the concepts of "tribe" and "chiefdom," but also that of "state" (21–28). "The Bible does not have 'states,' it has kingdoms and kings" (28). But the effort to describe an ancient culture in its own terms cannot be played off against the process of translation represented by every present-day attempt at understanding. If we were to abandon the effort we would not be able to get beyond the term "time of the judges"—which from a sociological point of view is inadequate—for the pre-state epoch. Methodologically it is a question of the difference between description and theory construction. The former is necessary for keeping us close to the unique reality; the latter is essential if we are to be able to make any comparisons at all between societies and societal epochs.

53. Henri J. M. Claessen and Peter Skalnik, eds., *The Early State* (New Babylon, Studies in the Social Sciences 32; The Hauge: Mouton, 1978), 22. Norman K. Gottwald, *The Politics of Ancient Israel* (Library of Ancient Israel; Louisville: Westminster John Knox, 2001), 183, uses similar terminology, speaking of the "incipient state" and "full-scale state."

54. Claessen and Skalnik, *The Early State*, 23.

55. Ibid.

56. James D. Martin, "Israel as a Tribal Society," in *The World of Ancient Israel: Sociological, Anthropological and Political Perspectives* (ed. Ronald E. Clements; Cambridge: Cambridge University Press, 1989), 95–117, quoting 113.

57. For resistance to the monarchy see Frank Crüsemann, *Der Widerstand gegen das Königtum. Die antiköniglichen Tete des Alten Testaments und der Kampf un dem frühen israelitischen Staat* (WMANT 49; Neukirchen-Vluyn: Neukirchener, 1978); Ansgar Moenikes, *Die grundsätzliche Ablehnung des Königtums in der hebräischen Bibel. Ein Beitrag zur Religionsgeschichte des alten Israel* (BBB 99; Weinheim: Beltz Athenaeum, 1995);

Reinhard Müller, *Königtum und Gottesherrschaft. Untersuchungen zur alttestamentlichen Monarchiekritik* (FAT 2, 3rd series; Tübingen: Mohr Siebeck, 2004); Timo Veijola, *Das Königtum in der Beurteilung der deuteronomistischen Historiographie. Eine redaktionsgeschichtliche Untersuchung* (AASF 198; Helsinki: Suomalainen Tiedeakatemia, 1977); and Keith W. Whitelam, "Israelite Kingship: The Royal Ideology and its Opponents," in *The World of Ancient Israel: Sociological, Anthropological and Political Perspectives* (ed. Ronald E. Clements; Cambridge: Cambridge University Press, 1989), 119–39.

58. On this see Veijola, *Das Königtum in der Beurteilung der deuteronomistischen Historiographie*, 13, for whom "linguistic usage" remains "the most reliable criterion for assigning individual pieces of tradition to the dtr redaction."

59. Veijola, *Das Königtum in der Beurteilung der deuteronomistischen Historiographie*, 112, sees in 1 Sam 8:10–17 and Judg 9:7–15 a pre-deuteronomistic "anti-royal stream of tradition . . . in which the monarchy is attacked by very intellectual, *secular* means." According to Moenikes, only this "critique of monarchy, directed against the social ruptures of the pre-state period, i.e., the socially and economic-politically motivated critique of monarchy" belongs to the early royal period, while he traces the "theologically motivated rejection of the monarchy" to newer layers (*Die grundsätzliche Ablehnung des Königtums*, 212).

60. Against this background, Crüsemann proposes, as his work's principal thesis: "This half-century of struggle, which we can trace, against the kingship as it was in the process of being established is the time from which come the anti-monarchical texts, and they were formulated by the circles that carried on the struggle" (*Der Widerstand gegen das Königtum*, 124).

61. See above, chapter 6, 61–62.

62. See the next section.

63. See below, 78–91.

64. For the evidence, see below, 53–54.

65. On this see David C. Hopkins, "Bare Bones: Putting Flesh on the Economics of Ancient Israel," in *The Origins of the Ancient Israelite States* (ed. Volkmar Fritz and Philip R. Davies; JSOTSup 228; Sheffield: Sheffield Academic, 1996), 121–39, esp. 125–26.

66. See the summary of my reflections on the royal economy, 88–91.

67. So Marvin L. Chaney, "Systemic Study of the Israelite Monarchy," *Semeia* 37 (1986): 53–76, quoting 55.

68. Frith Lambert, "The Tribe/State Paradox in the Old Testament," *SJOT* 8 (1994): 20–44.

69. See below, 92–103.

70. See below, 88–91.

71. *CWSS* nos. 11–19, 412–415; *HAE* 2/2, 111.

72. *CWSS* no. 30; *HAE* 2/2, 111–12.

73. For the Jerahmeel mentioned there, see the seal impression in *CWSS* no. 414; *HAE* 2/2, nos. 10, 74.

74. Manfred Görg, "Zum Titel BN HMLK ('Königssohn')," in *Ägyptiaca—Biblica. Notizen und Beiträge zu den Beziehungen zwischen Ägypten und Israel* (Ägypten und Altes Testament 11; Wiesbaden: Harrassowitz, 1991), 192–96, quoting 195; for "son of the king," see also Nahman Avigad, "A Seal of 'Manasseh Son of the King,'" *IEJ* 13(1963): 133–36; idem, (1978): 52–56; and idem, "Jerahmeel & Baruch, King's Son and Scribe," *BA* 42 (1979): 114–19.

75. See chapter 6, 53–55, above.

76. For the women of the Judahite court, see Anna Kiesow, *Löwinnen von Juda. Frauen als Subjekte politischer Macht in der judäischen Königszeit* (Theologische Frauenforschung in Europa 4; Münster: Lit, 2000).

77. *CWSS* nos. 6–10, 408–11; *HAE* 2/2, 112. See also Lachish ostracon 3,1. 18 (*HAE* 1, 419).

78. *CWSS* nos. 2–4, 407; *HAE* 2/2, 112–13.

79. For the officials, see Abraham Malamat, "Organs of Statecraft in the Israelite Monarchy," *BA* 28 (1965): 34–65; Tryggve N. D. Mettinger, *Solomonic State Officials: A Study of the Civil Government Officials of the Israelite Monarchy* (ConBOT 5; Lund: Gleerup, 1971); and Udo Rüterswörden, *Die Beamten der israelitischen Königszeit. Eine Studie*

zu śar und vergleichbaren Begriffen (BWANT 117; Stuttgart: Kohlhammer, 1985).

80. See 88–91, below.

81. See Mettinger, *Solomonic State Officials*, 19–24, 52–62; and Rütersworden, *Die Beamten der israelitischen Königszeit*, 89–91. The biblical evidence is in 2 Sam 8:16; 20:24; 1 Kgs 4:3; 2 Kgs 18:18, 37 = Isa 36:3, 22. Outside Israel and Judah, the title *mzkr* appears on a Moabite seal from the late eighth century, *CWSS* no. 1011.

82. Biblically attested in 2 Sam 8:17; 20:25; 1 Kgs 4:3; 2 Kgs 12:11; 2 Kgs 18:18, 37; 19:2 = Isa 36:3, 22; 37:2; 2 Kgs 22:3, 8-10, 12; Jer 36:10, 12, 20-21; 37:15, 20; epigraphically, see *CWSS* nos. 21–23; *HAE* 2/2, 115. One prominent representative is "Baruch ben Neriah the Scribe," who is represented both in the Bible (Jer 32:12-13, 16; 36:4-5, 8, 10, 13-19, 26-27, 32; 43:3, 6; 45:1-2) and on *bullae* (*CWSS* no. 417; *HAE* 2/2, nos. 2, 30).

83. Mentioned in the Bible under Solomon (1 Kgs 4:6) and then attested both in the northern kingdom (1 Kgs 16:9; 18:3; 2 Kgs 10:5) and in Judah (2 Kgs 15:5; 18:18, 37; 19:2 = Isa 36:3, 22; 37:2; Isa 22:15-25). There are five seal impressions with the combination of a name plus *ʾsr ʿl hbyt* (*CWSS* no. 1, 403–406; *HAE* 2/2, 113–14).

84. *HAE* 1:263–65.

85. *HAE* 1:425–27.

86. See also Rütersworden, *Die Beamten der israelitischen Königszeit*, 35–40.

87. *CWSS* no. 402; *HAE* 2/2, nos. 30.9 and 30.10. See also a seal with the inscription *lsr* = "belonging to the commandant/governor/officer" (*CWSS* no. 401; *HAE* 2/2, no. 30.7), as well as the possessive designation *lsr ʿir* = "belonging to the head of the city" on a storage jar from Kuntillet ʿAjrud (*HAE* 1, 55).

88. For this document, see 88–91, below, with literature.

89. Thus *HAE* 1:323–24.

90. Pierre Bordreuil, Felice Israel, and Dennis Pardee, "Deux ostraca paléo-hébreux de la collection Sh. Moussaïef," *Sem* 46 (1996): 49–76; the text is on 61. See also Jan A. Wagenaar, "'Give in the Hand of Your Maidservant the Property . . .' Some Remarks to the Second Ostrakon from the Collection of Sh. Moussaieff," *ZABR* 5 (1999): 15–27.

91. *HAE* 1:395.

92. *HAE* 1:412–19, 425–27. For a evaluation of the letters, see Rainer Kessler, *Staat und Gesellschaft im vorexilischen Juda. Vom 8. Jahrhundert bis zum Exil* (VTSup 47; Leiden: Brill, 1992), 178–82.

93. For the elders, see Joachim Buchholz, *Die Ältesten Israels im Deuteronomium* (GTA 36; Göttingen: Vandenhoeck & Ruprecht, 1988); Frank Crüsemann, "Das Gericht im Tor—eine staatliche Rechtsinstanz," in *Alttestamentlicher Glaube und Biblische Theologie. Festschrift für Horst Dietrich Preuss* (ed. Jutta Hausmann and Hans-Jürgen Zobel Stuttgart: Kohlhammer, 1992), 69–79; Jan Christian Gertz, *Die Gerichtsorganisation Israels im deuteronomischen Gesetz* (FRLANT 165; Göttingen: Vandenhoeck & Ruprecht, 1994); Hanoch Reviv, *The Elders in Ancient Israel: A Study of a Biblical Institution* (Jerusalem: Magnes, 1989); Volker Wagner, "Beobachtungen am Amt der Ältesten im alttestamentlichen Israel," *ZAW* 114 (2002): 391–411, 560–76; and Timothy M. Willis, *The Elders of the City: A Study of the Elders-Laws in Deuteronomy* (SBLMS 55; Atlanta: Scholars, 2001).

94. See above, chapter 6, 59–60.

95. Wagner demonstrates this in a comprehensive study whose methodological advance is that he not only distinguishes evidence for elders by the social institution to which they belong, "Beobachtungen am Amt der Ältesten," 404–405, but correlates the institution with the duties assigned to the elder, 396–99. The result is clear: "The elders of Israel were at no time to which the Old Testament can credibly witness related to tribes, clans, or families, but exclusively to cities and their populations" (411). Cf. also Willis, *The Elders of the City*; and Buchholz, *Die Ältesten Israels*, 81, who believes there were not only "city elders" but also "tribal elders," though his sole evidence for the latter is Exod 12:21*. [Ed.: The asterisk is the German way of indicating that some consider the portion of the verse containing "tribal elders" to be a later, possibly spurious, addition.]

96. Thus Willis's conclusion: ". . . such leaders perform a variety of functions: judicial . . . notarial

... representative ... and cultic. ..." (*The Elders of the City*, 307). Wagner attempts to restrict these to "executive function" and "notarial function," which is justified inasmuch as these are the principal functions of elders ("Beobachtungen am Amt der Ältesten," quoting 561).

97. See 91–97, below.

98. For the legal system, see 88–91, below.

99. Cf. Erhard Junge, *Der Wiederaufbau des Heerwesens des Reiches Juda unter Josia* (BWANT 75; Stuttgart: Kohlhammer, 1937); Gerhard von Rad, *Holy War in Ancient Israel* (trans. Marva J. Dawn and John Howard Yoder; Grand Rapids: Eerdmans, 1990; 5th ed. German original, 1969); Manfred Weippert, "'Heiliger Krieg' in Israel und Assyrien. Kritische Anmerkungen zu Gerhard von Rads Konzept des 'Heiligen Krieges im alten Israel,'" *ZAW* 84 (1972): 460–93.

100. For the ʿapiru see above, chapter 6, 41–44.

101. It is difficult here not to think of Augustine's famous account of the creation of the kingdom (Augustine, *The City of God* 4.4): "Justice being taken away, then, what are kingdoms but great bands of robbers? For what are robber bands themselves, but little kingdoms? ... If, by the admittance of abandoned men" (1 Sam 22:2) "this evil increases to such a degree that it holds places, fixes abodes, takes possession of cities, and subdues peoples" (1 Sam 27:6, 8-9; 30; 2 Sam 5:6-12; 8:1-15) "it assumes the more plainly the name of a kingdom..." (173).

102. Both are examples of how the fictional character of a narrative does not mean that it presumes conditions that are certainly familiar to the audience of such a narrative; see above, chapter 4, 26–28.

103. In the Lachish ostraca from the last days of the Kingdom of Judah, shortly before the Babylonian conquest of Jerusalem, we have epigraphical evidence of a named *sr hsb'*, Konyahu ben Elnathan (*HAE* 1:412–19).

104. *HAE* 1:347–403.

105. For the expansion of the meaning of "*Kittiyim*," which originally meant inhabitants of the city of Kition in Cyprus, to include all Cypriots,

then all Greeks, and finally all inhabitants of the western Mediterranean, see Paul-Eugène Dion, "Les *KTYM* de Tel Arad: Grecs ou Phéniciens?" *RB* 99 (1992): 70–97.

106. According to von Rad, *Holy War in Ancient Israel*, 33–38, 76–78, the levy ceased with the monarchy; according to Junge, *Der Wiederaufbau des Heerwesens*, it was only restored under Josiah. But Weippert, "'Heiliger Krieg' in Israel und Assyrien, 469, 491–92, shows that even in an empire like that of Assyria, and continuing into the Neo-Assyrian period, the levy existed alongside the standing army. Such a combination is all the more likely for small states like Israel and Judah.

107. *KAI* no. 81.

108. On socage, see Janne J. Nurmi, *Die Ethik unter dem Druck des Alltags. Die Impuse der gesellschaftlichen Änderungen und Situation zu der sozialkritischen Prophetie in Juda im 8. Jh. v. Chr.* (Åbo: Åbo Akademis, 2004), 118–22.

109. *CWSS* no. 20.

110. Even though no building works are mentioned here. For forced labor by daughters, see Willy Schottroff, "Der Zugriff des Königs auf die Töchter. Zur Fronarbeit von Frauen im alten Israels," in *Gerechtigkeit lernen. Beiträge zur biblischen Sozialgeschichte* (TB 94; Gütersloh: Kaiser/Gütersloher, 1999), 94–114.

111. Text and translations in *KAI* no. 200; *HAE* 1:315–29; *TUAT* 1:249–50; Lemaire 259–69; Jaroš no. 55; Smelik 87–93. For discussion, cf. J. D. Amusin and Michael L. Heltzer, "The Inscription from Mesad Hashavyahu: Complaint of a Reaper of the Seventh Century B.C.," *IEJ* 14 (1964): 148–57; Frank Crüsemann, "' ... damit er dich segne in allem Tun deiner Hand ... ' (Dtn 14.29). Die Produktionsverhältnisse der späten Königszeit dargestellt am Ostrakon von Mesad Hashavjahu, und die Sozialgesetzgebung des Deuteronomiums," in *Mitarbeiter der Schöpfung: Bibel und Arbeitswelt* (ed. Luise Schottroff and Willi Schottroff; Munich: Kaiser, 1983), 72–103; F. W. Dobbs-Allsopp, "The Genre of the Mesad Hashavyahu Ostracon," *BASOR* 295 (1994): 49–55; Alexander Fantalkin, "Mezad Hashavyahu: Its Material Culture and Historical Background," *Tel Aviv* 28 (2001): 3–165;

André Lemaire, "L'ostracon de Mesad Hashavjahu replacé dans son contexte," *Sem* 21 (1971): 57–79; Shemaryahu Talmon, "The New Hebrew Letter from the Seventh Century B.C.E. in Historical Perspective," in *King, Cult and Calendar in Ancient Israel: Collected Studies* (Leiden: Brill, 79–88, 1986); Robert Wenning, "Mesad Haśavyahu. Ein Stützpunkt des Jojakim?" in *Vom Sinai zom Horeb. Stationen alttestamentlicher Glaubensgeschichte* (ed. Frank-Lothar Hossfeld; Würzburg: Echter, 1989), 169–96.

112. We may think of the reign of Josiah or Jehoiakim; see the discussion in *HAE* 1:316.

113. For these payments, see Frank Crüsemann, "Der Zehnte in der israelitischen Königszeit," *WD* n.s. 18 (1985): 21–47; Henk Jagersma, "The Tithes in the Old Testament," *OTS* 21 (1981): 116–28; Rainer Kessler, "Gott und König, Grundeigentum und Fruchtbarkeit," *ZAW* 108 (1996): 214–32; Nurmi, *Die Ethik unter dem Druck des Alltags*, 113–18.

114. On 1 Kgs 4:7-19, cf. Paul S. Ash, "Solomon's? District? List," *JSOT* 67 (1995): 67–86; Volkmar Fritz, "Die Verwaltungsgebiete Salomos nach 1 Kön. 4,7–19," in *Meilenstein. Festgabe für Herbert Donner* (ed. Manfred Weippert and Stefan Timm; ÄAT 30; Wiesbaden: Harrassowitz, 1995), 19–26; Jens Kamlah, "Die Liste der Regionalfürsten in 1 Kön 4,7–19 als historische Quelle für die Zeit Salomos," *BN* 106 (2001): 57–78; Nadav Na'aman, "Solomon's District List (1 Kings 4:7–19) and the Assyrian Province System in Palestine," *UF* 33 (2001): 419–36; Hermann Michael Niemann, *Herrschaft, Königtum und Staat. Skizzen zur soziokulturellen Entwicklung im monarchischen Israel* (FAT 6; Tübingen: Mohr; 1993), 246–51.

115. This is more or less what Albrecht Alt proposed, "Israels Gaue unter Salomo," in *Kleine Schriften zur Geschichte des Volkes Israel* (Munich: Beck, 1964; original German essay, 1913), 2:76–89.

116. Strikingly, most of the place descriptions (as in vv. 8-10, 13, 15-19) begin with "in" (*be*) and not "over" (*ʿal*), as we would expect if these were governors; cf. 2 Sam 5:5: David is king "over" Judah, or Israel and Judah, "in" Hebron or Jerusalem. Thus the places listed in 1 Kgs 4:7-19 only indicate where the officials are located, not the district over which they rule. Only the secondary superscription in v. 7 makes this an authority "over all Israel."

117. Correspondingly, in the course of the Judaic kingdom, daughters of the rural aristocracy are frequently given in marriage to the king's sons; on this see below, 97–102.

118. For the view of 1 Kgs 4:7–19 presented here, see Niemann, *Herrschaft, Königtum und Staat*, 246–52; idem, "Taanach und Megiddo: Überlegungen zur strukturell-historischen Situation zwischen Saul und Salomo," *VT* 52 (2002): 93–102; and Kamlah, "Die Liste der Regionalfürsten in 1 Kön 4,7–19. For Fritz, this text is among "the few original documents appropriated by the Deuteronomistic History" ("Die Verwaltungsgebiete Salomos," 19). According to Ash, "Solomon's? District? List," the list contains pre-deuteronomistic material (79–85), handed on orally until the fall of the northern kingdom (84). "Only the names . . . suggest an early date" (85). Even if the glossing of the text developed by Ash himself (73–79) speaks more in favor of written tradition, the conclusion is similar to the one presented here: the list does not reflect an elaborate system of administration, but rather the interrelationships between local authorities and the court.

119. Crüsemann, "Der Zehnte in der israelitischen Königszeit".

120. *HAE* 1:195–96.

121. For a possible reason for the intertwining of state and sacral taxes ,Rainer Kessler, "Gott und König, Grundeigentum und Fruchtbarkeit," *ZAW* 108 (1996): 214–32, esp. 230–31.

122. Cf. also, for the obligation of tribute, only 2 Kgs 16:8; 17:4 ("year by year"); 18:14, and the epigraphical evidence in *TGI* nos. 24, 27, 28, 36, 39, 41, 44; for Judah's duty to pay tribute in the time of Manasseh, see the references in Gerhard Begrich, *Der wirtschaftliche Einfluss Assyriens auf Südsyrien und Palästina*. Diss. Berlin. (1975), esp. 201, 214–16.

123. Crüsemann, "Der Zehnte in der israelitischen Königszeit," 44–45. Michael Heltzer, "Some Questions Concerning the Economic

Policy of Josiah, King of Judah," *IEJ* 50 (2000): 105–108, discusses a series of *bullae* from the time of Josiah that can be best understood against the background of a system of taxes on agricultural products.

124. For the royal economy, see Albrecht Alt, "Der Rhythmus der Geschichte Syriens und Palästinas im Altertum," in *Kleine Schriften zur Geschichte des Volkes Israel* (Munich: Beck, 1964–68; original German essay 1944), 3:1–19; idem, "Israels Gaue unter Salomo," in [1913], *Kleine Schriften* (1964; original German essay, 1951), 2:76–89 ; idem, "Judas Gaue unter Josia," in *Kleine Schriften* (1964; original German essay, 1925), 2:276–88; idem, "Bemerkungen zu einigen judäischen Ortslisten des Alten Testaments," in *Kleine Schriften* (1964; original German essay, 1951), 2:289–305; Yitshak Avishur and Michael Heltzer, *Studies on the Royal Administration in Ancient Israel in the Light of Epigraphic Sources* (Tel Aviv: Archaeological Center, 2000); Zafrira Ben-Barak, "Meribaal and the System of Land Grants in Ancient Israel," *Bib* 62 (1981): 73–91; Zecharia Kallai, "Simeon's Town List: Scribal Rules and Geographical Patterns," *VT* 53 (2003): 81–96; Kessler, "Gott und König"; Raz Kletter, "Pots and Polities: Material Remains of Late Iron Age Judah in Relation to its Political Borders," *BASOR* 314 (1999): 19–54; Richard H. Lowery, *The Reforming Kings: Cult and Society in First Temple Judah* (JSOTSup 120; Sheffield: JSOT Press, 1991); Na'aman, "Solomon's District List; Martin Noth, "Das Krongut der israelitischen Könige und seine Verwaltung", in *Aufsätze zur biblishcne Landes- und Altertumskunde* (Neukirchen-Vluyn: Neukirchener Verlag, 1971, original German essay 1927), 1:159–82; Nurmi, *Die Ethik unter dem Druck des Alltags*, 122–32.

125. For the notion of crown estates, see Noth, "Das Krongut der israelitischen Könige"; for the role of the supposed crown estates in social development, see Alt, "Der Rhythmus der Geschichte Syriens und Palästinas".

126. Noth and Alt consistently mention the concept using such ideas.

127. Noth, "Das Krongut der israelitischen Könige".

128. See below, 91–97.

129. Nos. 20, 44, 53, 54, 61, 72, 73 (*HAE* 1:95, 101, 103–105, 107).

130. For the *lmlk* stamps, cf. Raz Kletter, "Temptation to Identify: Jerusalem, *mmšt*, and the *lmlk* Jar Stamps," *ZDPV* 118 (2002): 136–49; Darrell H. Lance, "The Royal Stamps and the Kingdom of Josiah," *HTR* 64 (1979): 315–32; André Lemaire, "Remarques sur la datation des estampilles 'lmlk,'" *VT* 25 (1975): 678–82; idem, "Classification des estampilles royales judéennes," *ErIsr* (1981): 53*–60*; Nadav Na'aman, "Sennacherib's Campaign to Judah and the Date of the lmlk Stamps," *VT* 29 (1979): 61–86; Nurmi, *Die Ethik unter dem Druck des Alltags*, 317–32; Anson F. Rainey, "Wine from the Royal Vineyards," *BASOR* 245 (1982): 57–62; David Ussishkin, "Royal Judean Storage Jars and Private Seal Impressions," *BASOR* 223 (1976): 1–13; Peter Welten, *Die Königs-Stempel. Ein Beitrag zur Militärpolitik Judas unter Hiskia und Josia* (ADPV; Wiesbaden: Harrassowitz, 1969).

131. *HAE* 2/2 lists "well over a thousand *lmlk* stamps" (81), but new examples are constantly being discovered.

132. See the chemical analyses in H. Mommsen, I. Perlman, and J. Yellin, "The Provenience of the lmlk Jars," *IEJ* 34 (1984): 89–113.

133. For the state of research on this, see Rainer Kessler, *Staat und Gesellschaft im vorexilischen Juda. Vom 8. Jahrhundert bis zum Exil.* (VTSup 47; Leiden: Brill, 1992); 144–48; Niemann, *Herrschaft, Königtum und Staat*, 157–60; and Kletter, "Temptation to Identify"; *HAE* 2/2, 102–106.

134. *HAE* 2/2, 102, and nos. 30.11–30.17; *CWSS* nos. 421 and 422.

135. *CWSS* 177 speaks of a "tax."

136. For the lists in Josh 15:21–44, 48–62; 18:21-28; 19:2-8, 41-46, which allow us to surmise a division of administration in the southern kingdom at the earliest in the late eighth century, see esp. Niemann, *Herrschaft, Königtum und Staat*, 251–72.

137. *HAE* 1:347–403. See also the significance of the ostraca for military organization, discussed above.

138. *HAE* 1:393–94.

139. For this office, see above, 79–88.

140. For judicial action see Elizabeth Belle-fontaine, "Customary Law and Chieftainship: Judicial Aspects of 2 Samuel 14.4–21," *JSOT* 38 (1987): 47–72; Zafrira Ben-Barak, "The Appeal to the King as the Highest Authority for Justice," in *"Wünschet Jerusalem Frieden." Collected Communications to the XIIIth Congress of the International Organization for the Study of the Old Testament* (ed. Matthias Augustin and Klaus-Dietrich Shunck; BEATAJ 13; Frankfurt: Peter Lang, 1986), 169–77; Frank Crüsemann, *The Torah: Theology and Social History of Old Testament Law* (trans. Allan W. Mahnke; Minneapolis: Fortress Press, 1996; German original, 1992), 80–95; Jan Christian Gertz, *Die Gerichtsorganisation Israels im deuteronomischen Gesetz* (FRLANT 165; Göttingen: Vandenhoeck & Ruprecht, 1994); Georg Christian Macholz, "Die Stellung des Königs in der israelitischen Gerichtsverfassung," *ZAW* 84 (1972): 157–82; idem, "Zur Geschichte der Justizorganisation in Juda," *ZAW* 84 (1972): 314–40; Herbert Niehr, *Rechtsprechung in Israel. Untersuchungen zur Geschichte der Gerichtsorganisation im Alten Testament* (SBS 130; Stuttgart: Katholisches Bibelwerk, 1987); Nurmi, *Die Ethik unter dem Druck des Alltags*, 147–94; Keith W. Whitelam, *The Just King: Monarchical Judicial Authority in Ancient Israel* (JSOTSup 12; Sheffield: JSOT Press, 1979); Timothy M. Willis, *The Elders of the City: A Study of the Elders-Laws in Deuteronomy* (SBLMS 55; Atlanta: Scholars, 2001); and Robert R. Wilson, "Israel's Judicial System in the Preexilic Period," *JQR* 74 (1983–84): 228–48.

141. For this view, see Crüsemann, *The Torah*, 80–95.

142. See above, 79–88, and at the beginning of this section.

143. On the role of elders in the local judicial system see above, 79–88.

144. See chapter 8, 114–117 below.

145. For the temple, see Matthias Delcor, "Le trésor de la maison de Yahweh des origines à l'exile," *VT* 12 (1962): 353–77; Otto Eißfeldt, "Eine Einschmelzstelle am Tempel zu Jerusalem," in *Kleine Schriften II* (Tübingen: Mohr, 1963), 107–109;

Kurt Galling, "Königliche und nichtkönigliche Stifter beim Tempel von Jerusalem," *ZDPV* 68 (1951), 134–42; Victor Hurowitz, "Another Fiscal Practice in the Ancient Near East: 2 Kings 12,5–17 and a Letter to Esarhaddon (LAS 277)," *JNES* 45 (1986): 289–94; Christoph Levin, "Die Instandsetzung des Tempels unter Joasch ben Ahasja," in *Fortschreibungen. Gesammelte Studien zum Alten Testament* (BZAW 316; Berlin: de Gruyter, 2003), 169–97; Joachim Schaper, "The Jerusalem Temple as an Instrument of the Achaemenid Fiscal Administration," *VT* 45 (2000): 528–39; Édouard Will, "Überlegungen und Hypothesen zur Entstehung des Münzgeldes," in *Seminar: Die Entstehung der antiken Klassengesellschaft* (ed. Hans G. Kippenberg; STW 130; Frankfurt: Suhrkamp, 1977), 205–22.

146. *KAI* no. 181,11. 17–18.

147. For "gift" as the basic figuration of the religious relationship between human and divine, see Marcel Mauss, *The Gift: The Form and Reason for Exchange in Archaic Societies* (trans. W. D. Halls; New York: Norton, 1990); and Maurice Godelier, *The Enigma of the Gift* (trans. Nora Scott; Chicago: University of Chicago Press, 1999; French original, 1996). Godelier rightly emphasizes the asymmetry in the relationship between divine gift and human reciprocation. Introductory discussion in Sarah Iles Johnston, ed., *Religions of the Ancient World: A Guide* (Cambridge: Belknap Press, 2004), 325–48, esp. 330–35.

148. See 88–91, above.

149. Disputed, but not to be decided here, is the question of the literary relationship of these two texts. Levin denies any possibility of giving a social-historical evaluation of the account in 2 Kings 12: "The account of the renovation of the temple under Jehoash ben Ahaziah has proved to be, in every part, a late, constructed narrative" ("Die Instandsetzung des Tempels," 197). The picture of the Davidides it paints is "closer to Chronicles in its essential features than to the deuteronomistic theology, to say nothing of the history of pre-exilic Judah" (197). The very fact that 2 Kgs 12:5 has been revised to fit later Torah regulations (Exod 30:13; Lev 27:1–8) shows that there must be

an older, underlying text. And Levin's late dating makes it hard to understand why Chronicles itself, in 2 Chronicles 22–24, tells the story again, in a quite different form, if it is supposed to have been written entirely in the spirit of those books.

150. For "votive offerings", see Tullia Linders and Gullög Nordquist, eds., *Gifts to the Gods: Proceedings of the Uppsala Symposium 1985* (Acta Universitatis Upsaliensis; Boreas: Uppsala Studies in Ancient Mediterranean and Near Eastern Civilizations 15; Uppsala: Academia Upsaliensis, 1987).

151. For discussion of the Josianic reform, see chapter 8, 104–8, below.

152. For Greece, see Will, "Überlegungen und Hypothesen"; for the connection between money as a means of circulation and also as a measure of value apart from its circulation (guaranteed, then, by the religious institution), see Godelier, *The Enigma of the Gift*, esp. 44–46; for the application to the Josianic reform see Schaper, *The Jerusalem Temple as an Instrument*, esp. 95–104.

153. See above, chapter 6, 41–44.

154. See above, chapter 6, 49–51.

155. Walter Dietrich, *Die frühe Königszeit in Israel. 10. Jahrhundert v. Chr.* (BE 3; Stuttgart: Kohlhammer, 1997), 239. This designation also avoids the misunderstanding that one should assert that the historical Philistines actually called the people with Saul "Hebrews." We are unable to say anything about that, one way or the other.

156. Martin Noth, *Könige* (BKAT 9/1; Neukirchen-Vluyn: Neukirchener, 1968), 1:217–18, shows that this view is not by itself improbable.

157. See above, 76–78.

158. Ibid.

159. See chapter 8, below.

160. Of course, the reverse is also possible: that the development of the Exodus narrative incorporated elements of the image of Jeroboam. For the exodus tradition as a tradition of the northern kingdom see Kessler, *Die Ägyptenbilder der Hebräischen Bibel. Ein Beitrag zur neueren Monotheismusdebatte* (SBS 197; Stuttgart: Katholisches Bibelwerk, 2002), esp. 91–101; and see also Felipe Blanco Wißmann, "Sargon, Mose und die Gegner Salomos. Zur Frage vor-neuassyrischer Ursprünge der Mose-Erzählung," *BN* 110 (2001): 42–54.

161. Dietrich, *Die frühe Königszeit in Israel*, 239.

162. Kessler, *Die Ägyptenbilder der Hebräischen Bibel*, 94.

163. Albrecht Alt, "The Monarchy in the Kingdoms of Israel and Judah," in *Essays on Old Testament History and Religion* (trans. R. A. Wilson; Garden City: Doubleday, 1967; original German essay, 1951),311–35; Tomoo Ishida, *The Royal Dynasties in Ancient Israel: A Study on the Formation and Development of Royal Dynastic Ideology* (BZAW 142; Berlin: de Gruyter, 1977); Stefan Timm, *Die Dynastie Omri. Quellen und Untersuchungen zur Geschichte Israels im 9. Jahrhundert vor Christus* (FRLANT 124: Göttingen: Vandenhoeck & Ruprecht, 1982).

164. For the many royal murders in Israel's last years, see also the clear allusions by the prophet Hosea (Hos 7:3–7; 8:4; 9:15); and see Jörg Jeremias, *Der Prophet Hosea* (ATD 24/1; Göttingen: Vandenhoeck & Ruprecht, 1983), 31–32, 95–97, 105–106, and 124–25.

165. See 97–102, below.

166. Ibid.

167. Alt, "The Monarchy in the Kingdoms of Israel and Judah," 320.

168. On this, see Ishida, *The Royal Dynasties in Ancient Israel*, 171–82.

169. This is Alt's thesis, "Der Stadtstaat Samaria," in *Kleine Schriften zur Geschichte des Volkes Israel* (Munich: Beck, 1968), 3:258–302.

170. See 88–91, above.

171. For the interpretation of 1 Kings 20, see, on the whole, Hermann Michael Niemann, *Herrschaft, Königtum und Staat. Skizzen zur soziokulturellen Entwicklung im monarchischen Israel* (FAT 6; Tübingen: Mohr, 1993), 67–69.

172. In Claessen and Skalnik's terminology this would be a "transitional early state" on its way to a "mature state" (Henri J. M. Claessen, and Peter Skalnik, eds., *The Early State* [New Babylon, Studies in the Social Sciences 32; The Hague: Mouton, 1978], 23; and see above, 74–76).

173. On this see chapter 8, 108–117, below.

174. See 76–78, above on resistance to the kingship.

175. For the text, interpretation, and bibliography, see *HAE* 1:79–109; and above, 88–91. See also the discussion in Yohanan Aharoni, *The Land of the Bible. A Historical Geography.* (2d rev. and emended ed; trans. A. F. Rainey; Philadelphia: Westminster, 1979), 356–68, as well as Anson F. Rainey, "Toward a Precise Date for the Samaria Ostraca," *BASOR* 272 (1988): 69–74.

176. Niemann, *Herrschaft, Königtum und Staat,* 82.

177. See chapter 8, 109–11, below.

178. For the Samaritan ivories—some five hundred pieces discovered, three hundred of them artistically carved—see Helga Weippert, *Palästina in vorhellenistischer Zeit* (Handbuch der Archäologie 2/1; Munich: Beck, 417–681, 1988), 654–60.

179. A payment of tribute from Menahem is recorded in one of Tiglath-pileser's tribute rolls; *TGI* no. 24.

180. See above, 64–72.

181. One only need see *TGI* nos. 28, 36, 39; see also no. 41.

182. On this see above, 88–91.

183. Probably Solomon's supposedly successful expeditions (1 Kgs 9:27-28; 10:11-12) are a backward projection of this failed attempt into the golden age of the past.

184. For *am-haʾarets*, see Samuel Daiches, "The Meaning of ʿm hʾrs in the O.T.," *JTS* 30, 245–49 (1929); Eva Gillischewski, "Der Ausdruck ʿm-hāʾārœs im AT," *ZAW* 40 (1922): 137–42; A. H. J. Gunneweg, "Die aramäische und die hebräische Erzählung über die nachexilische Restauration—ein Vergleich," *ZAW* 94 (1983): 299–302; Ihromi, "Die Königinmutter und der ʿamm haʾaretz im Reich Juda," *VT* 24 (1974): 421–29; John McKenzie, "The 'People of the Land' in the Old Testament," in *Akten des vierundzwanzigsten internationalen Orientalistenkongresses in München* (Wiesbaden: Harrassowitz, 1959), 206–208; J. Alberto Soggin, "Der judäische ʿamm haʾares und das Königtum in Juda," *VT* 13 (1963): 186–95; Shemaryahu Talmon, "The Judaean ʿam haʾarœs in Historical Perspective," in *King, Cult and Calendar in Ancient Israel: Collected Studies* (Leiden: Brill, 1986), 68–78; Thomas Willi, *Juda—Jehud—Israel. Studien zum Selbstverständnis des Judentums in persischer Zeit* (FAT 12; Tübingen: Mohr, 1995), 11–17; Ernst Würthwein, *Der 'amm haʾarœz im alten Testament* (BWANT 69; Stuttgart: Kohlhammer; 1936).

185. "Princes," *nesiʾeha,* as the probably original reading in v. 25; see *BHS*.

186. Thus Bernhard Lang, *Kein Aufstand in Jerusalem. Die Politik des Propheten Ezechiel* (2nd ed.; SBB Stuttgart: Katholisches Bibelwerk, 1981), at 56.

187. On this see above, 88–91.

188. Lachish ostracon 3; see *HAE* 1:412–19.

189. Rüterswörden's objection, *Die Beamten der israelitischen Königszeit. Eine Studie zu śr und vergleichbaren Begriffen* (BWANT 117; Stuttgart: Kohlhammer, 1985), 125, that landownership could not be the basis for officials' existence because the official could not farm it during his term of service is invalid, for two reasons: (1) if it was family property, another member of the family could work the land, and (2) there was also the possibility that a steward could manage the property, as both biblical examples (2 Sam 9:2; 19:18) and recovered seals with the designation "naʿar of PN" (*CWSS,* nos. 24–26.663; *HAE* 2/1, nos. 1.21; 1.81; 2.9; 13.37; 14.49) suggest; on this see, Hans-Peter Stähli, *Knabe—Jüngling—Knecht. Untersuchungen zum Begriff nʿr im Alten Testament* (BBET. Frankfurt: Peter Lang, 1978).

190. According to a suggestion by Talmon, "Kingship and the Ideology of the State," in *King, Cult and Calendar in Ancient Israel: Collected Studies* (Leiden: Brill, 1986), 9–38, at 25; as discussed in Rainer Kessler, *Staat und Gesellschaft im vorexilischen Juda. Vom 8. Jahrhundert bis zum Exil* (VTSup 47; Leiden: Brill, 1992), 202–7. For the form of the state as a whole, José Nunes Carreira, "Charisma und Institution. Zur Verfassung des Königtums in Israel und Juda," in *Prophetie und geschichtliche Wirklichkeit im Alten Israel. Festschrift für Siegfried Herrmann* (ed. Rüdiger Liwak and Siegfried Wagner; Stuttgart: Kohlhammer, 1991), 39–51; Georg Fohrer, "Israels Staatsordnung im Rahmen des

Alten Orients," in *Studien zur alttestamentlichen Theologie und Geschichte (1949–1966)* (BZAW 115; Berlin: Walter de Gruyter, 1969), 309–29; Kurt Galling, *Die israelitische Staatsverfassung in ihrer vorderorientalischen Umwelt* (AO 28, 3/4; Leipzig: J. C. Hinrichs, 1929); Baruch Halpern, *The Constitution of the Monarchy in Israel* (HSM 25; Chico: Scholars, 1981); Kessler, *Staat und Gesellschaft*; and Talmon, "Kingship and the Ideology of the State".

191. In the story of Joseph and his brothers, the contrast between despotic and participatory monarchy is an important theme. In Gen 47:13-26, Egypt is pictured as the land in which all the inhabitants lose their lands to the Pharaoh and become "Pharaoh's slaves" (vv. 19, 25). Joseph, in contrast, firmly rejects his brothers' offer to subject themselves to him ("behold, we are your slaves"). The monarchy does not make Israelites and Judahites the slaves of the king. For this interpretation of the Joseph story, see esp. Erhard Blum, *Die Komposition der Vätergeschichte* (WMANT 57. Neukirchen-Vluyn: Neukirchener, 1984), 234–44.

192. See above, n185.

193. *HAE* 1:392.

194. Talmon, "Kingship and the Ideology of the State," 29.

8. The Formation of an Ancient Class Society

1. See above, chapter 7, 64–72.

2. *TGI*, no. 39; *TUAT* 1:388–91; *COS* 2:302–3.

3. From the abundant literature, see Rainer Albertz, "Why a Reform like Josiah's Must Have Happened," in *Good Kings and Bad Kings* (ed. Lester L. Grabbe, Library of Hebrew Bible/Old Testament Studies 393; London: T&T Clark, 2005), 27–46; Boyd W. Barrick, *The King and the Cemeteries: Toward a New Understanding of Josiah's Reform* (VTSUP 88; Leiden: Brill, 2002); Herbert Niehr, "Die Reform des Joschija. Methodische, historische und religionsgeschichtliche Aspekte," in *Jeremia und die "deuteronomistische Bewegung"* (ed. Walter Groß; BBB 98; Weinheim: Beltz Athenaeum, 1995); Eckart Otto, "Josia/Josiareform,"

RGG, 4th ed., 4:587–89; Christoph Uehlinger, "Gab es eine joschianische Kultreform? Plädoyer für ein begründetes Minimum," in *Jeremia und die "deuteronomistische Bewegung"* (ed. Walter Groß; BBB 98; Weinheim: Beltz Athenaeum, 1995), 57–89; Ernst Würthwein, "Die Josianische Reform und das Deuteronomium," in *Studien zum Deuteronomistischen Geschichtswerk* (BZAW 227; Berlin: de Gruyter, 1994), 188–216.

4. So Würthwein, "Die Josianische Reform und das Deuteronomium," 211; and also Herbert Niehr, "historically improbable" ("Die Reform des Joschija, 51).

5. Thus Uehlinger, "Gab es eine joschianische Kultreform?" 57–89.

6. After an extensive analysis of the account of the reform in 2 Kings 23, Barrick, *The King and the Cemeteries*, concludes that there was a purification of the cult and its centralization in and around Jerusalem (the textual analysis is summarized on 107–8). Otto distinguishes between "a purification and centralization of the cult restricted to Jerusalem and its immediate surroundings" and an extension of these same methods to the entire land in "late pre-exilic Dtn.," which, however, "remained only a plan" ("Josia/Josiareform," 588).

7. For this view of Josiah's end, which knows nothing of a so-called "battle of Megiddo," see 2 Chr 35:20-24, cf. Rainer Kessler, *Die Ägyptenbilder der Hebräischen Bibel. Ein Beitrag zur neueren Monotheismusdebatte* (SBS 197; Stuttgart: Katholisches Bibelwerk, 2002), 42–43.

8. For prophetic social critique as a whole, see Herbert Donner, "Die soziale Botschaft der Propheten im Lichte der Gesellschaftsordnung in Israel," in *Das Prophetenverständnis in der deutschsprachigen Forschung seit Heinrich Ewald* (ed. Peter H. A. Neumann; WdF 307; Darmstadt: Wissenschaftliche Buchgesellschaft, 1979; original German essay, 1963), 493–514; Klaus Koch, "Die Entstehung der sozialen Kritik bei den Propheten," in *Gesammelte Aufsätze* (Neukirchen-Vluyn: Neukirchener, 1991; original German essay, 1971), 1:146–66; Hans-Joachim Kraus, "Die prophetische Botschaft gegen das soziale Unrecht Israels," *EvT* 15 (1955): 295–307; Bernhard Lang, "The

Social Organization of Peasant Poverty in Biblical Israel," *JSOT* 24 (1983) 47–63; idem, "Prophetie und Ökonomie im alten Israel," in *"Vor Gott sind alle gleich." Soziale Gleichheit, soziale Ungleichheit und die Religionen* (ed. Günter Kehrer; Düsseldorf: Patmos, 1983), 53–73; Ronald A. Simkins, "Patronage and the Political Economy of Monarchic Israel," *Semeia* 87 (1999): 123–44; Fritz Stolz, "Aspekte religiöser und sozialer Ordnung im alten Israel," *ZEE* 17 (1973): 145–59; and Wolfgang Zwickel,"Die Wirtschaftsreform des Hiskia und die Sozialkritik der Propheten des 8. Jahrhunderts," *EvT* 59 (1999): 356–77. For Amos' social critique in particular, see Marlene Fendler, "Zur Sozialkritik des Amos. Versuch einer wirtschafts- und sozialgeschichtlichen Interpretation alttestamentlicher Texte," *EvT* 33 (1973): 32–53; Gunther Fleischer, *Von Menschenverkäufern, Baschankühen und Rechtsverkehrern. Die Sozialkritik des Amos-Buches in historisch-kritischer, sozialgeschichtlicher und archäologischer Perspektive* (BBB 74; Frankfurt: Athenaeum, 1989); Rainer Kessler, "Die angeblichen Kornhändler von Amos VIII 4–7," *VT* 39 (1989): 13–22; and Haroldo Reimer, *Richtet auf das Recht! Studien zur Botschaft des Amos* (SBS 149; Stuttgart: Katholisches Bibelwerk, 1992).

9. Let me again emphasize that it is rather inconsequential for a social-historical evaluation whether and to what extent individual prophetic sayings go back to the very words of the prophet him- or herself, or whether the exact words were composed by disciples or followers—including those who took up the prophet's cause. When, in what follows, I speak of Amos, Isaiah, Micah, or others, I am in all cases referring to the writings attributed to them.

10. For this interpretation of the passage see Kessler, "Die angeblichen Kornhändler".

11. See above, chapter 7, 91–97.

12. In a methodological essay, Philip R. Davies asks: "How often is the social critique of Amos taken as an objective description?" ("The Society of Biblical Israel," in, *Second Temple Studies*, vol. 2, *Temple and Community in the Persian Period* [ed. Tamara C. Eskenazi and Kent H. Richards; JSOT-Sup 175; Sheffield: JSOT Press, 1994], 22–33,

quoting 29). He rightly points out the difference between literary reflection on social conditions and the conditions themselves. However, he swiftly turns the literature's own reflection of a social system into "invention," including the "invention of 'prophecy'" (31–32).

13. For Isaiah and Micah, see Hans Bardtke, "Die Latifundien in Juda während der zweiten Hälfte des achten Jahrhunderts v. Chr. (zum Verständnis von Jes 5,8–10)," in *Hommages à André Dupont-Sommer* (Paris: Adrien-Maisonneuve, 1971), 235–54; Walter Dietrich, *Die frühe Königszeit in Israel. 10. Jahrhundert v. Chr.* (BE 3; Stuttgart: Kohlhammer, 1976); Renatus Porath, *Die Sozialkritik im Jesajabuch. Redaktionsgeschichtliche Analyse* (European University Studies 23, Theology 503; Frankfurt: Peter Lang, 1994); D. M. Premnath, "Latifundalization and Isaiah 5.8–10," *JSOT* 40 (1988): 49–60.

14. On this see the next section.

15. See above, chapter 7, 98–102.

16. For this thesis and the interpretation of Micah as a whole, see Rainer Kessler, *Micha* (2nd ed.; HTKAT; Freiburg: Herder, 2000).

17. For the architectural history of Jerusalem, see Klaus Bieberstein and Hanswulf Bloedhorn, *Jerusalem. Grundzüge der Baugeschichte vom Chalkolithikum bis zur Frühzeit der osmanischen Herrschaft* (3 vols.; BTAVO 100; Wiesbaden: L. Reichert, 1994); Abraham Faust, "The Settlement of Jerusalem's Western Hill and the City's Status in Iron Age II Revisited," *ZDPV* 121 (2005): 97–118.

18. Cf. Wisser (1982).

19. See above, VII, 4, b.

20. For the bases and tendencies of this economic development, see Albrecht Alt,"Der Anteil des Königtums an der sozialen Entwicklung in den Reichen Israel und Juda," *Kleine Schriften zur Geschichte des Volkes Israel* (Munich: Beck, 1986; original German essay, 1955) 3:348–72; Hans Bobek, "Die Hauptstufen der Gesellschafts- und Wirtschaftsentfaltung in geographischer Sicht," in *Wirtschaftsgeographie* (ed. Eugen Wirth; WdF 219; Darmstadt: Wissenschaftliche Buchgesellschaft, 1969), 441–85; Moses I. Finley, "Die

Schuldknechtschaft," in *Seminar: Die Entstehung der antiken Klassengesellschaft* (ed. Hans G. Kippenberg, ed. STW 130; Frankfurt: Suhrkamp, 1977), 173–204; Rainer Kessler, "Das hebräische Schuldenwesen. Terminologie und Metaphorik," *WuD* n.s. 20 (1989): 181–95; idem, "Frühkapitalismus, Rentenkapitalismus, Tributarismus, antike Klassengesellschaft. Theorien zur Gesellschaft des alten Israel," *EvT* 54 (1994): 413–27; Hans G. Kippenberg, "Die Typik antiker Entwicklung," in *Seminar: Die Entstehung der antiken Klassengesellschaft* (ed. Hans G. Kippenberg; STW 130; Frankfurt: Surhkamp, 1977), 9–61; Oswald Loretz, "Die prophetische Kritik des Rentenkapitalismus. Grundlagen-Probleme der Prophetenforschung," *UF* 7 (1975): 271–78; and J. P. J. Olivier, "Money Matters: Some Remarks on the Economic Situation in the Kingdom of Judah During the Seventh Century B.C.," *BN* 73 (1994): 90–100.

21. See chapter 10, 148–51, below.

22. Finley, "Die Schuldknechtschaft," 181.

23. See the overview of research given by Janne J. Nurmi, *Die Ethik unter dem Druck des Alltags. Die Impuse der gesellschaftlichen Änderungen und Situation zu der sozialkritischen Prophetie in Juda im 8. Jh. v. Chr.* (Åbo: Åbo Akademis, 2004), 4–49.

24. Loretz, "Die prophetische Kritik des Rentenkapitalismus".

25. Ibid., 274.

26. The tributary concept comes from the Belgian sociologist of religion François Houtart, *Religion et modes de production précapitalistes* (Brussels: Éditions de l'Université de Bruxelles 1980). See the works of Carlos A. Dreher, "Das tributäre Königtum in Israel unter Salomo," *EvT* 51 (1991): 49–60; Milton Schwantes, "tributary model of production," "tributarism", *Das Land kann seine Worte nicht ertragen. Meditationen zu Amos* (KT 105; Munich: Kaiser, 1991), 73; and esp. Haroldo Reimer, *Richtet auf das Recht! Studien zur Botschaft des Amos* (SBS 149; Stuttgart: Katholisches Bibelwerk, 1992), 235–38. Norman K. Gottwald also speaks of a "Tributary Mode of Production (TMP)" ("Social Class as an Analytic and Hermeneutical Category in Biblical Studies," *JBL* 112 [1993], 3–22, quoting 5).

27. Karl Marx, "Ökonomische Manuskripte 1857/58," in Karl Marx and Friedrich Engels, *Gesamtausgabe (MEGA)* (2/1. 2. Berlin: Dietz, 1981), 381–83.

28. Kippenberg, "Die Typik antiker Entwicklung"; and Kessler, *Staat und Gesellschaft im vorexilischen Juda*, 12–17.

29. Loretz, "Die prophetische Kritik des Rentenkapitalismus," 272.

30. Kippenberg, "Die Typik antiker Entwicklung," 41.

31. "Social classes may be said to exist whenever one social group is able to appropriate a part of the surplus labor product of other groups" (Gottwald ["Social Class as an Analytic and Hermeneutical Category," 4]).

32. See above, chapter 7, 91–97.

33. See above, chapter 7, 97–102.

34. See above, chapter 7, 88–91.

35. See above, chapter 7, 78–88.

36. Henri Claessen and Peter Skalnik, *The Early State* (New Babylon, Studies in the Social Sciences 32; The Hauge: Mouton, 1978), 23, 643.

37. Friedrich Engels, *The Origin of the Family, Private Property, and the State* (Penguin Classics; Harmondsworth: Penguin, 1985).

38. Cited from *TUAT* 1:76.

39. Let me mention only Frank Crüsemann, *The Torah: Theology and Social History of Old Testament Law* (trans. Allan W. Mahnke; Minneapolis: Fortress Press, 1996); and Echart Otto, *Theologische Ethik des Alten Testaments* (Theologische Wissenschaft 3.2; Stuttgart: Kohlhammer, 1994), as summary accounts, both with additional bibliography.

40. On this see David W. Jamieson-Drake, *Scribes and Schools in Monarchic Judah: A Socio-Archaeological Approach* (JSOTSup 109; Sheffield: Almond; 1991).

41. Thus Otto, *Theologische Ethik des Alten Testaments*, 73, 180.

42. Thus Crüsemann, *The Torah*, 113–21.

43. Thus, for example, Otto, who calls the so-called laws of office "a utopian program of New Israel after the exile" (*Theologische Ethik des Alten Testaments*, 194). Noteworthy, though not

decisive, against this view is Timothy M. Willis's remark, *The Elders of the City: A Study of the Elders-Laws in Deuteronomy* (SBLMS 55; Atlanta: Scholars, 2001), that the ancient Near Eastern law codes are always related to "existing practices and institutions" (45) and the notion of a utopian program must presume "that the laws are being composed and redacted in something of a vacuum" (47).

9. Exiles and Their Consequences

1. See also *TGI*, no. 27.

2. *TGI*, no. 39.

3. See above, chapter 8, 104–8.

4. *TGI*, no. 46.

5. For the events of 605–597, see also the Babylonian Chronicle, reproduced in *TGI* no. 44; and *TUAT* 1:401–4.

6. Because the Babylonian Chronicle is not preserved for this period, the exact date is disputed. See the discussion in Rainer Albertz, *Israel in Exile: The History and Literature of the Sixth Century B.C.E.* (trans. David Green; Leiden: Brill, 2004), 79–80.

7. For Gedaliah and the Shaphanides, see above, chapter 7, 97–102. It is occasionally said that Gedaliah was installed as king in place of the Davidides; see Peter R. Ackroyd, "The History of Israel in the Exilic and Post-Exilic Periods," in *Tradition and Interpretation: Essays by Members of the Society for Old Testament Study* (New York: Oxford University Press, 1979), 320–50, esp. 324–25; and Francolino Conçalves, "Exílio babilónico de 'Israel.' Realidade histórica e propaganda," *Cadmo* 10 (2000): 177–79, esp. 167–96. It is hard to explain why the Babylonians would, in that case, have continued to regarded the Davidide Jehoiachin as king, just as it would be hard to understand the leading role of the Davidide Zerubbabel at the beginning of the Persian period.

8. On this see, Conçalves, "Exílio babilónico de 'Israel,'" 181.

9. Thus Albertz, *Israel in Exile*, 94–95.

10. On this, see chapter 10, 129–33, below. Albertz, ibid., 2, takes this event as a reason to extend his description of the exilic period to 520.

11. *TGI*, no. 46.

12. On this see below, chapter 10, 129–33.

13. See the full discussion in Albertz, *Israel in Exile*, 81–90.

14. See the description above in chapter 8.

15. Heinz Kreißig proposes that "the former day laborers . . . were now reinstated in possession—in possession, but most certainly not as owners, because the conquering king surely regarded this land as his property" (*Die sozialökonomische Situation in Juda zur Achämenidenzeit* [SGKAO 7; Berlin: Akademie, 1972], 24). That may be, but it cannot be proved. For the question of landownership in general, see also Walter Dietrich, "Wem das Land gehört. Ein Beitrag zur Sozialgeschichte Israels im 6. Jahrhundert v. Chr.," in *Theopolitik. Studien zur Theologie und Ethik des Alten Testaments* (Neukirchen-Vluyn: Neukirchener, 2002), 270–86.

16. We may set aside the question whether this is to be interpreted as "the occupation—by force if necessary—of the deserted villages" (so Albertz, *Israel in Exile*, 92).

17. Enno Janssen, *Juda in der Exilszeit. Ein Beitrag zur Frage der Entstehung des Judentums*; (FRLANT 69; Göttingen: Vandenhoeck & Ruprecht, 1956), 40, suggests that geographical differences may also have played a role: Jeremiah 40 is about Jeremiah, and therefore only about the region around Mizpah; things may have been quite different in other parts of the Land.

18. Kreißig on Lam 5:2: "One need only attribute the lament to a member of the class of Judean landowners. . ." (*Die sozialökonomische Situation in Juda*, 26).

19. Thus Ulrich Berges dates Lamentations 5 in the "period of the beginnings of return from Babylon (after 521 B.C.E.)," and yet rightly cites the text in reconstructing conditions at the beginning of the exilic era (*Klagelieder* [HTKAT; Freiburg: Herder, 2002], quoting 277).

20. Positions that regard the biblical picture of the exile and (in part) the return after the exile as a

myth that arose in order to give a common identity to the mixed population during the Persian period and in Hellenistic Judah are untenable: Thomas L. Thompson, "The Exile in History and Myth: A Response to Hans Barstad," in *Leading Captivity Captive: "The Exile" as History and Ideology* (ed. Lester L. Grabbe; JSOTSup 278; Sheffield: Sheffield Academic, 1998), 101–18; Philip R. Davies, "Exile? What Exile? Whose Exile?" in *Leading Captivity Captive: "The Exile" as History ad Ideology* (ed. Lester L. Grabbe; JSOTSup 278. Sheffield: Sheffield Academic, 1998), 128–38. In contrast, Lester L. Grabbe rightly insists that the "myth of the empty Land" represents the real mythical construction ("'The Exile' under the Theodolite: Historiography as Triangulation," in *Leading Captivity Captive: "The Exile" as History and Ideology* [ed. Lester L. Grabbe; JSOTSup 278; Sheffield: Sheffield Academic, 1998]). See also Joseph Blenkinsopp, "The Bible, Archaeology and Politics: or The Empty Land Revisited," *JSOT* 27 (2002): 169–87. On 2 Chr 36:20-21, see also the excursus in Thomas Willi, *Juda—Jehud—Israel. Studien zum Selbstverständnis des Judentums in persischer Zeit* (FAT 12; Tübingen: Mohr, 1995), 18–26.

21. See below, chapters 10, 151–53, and 11, 171–73.

22. Ran Zadok, *The Jews in Babylonia During the Chaldean and Achaemenian Periods According to the Babylonian Sources* (Studies in the History of the Jewish People and the Land of Israel Monograph Series 3; Haifa: University of Haifa, 1979), 35–38; idem, "Some Jews in Babylonian Documents," *JQR* 74 (1983/84): 294–97; and Bustenay Oded, "The Settlements of the Israelite and the Judan Exiles in Mesopotamia in the 8th-6th Centuries B.C.E.," in *Studies in Historical Geography and Biblical Historiography: Presented to Zecharia Kallai* (ed. Gershon Galil and Moshe Weinfeld; VTSUP 81; Leiden: Brill, 2000), 91–103.

23. Thus Albertz, *Israel in Exile*, 100.

24. Richard J. Coggins, "The Origins of the Jewish Diaspora," in *The World of Ancient Israel: Sociological, Anthropological, and Political Perspectives* (ed. Ronald E. Clements; Cambridge: Cambridge University Press, 1989), 163–81, esp. 164,

rightly points out the continued existence of a north-south distinction in such texts.

25. We will discuss below (chapter 10, 134–39) the conflicts that developed during the Persian period from this self-understanding of the Babylonian exile.

26. Zadok, *The Jews in Babylonia*, 34–43; and idem, "Some Jews in Babylonian Documents."

27. On this, see Bernhard Lang, *Kein Aufstand in Jerusalem. Die Politik des Propheten Ezechiel* (2nd ed.; SBB; Stuttgart: Katholisches Bibelwerk, 1981), 160–63.

28. Paolo Sacchi, *The History of the Second Temple Period* (JSOTSup 282; Sheffield: Sheffield Academic, 2000), 51–58, correctly points this out.

29. On the other hand, the opposite, that as Sacchi asserts, the contact between the deportees in their settlements and the king in Babylon, "which must have existed, could only have been stormy," is pure speculation (ibid., 53).

30. See above, chapter 7, 97–102.

31. On this question, see Albertz, *Israel in Exile*, 101–2.

32. See above, chapter 6, 53.

33. For the literary questions regarding these chapters, see Rainer Kessler, *Die Ägyptenbilder der Hebräischen Bibel. Ein Beitrag zur neueren Monotheismusdebatte* (SBS 197; Stuttgart: Katholisches Bibelwerk, 2002), esp. 57–63; Norbert Lohfink, "Die Gattung der 'Historischen Kurzgeschichte' in den letzten Jahren von Juda und in der Zeit des Babylonischen Exils," *ZAW* 90 (1978): 319–47; Winfried Thiel, *Die deuteronomistische Redaktion von Jeremia 26–45* (WMANT 52; Neukirchen-Vluyn: Neukirchener Verlag, 1981); Gunther Wanke, *Untersuchungen zur sogenannten Baruchschrift* (BZAW 122; Berlin: Walter de Gruyter, 1971).

34. See chapter 10, 152–53, below.

35. *TAD* A 4, 7 and A 4, 9. Also *TGI*, nos. 51–52.

36. Beyerlin, 268–69.

37. In contrast, Herbert Donner, writes: "The Jewish military colonists at Elephantine went their own, unique ways in their inherited Yahweh-religion as well" (*Geschichte des Volkes Israel und*

seiner Nachbarn in Grundzügen, part 2, *Von der Königszeit bis zu Alexander dem Großen* [3d ed.; GAT 4/2; Göttingen: Vandenhoeck & Ruprecht, 2001], 383). Those must, then, have consisted of adopting other Canaanite gods from the Aramaeans, who are also attested in Elephantine, and reverencing them together with their primary God, YHWH. That is not impossible, but it does not seem to have any positive attestation.

38. *OTP* 1:7–34.

10. Provincial Society under Persia

1. Gregor Ahn correctly emphasizes that the Persian religious policy had nothing to do with "tolerance," but was part and parcel of the "strategy of a comprehensive administrative and political-military dominance of the disparate regions of the empire" ("Israel und Persien," *RGG*[4] 4:309–11, esp. 309–10).

2. Xenophon, *Cyr.* 8.2.10–12; Herodotus, *Hist.* 1.114.

3. Cf. Hubertus C. M. Vogt according to whom "(the גולה) represents . . . the whole people of Israel" (*Studie zur nachexilischen Gemeinde in Esra-Nehemia* [Werl: Coelde, 1966], esp. 22–43, quoting 42).

4. For these two, see also Sara Japhet "Sheshbazzar and Zerubbabel—Against the Background of the Historical and Religious Tendencies of Ezra-Nehemiah," *ZAW* 94 (1982): 66–98; and idem, "Sheshbazzar and Zerubbabel. Against the Background of the Historical and Religious Tendencies of Ezra-Nehemiah II," *ZAW* 95 (1983): 218–29.

5. Albrecht Alt, "Die Rolle Samarias bei der Entstehung des Judentums," *Kleine Schriften zur Geschichte des Volkes Israel* (3d ed.; Munich: Beck, 1964; original German essay, 1934), 2:316–37; cautious agreement also from Sean E. McEvenue, "The Political Structure in Judah from Cyrus to Nehemiah," *CBQ* 43 (1981): 353–64.

6. For discussion of this material, see esp. Nahman Avigad, *Bullae and Seals from a Post-exilic Judean Archive* (Qedem 4; Jerusalem: Hebrew University, 1976), 5–7, 11–13, 22, 28, 32–36.

7. Avigad, ibid., 35, makes such an attempt; cf. Joachim Schaper, "Numismatik, Epigraphik, alttestamentliche Exegese und die Frage nach der politischen Verfassung des achämenidischen Juda," *ZDPV* 118 (2002): 150–68, esp. 163. Cf. also Hugh G. M. Williamson, *Studies in Persian Period History and Historiography* (FAT 38; Tübingen: Mohr Siebeck, 2004), 46–63.

8. Christiane Karrer, *Ringen um die Verfassung Judas. Eine Studie zu den theologisch-politischen Vorstellungen im Esra-Nehemia-Buch* (BZAW 308; Berlin: de Gruyter, 2001), 37.

9. Charles E. Carter, *The Emergence of Yehud in the Persian Period: A Social and Demographic Study* (JSOTSup 294; Sheffield: Sheffield Academic, 1999), 116–17. Cf. also earlier, Ephraim Stern's view that there had been an attempt at founding a province at the very beginning of Persian rule, but that there then took place under Nehemiah "a revival of the province, if not its re-establishment" ("The Province of Yehud: The Vision and the Reality," *The Jerusalem Cathedra* 1 [1981]: 9–21, esp. 12–14, quoting 14); and idem, "The Persian Empire and the Political and Social History of Palestine in the Persian Period," *CHJ* 1:70–87, esp. 72–74, 82–83. Similarly Lester L. Grabbe, "it seems likely that there were some governors over Judah before Nehemiah" (*Judaism from Cyrus to Hadrian* [Minneapolis: Fortress Press, 1992] 1:81–83, quoting 83) . In the same sense also Thomas Willi speaks of "initiatives toward provincial self-government" (*Juda—Jehud—Israel. Studien zum Selbstverständnis des Judentums in persischer Zeit* [FAT 12; Tübingen: Mohr,1995], 30).

10. See the first part of this section.

11. Karrer, *Ringen um die Verfassung Judas*, 42.

12. Douglas M. Gropp, "Sanballat," *Encyclopedia of the Dead Sea Scrolls* (New York: Oxford University Press, 2000), 2:823–25. Cf. also the older reconstructions of Kurt Galling, *Studien zur Geschichte Israels im persischen Zeitalter* (Tübingen: Mohr, 1964), 209–10; and Frank Moore Cross, "A Reconstruction of the Judean Restoration," *JBL* 94 (1975): 4–18, esp. 17.

13. Thus also Ulrich Kellermann, *Nehemia. Quelle, Überlieferung und Geschichte* (BZAW 102;

Berlin: Walter de Gruyter, 1967); Joseph Blenkinsopp, "The Nehemiah Autobiographical Memoir," in *Language, Theology and the Bible. Festschrift J. Barr* (ed. Samuel E. Balentine and John Barton; Oxford: Oxford University Press, 1994), 199–212; Grabbe, *Judaism from Cyrus to Hadrian* 1:131–36); Karrer, *Ringen um die Verfassung Judas*, 128–33); and esp. Titus Reinmuth, *Der Bericht Nehemias. Zur literarischen Eigenart, traditionsgeschichtlichen Prägung und innerbiblischen Rezeption des Ich-Berichts Nehemias* (OBO 183; Fribourg: Universitätsverlag, 2002). Reinmuth develops a two-stage origin for the memoir: at the beginning is the narrative of building the wall, "perhaps written already during the time when Nehemiah was governor," which was then expanded into a memoir "soon after his period of activity in Judah in the last quarter of the fifth century B.C.E." (336). The thesis that the Nehemiah account as a whole represents a construction by the Chronicler, as Joachim Becker proposes, *Der Ich-Bericht des Nehemiabuches als chronistische Gestaltung* (FB 87; Würzburg: Echter, 1998), has not withstood testing.

14. The most extended recent study is that of Karrer, *Ringen um die Verfassung Judas*. For a discussion of the Ezra material, see 147–48, below.

15. See above in this section.

16. For the date 445, see Reinmuth, *Der Bericht Nehemias*, 51–53; for the role of non-Persian interests within the imperial elite, see Joel Weinberg, "The International Elite of the Achæmenid Empire: Reality and Fiction," *ZAW* 111 (1999): 583–608.

17. Contrary to the biblical picture, according to which Ezra's mission began before that of Nehemiah and overlapped with it (accepted, for example, by Hans Heinrich Schaeder, *Esra der Schreiber* [BHT 5; Tübingen: Mohr, 1930]; Wilhelm Th. in der Smitten, *Esra. Quellen, Überlieferung und Geschichte* [SSN 15; Assen: Van Gorcum, 1973], 91–105; Peter Frei and Klaus Koch, *Reichsidee und Reichsorganisation im Perserreich* [2d. ed.; OBO 55; Fribourg: Universitätsverlag, 1996], 243–45), I assume that Ezra worked some fifty years after Nehemiah. The two are almost never connected in the books named for them; the two places where they appear simultaneously (Neh 8:9; 12:26) can

easily be recognized as redactional insertions. In particular, according to the present chronology, Ezra keeps the "law of the God of heaven" (Ezra 7) sealed for thirteen years before, according to Nehemiah 8–9, it is put into effect. It is much more probable that Nehemiah first set political affairs in order, and then Ezra organized religious matters. The dating of Ezra after Nehemiah, though in the year 428, is advocated by, among others, V. S. J. Pavlovský, "Die Chronologie der Tätigkeit Esdras. Versuche einer neuen Lösung," *Bib* 38 (1957): 275–305, 428–56. A thorough examination of the arguments led John A. Emerton, "Did Ezra Go to Jerusalem in 428 B.C." *JTS* n.s. 17 (1966): 1–19, to the conclusion that 398 is the more likely date.

18. See 147–48, below.

19. Thus Herbert Donner, *Geschichte des Volkes Israel und seiner Nachbarn in Grundzügen* (3d ed.; GAT 4/2; Göttingen: Vandenhoeck & Ruprecht, 2001), 2:467.

20. For the social structures of Jewish society in the Persian period, see the survey of research in Willy Schottroff, "Zur Sozialgeschichte Israels in der Perserzeit," *VF* 27 (1982): 46–88.

21. See chapter 4, 27–28, above, and the remarks of Christiane Karrer: "Belonging to a בית אבות was clearly regulated by genealogy. . . " (*Ringen um die Verfassung Judas. Eine Studie zu den theologisch-politischen Vorstellungen im Esra-Nehemia-Buch* [BZAW 308; Berlin: Walter de Gruyter, 2001], 88). For the "father's houses" as the basis for the family system in the Persian period, see also Hubertus C. M. Vogt, *Studie zur nachexilischen Gemeinde in Esra-Nehemia* (Werl: Coelde, 1966), 101–05; and Hans G. Kippenberg, *Religion und Klassenbildung im antiken Judäa. Eine religionssoziologische Studie zum Verhältnis von Tradition und gesellschaftlicher Entwicklung* (SUNT 14; Göttingen: Vandenhoeck & Ruprecht, 1978), 23–41.

22. The growing mass of epigraphical discoveries attests to the fact that, from the time of the exiles and associated population shifts, there was an increasing tendency for non-Israelite population groups to move into Judahite and Israelite territory. On this, see the overview in Israel Eph'al, "Changes in Palestine during the Persian Period

in Light of Epigraphic Sources," *IEJ* 48 (1998): 106–19.

23. See further details in the next section.

24. On this, see Friedrich Fechter, *Die Familie in der Nachexilszeit. Untersuchungen zur Bedeutung der Verwandtschaft in ausgewählten Texten des Alten Testaments* (BZAW 264; Berlin: de Gruyter, 1998).

25. See 134–39, below.

26. Tamara C. Eskenazi, "Out from the Shadows: Biblical Women in the Postexilic Era," *JSOT* 54 (1992): 25–43.

27. On this, see also Harold C. Washington, "The Strange Woman of Proverbs 1–9 and Post-Exilic Judaean Society," in *Second Temple Studies 2: Temple and Community in the Persian Period* (ed. Tamara C. Eskenazi and Kent H. Richards; JSOT-Sup 175; Sheffield: JSOT Press, 1994), 217–42; Daniel L. Smith-Christopher, "The Mixed Marriage Crisis in Ezra 9–10 and Nehemiah 13: A Study of the Sociology of the Post-Exilic Judaean Community," in *Second Temple Studies 2, Temple and Community in the Persian Period* (ed. Tamara C. Eskenazi and Kent H. Richards; JSOTSup 175; Sheffield: JSOT Press, 1994), 243–65.

28. Nahman Avigad, *Bullae and Seals from a Post-exilic Judean Archive* (Qedem 4; Jerusalem: Hebrew University, 1976), 17; and Eric M. Meyers, "The Shelomith Seal and the Judean Restoration. Some Additional Considerations," *ErIsr* 18 (1985): 33*–38*, date it in the sixth century; Ephraim Stern, *Material Culture of the Land of the Bible in the Persian Period 538-332 B.C.* (Warminster: Aris & Philips, 1982), 213; and Graham I. Davies in *AHI* 106.018 put it in the late fifth-early fourth century.

29. Avigad and Sass, in *CWSS*, 31. See also Stern: " . . . there is no doubt that Shelomith was a woman of high rank" (*Material Culture*, 207). Whether she is therefore to be identified with the Shelomith in 1 Chr 3:19 and traced to Davidic origins, as Meyers, "The Shelomith Seal and the Judean Restoration," 34*–35*, suggests, must remain an open question.

30. Eskenazi, "Out from the Shadows," 33.

31. See chapter 9, 121–23, above.

32. Ronny Reich and Eli Shukron, "The Jerusalem City Dump in the Late Second Temple Period," *ZDPV* 199 (2003): 12–18.

33. Ibid., 17.

34. For an interpretation of the conditions presumed by Nehemiah 5, see Hans G. Kippenberg, *Religion und Klassenbildung im antiken Judäa. Eine religionssoziologische Studie zum Verhältnis von Tradition und gesellschaftlicher Entwicklung* (SUNT 14; Göttingen: Vandenhoeck & Ruprecht, 1978), 55–62; and Willy Schottroff, "Arbeit und sozialer Konflikt im nachexilischen Juda," in *Gerechtigkeit lernen. Beiträge zur biblischen Sozialgeschichte* (TB 94; Gütersloh: Kaiser/Gütersloher, 1999), 52–93.

35. For the connection between the building of the wall and the threat of an uprising, see Heinz Kreißig, *Die sozialökonomische Situation in Juda zur Achämenidenzeit* (SGKAO 7; Berlin: Akademie, 1973), 109; and Schottroff, "Arbeit und sozialer Konflikt," 54–55.

36. Kreißig on the members of this group: "they must . . . be the owners of their land. And they are poor. They are typical smallholders, small farmers 'on their own soil'" (*Die sozialökonomische Situation in Juda*, 79).

37. See the next section.

38. This does not mean that they were part of the upper class in Babylon; see Ran Zadok: "The fact that Jews were integrated into Babylonian society does not however mean that they rose to the highest classes of that society" (*The Jews in Babylonia During the Chaldean and Achaemenian Periods According to the Babylonian Sources* [Studies in the History of the Jewish People and the Land of Israel Monograph Series 3; Haifa: University of Haifa, 1979], 86).

39. See above, chapter 9, 121–23.

40. According to Christiane Karrer, *Ringen um die Verfassung Judas. Eine Studie zu den theologisch-politischen Vorstellungen im Esra-Nehemia-Buch* [BZAW 308; Berlin: Walter de Gruyter, 2001], 144, 240, the identification of Israel = Qahal ("community") = exiles is typical of the book of Ezra.

41. Hubertus C. M. Vogt summarizes the analysis of the relevant terms in Ezra and Nehemiah by saying "that the author equates all the

contemporary inhabitants of the Land who did not belong to the community of the returnees with the pagan population at the time of the Exodus" (*Studie zur nachexilischen Gemeinde in Esra-Nehemia* [Werl, Germany: Coelde, 1966], 153). See also Enno Janssen, *Juda in der Exilszeit. Ein Beitrag zur Frage der Entstehung des Judentums* (FRLANT 69; Göttingen: Vandenhoeck & Ruprecht, 1956), 54.

42. Joseph Blenkinsopp formulates this thesis: "that there existed in the province a politically and economically dominant elite composed primarily of resettled Babylonian Jews" ("Temple and Society in Achaemenid Judah," in *Second Temple Studies 1: Persian Period* [ed. Philip R. Davies; JSOTSup 117; Sheffield: Sheffield Academic, 1991], 22–53, quoting 47). It is true that Kenneth Hoglund, "The Achaemenid Context," in *Second Temple Studies 1: Persian Period* (ed. Philip R. Davies; JSOTSup 117; Sheffield: Sheffield Academic, 1991), 54–72, questions this view, pointing to a supposed Persian settlement policy in which those who had appropriated others' previous property and those returning from the exile were equal. Apart from the fact that his demonstration of a deliberate Persian settlement policy can scarcely be called successful, even Hoglund must posit at least a conflict of interests between the two groups. For an archaeological testing of Hoglund's thesis, see Charles E. Carter, *The Emergence of Yehud in the Persian Period: A Social and Demographic Study* (JSOTSup 294; Sheffield: Sheffield Academic, 1999), 214–48; he concludes that "the traditional view of intra-province struggle between returnees and those who had remained on the land" can by no means be regarded as having been refuted (248).

43. The list of donations is a secondary addition to the list of returnees in Nehemiah 7, which is itself a composition made up of various elements; see the notes below. The parallel in Ezra 2:68-69 is also secondary to Neh 7:69-71.

44. So Lester L. Grabbe, *Judaism from Cyrus to Hadrian* (Minneapolis: Fortress Press, 1992), 39.

45. On this see the relevant title of Walter Dietrich's 2002 essay, "Wem das Land gehört" ("To whom the Land belongs)" ("Wem das Land gehört. Ein Beitrag zur Sozialgeschichte Isra-els im 6. Jahrhundert v. Chr.," in *Theopolitik. Studien zur Theologie und Ethik des Alten Testaments* [Neukirchen-Vluyn: Neukirchener, 2002], 270–86).

46. Daniel L. Smith, "The Politics of Ezra: Sociological Indicators of Postexilic Judaean Society," in *Second Temple Studies 1. Persian Period* (ed. Philip R. Davies; JSOTSup 117; Sheffield: Sheffield Academic, 1991), 73–97, at 93, also adduces Deut 28:43; 1 Kgs 8:33; Isa 5:17; Amos 5:11; Mic 6:15; Hag 2:10–14; and Zech 5:11. But only in some of these passages *might* there be the idea that the new landowners presumed by the text "were other Israelites."

47. For this interpretation of the passage see Dietrich, "Wem das Land gehört," 285. For Robert Hanhart, *Dodekapropheton 7.1. Sacharja 1–8* (BK 14/7.1; Neukirchen-Vluyn: Neukirchener, 1998), 324–51, in contrast, the text has nothing to do with real conflicts in the Persian era; stealing and false oaths are examples of violation of the Decalogue, and the punishment of house destruction is a conventional motif. In view of the text's obscure language, such an interpretation cannot be excluded. But the question remains why, in the first place, Zechariah, if he is only concerned about violation of the Decalogue, did not choose the otherwise so popular example of adultery, and second, whether the punishment should really be so completely unrelated to the deed. [Tr. note: The standard English translations of this passage reflect an entirely different interpretation of the Hebrew. For a critique of such an interpretation, and in agreement with Kessler, see Marvin A. Sweeney, *The Twelve Prophets* (Berit Olam; Collegeville: Liturgical, 2000), 617–18.]

48. For this interpretation of Leviticus 25, see Gerhard Wallis, "Das Jobeljahr-Gesetz, eine Novelle zum Sabbathjahr-Gesetz," *MIO* (1969): 337–45; Frank Crüsemann, *The Torah: Theology and Social History of Old Testament Law* (trans. Allan W. Mahnke; Minneapolis: Fortress Press, 1996), 330–31; Dietrich, "Wem das Land gehört," 279–81, 285–86; see now the extended discussion in Esias E. Meyer, *The Jubilee in Leviticus 25: A Theological-Ethical Interpretation from a South*

African Perspective (EXUZ 15; Münster: Lit, 2005). Differently John Sietze Bergsma, "The Jubilee: A Post-Exilic Priestly Attempt to Reclaim Lands?" *Bib* 84 (2003): 225–46.

49. Joel Weinberg, *The Citizen-Temple Community* (JSOTSup 151; Sheffield: JSOT Press, 1992). There is a good German summary in idem, *Der Chronist in seiner Mitwelt* (BZAW 239; Berlin: de Gruyter, 1996).

50. These numbers are in Weinberg, *The Citizen-Temple Community*, 43.

51. Among those discussing this thesis, one may note Blenkinsopp, "Temple and Society;" Peter Ross Bedford, "On Models and Texts: A Response to Blenkinsopp and Petersen," in *Second Temple Studies 1: Persian Period* (ed. Philip R. Davies; JSOTSup 117; Sheffield: Sheffield Academic Press, 1991), 154–62; and Richard A. Horsley, "Empire, Temple, and Community—but no Bourgeoisie! A Response to Blenkinsopp and Petersen," in *Second Temple Studies 1. Persian Period* (ed. Philip R. Davies; JSOTSup 117; Sheffield: Sheffield Academic, 1991), 163–74.

52. Thomas Willi, *Juda—Jehud—Israel. Studien zum Selbstverständnis des Judentums in persischer Zeit* (FAT 12; Tübingen: Mohr, 1995), 75.

53. Douglas M. Gropp, *Wadi Daliyeh II: The Samaria Papyri from Wadi Daliyeh* (DJD 28; Oxford: Clarendon, 2001), 1–116.

54. On interpreting the contents, see Rainer Kessler, "Samaria-Papyri und Sklaverei in Israel," in *"Einen Altar von Erde mache mir . . . ," Festschrift für Diethelm Conrad zu seinem 70. Geburtstag* (ed. Johannes F. Diehl, Reinhard Heitzenröder, and Markus Witte; KAANT 4/5; Waltrop: Spenner, 2003), 169–81.

55. See above, 129–33.

56. From the Behistun inscription: "Darius the king proclaims: These lands that have come to me—according to the will of Ahuramazda were they subjected to me. They brought me tribute" (*TUAT* 1:419–50).

57. For "Haggai's and Zechariah's expectations of the king," see Karl-Martin Beyse, *Serubbabel und die Königserwartungen der Propheten Haggai und Sacharja. Eine historische und traditi-*

onsgeschichtliche Untersuchung (AzTh 48; Stuttgart: Calwer, 1972), 50–103.

58. For an interpretation of Neh 6:1–14 in the sense that the Jewish male and female prophets mentioned there are not opposed to Nehemiah's politics—thus Robert P. Carroll, "Coopting the Prophets: Nehemiah and Noadiah," in *Priests, Prophets and Scribes: Essays on the Formation and Heritage of Second Temple Judaism in Honour of Joseph Blenkinsopp* (ed. Eugene Ulrich, et al.; JSOTSup 149; Sheffield: Sheffield Academic, 1992), 87–99—but rather intend to call him to become king, see Ulrich Kellermann, *Nehemia. Quelle, Überlieferung und Geschichte* (BZAW 102; Berlin: de Gruyter, 1967), 179–82; and then Rainer Kessler, "Mirjam und die Prophetie der Perserzeit," in *Gott an den Rändern. Sozialgeschichtliche Perspektiven auf die Bibel. Festschrift für Willi Schottroff* (ed. Ulrike Bail and Renate Jost; Gütersloh: Kaiser, 1996), 64–72, esp. 68–70. See also the modifying remarks of Ursula Rapp, *Mirjam. Eine feministisch-rhetorische Lektüre der Mirjamtexte in der hebräischen Bibel* (BZAW 317; Berlin: de Gruyter, 2002), 178–93.

59. See the previous section.

60. For these effects of Persian tax policies, see Hans G. Kippenberg, *Religion und Klassenbildung im antiken Judäa. Eine religionssoziologische Studie zum Verhältnis von Tradition und gesellschaftlicher Entwicklung* (SUNT 14; Göttingen: Vandenhoeck & Ruprecht, 1978), 50–52.

61. See the basic work of Joachim Schaper, "The Jerusalem Temple as an Instrument of the Achaemenid Fiscal Administration," *VT* 45 (1995): 528–39, esp. 535–38; also idem, *Priester und Leviten im achämenidischen Juda. Studien zur Kult- und Sozialgeschichte Israels in persischer Zeit* (FAT 31; Tübingen: Mohr Siebeck. 2000), 141–50.

62. See below, 143–47.

63. See above in this section.

64. Rainer Albertz, *A History of Israelite Religion in the Old Testament Period* (2 vols.; OTL; Louisville: Westminster John Knox, 1994), 2:453.

65. Christiane Karrer, *Ringen um die Verfassung Judas. Eine Studie zu den theologisch-politischen Vorstellungen im Esra-Nehemia-Buch* (BZAW 308;

Berlin: de Gruyter, 2001), 307, defends the view that the "diarchical principle" is a concept belonging to the final form of the books of Ezra-Nehemiah and was not found in the older, Aramaic portion of Ezra 1–6. The latter is certainly true, but if we look also at the text of Zechariah we will have to say that the initiative toward a secular and priestly equal exercise of power is present quite early. Only the development of this notion of equal power-sharing into a closed concept is due to a later point of view.

66. For the "elders" as part of the older Aramaic narrative, see A. H. J. Gunneweg, "Die aramäische und die hebräische Erzählung über die nachexilische Restauration—ein Vergleich," *ZAW* 94 (1982): 299–302, esp. 300; Karrer, *Ringen um die Verfassung Judas*, 91, 111.

67. Gesenius[17]; KBL; Zürcher Bibel. [Translator's note: Standard English translations include "rulers" (AV), "magistrates" (NAB), and "officials" (NIV, NRSV).]

68. So KBL.

69. Thus according to Ephraim Stern, who speaks of a "provincial official" and relates him to the governor ("The Province of Yehud: The Vision and the Reality," in *The Jerusalem Cathedra: Studies in the History, Archaeology, Geography, and Ethnography of the Land of Israel* 1 [ed. Lee I. Levine; Detroit: Wayne State University Press, 1981], 9–21, esp. 12). For the interpretation of the *seganim* as officials, see, emphatically, Albertz, *History of Israelite Religion*, 2:473 n. 21. In texts that speak of foreign peoples, we frequently find the combination of *pakhot* and *seganim*: see Jer 51:23, 28, 57; Ezek 23:6, 12, 23; and on this subject Karrer, *Ringen um die Verfassung Judas*, 161. It is true that the term *sar* by no means disappeared in the Persian era, but it was very broadly applied, for military officers (Neh 2:9; 4:10) and for the rulers of the administrative districts into which the province of Yehud was divided (Neh 3:9–19). There were also *sarim* among the priests, probably a leadership group among them (Ezra 8:24, 29; 10:5). The term is frequently used in a very broad sense, not so much as a title as in the sense of "officeholder" (thus in Ezra 9:1; 10:14; Neh 10:1; and frequently).

Such a variety of usage is surely due also to the numerous literary layers that are combined in Ezra and Nehemiah.

70. See above, 134–39.

71. English translations: K. C. Hanson, "Petition to Authorize Elephantine Temple Reconstruction," K. C. Hanson, www.kchanson.com/ANCDOCS/westsem/templeauth.html; Bezalel Porten, *The Elephantine Papyri in English: Three Millennia of Cross-Cultural Continuity and Change* (Documenta et monumenta Orientis antiqui 22; Leiden: Brill, 1996), B19, 139–44.

72. For the role of the *qahal*, see Hubertus C. M. Vogt, *Studie zur nachexilischen Gemeinde in Esra-Nehemia* (Werl, Germany: Coelde, 1966), 90–99; Stefan Stiegler, *Die naxexilische JHWH-Gemeinde in Jerusalem. Ein Beitrag zu einer alttestamentlichen Ekklesiologie* (BEATAJ 34 Frankfurt: Peter Lang, 1994), 109–16. It is quite in accord with the Chronicles-colored viewpoint when this assembly is called "the congregation of the exiles" (Ezra 10:8; see also, in the same vein, Neh 8:17). This certainly does not refer to a separate assembly of that group in contrast to an assembly of those who had not been exiled (thus Joseph Blenkinsopp, "Temple and Society in Achaemenid Judah," in *Second Temple Studies 1: Persian Period* [ed. Philip R. Davies; JSOTSup 117; Sheffield: Sheffield Academic, 1991], 22–53, esp. 44–46); in line with the concept of the "empty Land" during the exile, the presumption is that the genuine temple community is identical with the "congregation of the exiles."

73. Morton Smith, "Die Entwicklungen im Judäa des 5. Jh. v. Chr. aus griechischer Sicht," in *Seminar: Die Entstehung der antiken Klassengesellschaft* (ed. Hans G. Kippenberg; STW 130; Frankfurt: Suhrkamp, 1977), 313–27, quoting 319.

74. See 129–33, above.

75. Ibid.

76. For this overall picture, see Ephraim Stern, *Material Culture of the Land of the Bible in the Persian Period 538–332 B.C.* (Warminster: Aris & Philips, 1982), 215–28; and idem, "The Persian Empire and the Political and Social History of Palestine in the Persian Period," in *CHJ* 1:70–87, esp.

81. For coinage in the Persian era in particular, see the summary by Joachim Schaper, "Numismatik, Epigraphik, alttestamentliche Exegese und die Frage nach der politischen Verfassung des achämenidischen Juda," *ZDPV* 118 (2002): 150–68.

77. Stern, "The Persian Empire," 82.

78. Jon L. Berquist correctly points this out: ". . . Yehud received as much freedom in its internal affairs as would still allow the Persian Empire to gain the maximum amount of taxation and resources from it" (*Judaism in Persia's Shadow: A Social and Historical Approach* [Minneapolis: Fortress Press, 1995], 134). "Local autonomy was only partial but was still significant, allowing the formation of a local elite who could control the burden of the imperial intrusion . . ." (234).

79. See above, chapter 7, 97–102.

80. See above, chapter 8, 114–17.

81. See above, 129–33, as well as chapter 9, 120–23, and Rainer Albertz, *Israel in Exile: The History and Literature of the Sixth Century* B.C.E. (trans. David Green; SBLStBL 3; Atlanta: Society of Biblical Literature, 2003), 2, who continues his description of the period of the exile up to 520.

82. See above, 129–33.

83. See above, chapter 7, 88–91.

84. If older cult places remained in use in Persian-era Samaria, as József Zsengellér, *Gerizim as Israel: Northern Tradition of the Old Testament and the Early History of the Samaritans* (Utrechtse Theologische reeks 38; Utrecht, 1998), 157, suggests, there was no contradiction involved. What was crucial was that the north, until the building of a temple on Gerizim in the time of Alexander the Great (for this dating, see ibid., 150–55) had no central sanctuary.

85. *TAD* A 4.7 and A 4.9, in *TGI* nos. 51 and 52.

86. *TAD* A 4.1; Beyerlin, 270–71.

87. See also 148–51, below.

88. In certain phases of church history one could compare this with the double role of the Vatican as spiritual center for all Catholics and a political factor in Italian domestic politics.

89. See 139–43, above.

90. See chapter 11, 166–67.

91. The high position of the priest is attested by the fact that in fourth-century Yehud there was not only a state coinage with the inscription *yhd* (or the name of the governor with his title, *hpkhh*), but also a coinage with the inscription *ywkhnn hkhn* = Jochanan the priest; see Joachim Schaper, "Numismatik, Epigraphik, alttestamentliche Exegese und die Frage nach der politischen Verfassung des achämenidischen Juda," *ZDPV* 118 (2002), 150–68, esp. 156–58.

92. See Frank Moore Cross's attempts, "A Reconstruction of the Judean Restoration," *JBL* 94, 4–18 (1975); and Schaper, ibid., 160.

93. See above, chapter 7, 88–91.

94. Cf. Albertz, *A History of Israelite Religion*, 2:487–95.

95. For the state taxation system see above, 139–43.

96. Jürgen Kegler: "The petition for the overlord means, in fact, the acknowledgment of imperial rule; it accepts the status quo" ("Die Fürbitte für den persischen Oberherrn im tempel von Jerusalem (Esra 6,10). Ein imperiales Herrschaftsinstrument," in *Gott an den Rändern. Sozialgeschichteliche Perspektiven auf die Bibel. Festschrift für Willi Schottroff* [ed. Ulrike Bail and Renate Jost; Gütersloh: Kaiser, 1996], 73–82, quoting 79).

97. Joachim Schaper emphatically supports this position: "the Jerusalem temple administration acted as the interface between the tax-paying population of Judah and the Persian government" "The Jerusalem Temple as an Instrument of the Achaemenid Fiscal Administration," *VT* 45 (1995): 528–39, quoting 537.

98. Gesenius[18] s.v. יסר.

99. Schaper, "The Jerusalem Temple," 532.

100. For these passages, see Joachim Schaper, *Priester und Leviten im achämenidischen Juda. Studien zur Kult- und Sozialgeschichte Israels in persischer Zeit* (FAT 31; Tübingen: Mohr Siebeck, 2000), 1551; and idem, "The Temple Treasury Committee in the Times of Nehemiah and Ezra," *VT* 47 (1998): 200–206.

101. For an evaluation of this as a source see 133–43, above.

102. Ibid.

103. According to David Janzen, it is "a kind of midrash on the rest of the Ezra narrative" ("The 'Mission' of Ezra and the Persian-Period Temple Community," *JBL* 119 [2000]: 619–43, quoting 643). Sebastian Grätz , arguing from the "royal euergetism in the Hellenistic era," sees this as "the ideal background of Ezra 7:12–16)," and thus regards the text as a "fictional document" (*Das Edikt des Artaxerxes. Eine Untersuchung zum religionspolitischen und historischen Umfeld von Esra 7,12–26* [BZAW 337; Berlin: de Gruyter], 134). But it is questionable whether royal gifts, releases from taxation, and preservation of the sovereignty of law could be so thoroughly restricted to Hellenistic policy that Ezra 7 must necessarily come only from the Hellenistic era. See also, idem, "Esra 7 im Kontext hellenistischer Politik. Der königliche Euergetismus in hellenistischer Zeit als ideeller Hintergrund von Esr 7,12–16," in *Die Griechen und das antike Israel. Interdisziplinäre Studien zur Religions- und Kulturgeschichte des Heiligen Landes* (ed. Stefan Alkier and Markus Witte; OBO 121; Fribourg: Academic Press Fribourg, 2004), 131–54.

104. Peter Frei and Klaus Koch, *Reichsidee und Reichsorganisation im Perserreich* (2d ed.; OBO 55; Fribourg: Universitätsverlag, 1996), 52, 54.

105. Christiane Karrer: "Ezra 7:25-26 (and 14) thus contain elements that do not correspond conceptually to the overall context of the Ezra account, and so with a certain probability must belong to a model for the present letter text, which may in fact have been part of a historical document" (*Ringen um die Verfassung Judas. Eine Studie zu den theologisch-politischen Vorstellungen im Esra-Nehemia-Buch* (BZAW 308; Berlin: de Gruyter, 2001), 31. In this sense, also Erhard Blum, "Esra, die Mosetora und die persische Politik," in *Religion und Religionskontakte im Zeitalter der Achämeniden* (ed. Reinhard G. Kratz; VWGTH 22; Gütersloh: Gütersloher, 2002), 231–56, esp. 249–50. Klaus Koch, "Der Artaxerxes-Erlaß im Esrabuch," in *Meilenstein. Festgabe für Herbert Donner* (ed. Manfred Weippert and Stefan Timm; ÄAT 30; Weisbaden: Harrassowitz, 1995), 87–98 , also concludes from the difference between the Artaxerxes decree and

the Ezra account that the decree is genuine (98), but considers this more or less certain only in the case of vv. 12-20. According to Wilhelm Th. in der Smitten, vv. 12-19, 25-26 are "historical and genuine in their fundamental elements," although he excepts v. 14 from this (*Esra. Quellen, Überlieferung und Geschichte* (SSN 15; Assen: Van Gorcum, 1973], 19, 55). For the overall discussion, see also Frei and Koch, *Reichsidee und Reichsorganisation*, 54–61, 210–20.

106. Ernst Axel Knauf thinks in the case of the Passover letter of a "secretariat of religion for Jewish matters," probably in Babylon ("Elephantine und das vor-biblische Judentum," in *Religion und Religionskontakte im Zeitalter der Achämeniden* [ed. Reinhard G. Kratz; Veröffentlichungen der Wisenschaftlichen Gesellschaft für Theologie 22; Gütersloh: Kaiser, 2002], 179–88, quoting 186). He continues: "What was determined there had the force of law not on the basis of a 'law of Moses,' which did not yet exist, but by decree of the great king. . . ." However, that is too exclusive an alternative. For if Ezra, twenty years later, can present a finished 'law of Moses,' it would already have been available as a guideline for the secretariat.

107. Mantel's opinion (1973) that Ezra was only sent to the "sons of the exile," while the high priest continued to be responsible for the rest of the population of Yehud, is untenable. According to the final redaction of Ezra-Nehemiah the "sons of the exile" are identical with the YHWH-believing population of Yehud; all others are "people of the lands" (on which see above, 2, b).

108. Udo Rüterswörden wants to conclude from the fact that "the Passover letter from Elephantine shows that essential ordinances of the Torah appear to be known" that "Ezra's mission" is "essentially pointless" since "around the turn of the century the Torah was apparently known and did not need to be newly introduced" ("Die persische Reichsautorisation der Thora: Fact or Fiction?" *ZABR* 1 [1995], 47–61, quoting 60). But that short-circuits the matter, since Ezra 7 itself presumes that the Torah in principle is "apparently known" (v. 25). It is *not* being "newly introduced,"

but is merely being made universally applicable by the state authority.

109. So Karrer, *Ringen um die Verfassung Judas*, 30–32.

110. For the discussion see, Frei and Koch, *Reichsidee und Reichsorganisation*, 20–21, 51–54.

111. Thus, fundamentally, ibid.

112. For critique of the thesis of an imperial authorization, see Rüterswörden, "Die persische Reichsautorisation"; and Karrer, *Ringen um die Verfassung Judas*, 28–32.

113. Blum: Ezra's law "can . . . only be the Pentateuch in its essential substance" ("Esra, die Mosetora und die persische Politik," 25). According to in der Smitten, *Esra*, 124–30, to the contrary, it was only a conglomerate of D and P and other texts. Underlying this view is the mistaken opinion that a "law" could only be made up of texts that have the character of law in the strict sense. But "Torah," by its nature, contains both narrative and legal texts; the one cannot exist without the other. Cornelius Houtman's opinion, "Ezra and the Law. Observations on the Supposed Relation between Ezra and the Pentateuch," *OTS* 21 (1981): 91–115, that Ezra-Nehemiah refers to a law other than the Pentateuch because Ezra-Nehemiah does not speak only of laws drawn from the Pentateuch, but also to others that do not appear there (104–11) rests entirely on examples from Nehemiah 10 (105–106); for this chapter, see 148–51, below.

114. See chapter 11, 170–71, below.

115. See above, chapter 8, 114–17.

116. Frank Crüsemann, *The Torah: Theology and Social History of Old Testament Law* (trans. Allan W. Mahnke; Minneapolis: Fortress Press, 1996), 20.

117. Eckart Otto, "Mose und das Gesetz. Die Mose-Figur als Gegenentwurf Politischer Theologie zur neuassyrischen Königsideologie im 7. Jh. v. Chr.," in *Mose. Ägypten und das Alte Testament* (ed. Eckart Otto; SBS 189; Stuttgart: Katholisches Bibelwerk, 2000), 43–83, quoting 69.

118. See 143–47, above, and the text in *TAD* A 4.1; K. C. Hanson, "Petition to Authorize Elephantine Temple Reconstruction," K. C. Hanson, www.kchanson.com/ANCDOCS/westsem/

templeauth.html; and Bezalel Porten, *The Elephantine Papyri in English: Three Millennia of Cross-Cultural Continuity and Change* (DMOA 22; Leiden: Brill, 1996), B19, 139–44; and Beyerlin, 270–71.

119. For discussion of these aspects of the papyri, see Rainer Kessler, "Samaria-Papyri und Sklaverei in Israel," in "*Einen Altar von Erde mache mir . . . ," Festschrift für Diethelm Conrad zu seinem 70. Geburtstag* (ed. Johannes F. Diehl, Reinhard Heitzenröder, and Markus Witte; KAANT 4/5; Waltrop: Spenner, 2003), 169–81.

120. See chapter 11, 170–71, below.

121. Christiane Karrer, *Ringen um die Verfassung Judas. Eine Studie zu den theologisch-politischen Vorstellungen im Esra-Nehemia-Buch* (BZAW 308; Berlin: Walter de Gruyter, 2001), 258, interprets the tensions between the Artaxerxes letter in Ezra 7 and the Ezra document in Ezra 7–10 and Nehemiah 8 (without the letter) against this background. According to the royal letter, Ezra, with full authority, is to put the Torah into effect with a single stroke, while this portrait of Ezra is painted in the account of his actions: "His function was not, however, an authoritative imposition of the commandments of the Torah." In that case, the account would accommodate the claim that Ezra may really have publically proclaimed the Torah with the historical reality that the Torah succeeded in imposing its authority only gradually. Ezra becomes a "kind of 'catalyst' who enabled the population to act independently in accordance with the Torah."

122. For the disputed dating of Nehemiah 10, cf. on the one side, Hans G. Kippenberg, *Religion und Klassenbildung im antiken Judäa. Eine religionssoziologische Studie zum Verhältnis von Tradition und gesellschaftlicher Entwicklung* (SUNT 14; Göttingen: Vandenhoeck & Ruprecht; 1978, 69–76), who posits an origin under Nehemiah in the year 432, and on the other side, Ulrich Kellermann, *Nehemia. Quelle, Überlieferung und Geschichte* (BZAW 102; Berlin: de Gruyter, 1967), 37–41, for whom the document is post-Nehemiah. Titus Reinmuth, *Der Bericht Nehemias. Zur literarischen Eigenart, traditionsgeschichtlichen Prägung und*

innerbiblischen Rezeption des Ich-Berichts Nehemias (OBO 183; Fribourg: Universitätsverlag; Göttingen: Vandenhoeck & Ruprecht, 2002), 210–19, assumes a long growth process for the text, with its basic content in vv. 31–32, 38a*, 40b.

123. For this character of Nehemiah 10, see Crüsemann, *The Torah*, 395–97.

124. When Cornelius Houtman notes regarding some provisions in Nehemiah 10 that they do not appear at all in the Pentateuchal laws, he mistakes this character of legal interpretation, which is always at the same time an application to current circumstances ("Ezra and the Law. Observations on the Supposed Relation between Ezra and the Pentateuch," *OTS* 21 [1981]: 91–115, at 105–6). . "A prohibition to buy merchandise on sabbath or a holy day (v. 32a . . .) does not occur in the laws of the O. T." (105). Certainly not in that wording! But as an interpretation of law it certainly can be derived from the sabbath commandments.

125. After Reinmuth, *Der Bericht Nehemias*, 213–17, shows that by no means all the obligations in Nehemiah 10 have strict parallels in the Pentateuch, and that they also have an independent wording, he rightly interprets this to mean that the author of Nehemiah 10 was dealing creatively, not literally, with the ordinances of Torah, and that in doing so he gives an example of how Torah came to be in the post-exilic period.

126. See chapter 9, 119–20, above.

127. For the onomasticon of the Nippur documents, see Ran Zadok, *The Jews in Babylonia During the Chaldean and Achaemenian Periods According to the Babylonian Sources* (Studies in the History of the Jewish People and the Land of Israel Monograph Series 3; Haifa: University of Haifa, 1979), 44–78. David Coogan, "Life in the Diaspora: Jews at Nippur in the Fifth Century B.C.," *BA* 37 (1974): 6–12, emphasizes that Jews in Babylon could also adopt non-Hebraic, and as a rule Babylonian names.

128. Zadok, *The Jews in Babylonia*, 87–88.

129. For the texts, and for life in Elephantine, see Arthur E. Cowley, ed., *Aramaic Papyri of the Fifth Century B.C.* (Oxford: Clarendon, 1923; repr. Osnabrück: O. Zeller, 1967); Pierre Grelot, *Docu-*

ments araméens d'Égypte (LAPO 5; Paris: Cerf, 1972); Ernst Axel Knauf, "Elephantine und das vorbiblische Judentum," in *Religion und Religionskontakte im Zeitalter der Achämeniden* (ed. Reinhard G. Kratz; Veröffentlichungen der Wisenschaftlichen Gesellschaft für Theologie 22; Gütersloh: Kaiser, 2002), 179–88; Ingo Kottsieper, "Die Religionspolitik der Achämeniden und die Juden von Elephantine," in *Religion und Religionskontakte im Zeitalter der Achämeniden* (ed. Reinhard G. Kratz; Veröffentlichungen der Wisenschaftlichen Gesellschaft für Theologie 22; Gütersloh: Kaiser, 2002), 150–78; and Belazel Porten, *Archives from Elephantine: The Life of an Ancient Jewish Military Colony* (Berkeley: University of California Press, 1968); and idem, *The Elephantine Papyri in English: Three Millennia of Cross-Cultural Continuity and Change* (DMOA 22; Leiden: Brill, 1996). The text edition cited is *TAD*.

130. Knauf, "Elephantine und das vor-biblische Judentum," 181–82.

131. For slaves in Elephantine, see also Porten, *Archives from Elephantine*, 203–05.

132. For the Aramaeans, Porten, *Archives from Elephantine*, 16–19.

133. On this, see chapter 9, 126–27, above.

134. See the prosopography in Porten, *Elephantine Papyri in English*, 268–76.

135. See above, 139–43; 148–51.

136. Even Julius Wellhausen (⁶1905, 5) spoke of "hierocratic inclinations" in postexilic Judaism (*Prolegomena to the History of Israel: With a Reprint of the Article Israel from the "Encyclopaedia Britannica"* (5th ed.; trans. J. Sutherland Black and Allan Menzies [Edinburgh: Adam & Charles Black; repr., Scholars Press Reprints and Translations Series; Atlanta: Scholars, 1994). Lester L. Grabbe does the same today, without reference to any doubts: "Judah during most of that time could be best characterized as a theocracy" (*Judaism from Cyrus to Hadrian* [Minneapolis: Fortress Press, 1992], 74); "The Jewish Theocracy from Cyrus to Hadrian," 607.

137. See below, chapter 11, 170–75.

138. Peter R. Ackroyd, *Israel under Babylon and Persia* (Oxford: Oxford University Press, 1970), 162.

139. See also in Herbert Donner, *Geschichte des Volkes Israel und seiner Nachbarn in Grundzügen*, part 2, *Von der Königszeit bis zu Alexander dem Großen* (3d ed.; GAT 4/2; Göttingen: Vandenhoeck & Ruprecht, 2001), "Part VII: The Persian Era," with the sections "The beginning of the restoration in Jerusalem and Judah," and "The Completion of the Restoration in Jerusalem and Judah;" or Frank Moore Cross, "A Reconstruction of the Judean Restoration," *JBL* 94 (1975): 4–18.

140. See also Thomas Willi, *Juda—Jehud—Israel. Studien zum Selbstverständnis des Judentums in persischer Zeit* (FAT 12; Tübingen: Mohr, 1995), 172.

141. Max Weber, *Die Wirtschaftsethik der Weltreligionen. Das antike Judentum. Schriften und Reden 1911–1920* (MWG 1/21; Tübingen: Mohr, 2005), 724, emphasis supplied. For a critical discussion of Weber, see Frank Crüsemann (2003).

142. Wellhausen, *Prolegomena* ([6]1905), nn. 1, 3, 5.

143. Stefan Stiegler, coming from a Free Church background, emphasizes the "hypothesis . . . that the post-exilic YHWH-community in Jerusalem was not an ethnic group. Nor was it shaped in the first instance by economic, political, or sociological structures; the religious component was the decisive one" (*Die naxexilische JHWH-Gemeinde in Jerusalem. Ein Beitrag zu einer alttestamentlichen Ekklesiologie* [BEATAJ 34; Frankfurt: Peter Lang, 1994], 7, and quoting 52).

144. It should be noted that Isa 56:3-7 does not reflect the reality of Persian-era Israel, but "remained the utopia of a marginal group in opposition": so Frank Crüsemann, "Israel in der Perserzeit. Eine Skizze in Auseinandersetzung mit Max Weber," in *Kanon und Sozialgeschichte. Beiträge zum Alten Testament* (Gütersloh: Kaiser/Gütersloher, 2003; original German essay, 1985), 210–26, quoting 215.

145. Monika Bernett, "Polis und Politeia. Zur politischen Organisation Jerusalems und Jehuds in der Perserzeit," in *Die Griechen und das antike Israel. Interdisziplinäre Studien zur Religions- und Kulturgeschichte des Heiligen Landes* (ed. Stefan Alkier and Markus Witte; OBO 201; Fribourg: Academic Press Fribourg, 2004), 73–129—after an instructive review of research—also presumes that the social form of Persian-era Yehud should be described in terms not of religion, but of polity. Hence she suggests the concept of the city-state, seeing as constitutive thereof the status of Jerusalem, the formulation of binding legal principles, and belonging to particular social groups (100).

146. When Joachim Schaper calls Yehud "a semi-autonomous sub-state of the Achaemenid empire," he gives stronger emphasis to the element of independence; I do not see this as contradicting my view, but only as a different accentuation ("Numismatik, Epigraphik, alttestamentliche Exegese und die Frage nach der politischen Verfassung des achämenidischen Juda," *ZDPV* 118 [2002] 150–68, quoting 165).

147. See 143–51, above.

148. Christiane Karrer, *Ringen um die Verfassung Judas. Eine Studie zu den theologisch-politischen Vorstellungen im Esra-Nehemia-Buch* (BZAW 308; Berlin: de Gruyter, 2001), 27.

149. Cf. *TGI* no. 46.

150. See 152–53, above. Because of the usage in Elephantine, it is not certain whether this self-designation was really taken over from an originally Babylonian word for certain foreigners, as Rainer Albertz thinks (*Israel in Exile*, 22–23). "Judean" or German *"Jude"* = "Jew" is simply appropriate for people from Judah.

151. Cf. Karrer, *Ringen um die Verfassung Judas*, 149. Karrer prefers the German word "Judäer" (English "Judeans"), since the expression in the book of Ezra-Nehemiah is always applied to the Achaemenid province of Yehud. But since in other texts *yehudim* are clearly people outside the province—especially in the self-description of the people of Elephantine—it seems to me that even for Ezra-Nehemiah the translation "Jews" makes more sense.

152. On this, see Norman K. Gottwald, *The Politics of Ancient Israel* (Library of Ancient

Israel; Louisville: Westminster John Knox, 2001), 17–22.

153. For the different concepts of Israel in Ezra-Nehemiah cf. Karrer (2001) 73–77.

154. On this, see Willi, *Juda—Jehud—Israel*, 45; Karrer, *Ringen um die Verfassung Judas*, 303–04; and Peter Ross Bedford, "Diaspora: Homeland Relations in Ezra-Nehemiah," *VT* 52 (2002) 147–65.

155. See chapter 11, 170–71, below.

11. The Jewish *Ethnos* in the Hellenistic Age

1. Georg Fohrer, *Geschichte Israels. Von den Anfängen bis zur Gegenwart* (3d. ed.; UTB 708; Heidelberg: Quelle & Meyer, 1982), draws this conclusion; see also Salo Wittmayer Baron's multi-volume work, *A Social and Religious History of the Jews*, vol. 1, *To the Beginning of the Christian Era* (2d. ed.; New York: Columbia University Press, 1952).

2. This is what Herbert Donner ultimately does, though he only speaks of "additional pragmatic reasons" (*Geschichte des Volkes Israel und seiner Nachbarn in Grundzügen* [3d ed.; GAT 4/2; Göttingen: Vandenhoeck & Ruprecht, 2000–01], 2:474–75).

3. See above, chapter 1, 1–2.

4. Thus Israel Finkelstein and Neil A. Silberman, *The Bible Unearthed: Archaeology's New Vision of Ancient Israel and the Origin of its Sacred Texts* (2d ed.; New York: Free 2003), 336.

5. See Ernst Haag's description, *Das hellenistische Zeitalter. Israel und die Bibel im 4. bis 1. Jahrhundert v. Chr.* (BE 9; Stuttgart: Kohlhammer, 2003), 45–48, 53–56.

6. See ibid., 49–53.

7. The extent to which this prohibition was more strongly motivated by politics or religion and whether it was promoted more by the Seleucid king Antiochus IV or the Jewish Hellenists, are matters of dispute; "the only thing that is unquestioned is the political-juridical responsibility of the Seleucid king" (Klaus Bringmann, *Hellenistische Reform*

und Religionsverfolgung in Judäa. Eine Untersuchung zur jüdisch-hellenistischen Geschichte (175–163 v. Chr.) [AAWGPH 3/132; Göttingen: Vandenhoeck & Ruprecht, 1983], 12). For the active role of the Hellenists, see Dan 11:30-32.

8. See the genealogy in Josephus, *Ant.* 12.265, and the designation "Hasmoneans" (Asmoneans) in Josephus, *J.W.* 1.36.

9. Heinz Kreißig, *Wirtschaft und Gesellschaft im Seleukidenreich. Die Eigentums- und Abhängigkeitsverhältnisse* (Schriften zur Geschichte und Kultur der Antike 16; Berlin: Akademie, 1978) shows that the fundamental propertied situation on which the family relationships were based did not change in principle from the Persian to the Hellenistic epoch.

10. See above, chapter 10, 133–34.

11. For the role of women in the text-world of Tobit, see Helen Schüngel-Straumann, *Tobit* (HTKAT; Freiburg: Herder, 2000), *passim,* esp. 113–14; 139–41.

12. See above, chapter 10, 133–34.

13. Schüngel-Straumann, *Tobit*, 74–76 points also to *T. Job* 21 (*OTP* 2:829–68), according to which, after Job falls ill, his wife has to support the family through slave labor as a water-carrier.

14. See above, chapter 10, 134–39.

15. Josephus, *Ant.* 12.3–6.

16. See above, chapter 10, 134–39.

17. Ibid.

18. On this, see Otto Kaiser, "Arm und Reich bei Jesus Sirach," in *Theologie und Kirchenleitung. Festschrift für P. Steinacker zum 60. Geburtstag* (ed. Hermann Deuser, Geshe Linde, and Sigurd Rinke; Marburg: Elwert, 2003), 17–30.

19. Martin Hengel, *Judaism and Hellenism: Studies in Their Encounter in Palestine During the Early Hellenistic Period* (2 vols. in 1; trans. John Bowden; Philadelphia: Fortress Press, 1974), 1:48.

20. Ibid., 43–44.

21. Ibid., 270.

22. See chapter 7, 97–102, above.

23. See chapter 10, 129–33, above.

24. For the Tobiades and the Oniades, discussed below, see the summary in Hengel, *Judaism*

and Hellenism, 1:270–72; and Ernst Haag, *Das hellenistische Zeitalter. Israel und die Bibel im 4. bis 1. Jahrhundert v. Chr.* (BE 9; Stuttgart: Kohlhammer, 2003), 49–53.

25. *CPJ* 118–21. A "kleruchy" is to be understood as a piece of landed property given by the Ptolemies for purposes of military security; see Elias J. Bickerman, *The Jews in the Greek Age* (Cambridge: Harvard University Press, 1988), 72.

26. Josephus, *Ant.* 12.157–222, 224, 228–36; on this, see Hengel, *Judaism and Hellenism*, 1:48–50.

27. For the Ptolemaic system of government, see 164–65.

28. For the office of high priest in the Hellenistic period, see 164–65.

29. See 161–62.

30. Rainer Kessler, "Soziale Sicherung in vorstaatlicher, staatlicher und substaatlicher Gesellschaft: Das Beispiel des antiken Israel," in *Entstaatlichung und soziale Sicherheit. Verhandlungen des 31. Kongresses der Deutschen Gesellschaft für Soziologie in Leipzig 2002* (ed. Jutta Allmendinger; Opladen: Leske & Budrich, 2003); with CD-ROM.

31. For the role of alms in Jesus Sirach and Tobit, see Otto Kaiser, "Kultische und Sittliche Sühne bei Jesus Sirach," in *"Einen Altar von Erde mache mir . . . ," Festschrift für Diethelm Conrad zu seinem 70. Geburtstag* (ed. Johannes F. Diehl, Reinhard Heitzenröder, and Markus Witte; KAANT 4/5; Waltrop: Spenner, 2003), 151–67.

32. For this interpretation of the passage, see Rainer Kessler, "Armenfürsorge als Aufgabe der Gemeinde. Die Anfänge in Tempel und Synagoge," in *Dem Tod nicht glauben. Sozialgeschichte der Bibel. Festschrift für Luise Schottroff zum 70. Geburtstag* (ed. Frank Crüsemann et al.; Gütersloh: Gütersloher, 2004), 91–102.

33. Strabo 16.2.2.

34. Quoted from Hans G. Kippenberg, ed., *Seminar: Die Entstehung der antiken Klassengesellschaft* (STW 130; Frankfurt: Surhkamp, 1977), 372. For the resistance of the Near Eastern peoples against Hellenization, see Lester L. Grabbe, *Juda-ism from Cyrus to Hadrian* (Minneapolis: Fortress Press, 1992), 163–64.

35. For Ptolemaic administration as a whole, see Hengel, *Judaism and Hellenism*, 1:19.

36. Joachim Schaper, *Priester und Leviten im achämenidischen Juda. Studien zur Kult- und Sozialgeschichte Israels in persischer Zeit* (FAT 31; Tübingen: Mohr Siebeck, 2000), 174.

37. See Diodorus Siculus 40.2; Josephus, *Ant.* 12.162–166.

38. See also above, chapter 10, 143–47. For the high priestly office in the Hellenistic era, see Elias J. Bickerman, *The Jews in the Greek Age* (Cambridge: Harvard University Press, 1988), 141–45.

39. *TGI* no. 51,11.18–19, and above, chapter 10, 139–43.

40. So Hengel, *Judaism and Hellenism*, 1:25–27.

41. So Hans G. Kippenberg, *Religion und Klassenbildung im antiken Judäa. Eine religionssoziologische Studie zum Verhältnis von Tradition und gesellschaftlicher Entwicklung* (SUNT 14; Göttingen: Vandenhoeck & Ruprecht, 1978), 83, and 83n30), and Rainer Albertz, *A History of Israelite Religion in the Old Testament Period* (2 vols.; OTL; Louisville: Westminster John Knox, 1994), 2:592–93.

42. See above, chapter 10, 139–43.

43. So also Albertz, *History of Israelite Religion*, 2:593.

44. Kippenberg: "The system of tax farming fundamentally distinguished Greek from Persian rule" (*Religion und Klassenbildung im antiken Judäa*, 93).

45. See 162–64, above.

46. Citations from Josephus, *Ant.* 12.157–222.

47. Heinz Kreißig underscores that Jerusalem—as was true until the attempt we are here discussing, and which ultimately failed—was "never a πόλις in the classical sense, but rather the capital city of an ἔθνος with considerable autonomous rights" (*Wirtschaft und Gesellschaft im Seleukidenreich. Die Eigentums- und Abhängigkeitsverhältnisse* [Schriften zur Geschichte und Kultur der Antike 16; Berlin: Akademie, 1978], 74). Walter Ameling, "Jerusalem als hellenistische Polis: 2 Makk 4,9–12

und eine neue Inschrift," *BZ* n.s. 47 (2003): 105–11, adduces an interesting inscription documenting the bestowal of the *polis* rights on the Phrygian city of Toriaion. In both cases, constitution, laws, and gymnasium were the core of the new status.

48. For the backgrounds and motives of the Hellenistic reform in Jerusalem, see the description in Klaus Bringmann, *Hellenistische Reform und Religionsverfolgung in Judäa. Eine Untersuchung zur jüdisch-hellenistischen Geschichte (175–163 v. Chr.)* (AAWGPH 3/132; Göttingen: Vandenhoeck & Ruprecht, 1983), 66–74.

49. Hans G. Kippenberg: "The Maccabean fight for freedom was a fight against economic exploitation. It was at the same time … a struggle against the abolition of the religious tradition by part of the moneyed aristocracy. Because the religious symbolism expressed egalitarian interests, it was central for the revolutionary priests and farmers in this struggle" (*Religion und Klassenbildung im antiken Judäa. Eine religionssoziologische Studie zum Verhältnis von Tradition und gesellschaftlicher Entwicklung* (SUNT 14; Göttingen: Vandenhoeck & Ruprecht, 1978), 93.

50. Albertz, *History of Israelite Religion in the Old Testament Period,* 2:593.

51. See 173–75, below.

52. On this, see Samuel K. Eddy, "Gründe für den Widerstand gegen den Hellenismus in Asien," in *Seminar: Die Entstehung der antiken Klassengesellschaft* (ed. Hans G. Kippenberg; STW 130; Frankfurt: Suhrkamp, 1977), 328–50.

53. Albertz, *History of Israelite Religion,* 2:603.

54. On this see Adrian Schenker, "Die zweimalige Einsetzung Simons des Makkabäers zum Hohenpriester. Die Neuordnung des Hohepriestertums unter dem Hasmonäer Simon (1 Makk 14,25–49), in *Recht und Kult im Alten Testament. Achtzehn Studien* (OBO 172; Fribourg: Universitätsverlag, 2000), 158–69.

55. For this problem see chapter 10, 153–57, above.

56. Lester L. Grabbe writes in this sense, *Judaism from Cyrus to Hadrian* (Minneapolis: Fortress Press, 1992), 74.

57. See above, 166–67.

58. See above, chapter 10, 153–57.

59. For the Samaritans, see Reinhard Pummer, *The Samaritans* (Iconography of Religions Section 23 (Judaism), fasc. 5; Leiden: Brill, 1987); Shemaryahu Talmon, "Biblische Überlieferungen zur Frühgeschichte der Samaritaner," in *Gesellschaft und Literatur in der Hebräischen Bibel. Gesammelte Aufsätze 1* (Information Judentum 8; Neukirchen-Vluyn: Neukirchener, 1988), 132–51; József Zsengellér, *Gerizim as Israel. Northern Tradition of the Old Testament and the Early History of the Samaritans* (Utrechtse Theologische reeks 38; Utrecht: Faculteit de Godgeleerdheid, Universiteit Utrecht, 1998).

60. Josephus, *Ant.* 11.302–347, and Zsengellér, ibid., 151–55.

61. Ibid., 155–56.

62. Thus, for example, Herbert Donner, *Geschichte des Volkes Israel und seiner Nachbarn in Grundzügen,* part 2, *Von der Königszeit bis zu Alexander dem Großen* (3d ed.; GAT 4/2; Göttingen: Vandenhoeck & Ruprecht, 2001), 469.

63. Josephus, *Ant.* 12.228–236; and on this Hengel, *Judaism and Hellenism,* 1:272–74.

64. Josephus, *Ant.* 12.387–388; 13.62–73; 20.236.

65. To understand the differences between the Hebrew and Greek versions of the passage, see Zsengellér, *Gerizim as Israel,* 159–61.

66. Pummer: "The Samaritans are a branch of the Israelites" (*The Samaritans,* 2).

67. See the summary in Zsengellér, *Gerizim as Israel,* 167–68.

68. It is the achievement of Zsengellér's 1998 work, *Gerizim as Israel,* to have honored this Samaritan self-interpretation in appropriate fashion.

69. Here we cannot go into the different cultural conditions in the Diaspora in the Seleucid and Ptolemaic realms, to which Elias J. Bickerman, *The Jews in the Greek Age* (Cambridge: Harvard University Press, 1988), 81, points.

70. The references to Nineveh, which was destroyed in 612, and Ecbatana, which was not founded until the seventh century B.C.E., as places

of contemporary action attest to the narrative's fictional character.

71. For the beginnings of the Egyptian Diaspora, see above, chapter 9, 126–27.

72. See above, 162–64.

73. *CPJ* 1:11.

74. Ibid., 19.

75. *OTP* 2:7–34.

76. See chapter 9, 125–26, above.

77. *CJP* 1:136–37, no. 10..

78. Ibid., 45, on Egypt: "The temple of Jerusalem . . . was always highly esteemed by Egyptian Jews . . ."; and *CHJ* 2: 154: "In many respects Jerusalem was the focal point of all Jewish life."

79. Shemaryahu Talmon, "The Emergence of Jewish Sectarianism in the Early Second Temple Period," *King, Cult and Calendar in Ancient Israel. Collected Studies* (Leiden: Brill; Jerusalem: Magnes, 1986), 165–201.

80. See the overview of research in Norbert Lohfink, "Von der 'Anawim-Partei' zur 'Kirche der Armen.' Die bibelwissenschaftliche Ahnentafel eines Hauptbegriffs der 'Theologie der Befreiung,'" *Bib* 67 (1986): 153–76.

81. Thus Albertz, *History of Israelite Religion*, 596–76, the section "The 'piety of the poor' of the lower-class circles."

82. Johannes Un-Sok Ro, *Die sogenannte "Armenfrömmigkeit" im nachexilischen Israel* (BZAW 322; Berlin: de Gruyter, 2002).

83. See 168–70, above. For the Hasideans, see Hengel, *Judaism and Hellenism*, 1:175–80; Albertz, *History of Israelite Religion*, 598–600; and Ernst

Haag, *Das hellenistische Zeitalter. Israel und die Bibel im 4. bis 1. Jahrhundert v. Chr.* (BE 9; Stuttgart: Kohlhammer, 2003), 80–87.

84. Albertz, *History of Israelite Religion*, 603 (emphasis supplied).

85. Following Antonio Gramsci, *Prison Notebooks* (ed. Joseph A. Buttigieg; trans. Joseph A. Buttigieg and Antonio Callari; New York: Columbia University Press, 1992–94), n. 513; for the role of intellectuals as a whole see, 513–24.

86. See the summary of the discussion in Haag, *Das hellenistische Zeitalter*, 83–87.

87. Thus, ibid., 86.

88. On this, see Hartmut Stegemann, "Das Gesetzeskorpus der 'Damaskusschrift' (CD XI-XVI)," *RevQ* 14 (1989/1990): 409–34.

89. On this, see Joachim Schaper, *Priester und Leviten im achämenidischen Juda*; for the extension of the line into post-OT time, esp. 306–07.

12. Conclusion

1. Philip R. Davies, *In Search of "Ancient Israel"* (JSOTSup 148; Sheffield: Sheffield Academic Press, 1995), 59, quoted above, chapter 6, n24.

2. See the introduction, ix, above.

3. Entitled *Sozialgeschichtliches Wörterbuch zur Bibel* ["A Social-Historical Dictionary of the Bible"]; (Frank Crüsemann, Kristian Hungar, Claudia Janssen, Rainer Kessler, and Luise Schottroff, eds; Gütersloher Verlagshaus, forthcoming).

Glossary

Note that words in **boldface** are cross-references to other words in the glossary.

ᶜam-haᵓarets: Hebrew for "people of the land." This was an economically powerful upper class who were "landed aristocracy" or aristocrats whose socioeconomic power base lay in their extensive landholdings.

ᵓele-haᵓarets: Hebrew for "the elite of the land." The leading figures of the *ᶜam-haᵓarets*.

Agnatic descent: In genealogy, descent and relationship through the father's line.

Amphictyony: An association of ancient Greek tribes that were together maintained and defended a central cultic shrine. The German Hebrew Bible scholar Martin Noth adopted this idea to understand pre-state Israel's political organization. In Noth's understanding, pre-state Israel was an amphictyony in that Israel's tribes were united in their devotion to Yhwh and periodically gathered at Shechem to renew their covenant with Yhwh. Modern scholarship has discredited Noth's hypothesis.

Ancient class society: A class-based society that develops from the chronic indebtedness of one group to another.

anwe-haᵓarets: Hebrew for "the poor of the land." This was the lower class in ancient Israel, the "poorest of the poor," who were frequently exploited by the upper class, the *ᶜam-haᵓarets.*

Archaeological reconstruction (also just "reconstruction"): Once excavated, scholars must interpret the nature and use of artifacts and structures. Is a building a barn or is it a house? Or is it perhaps both? Is a small statue purely figurative or is it an image of a deity used for ritual purposes?

Biblical antiquities: The investigation of both the results of archaeological excavations of biblically related sites and ancient culture as reflected in the biblical text in order to elucidate the meaning of the biblical text. Synonymous with "biblical archaeology."

Biblical archaeology: A late nineteenth-, early twentieth-century synonym for biblical antiquities.

Bulla (pl. bullae): A seal impression in clay. Interpretation of the text and pictures on the seal impression provide important data in reconstructing an ancient society.

Canaan: Depending upon context, this word can mean either the land between the Mediterranean Sea and the Jordan River or all of Palestine. In either definition, it includes what is now Israel, the West Bank, and the Gaza Strip, plus adjoining coastal lands and parts of Lebanon and Syria.

Clan: The unit of social organization just below **tribe** in ancient Israel. Each clan consisted of a number of families, each of whom considered themselves related to the other families in the clan.

Confederation: According to German sociologist Max Weber, the farmers and semi-nomads of pre-state Israel developed "a community of interests," a similar group of socioeconomic concerns. These two groups, united in their community of interests, united with each other in a covenant of military cooperation "under and with Yhwh as the war god of the covenant." This unification of the farmers and semi-nomads, Weber called a "confederation" and understood it as having no enduring political institutions. Therefore the confederation was only a religiously united ad hoc military organization.

Conquest narrative: The narrative in Joshua that describes the Israelite's conquest of the Land after their exile from Egypt. Depending upon which scholar one reads this narrative extends from Joshua 2–9, 2–10, or 2–12 (and perhaps other variations as well).

Book of the Covenant (also called the Covenant Code): the material in Exodus 20:19—23:33

Criterion of datability: One of the two criteria (see also **criterion of temporal proximity**) that define a **primary source**. This criterion requires a relatively precise date for the historical source as based on archaeological data.

Criterion of temporal proximity: One of the two criteria (see also **criterion of datability**) define a **primary source**. This criterion requires that the historical source developed during or after the events it reports.

Deutero-Isaiah (also called Second Isaiah): Isaiah 40–55 (some scholars think that Deutero-Isaiah also includes Isaiah 56–66). According to the most commonly accepted theory about Isaiah's development, Isaiah consists of three collections of materials: First Isaiah related directly to the historical prophet Isaiah, Second Isaiah from the exilic period, and Third Isaiah (also called Trito-Isaiah) from the post-exilic period.

Deuteronomistic/deuteronomistic texts: Referring to exilic-age material compiled by a redactor (or redactors) known as the Deuteronomist(s), whose theological perspective aligns with Deuteronomy. The books Joshua, Judges, 1–2 Samuel and 1–2 Kings are regarded as the coherent product of such redactors and are together called the Deuteronomistic History.

Diachronic development: The development of something—be it a culture, concept, book, or what have you—through time.

Diadochoi: Greek for "successors." Used to refer to the generals who succeeded Alexander the Great after his death and divided up his kingdom.

Dyarchy: Rule by two. Used to describe Ezra's view that the high priest in Yehud, Jeshua, and Yehud's governor, Zerubbabel, always acted together and to describe Zechariah's vision of a future Israel in which the high priest and king always act in concert.

Egalitarian society: With reference to **segmented lineage societies**, each segment (tribe, clan, family) of the society have equal rights with respect to their mutual status in terms of their relationship to a common ancestor. An egalitarian society *does not* mean that these segments possess economic equality or similar size. Neither does it indicate anything about the social equality of individuals.

Endogamy: Marriage within one's own clan, so that one is marrying a distant relative. In ancient Israel, this insured that inherited property did not fall into the hands of non-Israelites (or later non-Jews) and that the traditional Israelite (or Jewish) faith would be preserved.

Epigraphy: The scholarly study of ancient texts inscribed on stone, metal, potsherds, and similar substances.

Ereignisgeschichte: German term for "political history" or what is here translated as "history of events."

Ethnology: That branch of anthropology that studies the nature of human societies cross-culturally.

Ethnos: The Hellenistic Greek term for an ethnic group that had long resided in one area. Such groups possessed a certain legal status under the rule of the Greeks and the various kingdoms that succeeded Alexander the Great. The Jews in Palestine and Egypt possessed this designation.

Exegesis: A critical analysis of a text, especially a biblical text, for the purposes of interpreting the text within its original cultural and historical setting.

Former Prophets (*Nevi'im Rishonim* in Hebrew): The books Joshua, Judges, 1–2 Samuel, and 1–2 Kings. In the Hebrew Bible, these books are part of the Nebiim (Hebrew for "prophets"). The Latter Prophets (*Nevi'im 'Aharonim*) consists of those books that are regarded as prophetic books in the Christian canon.

Gerousia: One of two bodies, the other being the priesthood, that represented the Jews during the Hellenistic era.

Hasidim: A poorly understood Jewish group in Seleucid era Palestine. It appears that this group professed the same devout piety as the poorer classes but are not necessarily to be identified as upper class. They may have also been a group that were "wise," that is, they taught the deeper aspects of Jewish life and faith to other Jews.

High chronology: The dating of various excavated Israelite structures to the tenth century, in other words, an early date that allows one to see these buildings as evidence of Solomonic building. See also **low chronology.**

Historical minimalism: A school of thought in the study of Israelite history that states that only external evidence, that is, nonbiblical texts and archaeological data, can be used to reconstruct Israelite history. According to this school of thought, it is doubtful that Saul, Solomon, or David and their respective kingdoms ever existed. Opposite: historical maximalism.

History of institutions: The history of a society from the perspective of its institutions. For example, we can write the history of Israel from the perspective of the monarchy, from the perspective of its legal systems, or from the perspective of the family.

History of time periods (epochs): A history of a society written from the perspective of its constituent eras. For Israel, this would include the pre-monarchic era, the United Monarchy, the Kingdoms of Israel and Judah, the exilic era, the postexilic era, and the Hellenistic period.

History over the long term: The historical relationship between a given society and its physical environment. For example, ancient Levantine cultures subsisted primarily by nomadism until the advent of agriculture.

Incomplete early state: A stage in a state's development in which there is a king who rules only over a territory occupied by his blood relations, a minimal bureaucracy consisting of the king's relatives, and no established income for the king except his own agricultural work.

Institution: An important organization, practice, or relationship within a culture such as marriage, kingship, initiation rituals, and similar phenomena.

Intentional tradition: The intended message of a biblical text. For example, Proverbs gives multiple examples of living wisely. See also **unintentional tradition.**

Judith: One of the books of the Apocrypha that narrates how the Jewish widow Judith single-handedly saves the Jews by killing the Assyrian general Holofernes. Judith is significant for Israelite/Jewish social history in providing an ideal portrait of widowhood in the Hellenistic era.

Kinship-based society: A society in which the family is the basic unit.

Lectura popular: Published Bible studies undertaken by groups of poor Latin American laypeople, which were done precisely in light of their poverty and their Christian faith.

Letter of Aristeas: A noncanonical text written by a Hellenistic Jew in the mid-second century BCE that fictionally describes how the **Septuagint** was written.

Letter of Jeremiah: Jer 29:1-23. A letter from the prophet Jeremiah to the exiles in Babylon offering them hope in their grim situation.

Levant: The area demarcated by modern Israel, Lebanon, Jordan, Syria, the West Bank, and the Gaza Strip.

Liberation theology: A branch of theology, Roman Catholic in origin, that emphasizes the Christian church's role in acting on behalf of society's poor and oppressed. Influenced by

Marxist ideas that society reflects economic class conflict, by philosophical notions about the need for philosophy not just to think about the nature of the world but to actively change it, and by biblical texts (especially the exodus from Egypt, the prophets, and the Gospels) that emphasize the need to care for the poor and oppressed.

Low chronology: The dating of various excavated Israelite structures to the eighth century, in other words, a late date that causes one to see these buildings as projects undertaken by the Northern Kingdom's monarchy. See also **high chronology.**

Maccabees: The name of the Jewish family that revolted against Seleucid rule in 167 BCE and ultimately founded a dynasty that lasted until 63 BCE.

Marxist biblical criticism: A form of academic biblical study that uses Marxist concepts to understand biblical texts. The major result of this approach is an emphasis on understanding economic class struggles that are either implied by the text or directly addressed by the text.

Minimalism: See **historical minimalism**

Narrated time: The supposed time that the text is set in. Anachronisms in Genesis 24 indicate that the author of the text lived in a much later time than the time in which the story is supposed to take place.

Norm (in legal texts): The legal text's author's ideal picture of what society should be and how people should behave. See also **reality (in legal texts)**.

Oniades: One of the great families, see also **Tobiads**, who had great influence in Jewish affairs during the Ptolemaic and Seleucid eras.

Palestine: That portion of the Mediterranean coast bounded by the Mediterranean Sea, the Jordan River, the Negev desert, and the Lake of Galilee.

Pariah people: German sociologist Max Weber's understanding of the Jews as a people isolated from surrounding society in a "self-chosen ghetto existence."

Participatory monarchy: With respect to ancient Judah, this was a monarchy in which the civil service aristocracy and the landed aristocracy both had the ability to limit the king's power. However, the king remained the final authority in all matters.

Patriarchal family: A family in which the husband is head of the household, represents the family in public, and in which the wife's role is restricted strictly to the domestic sphere.

Polis (**pl.** *poleis*): The Greek word for "city." However, this word also implied that the city's government ruled over the immediately surrounding countryside.

Pre-state period: That period of time in ancient Israel before the monarchy developed.

Primary sources: Historical sources whose relatively precise date has been determined using archaeological data and that originated during or shortly after the reported events. See also **criterion of datability** and **criterion of temporal proximity**. Such sources include artifacts and inscriptions.

Primary state-construction: When central government appears for the first time without a surrounding influence from other states in the surrounding environment.

Prostasia: The official representative of the Palestinian Jews before the Ptolemaic government, who also served as chief tax collector.

Provincial society: A society ruled by a governor who acts under the orders of a distant governmental authority.

Ptolemaic kleruchy: A group of soldiers in the Ptolemaic kingdom who served in return for a grant of land.

Realia: The physical objects (pottery, houses, altars, inscriptions, and similar items), places, and social institutions used by scholars to study a given society.

Reality (in legal texts): The real social situation that the legal text addresses. See also **norm (in legal texts)**.

Religious sociology: Synonym for **sociology of religion.**

Royal ideology: An idealized view of kingship in the ancient Near East in which the king protected the interests of the poor and needy.

Samaria: The name for the area that was originally the northern kingdom, the Kingdom of Israel. It had a history separate from Judah from the time of the northern kingdom's downfall in 722 BCE eventually culminating in the construction of a separate temple on Mount Gerazim in Samaria and the development of a religious tradition separate from, but closely related to, Judaism.

Secondary sources: Later historical sources that describe or depict earlier historical events. For the purposes of this book, the major secondary source is the text of the Hebrew Bible. Also included would be documents such as Josephus's various historical works.

Secondary state-construction: When a central government appears in a society under the influence of states in the society's environment.

Segmented lineage societies: Societies in which the constituent parts are organized by descent through the male line to a common ancestor. Further each constituent part, those parts or segments (tribes, clans, families) equally related to the same ancestor, have equal rights. See also **egalitarian society**.

Sensus literalis: The "literal sense" of a biblical text, that is, its plain grammatical sense in light of its historical sociocultural setting.

Septuagint: The Greek translation of the Hebrew Bible. It was developed by Diaspora Jewish scholars for the sake of Greek-speaking Jews who did not know Greek and includes books, now called the Apocrypha, that did not make it into the Hebrew Bible canon.

Sitz im Leben: "Life setting." A type of biblical exegesis in which the scholar attempts to reconstruct the social setting of a particular textual genre. For example, the *Sitz im Leben* of Psalm 8 is the enthronement of a new king in ancient Israel or Judah.

Social history: A history of the development of a particular aspect of a society: the evolution of the Israelite family over time, the development of the monarchy, the development of the Israelite priesthood, and so forth.

Social-historical biblical exegesis: synonym for **social-historical interpretation**.

Social-historical interpretation: The interpretation of a text using the methods of social history.

Sociology of religion: A subdivision of sociology that studies a given religion in terms of social categories (institutions, leaders, and so forth) and the relationship of that religion to the society that produced it.

Song of Deborah: A victory song recorded in Judg 5:2-31a that celebrates the triumph of Israel over a Canaanite army. This song is often thought to be the oldest text in the Hebrew Bible, possibly dating to the twelfth century BCE.

Stele: An ancient inscribed stone slab or pillar often erected for commemorative purposes.

Structural analogies: For social historical study, these are analogies between societies based on their simultaneous existence in the same environment or an ancient society and a similar society in the present. Both ancient Israel and various modern societies include some aspect(s) of nomadism in their history and/or structure. Therefore, one may draw analogies between these societies based on nomadism.

Syro-Palestine: The area bounded by modern Syria, Lebanon, the Gaza Strip, Israel, and the West Bank.

Tertiary sources: For the purposes of this book, a tertiary source is a descriptive analogy or theoretical model developed by anthropologists and ethnologist that is applied to ancient Israelite society.

Time of narrating (also time of the narrative): The actual time period in which the narrator of a text lives. The narrator of Jeremiah 32, based on the correlation between data in the text and the outside world, actually lived during the events he narrates.

Tobiades: One of two great families, see also
Oniads, who had great influence in Jewish
affairs during the Ptolemaic and Seleucid eras.
They were involved in banking in the Ptolemaic city of Alexandria. They held the office of
high priest and usually the **protasia**.

Tobit: One of the books of the Apocrypha that
narrates how the devout and generous Diaspora Jew Tobit regains his sight and gains a
sister-in-law through the adventures of his
son Tobias and the angel Raphael (disguised
as Azariah). The book is significant for the
information it provides about family life, marital customs, almsgiving, and other aspects of
Jewish life during the Hellenistic era.

Traditional authority: A phrase adopted from
German sociologist Max Weber to describe
patterns of authority in pre-state Israel. In this
model, "elders" are appointed to represent the
various families within a city to settle common
business including conflicts.

Tribe: The highest unit of social organization in
ancient Israel (below the level of *Israel* itself).
Each tribe consisted of a group of clans that
laid claim to the same male ancestor. Thus
the all the clans in the tribe of Benjamin
considered themselves to be descended from
Benjamin.

Typical early state: A stage in a state's development in which the king now rules over territory in which the population is not necessarily
related to the king, the royal bureaucracy has
expanded and consists of individuals other
than the king's relatives, and the king and his
court no longer participate in agricultural production.

Unintentional tradition: Information unintentionally passed on in a biblical text. The
book of Proverbs, in describing wise behavior,
unintentionally passes along information
about Israelite family life, economic activity,
and other social data. See also **intentional
tradition**.

Bibliography

Ackroyd, Peter R. *Exile and Restoration: A Study of Hebrew Thought of the Sixth Century BC*. London: SCM, 1968.

———. "The History of Israel in the Exilic and Post-Exilic Periods." In *Tradition and Interpretation: Essays by Members of the Society for Old Testament Study*. Ed. George W. Anderson. New York: Oxford University Press, 1979, 320–50.

———. *Israel under Babylon and Persia*. Oxford: Oxford University Press, 1970.

Aharoni, Yohanan. *The Land of the Bible: A Historical Geography*. Trans. A. F. Rainey. London: Burns & Oates, 1966.

Ahlström, Gösta W. "Pharaoh Shoshenq's campaign to Palestine." In *History and Traditions of Early Israel: Studies Presented to Eduard Nielsen*. Ed. André Lemaire and Benedikt Otzen. VTSup 50. Leiden: Brill, 1993, 1–16.

Ahn, Gregor. "Israel und Persien." *RGG*⁴ 4: 309–11.

Albertz, Rainer. "Ethnische und kultische Konzepte in der Politik Nehemias," in *Das Manna fällt auch heute noch. Beiträge zur Geschichte und Theologie des Alten, Ersten Testaments. FS Erich Zenger*. Ed. Frank-Lothar Hossfeld and Ludger Schwienhorst-Schönberger. HBS 44. Freiburg: Herder, 2004, 13–32.

———. *A History of Israelite Religion in the Old Testament Period*. Trans. John Bowden. 2 vols. OTL. Louisville: Westminster John Knox, 1994.

———. *Israel in Exile: The History and Literature of the Sixth Century B.C.E.* Trans. David Green. SBLStBL 3. Atlanta: Society of Biblical Literature, 2003.

———. "Why a Reform like Josiah's Must Have Happened." In *Good Kings and Bad Kings*. Ed. Lester L. Grabbe. Library of Hebrew Bible/ Old Testament Studies 393. London: T&T Clark, 2005, 27–46.

Albright, William F. "The Israelite Conquest of Canaan in the Light of Archaeology." *BASOR* 74 (1939): 11–23.

Alt, Albrecht. "Der Anteil des Königtums an der sozialen Entwicklung in den Reichen Israel und Juda." In *Kleine Schriften zur Geschichte des Volkes Israel*. 3 vols. Munich: Beck, 1964–68, 3:348–72. Original German article, 1955.

———. "Bemerkungen zu einigen judäischen Ortslisten des Alten Testaments." In *Kleine Schriften*, 2:289–305. Original German article, 1951.

———. "Erwägungen über die Landnahme der Israeliten in Palästina." In *Kleine Schriften*, 1:126–75. Original German article, 1939.

———. "Israels Gaue unter Salomo." In *Kleine Schriften*, 2:76–89. Original German article, 1913.

———. "Judas Gaue unter Josia." In *Kleine Schriften*, 2:276–88. Original German article, 1925.

———. *Kleine Schriften zur Geschichte des Volkes Israel*. 3 vols. Munich: Beck, 1964–68.

———. "The Monarchy in the Kingdoms of Israel and Judah." In *Essays on Old Testament History and Religion*. Trans. R. A. Wilson. Garden City: Doubleday, 1967, 311–35. Original German essay, 1951.

———. "Die Rolle Samarias bei der Entstehung des Judentums." In *Kleine Schriften,*, 2:316–37. Original German article, 1934.

—————. "Der Rhythmus der Geschichte Syriens und Palästinas im Altertum." In *Kleine Schriften*, 3:1–19. Original German article, 1944.

—————. "The Settlement of the Israelites in Palestine." In *Essays on Old Testament History and Religion*, 133–69. Original German essay, 1925.

—————. "Der Stadtstaat Samaria." In *Kleine Schriften* 3:258–302. Original German article, 1955.

Ameling, Walter. "Jerusalem als hellenistische Polis: 2 Makk 4,9–12 und eine neue Inschrift." *BZ* n.s. 47 (2003): 105–11.

Amusin, J. D., and Michael L. Heltzer. "The Inscription from Mesad Hashavyahu: Complaint of a Reaper of the Seventh Century B.C." *IEJ* 14 (1964): 148–57.

Ash, Paul S. *David, Solomon and Egypt. A Reassessment.* JSOTSup 297. Sheffield: Sheffield Academic, 1999.

—————. "Solomon's? District? List." *JSOT* 67 (1995): 67–86.

Athas, George. *The Tel Dan Inscription: A Reappraisal and a New Interpretation.* JSOTSup 360; Copenhagen International Seminar 12. Sheffield: Sheffield Academic, 2003.

Avigad, Nahman. "Baruch the Scribe and Jerahmeel the King's Son." *IEJ* 28 (1978): 52–56.

—————. *Bullae and Seals from a Post-exilic Judean Archive.* Qedem 4. Jerusalem: Hebrew University, 1976).

—————. *Hebrew Bullae from the Time of Jeremiah: Remnants of a Burnt Archive.* Jerusalem: Israel Exploration Society, 1986.

—————. "Jerahmeel & Baruch, King's Son and Scribe." *BA* 42 (1979): 114–19.

—————. "A Seal of 'Manasseh Son of the King.'" *IEJ* 13 (1963): 133–36.

Avishur, Yitshak, and Michael Heltzer. *Studies on the Royal Administration in Ancient Israel in the Light of Epigraphic Sources.* Tel Aviv: Archaeological Center Publication, 2000.

Axelsson, Lars Eric. *The Lord Rose up from Seir: Studies in the History and Traditions of the Negev and Southern Judah.* ConBOT 25. Stockholm: Almqvist & Wiksell, 1987.

Bächli, Otto. *Amphiktyonie im Alten Testament. Forschungsgeschichtliche Studie zur Hypothese von Martn Noth.* ThZS 6. Basel: Friedrich Reinhardt, 1977.

Bardtke, Hans. "Die Latifundien in Juda während der zweiten Hälfte des achten Jahrhunderts v. Chr. (zum Verständnis von Jes 5,8–10)." In *Hommages à André Dupont-Sommer.* Paris: Adrien-Maisonneuve, 1971, 235–54.

Baron, Salo Wittmayer. *A Social and Religious History of the Jews.* Vol. 1, *To the Beginning of the Christian Era.* 2d. ed. New York: Columbia University Press, 1952.

Barrick, Boyd W. *The King and the Cemeteries. Toward a New Understanding of Josiah's Reform.* VTSup 88. Leiden: Brill, 2002.

Barstad, Hans M. "The Strange Fear of the Bible: Some Reflections on the 'Bibliophobia' in Recent Ancient Israelite Historiography." In *Leading Captivity Captive: "The Exile" as History and Ideology.* Ed. Lester L. Grabbe. JSOTSup 278. Sheffield: Sheffield Academic, 1998, 120–27.

Baumgartner, Walter. Review of M. Lurje, *Studien zur Geschichte der wirtschaftlichen und sozialen Verhältnisse im iraelitisch-jüdischen Reiche.* ThLZ 52 (1927): 315–16.

Becker, Joachim. *Der Ich-Bericht des Nehemiabuches als chronistische Gestaltung.* FB 87. Würzburg: Echter, 1998.

Beckerath, Jürgen von. *Chronologie des pharaonischen Ägypten. Die Zeitbestimmung der ägyptischen Geschichte von der Vorzeit bis 332 v. Chr.* MÄS 46. Mainz: P. von Zabern, 1997.

Bedford, Peter Ross. "Diaspora: Homeland Relations in Ezra-Nehemiah." *VT* 52 (2002): 147–65.

—————. "On Models and Texts: A Response to Blenkinsopp and Petersen." In *Second Temple Studies 1. Persian Period.* Ed. Philip R. Davies. JSOTSup 117. Sheffield: Sheffield Academic, 1991, 154–62.

Begrich, Gerhard. *Der wirtschaftliche Einfluss Assyriens auf Südsyrien und Palästina.* Ph.D. diss., Berlin, 1975.

Bellefontaine, Elizabeth. "Customary Law and Chieftainship: Judicial Aspects of 2 Samuel 14.4–21." *JSOT* 38 (1987): 47–72.

Ben-Barak, Zafrira. "The Appeal to the King as the Highest Authority for Justice." In *"Wünschet Jerusalem Frieden." Collected Communications to the XIIIth Congress of the International Organization for the Study of the Old Testament.* Ed. Matthias Augustin and Klaus-Dietrich Shunck. BEATAJ 13. Frankfurt: Peter Lang, 1986, 169–77.

———. "Meribaal and the System of Land Grants in Ancient Israel." *Bib* 62 (1981): 73–91.

Bendor, Shunya. *The Social Structure of Ancient Israel: The Institution of the Family (beit 'ab) from the Settlement to the End of the Monarchy.* Jerusalem Biblical Studies 7. Jerusalem: Simor, 1996.

Benzinger, Immanuel. *Hebräische Archäologie.* 3d ed. Leipzig: Eduard Pfeiffer, 1927.

Ben Zvi, Ehud. "On the Reading 'bytdwd' in the Aramaic Stele from Tel Dan." *JSOT* 64 (1994): 25–32.

Berges, Ulrich. *Klagelieder.* HTKAT. Freiburg: Herder, 2002.

Bergsma, John Sietze. "The Jubilee: A Post-Exilic Priestly Attempt to Reclaim Lands?" *Bib* 84 (2003): 225–46.

Bernett, Monika. "Polis und Politeia. Zur politischen Organisation Jerusalems und Jehuds in der Perserzeit." In *Die Griechen und das antike Israel. Interdisziplinäre Studien zur Religions- und Kulturgeschichte des Heiligen Landes.* Ed. Stefan Alkier and Markus Witte. OBO 201. Fribourg: Academic Fribourg; Göttingen: Vandenhoeck & Ruprecht, 2004, 73–129.

Berquist, Jon L. *Judaism in Persia's Shadow: A Social and Historical Approach.* Minneapolis: Fortress Press, 1995.

Bertholet, Alfred. *Kulturgeschichte Israels.* Göttingen: Vandenhoeck & Ruprecht, 1919.

Beyse, Karl-Martin. *Serubbabel und die Königserwartungen der Propheten Haggai und Sacharja. Eine historische und traditionsgeschichtliche Untersuchung.* AzTh 48. Stuttgart: Calwer, 1972.

Bickerman, Elias J. *The Jews in the Greek Age.* Cambridge: Harvard University Press, 1988.

Bieberstein, Klaus, and Hanswulf Bloedhorn. *Jerusalem. Gründzüge der Baugeschichte vom Chalkolithikum bis zur Frühzeit der osmanischen Herrschaft.* 3 vols. BTAVO 100. Wiesbaden: L. Reichert, 1994.

Bimson, John J. "Merneptah's Israel and Recent Theories of Israelite Origins." *JSOT* 49 (1991): 3–29.

Biran, Avraham, and Joseph Naveh. "An Aramaic Stele Fragment from Tel Dan." *IEJ* 43 (1993): 81–98.

———. "A New Fragment." *IEJ* 45 (1995): 1–18.

Blenkinsopp, Joseph. "The Bible, Archaeology and Politics: or The Empty Land Revisited." *JSOT* 27/2 (2002): 169–87.

———. "The Nehemiah Autobiographical Memoir." In *Language, Theology and the Bible. FS J. Barr.* Ed. Samuel E. Balentine and John Barton. Oxford: Oxford University Press, 1994, 199–212.

———. "Temple and Society in Achaemenid Judah." In *Second Temple Studies 1. Persian Period.* JSOTSup 117. Ed. Philip R. Davies. Sheffield: Sheffield Academic, 1991, 22–53.

Blum, Erhard. "Esra, die Mosetora und die persische Politik." In *Religion und Religionskontakte im Zeitalter der Achämeniden.* Ed. Reinhard G. Kratz. VWGTH 22. Gütersloh: Gütersloher, 2002, 231–56.

———. *Die Komposition der Vätergeschichte.* WMANT 57. Neukirchen-Vluyn: Neukirchener Verlag, 1984.

Bobek, Hans. "Die Hauptstufen der Gesellschafts- und Wirtschaftsentfaltung in geographischer Sicht." In *Wirtschaftsgeographie.* Ed. Eugen Wirth. WdF 219. Darmstadt: Wissenschaftliche Buchgesellschaft, 1969, 441–85.

Boogaart, Thomas A. "Stone for Stone: Retribution in the Story of Abimelech and Schechem." *JSOT* 32 (1985): 45–56.

Bohanan, Paul. "Die Wanderung und Ausdehnung der Tiv." In *Ethnologische Texte 1. Vor- und Frühgeschichte Israels.* Ed. Christian Sigrist and Rainer Neu. Neukirchen-Vluyn: Neukirchener, 1989, 86–105.

Bordreuil, Pierre, Felice Israel, and Dennis Pardee."Deux ostraca paléo-hébreux de la collection Sh. Moussaïef." *Sem* 46 (1996): 49–76.

Borowski, Oded. *Agriculture in Iron Age Israel.* Winona Lake, Ind.: Eisenbrauns, 1987.

Bottéro, Jean. "Les Habiru, les Nomades et les Sédentaires." In *Nomads and Sedentary People.* Ed. Jorge Silva Castillo. Mexico City: El Colegio de México, 1981, 89–107.

———. *Le problème des ⁽Apiru à la 4ᵉ Rencontre Assyriologique Internationale.* Cahiers de la Société Asiatique 12. Paris: Impr. nationale, 1954.

Braudel, Fernand. *On History.* Trans. Sarah Matthews. Chicago: University of Chicago Press, 1982.

Brett, Mark G. "Israel's Indigenous Origins: Cultural Hybridity and the Formation of Israelite Ethnicity." *BibInt* 11 (2003): 400–12.

Briant, Pierre. *From Cyrus to Alexander. A History of the Persian Empire.* Trans. P. T. Daniels. Winona Lake: Eisenbrauns, 2002.

Briend, Jacques, André Caquot, Henri Cazelles, et al. *La protohistoire d'Israël. De L'exode à la monarchie.* Paris: Cerf, 1990.

Bringmann, Klaus. *Hellenistische Reform und Religionsverfolgung in Judäa. Eine Untersuchung zur jüdisch-hellenistischen Geschichte (175–163 v. Chr.).* AAWGPHK 3/132. Göttingen: Vandenhoeck & Ruprecht, 1983.

Buchholz, Joachim. *Die Ältesten Israels im Deuteronomium.* GTA 36. Göttingen: Vandenhoeck & Ruprecht, 1988.

Buhl, Frants, *Die socialen Verhältnisse der Israeliten.* Berlin: Reuther & Reichard, 1899.

Bultmann, Christoph, *Der Fremde im antiken Juda. Eine Untersuchung zum sozialen Typenbegriff "ger" und seinem Bedeutungswandel in der alttestamentlichen Gesetzgebung.* FRLANT 153. Göttingen: Vandenhoeck & Ruprecht, 1992.

Cahnman, Werner J."Der Pariah und der Fremde: Eine begriffliche Klärung." *AES* 15 (1974): 166–77.

Campbell, Edward F., Jr. "Judges 9 and Biblical Archaeology." In *The Word of the Lord Shall Go Forth: Essays in Honor of David Noel Freedman.* Ed. Carol L. Meyers and M. O'Connor. Winona Lake: Eisenbrauns, 1983, 263–71.

Carreira, José Nunes. "Charisma und Institution. Zur Verfassung des Königtums in Israel und Juda. In *Prophetie und geschichtliche Wirklichkeit im Alten Israel. Festschrift für Siegfried Herrmann.* Ed. Rüdiger Liwak and Siegfried Wagner. Stuttgart: Kohlhammer, 1991, 39–51.

Carroll, Robert P. "Coopting the Prophets. Nehemiah and Noadiah." In *Priests, Prophets and Scribes. Essays on the Formation and Heritage of Second Temple Judaism in Honour of Joseph Blenkinsopp.* Ed. Eugene Ulrich, et al. JSOTSup 149. Sheffield: Sheffield Academic, 1992, 87–99.

———. *Jeremiah: A Commentary.* OTL. London: SCM, 1986.

Carter, Charles E. *The Emergence of Yehud in the Persian Period: A Social and Demographic Study.* JSOTSup 294. Sheffield: Sheffield Academic, 1999.

Causse, Antonin. *Du groupe éthnique à la communauté religieuse. Le problème sociologique de la religion d'Israël.* Paris: Alcan, 1937.

Chaney, Marvin L. "Systemic Study of the Israelite Monarchy." *Semeia* 37 (1986): 53–76.

Claessen, Henri J. M., and Peter Skalnik, eds. *The Early State.* New Babylon, Studies in the Social Sciences 32. Hague: Mouton, 1978.

Clancy, Frank. "Shishak/Shoshenq's Travels." *JSOT* 86 (1999): 3–23.

Clastres, Pierre."Die Gesellschaft gegen den Staat." In *Ethnologische Texte zum Alten Testament 2. Die Entstehung des Königtums.* Ed. Christian Sigrist and Rainer Neu. Neukirchen-Vluyn: Neukirchener, 1997, 47–60. Original German essay, 1976.

Clauss, Manfred, *Gesellschaft und Staat in Juda und Israel.* Eichstätter Hochschulreden 48. Munich: Minerva, 1985.

Coggins, Richard J. "The Origins of the Jewish Diaspora." In *The World of Ancient Israel:*

Sociological, Anthropological, and Political Perspectives. Ed. Ronald E. Clements. Cambridge: Cambridge University Press, 1989, 163–81.

Conçalves, Francolino J. "Exílio babilónico de 'Israel.' Realidade histórica e propaganda." *Cadmo* 10 (2000): 167–96.

Coogan, David. "Life in the Diaspora. Jews at Nippur in the Fifth Century B.C." *BA* 37 (1974): 6–12.

Coote, Robert B. *Early Israel: A New Horizon.* Minneapolis: Fortress Press, 1990.

———. *The Emergence of Early Israel in Historical Perspective.* SWBA 5. Sheffield: Almond, 1987.

Coote, Robert B., and Keith W. Whitelam. "The Emergence of Israel: Social Transformation and State Formation Following the Decline in Late Bronze Age Trade." *Semeia* 37 (1986): 107–47.

Cowley, Arthur E., ed. *Aramaic Papyri of the Fifth Century B.C.* Oxford: Clarendon, 1923; repr. Osnabrück: O. Zeller, 1967.

Cross, Frank Moore. "A Reconstruction of the Judean Restoration," *JBL* 94 (1975): 4–18.

Cross, Frank Moore, and David Noel Freedman. "The Name of Ashdod." *BASOR* 175 (1964): 48–50.

Crüsemann, Frank. "Alttestamentliche Exegese und Archäologie. Erwägungen angesichts des gegenwärtigen Methodenstreits in der Archäologie Palästinas." *ZAW* 91 (1979): 177–93.

———. "' . . . damit er dich segne in allem Tun deiner Hand . . . ' (Dtn 14.29). Die Produktionsverhältnisse der späten Königszeit dargestellt am Ostrakon von Mesad Hashavjahu, und die Sozialgesetzgebung des Deuteronomiums." In *Mitarbeiter der Schöpfung: Bibel und Arbeitswelt.* Ed. Luise Schottroff and Willi Schottroff. Munich: Kaiser, 1983, 72–103.

———. "Das Gericht im Tor—eine staatliche Rechtsinstanz." In *Alttestamentlicher Glaube und Biblische Theologie. Festschrift für Horst Dietrich Preuss.* Ed. Jutta Hausmann and Hans-Jürgen Zobel. Stuttgart: Kohlhammer, 1992, 69–79.

———. "Israel in der Perserzeit. Eine Skizze in Auseinandersetzung mit Max Weber." In *Kanon und Sozialgeschichte. Beiträge zum Alten Testament.* Gütersloh: Kaiser/Gütersloher Verlagshaus, 2003, 210–26. Original German essay, 1985.

———. *The Torah. Theology and Social History of Old Testament Law.* Trans. Allan W. Mahnke. Minneapolis: Fortress Press, 1996.

———. *Der Widerstand gegen das Königtum. Die antiköniglichen Tete des Alten Testaments und der Kampf un dem frühen israelitischen Staat.* WMANT 49. Neukirchen-Vluyn: Neukirchener, 1978.

———. "Der Zehnte in der israelitischen Königszeit." *WD* n.s. 18 (1985): 21–47.

Cryer, Frederick H. "On the Recently Discovered 'House of David' Inscription." *SJOT* 8 (1994): 3–20.

Daiches, Samuel. "The Meaning of >m h<rs in the O.T." *JTS* 30 (1929): 245–49.

Dandamaev, M. A. *A Political History of the Achaemenid Empire.* Trans. W. J. Vogelsang. Leiden: Brill, 1989.

Davies, Philip R., ed. "Exile? What Exile? Whose Exile?" In *Leading Captivity Captive: "The Exile" as History and Ideology.* Ed. Lester L. Grabbe. JSOTSup 278. Sheffield: Sheffield Academic, 1998, 128–38.

———. *In Search of "Ancient Israel."* JSOTSup 148. Sheffield: Sheffield Academic Press, 1995.

———. *Second Temple Studies 1. Persian Period.* JSOTSup 117. Sheffield: JSOT Press, 1991.

———. "The Society of Biblical Israel." In *Second Temple Studies 2. Temple and Community in the Persian Period.* Ed. Tamara C. Eskenazi and Kent H. Richards. JSOTSup 175. Sheffield: JSOT Press, 1994, 22–33.

Davies, Philip R., and John M. Halligan, eds. (2002): *Second Temple Studies 3. Studies in Politics, Class and Material Culture.* JSOTSup 340. Sheffield: Sheffield Academic.

Davies, W. D., and Louis Finkelstein, eds. *The Cambridge History of Judaism.* 2 vols. Cambridge: Cambridge University Press, 1984–89.

Dearman, John Andrew. *Property Rights in the Eighth-Century Prophets: The Conflict and its Background.* SBLDS 106. Atlanta: Scholars, 1988.

Delcor, Mathias. "Le trésor de la maison de Yahweh des origines à l'exile." *VT* 12 (1962): 353–77.

Dever, William G. "Archaeology, Ideology, and the Quest for an 'Ancient' or 'Biblical' Israel." *NEA* 61 (1998): 39–52.

———. "Of Myths and Methods." *BASOR* 277/278 (1990): 121–30.

Dietrich, Walter. *Die frühe Königszeit in Israel. 10. Jahrhundert v. Chr.* BE 3. Stuttgart: Kohlhammer, 1997.

———. *Jesaja und die Politik.* BEvT 74. Munich: Kaiser, 1976.

———. "Staat/Staatsphilosophie I. Altes Testament." *TRE* 32: 4–8.

———. "Wem das Land gehört. Ein Beitrag zur Sozialgeschichte Israels im 6. Jahrhundert v. Chr." In *Theopolitik. Studien zur Theologie und Ethik des Alten Testaments.* Neukirchen-Vluyn: Neukirchener, 2002, 270–86.

Dietrich, Walter, and Stefan Münger. "Die Herrschaft Sauls und der Norden Israels." In *Saxa loquentur. Studien zur Archäologie Palästinas/Israels. Festschrift für Volkmar Fritz.* Ed. Cornelis G. den Hertog, Ulrich Hübner, and Stefan Münger, eds. AOAT 302. Münster: Ugarit, 2003, 39–59.

Dion, Paul-Eugène. "Les *KTYM* de Tel Arad: Grecs ou Phéniciens?" *RB* 99 (1992): 70–97.

Dobbs-Alsopp, F. W. "The Genre of the Mesad Hashavyahu Ostracon." *BASOR* 295 (1994): 49–55.

Donner, Herbert. *Geschichte des Volkes Israel und seiner Nachbarn in Grundzügen.* 3d ed. 2 vols. GAT 4. Göttingen: Vandenhoeck & Ruprecht, 2000–01.

———. "Die soziale Botschaft der Propheten im Lichte der Gesellschaftsordnung in Israel." In *Das Prophetenverständnis in der deutschsprachigen Forschung seit Heinrich Ewald.* Ed. Peter H. A. Neumann. WdF 307. Darmstadt: Wissenschaftliche Buchgesellschaft, 1979, 493–514. Original German essay, 1963.

Dreher, Carlos A. "Das tributäre Königtum in Israel unter Salomo." *EvT* 51 (1991): 49–60.

Drews, Robert. *The End of the Bronze Age: Changes in Warfare and the Catastrophe ca. 1200 B.C.* Princeton: Princeton University Press, 1993.

Eddy, Samuel K. "Gründe für den Widerstand gegen den Hellenismus in Asien." In *Seminar: Die Entstehung der antiken Klassengesellschaft.* Ed. Hans G. Kippenberg. STW 130. Frankfurt: Suhrkamp, 1977, 328–50.

Edel, Elmar. "Die Stelen Amenophis' II. aus Karnak und Memphis mit dem Bericht über die asiatischen Feldzüge des Königs." *ZDPV* 69 (1953): 97–169.

Edelman, Diana V., ed. *The Fabric of History: Text, Artifact and Israel's Past.* JSOTSup 127. Sheffield: JSOT Press, 1991.

Eißfeldt, Otto. "Eine Einschmelzstelle am Tempel zu Jerusalem." In *Kleine Schriften II.* Tübingen: Mohr, 1963, 107–109.

Emerton, John A. "Did Ezra Go to Jerusalem in 428 B.C." *JTS* n.s. 17 (1966): 1–19.

———. "The Values of the Moabite Stone as an Historical Source." *VT* 52 (2002): 483–92.

Engel, Helmut. "Die Siegesstele des Merenptah. Kritischer Überblick über die verschiedenen Versuche historischer Auswertung des Schlußabschnitts." *Bib* 60 (1979): 373–99.

———. *Die Vorfahren Israels in Ägypten. Forschungsgeschichtlicher Überblock über die Darstellungen seit Richard Lepsius (1849).* FTS 27. Frankfurt: Knecht, 1979.

Engels, Friedrich. *The Origin of the Family, Private Property, and the State.* Harmondsworth: Penguin, 1985. German original, 1892.

Eph'al, Israel. "Changes in Palestine during the Persian Period in Light of Epigraphic Sources." *IEJ* 48 (1998): 106–19.

Eskenazi, Tamara C. "Out from the Shadows: Biblical Women in the Postexilic Era." *JSOT* 54 (1992): 25–43.

Eskenazi, Tamara C., and Kent H. Richards, eds. *Second Temple Studies 2: Temple and Community in the Persian Period.* JSOTSup 175. Sheffield: JSOT Press, 1994.

Fantalkin, Alexander. "Mezad Hashavyahu: Its Material Culture and Historical Background." *TA* 28 (2001): 3–165.

Faust, Abraham. "Differences in Family Structure Between Cities and Villages in Iron Age II." *TA* 26 (1999): 233–52.

———. "The Settlement of Jerusalem's Western Hill and the City's Status in Iron Age II Revisited." *ZDPV* 121 (2005): 97–118.

Fecht, Gerhard. "Die Israelstele, Gestalt und Aussage." In *Fontes atque Pontes: eine Festgabe für Hellmut Brunner*. Ed. Manfred Görg. ÄAT 5. Wiesbaden: In Kommission by O. Harrassowitz, 1983, 106–38.

Fechter, Friedrich. *Die Familie in der Nachexilszeit. Untersuchungen zur Bedeutung der Verwandtschaft in ausgewählten Texten des Alten Testaments*. BZAW 264. Berlin: de Gruyter, 1998.

Feinman, Gary M., and Joyce Marcus, eds. *Archaic States*. Santa Fe: School of American Research Press, 1998.

Fendler, Marlene. "Zur Sozialkritik des Amos. Versuch einer wirtschafts- und sozialgeschichtlichen Interpretation alttestamentlicher Texte." *EvT* 33 (1973): 32–53.

Fiensy, David. "Using the Nuer Culture of Africa in Understanding the Old Testament: An Evaluation." *JSOT* 38 (1987): 73–83.

Finkelstein, Israel. *The Archaeology of the Israelite Settlement*. Jerusalem: Israel Exploration Society, 1988.

———. "The Archaeology of the United Monarchy: An Alternative View." *Levant* 28 (1996): 177–87.

———. "The Campaign of Shoshenq I to Palestine. A Guide to the 10ᵗʰ Century B.C.E. Polity." *ZDPV* 118 (2002): 109–35.

———. *The Land of Ephraim Survey 1980–1987: Preliminary Report*. Tel Aviv: Institute of Archaeology of Tel Aviv University, 1988–89, 15–16, 117–83.

Finkelstein, Israel, and Nadav Na'aman, eds. *From Nomadism to Monarchy: Archaeological and Historical Aspects of Early Israel*. Washington: Biblical Archaeology Society, 1994.

Finkelstein, Israel, and Neil A. Silberman. *The Bible Unearthed: Archaeology's New Vision of Ancient Israel and the Origin of its Sacred Texts*. New York: Free, 2001.

Finley, Moses I. "Die Schuldknechtschaft." In *Seminar: Die Entstehung der antiken Klassengesellschaft*. Ed. Hans G. Kippenberg. STW 130. Frankfurt: Suhrkamp, 1977, 173–204.

Flanagan, James W. "Chiefs in Israel," *JSOT* 20 (1981): 47–73.

Fleischer, Gunther. *Von Menschenverkäufern, Baschankühen und Rechtsverkehrern. Die Sozialkritik des Amos-Buches in historisch-kritischer, sozialgeschichtlicher und archäologischer Perspektive*. BBB 74. Frankfurt: Athenaeum, 1989.

Fohrer, Georg. "Die Familiengemeinschaft." In *Studien zu alttestamentlichen Texten und Themen*. BZAW 155. Berlin: de Gruyter, 1981, 161–71.

———. "Israels Staatsordnung im Rahmen des Alten Orients." In *Studien zur alttestamentlichen Theologie und Geschichte (1949–1966)*. BZAW 115. Berlin: de Gruyter, 1969, 309–29.

———. *Geschichte Israels. Von den Anfängen bis zur Gegenwart*. UTB 708. 3d ed. Heidelberg: Quelle & Meyer, 1982.

Frei, Peter, and Klaus Koch. *Reichsidee und Reichsorganisation im Perserreich*. OBO 55. 2d ed. Fribourg: Universitätsverlag; Göttingen: Vandenhoeck & Ruprecht, 1996.

Frick, Frank S. (1985): *The Formation of the State in Ancient Israel: A Survey of Models and Theories*. SWBA 4. Sheffield: Almond.

———. "Social Science Methods and Theories of Significance for the Study of the Israelite Monarchy: A Critical Review Essay." *Semeia* 37 (1986): 9–52.

Friedl, Corinna. *Polygynie in Mesopotamien und Israel. Sozialgeschichtliche Analyse polygyner Beziehungen anhand rechtlicher texte aus dem 2. und 1. Jahrtausend v. Chr.* AOAT 277. Münster: Ugarit, 2000.

Fritz, Volkmar. "Abimelech und Sichem in Jdc. IX." *VT* 32 (1982): 129–44.

————. "Conquest or Settlement? The Early Iron Age in Palestine." *BA* 50 (1987): 84–100.

————. *Die Entstehung Israels im 12. und 11. Jahrhundert v. Chr.* BE 2. Stuttgart: Kohlhammer, 1996.

————. "Erwägungen zur Siedlungsgeschichte des Negeb in der eisen-I-Zeit (1200–1000 v. Chr.) im Lichte der Ausgrabungen auf der Hirbet-el-Mšaš." *ZDPV* 91 (1975): 30–45.

————. "Die Landnahme der israelitischen Stämme in Kanaan." *ZDPV* 106 (1990): 63–77.

————. "Die Verwaltungsgebiete Salomos nach 1 Kön. 4,7–19." In *Meilenstein. Festgabe für Herbert Donner.* Ed. Manfred Weippert and Stefan Timm. ÄAT 30. Wiesbaden: Harrassowitz, 1995, 19–26.

Fritz, Volkmar, and Philip R. Davies, eds. *The Origins of the Ancient Israelite States.* JSOTSup 228. Sheffield: Sheffield Academic, 1996.

Gal, Zwi. *Lower Galilee During the Iron Age.* ASORDS 8. Winona Lake: Eisenbrauns, 1992.

Galazzi, Sandro. (*A teocracia sadacita. Su história e ideologia.* Macapá—AP, Brazil, n.p., 2002.

Galling, Kurt. *Die israelitische Staatsverfassung in ihrer vorderorientalischen Umwelt.* AO 28, 3/4. Leipzig: J. C. Hinrichs, 1929.

————. "Königliche und nichtkönigliche Stifter beim Tempel von Jerusalem." *ZDPV* 68 (1951): 134–42.

————. *Studien zur Geschichte Israels im persischen Zeitalter.* Tübingen: Mohr (Siebeck), 1964.

Gerstenberger, Erhard S. *Israel in der Perserzeit. 5. u. 4. Jahrhundert v. Chr.* BE 8. Stuttgart: Kohlhammer, 2005.

————. *Theologies in the Old Testament.* Trans. John Bowden. Minneapolis: Fortress Press, 2002.

Gertz, Jan Christian. *Die Gerichtsorganisation Israels im deuteronomischen Gesetz.* FRLANT 165. Göttingen: Vandenhoeck & Ruprecht, 1994.

Geus, C. H. J. De. *The Tribes of Israel: An Investigation into Some of the Presuppositions of Martin Noth's Amphictyony Hypothesis.* SSN 18. Assen: Van Gorcum, 1976.

Geus, Jan Kees de. "Die Gesellschaftskritik der Propheten und die Archäologie." *ZDPV* 98 (1982) 50–57.

Gillischewski, Eva, "Der Ausdruck '*m-hā'āræs* im AT." *ZAW* 40 (1922): 137–42.

Godelier, Maurice. *The Enigma of the Gift,* Trans. Nora Scott. Chicago: University of Chicago Press, 1999.

Gonen, Rivka. "Urban Canaan in the Late Bronze Period." *BASOR* 253 (1984): 61–73.

Görg, Manfred. "Zum Titel BN HMLK ('Königssohn')." In *Ägyptiaca—Biblica. Notizen und Beiträge zu den Beziehungen zwischen Ägypten und Israel.* ÄAT 11. Wiesbaden: Harrassowitz, 1991, 192–96.

Gottwald, Norman K. "Domain Assumptions and Social Models in the Study of Premonarchic Israel." *Congress Volume Edinburgh 1974.* VTSup 28. Leiden: Brill, 1975, 89–100.

————. "The Israelite Settlement as a Social Revolutionary Movement." In *Biblical Archaeology Today: Proceedings of the International Congress on Biblical Archaeology, Jerusalem, April 1984.* Jerusalem: Israel Exploration Society, 1985, 34–46.

————. *The Politics of Ancient Israel.* Library of Ancient Israel. Louisville: Westminster John Knox, 2001.

————. "Social Class as an Analytic and Hermeneutical Category in Biblical Studies." *JBL* 112 (1993): 3–22.

————. *The Tribes of Yahweh: A Sociology of the Religion of Liberated Israel 1250–1050 B.C.E.* Maryknoll: Orbis, 1979.

Grabbe, Lester L., ed. *Can a "History of Israel" Be Written?* JSOTSup 245. Sheffield: Sheffield Academic, 1997.

————ed. *Did Moses Speak Attic? Jewish Historiography and Scripture in the Hellenistic Period.* JSOTSup 317. Sheffield: Sheffield Academic, 2001.

————. "'The Exile' under the Theodolite: Historiography as Triangulation." In *Leading Captivity Captive: "The Exile" as History and Ideology.* Ed. Lester L. Grabbe. JSOTSup 278. Sheffield: Sheffield Academic, 1998.

———. *Judaism from Cyrus to Hadrian.* Minneapolis: Fortress Press, 1992.

———, ed. *Leading Captivity Captive: "The Exile" as History and Ideology.* JSOTSup 278. Sheffield: Sheffield Academic, 1998.

———. "Writing Israel's History at the End of the Twentieth Century." In *Congress Volume Oslo 1998.* Ed. André Lemaire and Magne Sæbø. VTSup 80. Leiden: Brill, 2000, 203–18.

Gramsci, Antonio. *Prison Notebooks,* ed. Joseph A. Buttigieg; Trans. Joseph A. Buttigieg and Antonio Callari. New York: Columbia University Press, 1992–.

Grätz, Sebastian. *Das Edikt des Artaxerxes. Eine Untersuchung zum religionspolitischen und historischen Umfeld von Esra 7,12–26.* BZAW 337. Berlin: de Gruyter, 2004.

———. "Esra 7 im Kontext hellenistischer Politik. Der königliche Euergetismus in hellenistischer Zeit als idealler Hintergrund von Esr 7,12–16." In *Die Griechen und das antike Israel. Interdisziplinäre Studien zur Religions- und Kulturgeschichte des Heiligen Landes.* Ed. Stefan Alkier and Markus Witte. OBO 121. Fribourg: Academic Fribourg; Göttingen: Vandenhoeck & Ruprecht, 2004, 131–54.

Grelot, Pierre. *Documents araméens d'Égypte.* Littératures anciennes du Proche-Orient 5. Paris: Cerf, 1972.

Gropp, Douglas M. "Sanballat." *Encyclopedia of the Dead Sea Scrolls.* Oxford: Oxford University Press, 2000, 2:823–25.

———. *Wadi Daliyeh II. The Samaria Papyri from Wadi Daliyeh.* DJD 28. Oxford: Clarendon, 2001, 1–116.

Gunneweg, A. H. J. "Die aramäische und die hebräische Erzählung über die nachexilische Restauration—ein Vergleich." *ZAW* 94 (1982): 299–302.

———. "'m ha-ar'rs—A Semantic Revolution." *ZAW* 95 (1993): 437–40.

Gutiérrez, Gustavo. *A Theology of Liberation: History, Politics, and Salvation,* Trans. and ed. Sr. Caridad Inda and John Eagleson. Maryknoll: Orbis, 1973.

Guttmann, Julius. "Max Webers Soziologie des antiken Judentums." In *Max Webers Studie über das antike Judentum. Interpretation und Kritik.* Ed. Wolfgang Schluchter. STW 340. Frankfurt: Suhrkamp, 1981, 289–326. Original German essay, 1925.

Haag, Ernst. *Das hellenistische Zeitalter. Israel und die Bibel im 4. bis 1. Jahrhundert v. Chr.* BE 9. Stuttgart: Kohlhammer, 2003.

Halpern, Baruch. *The Constitution of the Monarchy in Israel.* HSM 25. Chico: Scholars, 1981.

———. "The Construction of the Davidic State: An Exercise in Historiography," in Volkmar Fritz and Philip R. Davies, eds., *The Origins of the Ancient Israelite States.* JSOTSup 228. Sheffield: Sheffield Academic, 1996, 44–75.

———. *The Emergence of Israel in Canaan.* SBLMS 29. Chico: Scholars, 1983.

———. "The Gate of Megiddo and the Debate on the 10th Century." In *Congress Volume Oslo 1998.* Ed. André Lemaire and Magne Sæbø. VTSup 80. Leiden: Brill, 2000, 79–121.

Handy, Lowell K., ed. *The Age of Solomon: Scholarship at the Turn of the Millennium.* SHCANE 11. Leiden: Brill, 1997.

Hanhart, Robert (1998): *Dodekapropheton 7.1. Sacharja 1–8.* BK XIV/7.1. Neukirchen-Vluyn: Neukirchener.

Hanson, K. C. "Petition to Authorize Elephantine Temple Reconstruction." K. C. Hanson, www.kchanson.com/ANCDOCS/westsem/templeauth.html.

Hasel, Michael G. (2004): "The Structure of the Final Hymnic-Poetic Unit on the Merenptah Stela," *ZAW* 116, 75–81.

Helck, Wolfgang (1961): *Urkunden der 18. Dynastie. Übersetzung zu den Heften 17–22.* Berlin: Akademie-Verlag. English: *Egyptian Historical Records of the Later Eighteenth Dynasty,* Trans. Barbara Cumming from the original hieroglyphic text as published in W. Helck, "Urkunden der 18. Dynastie," Heft 17–19, with reference to Professor Helck's German translation. Warminster, England: Aris & Phillips, 1982–84.

Heltzer, Michael (2000): "Some Questions Concerning the Economic Policy of Josiah, King of Judah," *IEJ* 50, 105–108.

Hengel, Martin. *Judaism and Hellenism: Studies in Their Encounter in Palestine During the Early Hellenistic Period.* Trans. John Bowden. Philadelphia: Fortress Press, 1974.

Hentschel, Georg. *Saul. Schuld, Reue und Tragik eines "Gesalbten."* Biblische Gestalten 7. Leipzig: Evangelische, 2003.

Herion, Gary A. "The Impact of Modern and Social Science Assumptions on the Reconstruction of Israelite History." *JSOT* 34 (1986): 3–33.

Herrmann, Siegfried. "Basic Factors of Israelite Settlement in Canaan." In *Biblical Archaeology Today: Proceedings of the International Congress on Biblical Archaeology, Jerusalem, April 1984.* Jerusalem: Israel Exploration Society, 1985, 47–53.

———. *A History of Israel in Old Testament Times.* Trans. John Bowden. Philadelphia: Fortress Press, 1981.

Hoglund, Kenneth (1991): "The Achaemenid Context," in Philip R. Davies, ed., *Second Temple Studies 1. Persian Period.* JSOTSup 117. Sheffield: Sheffield Academic, 54–72.

Holm-Nielsen, Svend. "Die Sozialkritik der Propheten." In *Denkender Glaube. Festschrift: Carl Heinz Ratschow zur Vollendung seines 65. Lebensjahres am 22. Juli 1976 gewidmet von Kollegen, Schülern u. Freunden.* Ed. Otto Kaiser. Berlin: de Gruyter, 1976, 7–23.

Hopkins, David C. "Bare Bones: Putting Flesh on the Economics of Ancient Israel." In *The Origins of the Ancient Israelite States.* Ed. Volkmar Fritz and Philip R. Davies. JSOTSup 228. Sheffield: Sheffield Academic, 1996, 121–39.

———. *The Highlands of Canaan: Agricultural Life in the Early Iron Age.* SWBA 3. Decatur: Almond, 1985.

Hornung, Erik. "Die Israelstele des Merenptah." In *Fontes atque Pontes: eine Festgabe für Hellmut Brunner.* Ed. Manfred Görg. ÄAT 5. Wiesbaden: in Kommission by O. Harrassowitz, 1983, 106–38.

Horsley, Richard A. "Empire, Temple and Community—but no Bourgeoisie! A Response to Blenkinsopp and Petersen." In *Second Temple Studies 1: Persian Period.* Ed. Philip R. Davies. JSOTSup 117. Sheffield: Sheffield Academic, 1991, 163–74.

Houtart, François. *Religion et modes de production précapitalistes.* Brussels: Éditions de l'Université de Bruxelles, 1980.

Houtman, Cornelis. "Ezra and the Law. Observations on the Supposed Relation between Ezra and the Pentateuch." *OTS* 21 (1981): 91–115.

Hurowitz, Victor. "Another Fiscal Practice in the Ancient Near East: 2 Kings 12,5–17 and a Letter to Esarhaddon (LAS 277)." *JNES* 45 (1986): 289–94.

Ihromi. "Die Königinmutter und der 'amm ha'aretz im Reich Juda." *VT* 24 (1974): 421–29.

Ishida, Tomoo. *The Royal Dynasties in Ancient Israel: A Study on the Formation and Development of Royal Dynastic Ideology.* BZAW 142. Berlin: de Gruyter, 1977.

Jagersma, Henk. "The Tithes in the Old Testament." *OTS* 21 (1981): 116–28.

Jamieson-Drake, David W. *Scribes and Schools in Monarchic Judah: A Socio-Archaeological Approach.* JSOTSup 109. Sheffield: Almond, 1991.

Janssen, Enno. *Juda in der Exilszeit. Ein Beitrag zur Frage der Entstehung des Judentums.* FRLANT 69. Göttingen: Vandenhoeck & Ruprecht, 1956.

Janzen, David. "The 'Mission' of Ezra and the Persian-Period Temple Community." *JBL* 119 (2000): 619–43.

Japhet, Sara. *1 Chronik.* HTKAT. Freiburg: Herder, 2002.

———. "Sheshbazzar and Zerubbabel—Against the Background of the Historical and Religious Tendencies of Ezra-Nehemiah." *ZAW* 94 (1982): 66–98.

———. "Sheshbazzar and Zerubbabel. Against the Background of the Historical and Religious Tendencies of Ezra-Nehemiah II." *ZAW* 95 (1983): 218–29.

Jeremias, Jörg. *Der Prophet Hosea.* ATD 24/1. Göttingen: Vandenhoeck & Ruprecht, 1983.

Junge, Ehrhard. *Der Wiederaufbau des Heerwesens des Reiches Juda unter Josia.* BWANT 75. Stuttgart: Kohlhammer, 1937.

Kaiser, Otto. "Arm und Reich bei Jesus Sirach." In *Theologie und Kirchenleitung. Festschrift für P. Steinacker zum 60. Geburtstag.* Ed. Hermann Deuser, Geshe Linde, and Sigurd Rinke. Marburg: Elwert, 2003, 17–30.

———. *Das Buch des Propheten Jesaja. Kapitel 1–12.* 5th ed. ATD 17. Göttingen: Vandenhoeck & Ruprecht, 1981.

———. "Kultische und Sittliche Sühne bei Jesus Sirach." In *"Einen Altar von Erde mache mir . . . ," Festschrift für Diethelm Conrad zu seinem 70. Geburtstag.* Ed. Johannes F. Diehl, Reinhard Heitzenröder, and Markus Witte. KAANT 4/5. Waltrop: Spenner, 2003, 151–67.

Kallai, Zecharia. "Simeon's Town List: Scribal Rules and Geographical Patterns." *VT* 53 (2003): 81–96.

Kamlah, Jens. "Die Liste der Regionalfürsten in 1 Kön 4,7–19 als historische Quelle für die Zeit Salomos." *BN* 106 (2001): 57–78.

Kamp, Kathryn A., and Norman Yoffee. "Ethnicity in Ancient Western Asia During the Early Second Millennium B.C.: Archaeological Assessments and Ethnoarchaeological Prospectives." *BASOR* 237 (1980): 85–99.

Karrer, Christiane. *Ringen um die Verfassung Judas. Eine Studie zu den theologisch-politischen Vorstellungen im Esra-Nehemia-Buch.* BZAW 308. Berlin: de Gruyter, 2001.

Kegler, Jürgen. "Debora—Erwägungen zur politischen Funktion einer Frau in einer patriarchalistischen Gesellschaft." In *Traditionen der Befreiung. Sozialgeschichtliche Bibelauslegungen 2: Frauen in der Bibel.* Ed. Willi Schottroff and Wolfgang Stegemann. Munich: Kaiser, 1980, 37–59.

———. "Die Fürbitte für den persischen Oberherrn im tempel von Jerusalem (Esra 6,10). Ein imperiales Herrschaftsinstrument." In *Gott an den Rändern. Sozialgeschichteliche Perspektiven auf die Bibel. Festschrift für Willi Schottroff.* Ed. Ulrike Bail and Renate Jost. Gütersloh: Kaiser, 1996, 73–82.

Kellermann, Ulrich. *Nehemia. Quelle, Überlieferung und Geschichte.* BZAW 102. Berlin: de Gruyter, 1967.

Kessler, Rainer. *Die Ägyptenbilder der Hebräischen Bibel. Ein Beitrag zur neueren Monotheismusdebatte.* SBS 197. Stuttgart: Katholisches Bibelwerk, 2002.

———. "Die angeblichen Kornhändler von Amos VIII 4–7." *VT* 39 (1989): 13–22.

———. "Armenfürsorge als Aufgabe der Gemeinde. Die Anfänge in Tempel und Synagoge." In *Dem Tod nicht glauben. Sozialgeschichte der Bibel. Festschrift für Luise Schottroff zum 70. Geburtstag.* Ed. Frank Crüsemann. Gütersloh: Gütersloher, 2004, 91–102.

———. "Chiefdom oder Staat? Zur Sozialgeschichte der frühen Monarchie." In *Freiheit und Recht. Festschrift für Frank Crüsemann zum 65. Geburtstag.* Ed. Christhof Hardmeier, Rainer Kessler, and Andreas Ruwe, et al. Gütersloh: Kaiser/Gütersloher, 2003, 121–40.

———. "Frühkapitalismus, Rentenkapitalismus, Tributarismus, antike Klassengesellschaft. Theorien zur Gesellschaft des alten Israel." *EvT* 54 (1994): 413–27.

———. "Gott und König, Grundeigentum und Fruchtbarkeit." *ZAW* 108 (1996): 214–32.

———. "Das hebräische Schuldenwesen. Terminologie und Metaphorik." *WD* n.s. 20 (1989): 181–95.

———. *Micha.* HTKAT. 2d ed. Freiburg: Herder, 2000.

———. "Mirjam und die Prophetie der Perserzeit." In *Gott an den Rändern. Sozialgeschichtliche Perspektiven auf die Bibel. Festschrift für Willi Schottroff.* Ed. Ulrike Bail and Renate Jost. Gütersloh: Kaiser, 1996, 64–72.

———. "Samaria-Papyri und Sklaverei in Israel." In *"Einen Altar von Erde mache mir . . . ," Festschrift für Diethelm Conrad zu seinem 70. Geburtstag.* KAANT 4/5. Ed. Johannes F. Diehl, Reinhard Heitzenröder, and Markus Witte. Waltrop: Spenner, 2003, 169–81.

————."Soziale Sicherung in vorstaatlicher, staatlicher und substaatlicher Gesellschaft: Das Beispiel des antiken Israel." In *Entstaatlichung und soziale Sicherheit. Verhandlungen des 31. Kongresses der Deutschen Gesellschaft für Soziologie in Leipzig 2002*. Ed. Jutta Allmendinger. Opladen: Leske & Budrich, 2003. With CD-ROM.

————. *Staat und Gesellschaft im vorexilischen Juda. Vom 8. Jahrhundert bis zum Exil*. VTSup 47. Leiden: Brill, 1992.

Kiesow, Anna. *Löwinnen von Juda. Frauen als Subjekte politischer Macht in der judäischen Königszeit*. Theologische Frauenforschung in Europa 4. Münster: Lit, 2000.

Kinet, Dirk. *Geschichte Israels*. NEB. Ergänzungsband zum Alten Testament 2. Würzburg: Echter, 2001.

Kippenberg, Hans G., ed. *Religion und Klassenbildung im antiken Judäa. Eine religionssoziologische Studie zum Verhältnis von Tradition und gesellschaftlicher Entwicklung*. SUNT 14. Göttingen: Vandenhoeck & Ruprecht, 1978.

————. *Seminar: Die Entstehung der antiken Klassengesellschaft*. STW 130. Frankfurt: Surhkamp, 1977.

————. "Die Typik antiker Entwicklung." In *Seminar: Die Entstehung der antiken Klassengesellschaft*. Ed. Hans G. Kippenberg. STW 130. Frankfurt: Surhkamp, 1977, 9–61.

Kittel, Rudolf. *Geschichte des volkes Israel*. 2 vols. 5th/6th eds. Stuttgart: Kohlhammer, 1909–29; Gotha: F. A. Perthes, 1923–25.

Klengel, Horst. *Zwischen Zelt und Palast. Die begegnung von Nomaden und Seßhaften im alten Vorderasien*. Vienna: Schroll, 1972.

Kletter, Raz. "Chronology and United Monarchy. A Methodological Review." *ZDPV* 120 (2004): 13–54.

————. "Pots and Polities: Material Remains of Late Iron Age Judah in Relation to its Political Borders." *BASOR* 314 (1999): 19–54.

————. "Temptation to Identify: Jerusalem, *mmšt*, and the *lmlk* Jar Stamps." *ZDPV* 118 (2002): 136–49.

Knauf, Ernst Axel. "Elephantine und das vorbiblische Judentum." In *Religion und Religionskontakte im Zeitalter der Achämeniden*. Ed. Reinhard G. Kratz. Veröffentlichungen der Wisenschaftlichen Gesellschaft für Theologie 22. Gütersloh: Kaiser, 2002, 179–88.

————. "From History to Interpretation." In *The Fabric of History: Text, Artifact and Israel's Past*. Ed. Diana V. Edelman. JSOTSup 127. Sheffield: JSOT Press, 1991, 26–64.

————. "Das 'Haus Davids' in der alt-aramäischen Inschrift vom Tel Dan." *BK* 51 (1996): 9–10.

————. "Saul, David, and the Philistines: From Geography to History." *BN* 109 (2001): 15–18.

————. *Die Umwelt des Alten Testament*. NSKAT 29. Stuttgart: Katholisches Bibelwerk, 1994.

Knauf, Ernst Axel, Albert de Pury, and Thomas Römer. "*Bayt Dawid ou *Bayt Dod? Une relecture de la nouvelle inscription de Tel Dan." *BN* 72 (1994): 60–69.

Knudtzon, Jørgen A. *Die El-Amarna-Tafeln*. Leipzig: J. C. Hinrichs, 1915.

Koch, Heidemarie. *Es kündet Dareios der König . . . Vom Leben im persischen Großreich*. 2d ed. Kulturgeschichte der antiken Welt 55. Mainz: P. von Zabern, 1996.

Koch, Klaus. "Der Artaxerxes-Erlaß im Esrabuch." In *Meilenstein. Festgabe für Herbert Donner*. Ed. Manfred Weippert and Stefan Timm. ÄAT 30. Weisbaden: Harrassowitz, 1995, 87–98.

————. "Die Entstehung der sozialen Kritik bei den Propheten." In *Spuren des hebräischen Denkens. Beiträge zur alttestamentlichen Theologie. Gesammelte Aufsätze 1*. Neukirchen-Vluyn: Neukirchener, 1991, 146–66. Original German essay, 1971.

————. "Die Hebräer vom Auszug aus Ägypten bis zum Großreich Davids." *VT* 19 (1969): 37–81.

Kottsieper, Ingo. "Die Religionspolitik der Achämeniden und die Juden von Elephantine." In *Religion und Religionskontakte im Zeitalter der Achämeniden*. Ed. Reinhard G. Kratz. Veröffentlichungen der Wisenschaftlichen

Gesellschaft für Theologie 22. Gütersloh: Kaiser, 2002, 150–78.

Kraus, Hans-Joachim. "Die Anfänge der religionssoziologischen Forschungen in der alttestamentlichen Wissenschaft. Eine forschungsgeschichtliche Orientierung." In *Biblisch-theologische Aufsätze*. Neukirchen-Vluyn: Neukirchener, 1972, 296–310.

———. "Die prophetische Botschaft gegen das soziale Unrecht Israels." *EvT* 15 (1955) 295–307.

Kreissig, Heinz. *Die sozialökonomische Situation in Juda zur Achämenidenzeit*. SGKAO 7. Berlin: Akademie, 1973.

———. *Wirtschaft und Gesellschaft im Seleukidenreich. Die Eigentums- und Abhängigkeitsverhältnisse*. Schriften zur Geschichte und Kultur der Antike 16. Berlin: Akademie, 1978.

Kreuzer, Siegfried. "Max Weber, George Mendenhall und das sogenannte Revolutionsmodell für die 'Landnahme' Israels." In *Altes Testament: Forschung und Wirkung. Festschrift für Henning Graf Reventlow*. Ed. Peter Mommer and Winfried Thiel. Frankfurt: Peter Lang, 1994, 238–305.

———. "'Saul war noch zwei Jahre König . . . .'" Textgeschichtliche, literarische und historische Beobachtungen zu 1 Sam 13,1." *BZ* n.s. 40 (1996): 263–70.

———. "'War Saul auch unter den Philistern?' Die Anfänge des Königtums in Israel." *ZAW* 113 (2001): 56–73.

Kupper, Jean-Robert. *Les nomades en Mésopotamie au temps des rois de Mari*. Paris: Les Belles Lettres, 1957.

Lambert, Frith. "The Tribe/State Paradox in the Old Testament." *SJOT* 8 (1994): 20–44.

Lance, Darrell H. "The Royal Stamps and the Kingdom of Josiah." *HTR* 64 (1979): 315–32.

Lang, Bernhard. *Kein Aufstand in Jerusalem. Die Politik des Propheten Ezechiel*. 2d ed. SBB. Stuttgart: Katholisches Bibelwerk, 1981.

———. "Prophetie und Ökonomie im alten Israel." In*"Vor Gott sind alle gleich." Soziale Gleichheit, soziale Ungleichheit und die Religio-nen*. Ed. Günter Kehrer. Düsseldorf: Patmos, 53–73, 1983.

———. "The Social Organization of Peasant Poverty in Biblical Israel." *JSOT* 24 (1982): 47–63.

Lehmann, Reinhard, and Marcus Reichel. "DOD und ASIMA in Tell Dan." *BN* 77 (1995): 29–31.

Lemaire, André. "Classification des estampilles royales judéennes." *EI* 15 (1981): 53*–60*.

———. "L'ostracon de Mesad Hashavjahu replacé dans son contexte." *Sem* 21 (1971): 57–79.

———. "Remarques sur la datation des estampilles 'lmlk.'" *VT* 25 (1975): 678–82.

Lemche, Niels Peter. *Ancient Israel. A New History of Israelite Society*. Sheffield: JSOT Press, 1988.

———. *Early Israel: Anthropological and Historical Studies on the Israelite Society Before the Monarchy*. VTSup 37. Leiden: Brill, 1985.

———. "From Patronage Society to Patronage Society." In *The Origins of the Ancient Israelite States*. Ed. Volkmar Fritz and Philip R. Davies. JSOTSup 228. Sheffield: Sheffield Academic, 1996, 106–20.

———. "Is it Still Possible to Write a History of Ancient Israel?" *JSOT* 8 (1994): 165–90.

———. "On Sociology and the History of Israel. A Reply to Eckhart Otto—and some Further Considerations." *BN* 21 (1983): 48–58.

———. *Prelude to Israel's Past: Background and Beginnings of Israelite History and Identity*. Trans. E. F. Maniscalco. Peabody, Mass.: Hendrickson, 1998.

Lemche, Niels Peter, and Thomas L. Thompson. "Did Biran Kill David? The Bible in the Light of Archaeology." *JSOT* 64 (1994): 3–22.

Levin, Christoph. "Die Instandsetzung des Tempels unter Joasch ben Ahasja." In *Fortschreibungen. Gesammelte Studien zum Alten Testament*. BZAW 316. Berlin: de Gruyter, 2003, 169–97.

———. "The Poor in the Old Testament. Some Observations." In *Fortschreibungen. Gesammelte Studien zum Alten Testament*. BZAW 316. Berlin: de Gruyter, 2003, 322–38.

————. "Das vorstaatliche Israel." In *Fortschreibungen. Gesammelte Studien zum Alten Testament*. BZAW 316. Berlin: de Gruyter, 2003, 142–57.

Lohfink, Norbert. "Die Gattung der 'Historischen Kurzgeschichte' in den letzten Jahren von Juda und in der Zeit des Babylonischen Exils." *ZAW* 90 (1978): 319–47.

————. "Von der 'Anawim-Partei' zur 'Kirche der Armen.' Die bibelwissenschaftliche Ahnentafel eines Hauptbegriffs der 'Theologie der Befreiung.'" *Bib* 67 (1986): 153–76.

Long, V. Philips. "How Reliable are Biblical Reports? Repeating Lester Grabbe's Comparative Experiment." *VT* 52 (2002): 367–84.

Loretz, Oswald. *Habiru—Hebräer. Eine soziolinguistische Studie über die Herkunft des Gentilizismus 'ibri vom Appellativum habiru*. BZAW 160. Berlin: de Gruyter, 1984.

————."Die prophetische Kritik des Rentenkapitalismus. Grundlagen-Probleme der Prophetenforschung." *UF* 7 (1975): 271–78.

Lowery, Richard H. *The Reforming Kings: Cult and Society in First Temple Judah*. JSOTSup 120. Sheffield: JSOT Press, 1991.

Lurje, M. *Studien zur Geschichte der wirtschaftlichen und sozialen Verhältnisse im israelitisch-jüdischen Reiche von der Einwanderung in Kanaan bis zum babylonischen Exil*. BZAW 45. Gießen: Töpelmann, 1927.

Macholz, Georg Christian. "Zur Geschichte der Justizorganisation in Juda." *ZAW* 84 (1972): 314–40.

————. "Die Stellung des Königs in der israelitischen Gerichtsverfassung." *ZAW* 84 (1972):157–82.

Malamat, Abraham. "Charismatische Führung im Buch der Richter." In *Max Webers Studie über das antike Judentum. Interpretation und Kritik*. Ed. Wolfgang Schluchter. STW 340. Frankfurt: Suhrkamp, 1981, 110–33.

————. "Organs of Statecraft in the Israelite Monarchy." *BA* 28 (1965): 34–65.

————. "The Proto-History of Israel: A Study in Method." In *The Word of the Lord Shall Go Forth. Festschrift for David Noel Freedman*. Ed.

Carol L. Meyers and M. O'Connor. Winona Lake: Eisenbrauns, 1983, 303–13.

Mantel, Hugo (Haim Dov). "The Dichotomy of Judaism During the Second Temple." *HUCA* 44 (1973): 55–87.

Marcus, Joyce, and Gary M. Feinman. "Introduction." In *Archaic States*. Ed. Gary M. Feinman and Joyce Marcus. Santa Fe: School of American Research Press, 1998, 3–14.

Martin, James D. "Israel as a Tribal Society." In *The World of Ancient Israel: Sociological, Anthropological and Political Perspectives*. Ed. Ronald E. Clements. Cambridge: Cambridge University Press, 1989, 95–117.

Marx, Karl."Ökonomische Manuskripte 1857/58." In Karl Marx and Friedrich Engels, *Gesamtausgabe (MEGA)* II/1, 2. Berlin: Dietz, 1981.

Matthews, Victor H., and Don. C. Benjamin. *Social World of Ancient Israel 1250–587 B.C.E.* 2d ed. Peabody: Hendrickson, 1995.

Mauss, Marcel. *The Gift: The Form and Reason for Exchange in Archaic Societies*. Trans. W. D. Halls. New York: W. W. Norton, 2000.

Mayes, Andrew D. H. "Sociology and the Old Testament." In *The World of Ancient Israel. Sociological, Anthropological and Political Perspectives*. Ed. Ronald E. Clements. Cambridge: Cambridge University Press, 1989, 39–63.

McEvenue, Sean E. "The Political Structure in Judah from Cyrus to Nehemiah." *CBQ* 43 (1981): 353–64.

McKenzie, John. "The 'People of the Land' in the Old Testament." In *Akten des vierundzwanzigsten internationalen Orientalistenkongresses in München*. Wiesbaden: Harrassowitz, 1959, 206–208.

McNutt, Paula. *Reconstructing the Society of Ancient Israel*. Library of Ancient Israel. Louisville: Westminster John Knox, 1999.

Mendenhall, George E. "The Hebrew Conquest of Palestine." *BA* 25 (1962) 66–87. Repr., *BARev* 3 (1970): 100–120.

Mettinger, Tryggve N. D. *Solomonic State Officials: A Study of the Civil Government Officials of the Israelite Monarchy*. ConBOT 5. Lund: Gleerup, 1971.

Meyer, Esias E. *The Jubilee in Leviticus 25: A Theological-Ethical Interpretation from a South African Perspective.* EXUZ 15. Münster: Lit, 2005.

Meyers, Carol L. *Discovering Eve: Ancient Israelite Women in Context.* New York: Oxford University Press, 1988.

Meyers, Eric M. "The Shelomith Seal and the Judean Restoration: Some Additional Considerations." *EI* 18 (1985): 33*–38*.

Milgrom, Jacob. "Religious Conversion and the Revolt Model for the Formation of Israel." *JBL* 101 (1982): 169–76.

Miller, J. Maxwell. "Is it Possible to Write a History of Israel without Relying on the Hebrew Bible?" In *The Fabric of History: Text, Artifact and Israel's Past.* Ed. Diana V. Edelman. JSOTSup 127. Sheffield: JSOT Press (1991): 93–102.

Mittmann, Siegfried. *Beiträge zur Siedlungs- und Territorialgeschichte des nördlichen Ostjordanlandes.* ADPV. Wiesbaden: Harrassowitz, 1970.

Moenikes, Ansgar. *Die grundsätzliche Ablehnung des Königtums in der hebräischen Bibel. Ein Beitrag zur Religionsgeschichte des alten Israel.* BBB 99. Weinheim: Beltz Athenaeum, 1995.

Mommsen, H., I. Perlman, and J. Yellin. "The Provenience of the lmlk Jars." *IEJ* 34 (1984): 89–113.

Müller, Reinhard. *Königtum und Gottesherrschaft. Untersuchungen zur alttestamentlichen Monarchiekritik.* FAT 2/3. Tübingen: Mohr Siebeck, 2004.

Na'aman, Nadav. "The Kingdom of Judah under Josiah." *TA* 18 (1991): 3–71.

———. "Sennacherib's Campaign to Judah and the Date of the lmlk Stamps." *VT* 29 (1979): 61–86.

———. "Solomon's District List (1 Kings 4:7–19) and the Assyrian Province System in Palestine." *UF* 33 (2001): 419–36.

Neu, Rainer. "'Israel' vor der Entstehung des Königtums." *BZ* n.s. 30 (1986): 204–21.

———. *Von der Anarchie zum Staat. Entwicklungsgeschichte Israels vom Nomadentum*

zur Monarcie im Spiegel der Ethnosoziologie. Neukirchen-Vluyn: Neukirchener, 1992.

Niehr, Herbert. *Herrschen und Richten. Die Wurzel špṭ im Alten Orient und im Alten Testament.* FB 54. Würzburg: Echter, 1986.

———. *Rechtsprechung in Israel. Untersuchungen zur Geschichte der Gerichtsorganisation im Alten Testament.* SBS 130. Stuttgart: Katholisches Bibelwerk, 1987.

———. "Die Reform des Joschija. Methodische, historische und religionsgeschichtliche Aspekte." In *Jeremia und die "deuteronomistische Bewegung."* BBB 98. Ed. Walter Groß. Weinheim: Beltz Athenaeum, 1995, 33–55.

———. "Some Aspects of Working with the Textual Sources." In *Can a "History of Israel" Be Written?* Ed. Lester L. Grabbe. JSOTSup 245. Sheffield: Sheffield Academic, 1997, 156–65.

Niemann, Hermann Michael. *Herrschaft, Königtum und Staat. Skizzen zur soziokulturellen Entwicklung im monarchischen Israel.* FAT 6. Tübingen: Mohr, 1993.

———. "Taanach und Megiddo: Überlegungen zur strukturell-historischen Situation zwischen Saul und Salomo." *VT* 52 (2002): 93–102.

Norin, Stig. "Response to Lemche, 'Ist es noch möglich die Geschichte des alten Israels zu schreiben?'" *SJOT* 8 (1994): 191–97.

Noth, Martin. *The History of Israel.* Trans. from the 2d ed. by Stanley Godman. London: A & C. Black, 1958.

———. *Könige. 1. Teilband.* BK 9/1. Neukirchen-Vluyn: Neukirchener, 1968.

———. "Das Krongut der israelitischen Könige und seine Verwaltung." In *Aufsätze zur biblischen Landes- und Altertumskunde.* Neukirchen-Vluyn: Neukirchener, 1971, 1:159–82. Original German essay, 1927.

———. *Das System der zwölf Stämme Israels.* BWANT 52. Darmstadt: Wissenschaftliche Buchgesellschaft, 1930.

Nurmi, Janne J. *Die Ethik unter dem Druck des Alltags. Die Impuse der gesellschaftlichen Änderungen und Situation zu der sozialkritischen*

Prophetie in Juda im 8. Jh. v. Chr. Åbo: Åbo Akademis, 2004.

Oded, Bustenay. "The Settlements of the Israelite and the Judan Exiles in Mesopotamia in the 8th-6th Centuries B.C.E." In *Studies in Historical Geography and Biblical Historiography: presented to Zecharia Kallai.* Ed. Gershon Galil and Moshe Weinfeld. VTSup 81. Leiden: Brill, 2000, 91–103.

Olivier, J. P. J. "Money Matters: Some Remarks on the Economic Situation in the Kingdom of Judah During the Seventh Century B.C." *BN* 73 (1994): 90–100.

Olmstead, Albert T. *History of the Persian Empire.* 2d ed. Chicago: University of Chicago Press, 1959.

Ortiz, Steven M. "Methodological Comments on the *Low Chronology:* A Reply to Ernst Axel Knauf." *BN* 111 (2002): 34–39.

Otto, Eckart. "Hat Max Webers Religionssoziologie des antiken Judentums Bedeutung für eine Theologie des Alten Testaments"? *ZAW* 94 (1982): 187–203.

―――. "Historisches Geschehen—Überlieferung—Erklärungsmodell. Sozialhistorische Grundsatz- und Einzelprobleme in der Geschichtsschreibung des frühen Israel—Eine Antwort auf N. P. Lemches Beitrag zur Diskussion um eine Sozialgeschichte Israels." *BN* 23 (1984): 63–80.

―――. "Josia/Josiareform." *RGG*⁴ 4:587–89.

―――. *Max Webers Studien des Antiken Judentums. Historische Grundlegung einer Theorie der Moderne.* Tübingen: Mohr Siebeck, 2002.

―――. "Mose und das Gesetz. Die Mose-Figur als Gegenentwurf Politischer Theologie zur neuassyrischen Königsideologie im 7. Jh. v. Chr." In *Mose. Ägypten und das Alte Testament.* Ed. Otto Eckhart. SBS 189. Stuttgart: Katholisches Bibelwerk, 2000, 43–83.

―――. "Sozialgeschichte Israels. Probleme und Perspektiven. Ein Diskussionspapier." *BN* 15 (1981): 87–92.

―――. *Theologische Ethik des Alten Testaments.* Theologische Wissenschaft 3.2. Stuttgart: Kohlhammer, 1994.

Pavlovskyœ, V. S. J. "Die Chronologie der Tätigkeit Esdras. Versuche einer neuen Lösung." *Bib* 38 (1957): 275–305, 428–56.

Pedersen, Johannes. *Israel: Its Life and Culture.* 4 vols. London: Oxford University Press 1926–1940. Repr. with additions, 1959.

Perdue, Leo G., Joseph Blenkinsopp, John J. Collins, and Carol Meyers. *Families in Ancient Israel.* Louisville: Westminster John Knox, 1997.

Pleins, J. David. *The Social Visions of the Hebrew Bible: A Theological Introduction.* Louisville: Westminster John Knox, 2001.

Porath, Renatus. *Die Sozialkritik im Jesajabuch. Redaktionsgeschichtliche Analyse.* EHS Theologie 503. Frankfurt: Peter Lang, 1994.

Porten, Bezalel. *Archives from Elephantine: The Life of an Ancient Jewish Military Colony.* Berkeley: University of California Press, 1968.

―――. *The Elephantine Papyri in English: Three Millennia of Cross-Cultural Continuity and Change.* DMOA 22. Leiden: Brill, 1996.

Premnath, D. M. "Latifundalization and Isaiah 5.8–10." *JSOT* 40 (1988): 49–60.

Pummer, Reinhard. *The Samaritans.* Iconography of Religions Section 23 (Judaism), fasc. 5. Leiden: Brill, 1987.

Rad, Gerhard von. *Holy War in Ancient Israel.* Trans. Marva J. Dawn and John Howard Yoder. Grand Rapids: Eerdmans, 1990.

Rainey, Anson F. "Israel in Merenptah's Inscription and Reliefs." *IEJ* 51 (2001): 57–75.

―――. "Toward a Precise Date for the Samaria Ostraca." *BASOR* 272 (1988): 69–74.

―――. "Wine from the Royal Vineyards." *BASOR* 245 (1982): 57–62.

Rapp, Ursula. *Mirjam. Eine feministisch-rhetorische Lektüre der Mirjamtexte in der hebräischen Bibel.* BZAW 317. Berlin: de Gruyter, 2002.

Redford, Donald B. "The Ashkelon Relief at Karnak and the Israel Stela." *IEJ* 36 (1986): 188–200.

Reich, Ronny, and Eli Shukron. "The Jerusalem City Dump in the Late Second Temple Period." *ZDPV* 199 (2003): 12–18.

Reimer, Haroldo. *Richtet auf das Recht! Studien zur Botschaft des Amos.* SBS 149. Stuttgart: Katholisches Bibelwerk, 1992.

Reinmuth, Titus. *Der Bericht Nehemias. Zur literarischen Eigenart, traditionsgeschichtlichen Prägung und innerbiblischen Rezeption des Ich-Berichts Nehemias.* OBO 183. Fribourg: Universitätsverlag; Göttingen: Vandenhoeck & Ruprecht, 2002.

Rendtorff, Rolf. *The Canonical Hebrew Bible: A Theology of the Old Testament,* Trans. David E. Orton. Tools for Biblical Study 7. Leiden: Deo, 2005.

Reviv, Hanoch. *The Elders in Ancient Israel: A Study of a Biblical Institution.* Jerusalem: Magnes, 1989.

———. "The Government of Shechem in the El-Amarna Period and in the Days of Abimelech." *IEJ* 16 (1966): 252–57.

Ro, Johannes Un-Sok. *Die sogenannte "Armenfrömmigkeit" im nachexilischen Israel.* BZAW 322. Berlin: de Gruyter, 2002.

Rogerson, John W. "The Use of Sociology in Old Testament Studies." In *Congress Volume Salamanca 1983.* Ed. John A. Emerton. VTSup 36. Leiden: Brill, 1985, 245–56.

———. "Was Early Israel a Segmentary Society?" *JSOT* 36 (1986): 17–26.

Rösel, Hartmut N. "The Emergence of Ancient Israel—Some Related Problems." *BN* 114/115 (2002): 151–60.

———. *Israel in Kanaan. Zum Problem der Entstehung Israels.* BEATAJ 11. Frankfurt: Peter Lang, 1992.

———. "Überlegungen zu 'Abimelech und Sichem in Jdc. IX." *VT* 33 (1983): 500–503.

Rostovzeff, Michael Ivanovitch. *The Social and Economic History of the Hellenistic World.* 3 vols. Oxford: Clarendon, 1941.

Rowton, Michael B. "Dimorphic Structure and the Parasocial Element." *JNES* 36 (1977): 181–98.

———. "Dimorphic Structure and the Problem of the ʿApiru-ʿIbrîm." *JNES* 35 (1976): 13–20.

———. "Urban Autonomy in a Nomadic Environment." *JNES* 32 (1973): 201–15.

Rüterswörden, Udo. *Die Beamten der israelitischen Königszeit. Eine Studie zu ∞r und vergleichbaren Begriffen.* BWANT 117. Stuttgart: Kohlhammer, 1985.

———. "Die persische Reichsautorisation der Thora: Fact or Fiction?" *ZABR* 1 (1995): 47–61.

Sacchi, Paolo. *The History of the Second Temple Period.* JSOTSup 282. Sheffield: Sheffield Academic, 2000.

Sasse, Markus. *Geschichte Israels in der Zeit des Zweiten Tempels. Historische Ereignisse—Archäologie—Sozialgeschichte—Religions- und Geistesgeschichte.* Neukirchen-Vluyn: Neukirchener, 2004.

Schaeder, Hans Heinrich. *Esra der Schreiber.* BHT 5. Tübingen: Mohr, 1930.

Schäfer-Lichtenberger, Christa. "Michal—eine literarische Figur mit Vergangenheit." *WD* 27 (2003): 89–105.

———. "Sociological and Biblical Views of the Early State." In *The Origins of the Ancient Israelite States.* Ed. Volkmar Fritz and Philip R. Davies. JSOTSup 228. Sheffield: Sheffield Academic, 1996, 78–105.

———. *Stadt und Eidgenossenschaft im Alten Testament. Eine Auseinandersetzung mit Max Webers Studie "Das antike Judentum."* BZAW 156. Berlin: de Gruyter, 1983.

———. "Zur Funktion der Soziologie im Studium des Alten Testaments." In *Congress Volume Oslo 1998.* Ed. André Lemaire and Magne Sæbø. VTSup 80. Leiden: Brill, 2000, 179–202.

Schaper, Joachim. "The Jerusalem Temple as an Instrument of the Achaemenid Fiscal Administration." *VT* 45 (1995): 528–39.

———. "Numismatik, Epigraphik, alttestamentliche Exegese und die Frage nach der politischen Verfassung des achämenidischen Juda." *ZDPV* 118 (2002): 150–68.

———. *Priester und Leviten im achämenidischen Juda. Studien zur Kult- und Sozialgeschichte Israels in persischer Zeit.* FAT 31. Tübingen: Mohr Siebeck, 2000.

—————. "The Temple Treasury Committee in the Times of Nehemiah and Ezra." *VT* 47 (1998): 200–206.

Schenker, Adrian. "Die zweimalige Einsetzung Simons des Makkabäers zum Hohenpriester. Die Neuordnung des Hohepriestertums unter dem Hasmonäer Simon (1 Makk 14,25–49). In *Recht und Kult im Alten Testament. Achtzehn Studien.* OBO 172. Fribourg: Universitätsverlag, 2000, 158–69.

Schipper, Bernd Ulrich. *Israel und Ägypten in der Königszeit. Die kulturellen Kontakte von Salomo bis zum Fall Jerusalems.* OBO 170. Fribourg: Universitätsverlag; Göttingen: Vandenhoeck & Ruprecht, 1999.

Schluchter, Wolfgang, ed. *Max Webers Sicht des antiken Christentums. Interpretation und Kritik.* STW 548. Frankfurt: Suhrkamp, 1985.

—————, ed. *Max Webers Studie über das antike Judentum. Interpretation und Kritik.* STW 340. Frankfurt: Suhrkamp, 1981.

Schmid, Herbert. "Die Herrschaft Abimelechs (Jdc 9)." *Jud* 26 (1970): 1–11.

Schoors, Antoon. *Die Königreiche Israel und Juda im 8. und 7. Jahrhundert v. Chr. Die assyrische Krise.* BE 5. Stuttgart: Kohlhammer, 1998.

Schottroff, Willy. "Arbeit und sozialer Konflikt im nachexilischen Juda." In *Gerechtigkeit lernen. Beiträge zur biblischen Sozialgeschichte.* ThB 94. Gütersloh: Kaiser/Gütersloher, 1999, 52–93.

—————. "Soziologie und Altes Testament." *VF* 19/2 (1974): 46–66.

—————. "Zur Sozialgeschichte Israels in der Perserzeit." *VF* 27 (1982): 46–88.

—————. "Thesen zur Aktualität und theologischen Bedeutung sozialgeschichtlicher Bibelauslegung im Kontext christlicher Sozialethik." In *Gerechtigkeit lernen. Beiträge zur biblischen Sozialgeschichte.* ThB 94. Gütersloh: Kaiser/Gütersloher, 1999, 1–4. Original German essay, 1987.

—————. "Der Zugriff des Königs auf die Töchter. Zur Fronarbeit von Frauen im alten Israels." In *Gerechtigkeit lernen. Beiträge zur biblischen*

Sozialgeschichte. ThB 94. Gütersloh: Kaiser/Gütersloher, 1999, 94–114.

Schulte, Hannelis. "Beobachtungen zum Begriff der *Zônâ* im alten Testament." *ZAW* 104 (1992): 255–62.

Schüngel-Straumann, Helen. *Tobit.* HTKAT. Freiburg: Herder, 2000.

Schwantes, Milton. *Das Land kann seine Worte nicht ertragen. Meditationen zu Amos.* KT 105. Munich: Kaiser, 1991.

Seiffert, Helmut. *Einführung in die Wissenschaftstheorie.* Vol. 2: *Geisteswissenschaftliche Methoden: Phänomenologie—Hermeneutik und historische Methode—Dialektik.* Beck'sche Schwarze Reihe 61. Munich: Beck, 1970.

Sicre, José Luis. *"Con los pobres de la tierra." La justicia social en los profetas de Israel.* Madrid: Ediciones Christiandad, 1984.

—————. *Los dioses olvidados. Poder y riqueza en los profetas preexílicos.* Madrid: Ediciones Christiandad, 1979.

Sigrist, Christian. *Regulierte Anarchie. Untersuchungen zum Fehlen und zur Entstehung politischer Herrschaft in segmentären Gesellschaften Afrikas.* Texte und Dokumente zur Soziologie. Olten: Walter, 1979.

—————. "Segmentäre Gesellschaft," in idem and Rainer Neu, eds., *Ethnologische Texte I. Vor- und Frühgeschichte Israels.* Neukirchen-Vluyn: Neukirchener, 1989, 106–22.

Sigrist, Christian, and Rainer Neu, eds. *Ethnologische Texte zum Alten Testament.* 2 vols. Neukirchen-Vluyn: Neukirchener, 1989–97.

Silva Castillo, Jorge, ed. *Nomads and Sedentary People.* Mexico City: El Colegio de México, 1981.

Silver, Morris. *Prophets and Markets. The Political Economy of Ancient Israel.* Boston: Kluwer-Nijhoff, 1983.

Simkins, Ronald A. "Patronage and the Political Economy of Monarchic Israel." *Semeia* 87 (1999): 123–44.

Smith, Daniel L. "The Politics of Ezra: Sociological Indicators of Postexilic Judaean Society." In *Second Temple Studies 1: Persian Period.*

Ed. Philip R. Davies. JSOTSup 117. Sheffield: Sheffield Academic, 1991, 73–97.

Smith-Christopher, Daniel L. "The Mixed Marriage Crisis in Ezra 9–10 and Nehemiah 13: A Study of the Sociology of the Post-Exilic Judaean Community." In *Second Temple Studies 2. Temple and Community in the Persian Period*. Ed. Tamara C. Eskenazi and Kent H. Richards. JSOTSup 175. Sheffield: JSOT Press, 1994, 243–65.

Smith, Morton. "Die Entwicklungen im Judäa des 5. Jh. v. Chr. aus griechischer Sicht." In *Seminar: Die Entstehung der antiken Klassengesellschaft*. Ed. Hans G. Kippenberg. STW 130. Frankfurt: Suhrkamp, 1977, 313–27.

Smitten, Wilhelm Th. in der. *Esra. Quellen, Überlieferung und Geschichte*. SSN 15. Assen: Van Gorcum, 1973.

Soggin, J. Alberto. "Ancient Israel: An Attempt at a Social and Economic Analysis of the Available Data." In *Text and Context. Old Testament and Semitic Studies for F. C. Fensham*. Ed. Walter T. Claassen. JSOTSup 48. Sheffield: JSOT Press, 1988, 201–8.

———."Bemerkungen zur alttestamentlichen Topographie Sichems mit besonderem Bezug auf Jdc. 9." *ZDPV* 83 (1967): 183–98.

———. *Einführung in die Geschichte Israels und Judas. Von den Ursprüngen bis zum Aufstand Bar Kochbas*. Darmstadt: Wissenschaftliche Buchgesellschaft, 1991.

———. "Der judäische *'amm ha'ares* und das Königtum in Juda." *VT* 13 (1963): 186–95.

———. "Probleme einer Vor- und Frühgeschichte Israels." *ZAW* 100 (1988): Supplement 255–67.

Southall, Aidan W. "Zum Begriff des segmentären Staates. Das Beispiel der Alur." In *Ethnologische Texte zum Alten Testament*. Ed. Christian Sigrist and Rainer Neu. Neukirchen-Vluyn: Neukirchener, 1997, 2:67–92. Original English article, 1953.

Stähli, Hans-Peter. *Knabe—Jüngling—Knecht. Untersuchungen zum Begriff n'r im Alten Testament*. BBET. Frankfurt: Peter Lang, 1978.

Staubli, Thomas. *Das Image der Nomaden im Alten Israel und in der Ikonographie seiner sesshaften Nachbarn*. OBO 107. Fribourg: Universitätsverlag; Göttingen: Vandenhoeck & Ruprecht, 1991.

Stegemann, Hartmut."Das Gesetzeskorpus der 'Damaskusschrift' (CD XI-XVI)." *RevQ* 14 (1989/1990): 409–34.

Stern, Ephraim. *Material Culture of the Land of the Bible in the Persian Period 538–332 B.C.* Warminster: Aris & Philips, 1982.

———. "The Persian Empire and the Political and Social History of Palestine in the Persian Period." In *The Cambridge History of Judaism*. Vol. 1, *Introduction; The Persian Period*. Ed. W. D. Davies and Louis Finkelstein. Cambridge: Cambridge University Press, 1984, 70–87.

———. "The Province of Yehud: The Vision and the Reality." Pages 9–21 in *The Jerusalem Cathedra: Studies in the History, Archaeology, Geography, and Ethnography of the Land of Israel 1*. Detroit: Wayne State University Press, 1981.

Stiegler, Stefan. *Die naxexilische JHWH-Gemeinde in Jerusalem. Ein Beitrag zu einer alttestamentlichen Ekklesiologie*. BEATAJ 34. Frankfurt: Peter Lang, 1994.

Stolz, Fritz. "Aspekte religiöser und sozialer Ordnung im alten Israel." *ZEE* 17 (1973) 145–59.

Tadmor, Hayim. "The Decline of Empires in Western Asia ca. 1200 B.C.E." In *Symposia Celebrating the Seventy-fifth Anniversary of the Founding of the American Schools of Oriental Research (1900–1975)*. Ed. Frank M. Cross. Cambridge: American Schools of Oriental Research, 1979, 1–14.

Talmon, Shemaryahu. "Biblische Überlieferungen zur Frühgeschichte der Samaritaner." In idem, *Gesellschaft und Literatur in der Hebräischen Bibel. Gesammelte Aufsätze 1*. Information Judentum 8. Neukirchen-Vluyn: Neukirchener, 1988, 132–51.

———. "The Emergence of Jewish Sectarianism in the Early Second Temple Period." In *King, Cult and Calendar in Ancient Israel: Collected Studies*. Leiden: Brill, 1986, 165–201.

———. "The Judaean *'am ha'arœs* in Historical Perspective." In *King, Cult and Calendar in Ancient Israel: Collected Studies*. Leiden: Brill, 1986, 68–78.

———. "Kingship and the Ideology of the State." In *King, Cult and Calendar in Ancient Israel: Collected Studies*. Leiden: Brill, 1986, 9–38.

———. "The New Hebrew Letter from the Seventh Century B.C.E. in Historical Perspective." In *King, Cult and Calendar in Ancient Israel. Collected Studies*. Leiden: Brill, 1986, 79–88.

Tcherikover, Viktor A., and Alexander Fuks, eds. *Corpus Papyrorum Judaicarum*. Vol. 1. Cambridge: Harvard University Press, 1957.

Thiel, Winfried. *Die deuteronomistische Redaktion von Jeremia 26–45*. WMANT 52. Neukirchen-Vluyn: Neukirchener, 1981.

———. *Die soziale Entwicklung Israels in vorstaatlicher Zeit*. 2d ed. Neukirchen-Vluyn: Neukirchener, 1985.

Thompson, Thomas L. *Early History of the Israelite People: From the Written and Archaeological Sources*. SHANE 4. Leiden: Brill, 1994.

———. "The Exile in History and Myth: A Response to Hans Barstad." In *Leading Captivity Captive: "The Exile" as History and Ideology*. Ed. Lester L. Grabbe. JSOTSup 278. Sheffield: Sheffield Academic, 1998, 101–18.

———. "Problems of Genre and Historicity with Palestine's Inscriptions." In *Congress Volume Oslo 1998*. Ed. André Lemaire and Magne Sæbø. VTSup 80. Leiden: Brill, 2000, 321–26.

Timm, Stefan. *Die Dynastie Omri. Quellen und Untersuchungen zur Geschichte Israels im 9. Jahrhundert vor Christus*. FRLANT 124. Göttingen: Vandenhoeck & Ruprecht, 1982.

Uehlinger, Christoph. "Gab es eine joschianische Kultreform? Plädoyer für ein begründetes Minimum." In *Jeremia und die "deuteronomistische Bewegung."* Ed. Walter Groß. BBB 98. Weinheim: Beltz Athenaeum, 1995, 57–89.

Ussishkin, David. "Note on Megiddo, Gezer, Ashdod, and tel Batash in the Tenth to Ninth Centuries B.C." *BASOR* 277/278 (1990): 71–91.

———. "Royal Judean Storage Jars and Private Seal Impressions." *BASOR* 223 (1976): 1–13.

Vaux, Roland de. *Ancient Israel: Its Life and Institutions*. Trans. John McHugh. New York: McGraw-Hill, 1961. Repr., Biblical Resource Series. Grand Rapids: Eerdmans, 1997.

———. "Le problème des Hapiru après quinze années." *JNES* 27 (1968): 221–28.

Veijola, Timo. *Das Königtum in der Beurteilung der deuteronomistischen Historiographie. Eine redaktionsgeschichtliche Untersuchung*. AASF 198. Helsinki: Suomalainen Tiedeakatemia, 1977.

Vieweger, Dieter. *Archäologie der biblischen Welt*. UTB 2394. Göttingen: Vandenhoeck & Ruprecht, 2003.

———. "Überlegungen zur Landnahme israelitischer Stämme unter besonderer Berücksichtigung der galiläischen Berglandgebiete." *ZDPV* 109 (1993): 20–36.

Vogt, Hubertus C. M. *Studie zur nachexilischen Gemeinde in Esra-Nehemia*. Werl: Coelde, 1966.

Volz, Paul. *Die biblischen Altertümer*. Calw: Verlag der Vereinsbuchhandlung, 1914. Repr. Wiesbaden: Fournier, 1989.

Wagenaar, Jan A. "'Give in the Hand of Your Maidservant the Property . . . ' Some Remarks to the Second Ostrakon from the Collection of Sh. Moussaieff." *ZABR* 5 (1999): 15–27.

Wagner, Volker. "Beobachtungen am Amt der Ältesten im alttestamentlichen Israel." *ZAW* 114 (2002): 391–411, 560–76.

Wallis, Gerhard. "Das Jobeljahr-Gesetz, eine Novelle zum Sabbathjahr-Gesetz." *MIOF* 15 (1969): 337–45.

Wanke, Gunther. *Untersuchungen zur sogenannten Baruchschrift*. BZAW 122. Berlin: de Gruyter, 1971.

———. "Zu Grundlagen und Absicht prophetischer Sozialkritik." *KD* 18 (1972): 2–17.

Washington, Harold C. "The Strange Woman of Proverbs 1–9 and Post-Exilic Judaean Society." In *Second Temple Studies 2: Temple and Community in the Persian Period*. Ed. Tamara C. Eskenazi and Kent H. Richards.

JSOTSup 175. Sheffield: JSOT Press, 1994, 217–42.

Weber, Max. *Ancient Judaism*. Trans. and ed. Hans H. Gerth and Don Martindale. New York: Free, 1952.

———.*Economy and Society: An Outline of Interpretive Sociology*. Ed. Günther Roth and Claus Wittich. Trans. Ephraim Fischoff et al. Berkeley: University of California Press, 1978.

———. *Die Wirtschaftsethik der Weltreligionen. Das antike Judentum. Schriften und Reden 1911–1920*. MWG 1/21. Tübingen: Mohr, 2005.

Weinberg, Joel. *The Citizen-Temple Community*. JSOTSup 151. Sheffield: JSOT Press, 1992.

———. *Der Chronist in seiner Mitwelt*. BZAW 239. Berlin: Walter de Gruyter, 1996.

———. "The International Elite of the Achæmenid Empire: Reality and Fiction." *ZAW* 111 (1999): 583–608.

Weinfeld, Moshe. "Historical Facts Behind the Israelite Settlement Pattern." *VT* 38 (1988): 324–32.

Weippert, Helga. *Palästina in vorhellenistischer Zeit*. Handbuch der Archäologie 2.1. Munich: Beck, 1988, 417–681.

Weippert, Manfred. "'Heiliger Krieg' in Israel und Assyrien. Kritische Anmerkungen zu Gerhard von Rads Konzept des 'Heiligen Krieges im alten Israel.'" *ZAW* 84 (1972): 460–93.

———. *Die Landnahme der israelitischen Stämme in der neueren wissenschaftlichen Diskussion. Ein kritischer Bericht*. FRLANT 92. Göttingen: Vandenhoeck & Ruprecht, 1967.

Weisman, Ze'ev. "Charismatic Leaders in the Era of the Judges." *ZAW* 89 (1977): 399–411.

Wellhausen, Julius. *Prolegomena to the History of Israel: With a Reprint of the Article Israel from the "Encyclopaedia Britannica."* Trans. J. Sutherland Black and Allan Menzies. 5th ed. Edinburgh: Adam & Charles Black. Repr., Atlanta: Scholars, 1994.

Welten, Peter. *Die Königs-Stempel. Ein Beitrag zur Militärpolitik Judas unter Hiskia und Josia*. ADPV. Wiesbaden: Harrassowitz, 1969.

———. "Ansätze sozialgeschichtlicher Betrachtungsweise des Alten Tetaments im 20. Jahrhundert." *BTZ* 6 (1989): 207–21.

Wenning, Robert. "Mesad Hašavyahu. Ein Stützpunkt des Jojakim?" In *Vom Sinai zom Horeb. Stationen alttestamentlicher Glaubensgeschichte*. Ed. Frank-Lothar Hossfeld. Würzburg: Echter, 1989, 169–96.

Whitelam, Keith W. "The Identity of Early Israel: The Realignment and Transformation of Late Bronze-Iron Age Palestine." *JSOT* 63 (1994): 57–87.

———. *The Invention of Ancient Israel. The Silencing of Palestinian History*. London: Routledge, 1996.

———. "Israelite Kingship. The Royal Ideology and its Opponents." In *The World of Ancient Israel: Sociological, Anthropological and Political Perspectives*. Ed. Ronald E. Clements. Cambridge: Cambridge University Press, 1989, 119–39.

———. *The Just King: Monarchical Judicial Authority in Ancient Israel*. JSOTSup 12. Sheffield: JSOT Press, 1979.

———. "Recreating the History of Israel." *JSOT* 35 (1986): 45–70.

Wiesehöfer, Josef. *Ancient Persia: from 550 BC to 650 AD*. 2d. ed. Trans. Azizeh Azodi. London: I. B. Tauris, 2001.

Will, Édouard. "Überlegungen und Hypothesen zur Entstehung des Münzgeldes." In *Seminar: Die Entstehung der antiken Klassengesellschaft*. Ed. Hans G. Kippenberg. STW 130. Frankfurt: Suhrkamp, 1977, 205–22.

Willi, Thomas. *Juda—Jehud—Israel. Studien zum Selbstverständnis des Judentums in persischer Zeit*. FAT 12. Tübingen: Mohr Siebeck, 1995.

Williamson, Hugh G. M. *Studies in Persian Period History and Historiography*. FAT 38. Tübingen: Mohr Siebeck, 2004.

Willis, Timothy M. *The Elders of the City. A Study of the Elders-Laws in Deuteronomy*. SBLMS 55. Atlanta: Scholars, 2001.

Wilson, Robert R. *Genealogy and History in the Biblical World*. Yale Near Eastern Researches

7. New Haven and London: Yale University Press, 1977.

———. "Israel's Judicial System in the Preexilic Period." *JQR* 74 (1983/84): 228–48.

Wisser, Laurent. *Jérémie, critique de la vie sociale. Justice sociale et connaissance de Dieu dans le livre de Jérémie.* Geneva: Labor et Fides, 1982.

Wißmann, Felipe Blanco. "Sargon, Mose und die Gegner Salomos. Zur Frage vor-neuassyrischer Ursprünge der Mose-Erzählung." *BN* 110 (2001): 42–54.

Wit, Johan Hendrik de. ( ): *Leerlingen van de armen. Een onderzoek naar de betekenis van de Latijnamerikaanse volkse lezing van de bijbel in de hermeneutische ontwerpen en exegetische praktijk van C. Mesters, J. S. Croatto en M. Schwantes.* Ph.D. diss., Amsterdam, 1991.

Würthwein, Ernst. "Abimelech und der Untergang Sichems—Studien zu Jdc. 9." In *Studien zum Deuteronomistischen Geschichtswerk.* BZAW 227. Berlin: de Gruyter, 1994, 12–28.

———. *Der 'amm ha'aræz im alten Testament.* BWANT 69. Stuttgart: Kohlhammer, 1936.

———. "Die Josianische Reform und das Deuteronomium." In *Studien zum Deuteronomistischen Geschichtswerk.* BZAW 227. Berlin: de Gruyter, 1994, 188–216.

Yamauchi, Edwin M. *Persia and the Bible.* 2d ed. Grand Rapids: Baker, 1991.

Yoffee, Norman. *Myths of the Archaic State. Evolution of the Earliest Cities, States, and Civilizations.* Cambridge: Cambridge University Press, 2005.

Zadok, Ran. *The Jews in Babylonia During the Chaldean and Achaemenian Periods According to the Babylonian Sources.* Studies in the History of the Jewish People and the Land of Israel Monograph Series 3. Haifa: University of Haifa, 1979.

———. "Some Jews in Babylonian Documents." *JQR* 74 (1983/84): 294–97.

Zertal, Adam. "An Early Iron Age Cultic Site on Mount Ebal: Excavation Seasons 1982–1987. Preliminary Report." *TA* 13–14 (1986/1987): 104–65.

Zsengellér, József. *Gerizim as Israel: Northern Tradition of the Old Testament and the Early History of the Samaritans.* Utrechtse Theologische reeks 38. Utrecht: Faculteit der Godgeleerdheid, Universiteit Utrecht, 1998.

Zwickel, Wolfgang. "Die Wirtschaftsreform des Hiskia und die Sozialkritik der Propheten des 8. Jahrhunderts." *EvT* 59 (1999): 356–77.

———. *Einführung in die biblische Landes- und Altertumskunde.* Darmstadt: Wissenschaftliche Buchgesellschaft, 2002.

Index of Selected Topics

administration, 18
    central, 81–82
    chiefdoms, 63, 74–75, 200 n. 83, 206 n. 49
    division of, 95
    Hellenistic, 165–70, 177, 178
    local, 42, 82, 141
    monarchical, 42, 55, 63, 72, 73–83, 89, 103–4,
        134, 153, 171, 173, 176–78
    Persian, 128–30, 139–43, 147, 155, 170, 177
    pre-state, 51, 59–60, 62, 74, 76, 200 n. 83
    provincial, 64, 141–43, 149
    Ptolemaic, 164, 166–67
    roles, 80
    state, 64, 74, 83, 85, 206 n. 49
    temple, 85, 132
alms, 162, 164–65. *See also* gifts/gift giving
ᶜam-haᵓarets. *See* landed nobility
ᶜApiru, 40, 42, 43–44, 47, 50, 51, 83, 91–92
archeology, 5
    on economy, 59
    interpreting, 23, 45, 67, 179
    as primary sources, 19–21, 35, 53, 189 n. 4
    on social structures, 33, 61, 135
armed bands. *See* gangs

cities
    capital, 66
    city-states, 40, 42, 45, 46, 51, 53, 72
    and nomadism, 42
    populations, 46
    and temples, 145
    See also Jerusalem
class. *See* landed nobility; lower classes; nomads;
    upper classes
coinage
    increase of, 131

inscriptions, 22, 226 n. 91
    introduction of, 23, 163
    silver, 28, 89, 91, 97, 109
    as source material, 21
    See also money
commerce/trade
    and coinage, 23
    development of, 40, 46–47, 89, 196 n. 35
    and Diaspora, 171–73
    and gift giving, 64
    money-changers, 110–11
    Sabbath prohibition, 167, 229 n. 124
    and wealth, 42

debt
    of peasants, 32, 62, 103, 114, 122, 135, 164
    slavery, 32, 103, 106, 111, 112, 133–36, 141,
        152
destitution, 135, 162. *See also* poor/poverty
dyarchy. *See* administration

economy. *See* commerce/trade; money
elders, 41, 60, 63, 64, 74, 83, 87–88, 141, 147, 166,
    208 n. 95, 208–9 n. 96
Elephantine, 23, 118, 127, 130, 131, 144–45, 147,
    149, 152–53, 166, 219 n. 37
epigraphy, 22–23, 50, 81, 84–85, 86, 98, 131, 151

family
    and clans, 4, 55, 57, 79
    conflicts, 41, 62
    and Diaspora, 172
    and economics, 41
    history of, 3
    and house, 178–79
    and marriage, 35

Index of Selected Biblical Passages